Making: The Proper Habit of Our Being

Teach us to care and not to care
Teach us to sit still
Even among these rocks,
Our peace in His will. . . .
– T. S. Eliot, "Ash-Wednesday"

Thomistic personalism stresses the metaphysical distinction between individuality and personality. . . . it is the human *person* who enters society; as an individual, it enters society as a part whose proper good is inferior to the good of the whole. . . . [B]ut because of the highest requirements of personality as such, the human person, as a spiritual totality referred to the transcendent whole, *surpasses* and is superior to all temporal societies. . . . With respect to the eternal destiny of the soul, society exists for each person and is subordinate to it.

– Jacques Maritain, *The Person and the Common Good*

Making
The Proper Habit of Our Being
Essays Speculative, Reflective, Argumentative

Marion Montgomery

St. Augustine's Press
South Bend, Indiana
2000

Manufactured in the United States of America.

Library of Congress Cataloging in Publication Data
Montgomery, Marion.
Making : the proper habit of our being / Marion Montgomery.
p. cm.
Includes bibliographical references.
ISBN 1-890318-39-6 (cloth : alk. paper)
1. Creative ability—Religious aspects—Christianity. 2. Intellect—Religious aspects—Christianity. I. Title.
BT709.5.M66 1999
233'.5—dc21 99-19017
CIP

∞*The paper used in this publication meets the minimum requirements of the American National Standard for Information Sciences—Permanence of Paper for Printed Materials, ANSI Z39.48-1984.*

The publisher gratefully acknowledges the creative work of Kevin Cawley in the production of this book.

Foreword

In these pages some of my assertions about "making" depend from arguments about and analysis of literature in earlier critical works, for instance, in my trilogy *The Prophetic Poet and the Spirit of the Age* and in *Possum, and Other Receits for the Recovery of "Southern" Being*. The present work also depends rather heavily on two more recent works, and is in effect the third of a series, of which the first is *Romantic Confusions of the Good: Beauty as Truth, Truth Beauty*, the second, *Intellectual Philandering: Poets and Philosophers, Priests and Politicians*. I have for many years attempted to deal with philosophical, theological, and aesthetic dimensions of literature as desirably inseparable in our response to the work of art. Insofar as the analysis of particular works (poems, stories, plays) in my earlier work demonstrates a competence in such matters, I trust it relieves me of the necessity of extensive explication and argument based in the particular works summoned to this present argument.

I have a confidence in my reader's judgment in weighing my assertions, only suggesting that justification of them to my own mind rests in that earlier work. I beg only an initial open response, a willing suspension of disbelief in respect to the argument, after which the necessity of a judgment of its validity must of course follow. Even in that deportment as Coleridge advocates to the poem, that suspension must at last be set aside, since otherwise we should lose the principal necessity to rational intellect: discrimination. Some poems and some arguments are better than others, both within a single work and among works.

As for this single work, I am grateful for encouragement and support by both the Earhart Foundation and by Bruce Fingerhut, its editor and publisher who has labored to bring it to issue, trusting that their discrimination proves warranted by it.

Preface

I move in the present argument from a principle, established in Christian orthodoxy, that man is a created intellectual creature. I believe my reader may follow me out of this principle, however he may rationalize it in respect to that element of the definition, *created*, which is not to say that any reader will agree at last with the consequences of my argument. If he holds resolutely to the popular position – that intellect is a dimension of human existence evolved out of temporal nature – he will not consent to my argument, though in making it I will have raised certain questions to which he must respond, insofar as he is committed to a concern for the truth of things. Although I value the response of orthodox minds to my arguments, my intention is not primarily to address the converted, though I depend as always upon those good minds, likewise committed to the truth of how things stand, to examine me most closely on my argument.

I am especially concerned that the orthodox philosopher and theologian examine me on my central thesis, that man is *by* his very created nature preeminently a maker. I shall contend that acts of the mind are precisely acts of making, whatever the nature of the "thing" made by such acts. In this respect my argument will appear initially not sufficiently orthodox, given the Thomistic distinctions between the practical and speculative intellects and the ends of action out of those intellects as separately considered, as those distinctions are usually made. In my sense of *making*, I suggest that concept itself is a made thing, and further that as such it bears the marks of the particular maker. And I believe the position supported by Thomas himself. Here indeed is the center of my concern, which I take to be vital to any mind, orthodox or not.[1] I take it as a very particular principle, made by intellectual

1 Concerning my use of *thing*, consider Jacques Maritain's distinction in "Thing and Object," *The Degrees of Knowledge*: "Whereas the word 'thing' primarily refers to the sensible and visible thing in which our intellect naturally finds . . . the simplest paradigm of reality (because its concepts come from the senses), it also refers to any reality, whatsoever it may be, whether spiritual or corporeal, to any actual or possible datum that is or can

action in response to the reality of existence itself, that man is a created intellectual creature, a definition formal in my meaning of it in relation to scholastic thought. But it is evidenced beyond such dependence by the action of such a creature out of its given nature and is not primarily dependent upon scholastic formulation, which is rather a mediator, a clarifier of, actual experience. Thus one may recognize the action of making as a reflection of, though significantly different from, the action of its necessary cause, whose action is not a *making* but a *creating*.

I take this definition, then, and its implications in relation to our humanity as self-evident, certified by any person's thoughtful reflection upon the experience of immediacy. Immediacy here is the present experience of self-evident self-existence in relation to the complex of creation of which that existing awareness is a part. I believe that my understanding of this principle of our being is rationalized succinctly by St. Thomas, but it must be emphasized that *succinctness* in intellectual response to the complexity of creation and to the person's immediacy of experience of that complexity is not the same as *brevity*. The arresting virtue of art in St. Thomas's *Summa Theologiae* is precisely its succinctness. Our discursive nature, determined by the finitudes of our nature, commits intellect to pursue simplicity, but not simplistically, so that *succinctness* proves relative, sometimes to the weariness of our desire for the immediacy of vision.

In this train of thought, I emphasize at once that I depend upon St. Thomas's rationalizations of principles, not because he rationalizes them, but because his arguments seem best to enlighten my own conscious experiences of mind's actions in the world. And I find in others, even in un-Thomistic poets such as William Wordsworth or cautious skeptics of scholastic Thomism such as Eric Voegelin, testimony through their own made things compatible to my experiences and – I believe – compatible to St. Thomas's own experiences of reality. St. Thomas says in his "Prologue" to Part I of the Second Part of the *Summa Theologiae*, that "man is said to be made to the image of God, 'image' in this context signifying an intellectual being who is free to judge what he shall do and has the power to act or not to

---

be put into existence independently of our mind." (note, page 91) Maritain intends *object* to be taken "in the strictest scholastic sense (formal object). . . . In current modern language it has received a very different meaning inasmuch as the opposition of *objective* to *subjective* has finally made the values proper to 'thing' or the 'real' pass on to the object." (n. page 91)

act." There are principles underlying such words as *being, judge, act, do* and so on, with which we shall have to come to terms as we go along.

Most centrally, however, we shall have to consider distinctions made by St. Thomas between *doing* and *making*, so that here I may anticipate somewhat the drift of my argument, which I trust is not without sufficient anchor in St. Thomas, in respect to his distinctions. Especially the relation of *doing* and *making* in relation to the gifts of the *practical* and *speculative* intellect will be at issue. I shall tend toward a conclusion in my argument that intellectual action, when ordered by a right will in its relation to the complexity of created reality (including the intellect's own existence as created), is at last – that is, in its proximation to its own inherent desire – a simple action in which distinctions between practical and speculative intellect, as between doing and making, are transformed into a simplicity beyond the necessity of such terms to that intellect.

The divisions analytically perceived by finite intellect in its response to existential reality are nevertheless analytically perceived as a necessary accompaniment to the person's – the created soul's – journey of becoming within the created limits of his participation in being. We speak analytically of this relation as that between actual and potential existence to a person. Because man as intellectual creature differs not only from God in the mode of possible action but from that angelic mode of action which he nevertheless shares as intuitive action, he is primarily discursive intellect in his setting out toward perfection of potential being. Certain intellectual actions are required that are peculiar to man because specific to his created nature. The labors of the practical intellect as opposed to the speculative, the rational as opposed to the intuitive, of the necessity of his nature as an existing intellectual creature, these require analytical "makings" in response to intuitive recognition of existence as actual. That is intellect's point of departure in response to existence out of its own awareness of its own existence.

Insofar as the discrete intellect approaches the perfection of its potential as intellectual creature, a journey not denied even by those who would deny to man his nature as created, I suggest that it approaches a simplicity to which analytical distinctions appear less and less persuasive as actual, present demarcations in his simple being as intellectual creature. Thus in a person's moving from the intellectual arena of *knowledge* to an enlarged *understanding*, and thence to that state called *wisdom*, the discrete person moves beyond the adequacy of rational intellect as dominant guide to that person's becoming. That is a point made dramatically by Dante in his *Di-*

vine Comedy when on the top of Purgatory Mountain his guide Virgil, as rational intellect (albeit as poet infused intuitively as well), yields guidance to Beatrice. She in turn yields guidance at that subsequent moment of full vision at the end of the *Paradiso*. One would not say that the rational and the intuitive, the practical and the speculative, represented respectively by Virgil and Beatrice, are *erased* from Dante's state as person, his nature as created intellectual creature. It is rather as if he has grown *through* them to a simplicity beyond the necessity of such distinction, though he does so as a person destined to return to the limits of his finitude in the world and to his task as poet, which is to re-enact that journey of growth in the interest of recovering the straight way beyond the handicaps to created man's finitudes. That is a journey he recognizes, of course, as made possible only through grace, as Dante insists.

If that person, the discrete intellectual creature, is so graced as to move beyond the inadequacy of his rational intellect anchored in his enduring finitudes – beyond the rational intellect's power to give sufficient account of the state of existence to which he is arrived as a wise person – there emerges in that new state a more comforting assurance described as the state of wisdom. We recall from history the deportment of Socrates, which gives many signs of his contentment with his own intellectual finitude in relation to the mystery of existence. For by patience Socrates accepts that mystery as not fully open to him as intellectual creature. In another instance from history, St. Thomas Aquinas himself reaches a point where he declares, "All that I have written seems to me nothing but straw . . . compared to what I have seen and what has been revealed to me." And so, he says to his friend Reginald, "I can write no more." His journey is resolved on the threshold of death, and through death he both hopes and believes, out of what has been revealed to him, that the resolution in that ultimate state we speak of as Beatitude.

Meanwhile, there is for most of us the continuing necessity, not necessarily of writing, but of some aspect of making, until we may through grace arrive at a recognition that all intellectual labors are as straw in respect to their manifestations in our made things. This is to recognize that our "making" is, in its proximate character, an intellectual action through our rational intellect's support of our intuited relation to that Being whose pulsing presence we encounter within the structures of reality. Thus we recognize that all our "making" is insufficient to an account of that pulsing "something," whose immediate formal name is the Lord and Giver of Life, the Holy

Spirit. Such is the limit of our making. After his visionary moment, through which Dante becomes reconciled to his limits, he must nevertheless labor at his making of his great poem, imitating succinctly, though at length, his progress toward his visionary moment which is the precedent experience to the poem. In contrast to Dante, we might say that St. Thomas writes his own "poem" as he goes, arriving at last at that state where he sets aside his uncompleted treatise on the Sacrament of Penance. We, most of us, go on with our making, whether that making is manifested as an argument such as ours here, or a poem or a play or a statue or a watercolor or dance or garden or the ordered books appropriate to our public office or business office, or whatever. We do so (I suspect) not because we do not experience such moments of vision as those of Dante or St. Thomas, but because we do not recognize such moments, lacking habits of devotion to fulfilling our intellectual nature.

In this arena of limit upon our human capacity as maker, upon our freedom consequent to being created in the "image" of God, our intellectual actions bear always the mark of exercise toward fulfillment. Thus our "worldly" labors are marked by exercise, the mark itself being against that simplicity through grace which we desire and perhaps at some moment or moments find revealed to us also. This is to say that our acts of making speak always our incompleteness. Yeats speaks tellingly to rare moments of simplicity, with an awe caught in words that make those words memorable, and very much to our point:

> O body swayed to music, O brightening glance,
> How can we know the dancer from the dance?

Such moments, we are saying, are rare. They are what Eliot spoke of as the "still point" and of them we suggest such a point to be beyond the rational "makings" of the practical intellect, though possible to us only through such makings. It is in our makings, in other words, that we may remove obstacles that otherwise prevent – or tend to refuse – the actions of grace. It is such an opening of our desire for that divine simplicity of being under the auspices of grace that we labor toward in our exercises of making. If we in a moment achieve an openness of the desire which is native to our specific nature in respect to potential being, it is also consequent to the very gift of our specific existence as intellectual creature. We must inevitably conclude that our labor of making though it yield a made thing – this book for instance – will itself be as straw.

What justifies that judgment, however, is not that it lacks validity within the limited arena of our fallible rational making (though that might well be so as well), but it is as straw because we will have come to see it, in turning from it, not in relation to what other better intellects that our own have said on the question of man as maker perhaps. It will be because we have recovered the true tendency of our journey, toward God. We remember, as St. Thomas remembers in judging his own monuments of unaging intellect in the world, this point as a recovery toward ultimate good. Our made thing, then, is as straw because of a moment's experience of or intimation of the possibility of a divine simplicity to our own existence through grace, through what has been revealed to us as an ultimate relation to that Love which is our initiating cause, in whose image we exist.

– Crawford, Georgia

I

Let us accept, for the moment at least, that portion of St. Thomas's statement which defines man as an intellectual being who judges and acts. We defer the gnawing Modernist concern with whether man in reality may be said to be "free" or has only an apparent freedom of judgment and act. For we shall arrive not at all if we do not deal with such concepts by Thomas in recognizing that they neither say, nor intend in our use of them, to pronounce an absolute degree of freedom. Our concern must be with the *limits* of man's freedom to act and to judge. The question turns upon the nature of the actual *limits* of man's freedom as discovered within the context of his actual existence. One may have intimations of degrees of absolute freedom, but such is our limited nature that at best they are only intimations. That is why, in attempting to verbalize that actuality beyond all finitudes, that being as being who reveals Himself in *Exodus* in the words *ego sum cui sum*, St. Thomas insists that "Because we are not capable of knowing what God is but only what He is not, we cannot contemplate how God is but only how he is not."[1]

In that recognition we find ourselves in the limited arena, concerned with man as maker, including his "making" of concepts of existential realities from the lowest structures of being constituting "Creation" to the transcendent creator whom we approach, with our rational intellect as "knower," by negative makings. This is to say that our acts of knowing involve a making dependent upon our setting aside the thing we would know, through the act of our making it, from all else. Figuratively, the divine simplicity of the marble stone requires our setting aside from it the portions of stone captive of the figure. We come to the figure in the stone, in a sense, by unmaking the stone, by setting aside, and in overlooking this dimension upon our gift as maker we easily mistake ourselves as maker to be the Prime Cause of

1 The passage is in *Questionaes Disputatae de Veritate*. On the importance of this revelation in Exodus as it affects Christian philosophy and distinguishes it from Greek philosophy, see Etienne Gilson's "Being and Its Necessity" and "Beings and Their Contingence" in *The Spirit of Mediaeval Philosophy*.

the created thing. For such is our fascination with the imagined figure that the gift of the stone itself becomes neglected. To suppose art as primary, as opposed to a secondary "creation" is to confuse the sculptor and God, a confusion easily succumbed to when the rational intellect is overwhelmed by the intuitive intellect. On the other hand, when the rational intellect overwhelms the intuitive the released figure is yet strangely somehow yet confined by the stone – is not "alive," as we say metaphorically.

We are attempting to characterize the arena within which man as maker is constricted from absolute making, that is, from actual creation. This dangerous freedom, without which we would have no freedom at all, is the necessity also: it requires our "setting aside" our made things, within complex creation, in order to accommodate some of the whole of creation to the limits of our own finitude. By that setting aside we "make" creation proportionate to our own finitude. That is the necessity to practical intellect, namely, the necessity of rational discrimination. What is at primary risk, of course, is not complex creation (though creation may suffer secondary effects) but the discrete, finite intellect engaged in its necessary action of discrimination. It is perhaps less an arena, however, than a seeming jungle within which we must find the limits of our capacity as makers. Given our recent intellectual history, it is pressingly important to intellect in all its varieties of particularities, in the multitude of its assumptions about such terms as *freedom* and *judgment* and *action*, to attempt some understanding which does not disallow the terms, while at the same time seeing them in their limits in respect to reality. The attempt is at once confused by and justified by desire in the human spirit, *as human spirit*, to move beyond rationalizations of the nature of limit such as we here attempt to characterize. The intellectual chaos of our moment of history, not only that effected by the relativistic detachment of the philosopher but of the theologian or statesman or business man or doctor or any calling within the intellectual world as well, is an effect out of our loss of understanding of limit. Given an insatiable hunger for freedom which, in consort with Original Sin and the ascendancy of that relativism which posits intellect itself as the only transcendent of complex reality, we complicate the community of spiritual creatures as we participate in that community. In that chaos of intellectual community, there is no shortage of rationalizations with and about terms, but the tendency of rationalization is to deny the limit of intellect itself in its rational action. That is the strategy whereby existence as relativistically posited nevertheless implies the positing of human intellect itself as an absolute.

If we may accept for the moment this argument by St. Thomas on the impossibility of limited intellect's "knowing" the ineffable, we might discover intellect at this historical juncture at a crucial fork in the road of its intellectual journey. From Thomas's position, the one branch is taken through a steady faith, beyond reason, in the existence of the ineffable Other, whom he calls God. The way thenceforth is most narrow, straitened increasingly and so a labored journey, in that intellect is moved repeatedly to engage the straitening jungle which is contingent to the faint path it would travel. Repeatedly, intellect recognizes a *good* in the jungle itself such as tempts it to embrace that good as ultimate, rather than a lesser good. It is nevertheless a good, though abused, in that it necessarily speaks by indirection of a greater good. The jungle is not to be rejected as in that older gnostic error whereby creation itself was rejected. What is rather necessary is the holding of the good, but holding it as lesser. That is to hold it for its good, but to see as well that it is not itself the absolute Good, God. It is in this precariously constant engagement of reality by the intellect that intellect may in the end open itself toward the absolute, having removed those obstacles to visionary openness which are consequent less upon deliberate evil than upon lesser, mediate good mistaken by finite intellect as greater good. The lesser good, once we take it as leading to the greater, occasions the moment of panic when we "find" ourselves as Dante did. That is a less than a instantly happy finding and so appears not to be good. It is only the first step of the journey. One "comes to himself" and finds himself lost in a dark wood. And that is where we truly begin our proper journey.

As for that other path at the crossroad which intellect may choose, that is the path chosen by intellectual gnosis. It is chosen through faith also, but through a faith in the self as absolute in its freedom, requiring only a will to that absoluteness. We may put it in theological terms: The will in this error of free choice of the way intends self-redemption, rejecting redemptive grace in any agency other than itself as operative cause. If we observe this action in its intense determination to self-rescue, we might say it shares a fanaticism we find popularly attributed to Christian "fundamentalism" in current ideological wars. But it does not follow, therefore, as the sophisticated, simplistic intellectualism of our age inclines to take it in relation to Christian fundamentalism, that we mean to describe the merely primitive, pre-intellectual. Perhaps that point is sufficiently made by recalling one of our age's arresting intellectuals, who but recently was of lively interest to the academic community. He wrote parables of the Modernist dead-end so disturbing as to require of such intellectuals an escape from the excruciating burden of his parables. He attempted, through elaborate analysis concentrating upon the game with idea, upon an abstract accounting for the things he made. His good intention was to lessen the burden echoing in those made things lest they be too intimidating to intellect. The game was but a game, or so is the suggestion in his attempt at our relief.

That fascinating intellectual we at once recognize when I name some of his works: *The Rebel*, *The Stranger*, or *The Plague*. Those works reveal the state of a soul arrested at the parting of the ways we have described, arrested by his faith suspended. For Camus could rest faith neither in the ineffable God nor in the presumptuous self as redeemer through its games. The poignancy of Camus is in this suspension, which he recognized in himself. In a telling moment he says (as reported by Julian Green in his diary), responding to an insistent demand that he abandon the suspense, "I am your Augustine, before his conversion, I am struggling with the problem of evil and can't get to the end of it."

The poignancy in such an admission, like that poignancy residual in his works, including his philosophical essays no less than his imaginative makings, is most unsettling to intellectuals, but it is so in proportion to their sense of their own Modernist resolutions. For Camus is a disturbing but more importantly a disturbed Modernist, upsetting a range of liberated intellects from Sartre through the enlightened academics of established academic centers of intellectual "enlightenment," down to even the level of the provincial academies. It is the provincial academic intellect who more and more must deal with the effects of what Eric Voegelin calls the "modern gnostic" intent upon power over being. He must reconcile that desire for power with the daily acceleration of effects of his presumptions – effects that speak more and more clearly the presence of an evil in operation, an evil virus infecting intellect when self is unleashed by gnostic intentionality. It affects the community of mankind at the most elementary levels of human existence.

Father James Schall observes Camus' reflections on the local, elementary condition to human life in Algiers. Camus, says Father Schall, recognized that "Pleasure without hope is next to despair," while "Joy is most poignant when it is most joy," since that fleeting joy says to us inescapably that "we have here 'no lasting city,'" Fr. Schall recalls St. Paul and especially St. Augustine to the point. He then quotes a most telling passage from Camus, which makes us aware of what Camus means by describing himself as an "Augustine, before his conversion." Looking at the city and country and people he loves in Algiers, Camus says of those lesser goods through which he is still unable to move toward that greater good:

> One can find a certain moderation as well as a constant excess in the strained and violent faces of these people, in this summer sky emptied of tenderness, beneath which all truths can be told and on which no deceitful divinity has traced the signs of hope or redemption. Beneath this sky and the faces turned toward it there is nothing on which to hang a mythology, a literature, an ethic, or a religion – only stones, flesh, stars, and those truths the hand can touch.[2]

Joy without hope, which is spiritual despair. There seems, in Camus's art, an arrest which speaks *acedia*. And this is the moment we meet in a telling poem by one of our own poets who was himself at that branching of the ways in the dark wood of the world, discovering this same joy without hope which can yield only despair within the tangles of memory with desire. T. S. Eliot has his little old man in "Gerontion" reflect on his own world in a

---

2 Fr. Schall's "No Point in the Happiness of Angels?" is in *Crisis* (May 1991). History answers Camus's lament of Algerian sterility as I write. That unhappy country has just accomplished a final overthrow of its Marxist regime, through the instrument of "democratic" election. Involved were 49 political parties. In the contested event the "Muslim fundamentalists," the Islamic Salvation Front, reportedly won 386 of the 430 parliamentary seats, lacking only forty nine for absolute control. Charles Tripp, a student of that political scene, at the School of Oriental and African Studies (London), is reported to find the appeal of the ISF to be that of "a third way that is neither capitalist nor socialist" (Atlanta *Journal* [December 28, 1991]). Not only many Algerians, but neighboring countries (let alone European states), are disturbed anew by the waywardness of the "democratic" process. The ISF ran successfully on the slogan: "No constitution and no laws. The only rule is the Koran and the law of God." On the eve of run-off elections for contested seats, Imam Abdelkader Moghini attempted to reassure the wary: His party will "allow all political voices." A fellow Imam, Sheik Mohammed Said, meanwhile called on all Algerians to be prepared to change their habits, as for instance those involving dress, food, drink. Such is the "third way," under construction with the instrument of Western-style "democracy," which appears (in the shadow of Iran's recent history) to be rather surely a totalitarian state run by an oligarchy of imams. Such is one possible emergence of "mythology. . . literature . . . ethic . . . religion" Camus lamented as absent from his beloved Algeria.

mood very like this in Camus, an old man in a dry month remembering "strained and violent faces" still given to pleasure without hope, longing only for the springing of "Christ the tiger" to resolve the intellectual impasse of "the word within a word, unable to speak a word," Theirs is the dead-end of sign when sign is divorced from the complexity of existence itself. That divorce leaves creation itself a decayed house inhabited by strange and disturbing ghosts as far as the isolated intellect can see. And such is the circumstance to the honest intellectual in our century, for whom the spiritual failure termed *acedia* leads not to the elegiac arrest reflected by Camus and Eliot but to a busy-ness through which to distract attention from intellectual arrest. In these distractions, these manipulations of signs, often in "explication" of words in other men's made things of art, the "academic" intellect may avoid the necessity of spiritual choice which insists on being recognized and accepted as spiritual choice.

In that emptiness of action so typical of academic intellectuals, I suggest, one finds the impetus to destructions of reality which affect the fabric of society itself and exacerbate the very evil which those actions would avoid. For those actions are in the end perversions of reality through signs, whereby signs become defenses against reality rather than means to an intellectual openness to reality. That was what Eliot at last recognized in himself, at a turning point, leading him to accept the world as created, a creation mediating the way beyond intellect's entrapment in its dark wood. Intellect found itself entrapped by its own false acceptance of the self as the only acceptable mediator of an absolute freedom of the self. It is the consequences of such spiritual failure of intellect, in persons high and low, which yields the spectacles of community decay all about us. And that decay is exacerbated by a certain desperateness in our abuse of sign, of our common words, affecting us all. That intentionality of will to absolute freedom has the tragic consequence, as Camus saw clearly, of our inevitable entrapment in a world of sterilized vision, in which "there is nothing on which to hang a mythology, a literature, an ethic or a religion." Those few "truths the hand can touch" prove again and again to be only the limited truths of our willful separation from a rich, living reality, leaving us to lament our alienation more desperately than ever the old Psalmist lamented his exile.

Meanwhile, there are the surface effects in our social deportments, those spectacles through dislocated signs, which would encourage us to a severe, caustic, satiric recovery of signs, could we but recover some measure of our dislocations that lie beneath spectacle, beneath our signs. The

Modernist error has been to push freedom to an absolute degree through its presumption in denying all limit upon freedom of intellect. But deep in us, common sense alone is sufficient to call that absolute in question. That does not, of course, prevent man's intention to absolutism. There is the continuing quest for the Fountain of Youth always with us, and nowhere better represented than in the spectacle of the accomplishments of modern medicine. Those accomplishments exercise a trickle-down effect, to borrow a popular economic term contingent to if not lineally effected by scientific "Progress." One sees it in those lively ads on television, in which alchemy through trick effects transforms reality: The mass-produced hamburger is vibrantly alive – if only through sprayed oils suited to the camera's imitations of our dream hungers about reality. Facial creams remove wrinkles – albeit by swelling the surface of the face. One need not worry, for the duration of this evening's Olympian adventures at least, about what will appear when the swelling goes down.

Our concern here, beyond satiric irony, is that Modernist forms of alchemy are executed through the manipulation of our signs in such a way as to distort our relation to reality. Those visual images of the sizzling sandwich or the subtle association of sex with the latest thrust of engine in the new sleek "Sports" car carry with them all the "conveniences" needed in our work-a-day existence to forget it as work-a-day. Such are the promised gifts of Calypso in a current cereal or face lotion, the promise of eternal youth and all the pleasures of the body. And this is to say that there is at work a subversion of intellect, one as old as the temptation to free apples in the Garden of Eden. With the secret which intellect may itself seize in an act of freeing itself absolutely from reality, it may become "as the gods." One might even put it that our seduction by the alchemy of signs is the continuing evidence that we suffer Original Sin, though one need not grant that point as an accepted doctrine to grant our self-manipulation through sign to illusions of reality.

It is important to see in this context that what I call our self-manipulation through sign is not dependent on intellectual sophistications such as we usually associate with an intelligentsia. Unless we see the point, we shall too easily separate the intelligentsia as "intellectual" from the rest of humanity, as if humanity did not share common nature as intellectual creatures. And because such a separation is fatal to the prospect of our intellectual recovery to reality at every level of social, political, intellectual community, we must emphasize this elementary point. In addition, our term is quite deliberately "intellectual creature," as opposed to "rational creature." The phrase "rational creature" has led to an unwarranted reduction by definition of the nature of man, a reduction gradually accomplished since the Renaissance whereby there is an estrangement of intellectual nature from its commonality.

It is an estrangement increasingly deliberate on both sides. The "egghead" and the *hoi polloi* at best are uneasy with each other. A reduction of the complexity of man as intellectual to the specialized concept of some men as rational plagues modern thought in its attempt to understand, beyond "rational" delineations, the full, existential nature of man. It is a consequence especially since the Enlightenment, through which there enter distortions of thought and action resulting in a more and more fragmented community. Usually we find justification by separating in intellect itself "thought" from "feeling." The "dissociation of sensibilities," which was a popular concept in literary theory for a time, following Eliot's famous argument for the term, speaks a breach in the unity of intellectual action affecting all our makings consequent to the breach, whether we speak of the selling of soap or of political shibboleths. It is not merely a "literary" problem.

That analytical separation of what is by essence a unity of nature specific to mankind has made it increasingly difficult to maintain a community of mind through consent to the complexity of this undeniable reality: man, a creature judging and acting and affecting the body of community and the body of nature itself through his judgment and action as intellectual creature. Without common consent to a common nature, community dissolves to fragments of specialized structures devoid at last of communal unity. Consequently we seem to require forced structures of community through mechanisms of abstractionism. The instrument necessary to that forced construction of reality by intellect turned gnostic, operative as gnostic at each level of the imposed structure, is the sign. But it is sign divorced from reality, whereby sign becomes the instrument of will, rather than a mediator of reality among consenting intellects. It is only when common sense intrudes upon these manipulations that intellect is for a moment at least recovered toward the ordinate use of sign, and with an immediacy salvific to intellectual rescue. The effect is a rescue from the distortions of theoretical semiotics – as semiotics has come to dominate thought in restrictive, "scientific" ways. My concern here is not with the science of signs in its own limits as necessary to the intellectual pursuit of reality, but with the presumptions in many of its practitioners of an absoluteness of their science, whereby the complexity of reality is denied or avoided. That was the objection made effectively by Etienne Gilson in *Philosophy and Linguistics*. It is the objection as well of Walker Percy in essays and through fictions, so that by reference to both we shall come to depend upon philosopher and poet presently.

The term "rational creature" (Aristotle's "rational animal") involves for our age a reduction of the nature of man, as it did not in the pre-Renaissance world, from St. Thomas back to Aristotle and Plato. For not only was the term *rational* subsequently reduced in its reference, but the emergence of anthropology and the eventual dominance of Darwinian thought, extended by Freud and others, centered rationality in our animal nature as opposed to our spiritual nature. Thought comes thereby to be a sort of spume played upon the surface of material existence through an unaccountable evolutionary force. The term *intellectual creature* to the contrary may be urged as encompassing not only the rational dimension but other powers of intellect as well, powers which will emerge in our discussion but which are not sufficiently accounted for by deterministic mechanism as the principle of existence in general. Power as imminent in man in relation to the structure of existence, we shall hold, is a reality, but it is a limited reality. In avoiding the implications of limit, man may mistake the significance of limit to his intellectual power, endangering himself by self-abolition as man.

It is not that certain intellectual creatures have not opposed such reductionism, as my allusion to C. S. Lewis's famous little book, *The Abolition of Man*, indicates. Nor is that opposition only recent. We might recall the opposition to Enlightenment reductionism which emerges in the nineteenth century as "Romanticism," with the poets the principal objectors. What the poets began to insist upon is that reality itself calls in question rationalistic reductions of existence. Individual minds, in their experiences of their own existence, discovered (or rediscovered) dimensions of awareness not included in the merely "rational." The intimations of reality disallowed by the strictly rationalistic deconstructions of intellect as of all existence led to attempts to recover reality in its complexities to the auspices of an intellect more largely conceived than by strict rationalism. Kant's attempt to establish as a reality of individual action the "categorical imperative" is a sign of that resistance, and Kantian thought in general, as an influence upon the Romantic poet from Coleridge to John Crowe Ransom, is in this sense reactionary to Enlightenment rationalism, whatever difficulties there are attendant upon Kant's attempt.

More largely put, in relation to the Romantic poet as antagonist to rationalistic reduction of man to rational animal, that poet's concern for the relation of imagination to reason, of thought to feeling, and so on, suggests that the gnostic reductions of reality by intellectual presumptions of intellect's own transcendence over reality met opposition, though such presumption nevertheless proved dominant in intellectual community well into our own century. The attempt to establish mind as in control of a mechanistic universe, whether by Comte or Darwin or Marx, initially dominant in Western thought after the eighteenth century, began to decay with the uncertainty of the presumption of its own transcendence. The seed out of Kant begins to germinate in Bergson, let us say, after which the contention between rationalist and intuitionist, between scientist and poet, becomes more and more intense. We shall be holding, as our argument unfolds, that the contention between the two is a false contention, resulting from the common loss of an understanding of the complex nature of intellect itself.

Meanwhile, the larger questions about individual consciousness as it relates to its presence in an actual natural body – that complex called *person* – continue to be pressing concerns because consciousness itself cannot rest in the dualism implied. The concern increases as the marvels of technology unfold, speaking a power in intellect – it supposes – whereby it may control chaos in social, political, military affairs of community. The consequences in our century have been initially arresting and pleasing to intellectual presumptions, but then more arresting than pleasing, given the catastrophic events of the late twentieth century. At the end of our century we are at last, perhaps, prepared to consider again the nature of man, so that we may recover an understanding of his limits as intellectual creature.

II

In our attempt to *understand*, beyond *knowing* the formulations of our tacitly or consciously accepted first principle, we must explore the formulations. That principle: Man is intellectual creature. And since the issue of understanding is crucial to our very being as intellectual creature, we welcome any aid to our understanding. The aids are various, but I shall depend primarily upon one considerable intellectual creature, who has had effectively rationalized the principle out of his reflective considerations. I mean the scholastic rationalization of man's being by St. Thomas Aquinas. For though we may popularly consider St. Thomas as ancient and therefore remote from our concern for present reality, insofar as he reveals truths about the nature of man as intellectual creature those revelations prove very immediate. They are immediate, not because St. Thomas revealed them, but because truth continues unwavering in itself, and valid testimony to it therefore also continues valid. The formulations are measured by truth, and not truth by formulation, and that is an article of faith in St. Thomas which justified for him his long pursuit of the truth of things, knowing the problems of a formulation as a recent poet came to engage those problems – a poet whom we call to witness how abiding those problems. Signs, words, as Eliot said, are notorious, in that words "Crack and sometimes break." They "Decay with imprecision, will not stay in place, will not stay still." But if too often we are distressed to discover that "last year's words" belong to last year's language about the sign and next year's words "await another voice," that uncertainty is due less to the fixity of the word once spoken in the time of its spokenness than to our own movement beyond or away from the understanding at the moment we utter the words. From that we may discover, though with difficulty, the necessary caution toward signs occasioned by intellect's fallibility as sign-maker toward truth. Some signs prove steadier than the mere fixity of last year's words or the slipperiness or brittleness of some of our words. *Truth*, like *love*, is one of those fixed signs, though in our journeying those signs seem at times kaleidoscopes distorting the color of reality, from dark to bright, as intellect attempts to move through them to the reality that must steady signs rightly taken, despite our shifting uses of them.

And so, if we accept man as intellectual creature and if we recognize that the sign of that reality is intellectually formulated, we shall then have to consider the complicated question of the relation of man's signs, the evidence of his intellectual actions, as those signs are governed by truth. Signs must be steadily put to the test by truth, as we pursue the reality of existence itself. That is the import of St. Thomas's reminding us that the truth of things is the object of intellectual action. And so we must continue aware of the complicated question of the word's relation to the thought, from which and by which the word is justified. In doing so we may find that the reality of things, and the truth signified by the thing itself *as thing*, at last justifies thought, and not thought reality, from which justification the sign (the word) mediates intellectual action for intellect's sake. It does not, however, do so for the sake of the thing itself. To miss this point is to become too easily the justifier, rather than the justified. It is through signs that man justifies his own judgment and action, measures himself against the truth. But truth is the justifier of sign and not man himself. This is to say that by the felicity of sign, intellect measures the rightness of its own responsive action to the truth it holds of things.

How necessary signs are to any movement of mind! Even when man would deny a relation of sign to reality, his denial must be by a resort to words. And denial itself through words makes the words dependent upon that which is denied, reality itself. Existence, this is to say, is prior to any action of an particular existent thing, among whose number is the particular intellect itself. Only if the word were absolutely independent of existence would it be possible that our intellectual action might become the principal cause of being. The attempt to declare that this false principle is true, the gnostic attempt, is only possible in relation to the true principle itself, recognized if not acknowledged by a denial of it. The agonies of the isolated mind, pronouncing out of that agony that mind itself is the only absolute principle, reveals mind as at best but singing in the chains of being, to echo that much-troubled poet who attempts by poetry to escape Modernist reductions of the mystery of intellect. I mean Dylan Thomas, and refer to his "Fern Hill."

We have been using words with an intention of restricted meaning: *principle*, *intellect*, *reality*, *rational*, and the like. There shall be many more in the pages that follow, the whole argument depending at last upon the care with which we use the word. The ever-present difficulty is that by words one may sing, yet be forgetful of the limits of song in existence itself. The inclination, we affirm, is nevertheless out of a proper desire for a fulfillment of intellect. The desire is to move at last beyond the necessity of any sign, to what we might term an earned silence, a fulfillment of hope. It is in this light that we may better understand what St. Thomas means when he says that all his own singing appears to him, at the high moment of his earthly journey, but as "straw" destined for the fires of time.

We test our terms against the definitions at hand in unabridged dictionaries. A suitable enough beginning, in that such definitions give a guide to the current understanding of a word as inherited from the complexity of its historical uses. But we puzzle over it beyond dictionary incarceration, as we find it in contextual exposition by a particular mind. But that is a beginning at the level of its own grammar of being, and what remains necessary in our concern for understanding is the term's *significant* weight in relation to the experience of our own minds as actively responding to a reality inclusive of and larger than dictionaries or formulated arguments, even our own. We test them by the complexity of our own particular life as a specific mind in creation. Our proper end, Thomas says in that lighted and lighting formulation of his words which we bear with us, is *the truth of things in themselves* – not the truth as abstracted from things and thereby separated from things, which separation is in some degree a necessity to our formulation of thought through signs. For, given created intellect's nature as discursive, formulation is the necessary guard against presumption of intellect to an authority of intuitive knowledge which is as yet unjustified by the labor of discursiveness. We need only recall the tendency to intellectual irresponsibility in the course of the Romantic movement whenever the Romantic mind sees its intuitive knowledge as an evidence of its omniscience.

The mind's journey is through the dark wood of creation, not dark in itself but strict in its yielding of light to the discursive intellect, to discursive formulation – that is, concept advanced through sign to our reflective consideration. The formulation becomes a campsite along the way. Secured by discursive reflections against what may appear an overwhelming darkness, our small campfires blaze a moment, reassuring of our necessary journey toward light. But such moments of rest do not in themselves yield the light desired.

That is, intellect is required a venturing beyond the local, husbanded light, and each venture is a new beginning, with intellect newly at risk, as

T. S. Eliot puts in *East Coker*. With each attempt, we leave the safety of the local light which we have shored against the intellect's ruin, to venture into a new darkness. The "shabby equipment" of our words is "always deteriorating" under the pressures of the act of our "raid on the inarticulate." It is a raid most subject to our own abusive uses of that equipment, and that is so because of "the general mess of imprecision of feeling" moving in us, those "Undisciplined squads of emotion" that threaten a rout of our intellectual forces.

By such metaphors we have underlined the significant theme of St. Augustine's *Confessions* or Dante's *Divine Comedy*. That these are companionable works to our metaphoric presentation of the intellectual journey suggests a constancy of the drama of those journeys toward the light. In one dimension they are aesthetically rewarding to our reflection, but that is not a sufficient response. What we want to add here is that even the less dramatic, the seemingly less "literary" virtues of something like the *Summa Theologiae* should not hide from us that the same dramatic journey is underway by St. Thomas himself, whose arguments justify St. Augustine in this respect, even as they prepare for that great poem, *The Divine Comedy*. As for the dramatic context of Thomas's academic situation, his jousting is not only with a Siger of Brabant or Duns Scotus or William of Ockham. To name near contemporaries already suggests the enlarged arena of the philosopher's attempt. For in pursuit of the truth of things as undertaken through signs, the necessity of the sign's anchor in the truth calls into the arena Plato and Aristotle and St. Augustine, but also Bacon and Locke and Hegel and Marx and Heidegger and so on. That is why a concern limited to history or to the literary drama of a single poem, even such a great poem as *The Divine Comedy*, if taken merely as a fragment of History, of intellect's art, at last proves insufficient to the intellect's progress toward the fullness of light by its making.

To be content with knowing what men have said of the truth of things, our point of departure on the intellectual journey toward the light, will leave intellect unfulfilled, however much it might feel fashionable among intellects to have achieved such a learnedness. The concern here turns on this point: Discursiveness is the necessary limit of intellectual action; discursiveness requires of intellect its careful attention to what intellects have said of the truth of things. But neither discursiveness in all its virtues nor intellectual command of what men have said of the truth of things is acceptable *except as means toward a proper end* of that actual intellect. One remembers, for instance, such a towering intellect as John Milton's, a mind suggested by literary historians to be the last in the Western tradition that *knew* first-hand all that minds in that tradition had said of truth. But for all his power through knowledge, Milton cannot in the end be accepted as understanding sufficiently the truth of things in relation to his own intellectual journey. For instance, one is properly awed by the wealth of knowledge he brings to his argument in the "Treatise of Civil Power in Ecclesiastical Causes" or in his *Christian Doctrine* or "The Reason of Church Government Urged against Prelaty." But one is not at last persuaded of a fullness of Milton's understanding out of his encyclopedic knowledge of what men have said. There lies in his argument, undermining it, an irresolution occasioned by the immediacy of circumstances to him.

I would put it, in brief, that Milton's fundamentalism as philosophical theologian is forced to the severely radical. It is forced to that point of an intellectual primitivism. His absolute principle, increasingly forced upon him by immediate circumstance, is that individual conscience is the only supreme authority. He reveals himself out of his circumstances to be an intellectual libertarian, besieged on the one hand by what he calls the "forcing protestant" represented by Parliament and on the other by a prelacy which he centers in the Pope, the "forcing Pope." Milton is consequently a traditionalist laboring against tradition, and in the end he declares tradition itself heretical. As poet, he is not only a traditionalist, but specifically so in respect to ceremony, without which formalities neither prosody nor drama can be effective in his art. He nevertheless finds himself declaring ceremony itself heretical.[1]

---

1 Milton's problem as polemicist is that he must argue from certain givens, and that means that he must argue from both tradition and ceremony. But as "protestant" he must reject both, as he does explicitly in his "Treatise of Civil Power in Ecclesiastical Causes," addressed to the Parliament summoned on January 27, 1659. One must "do by scripture and the gospel, according to conscience," if one is "not to do evil." But what is in suspense is the relative authority of consciences. Milton is thus put in the awkward position of defending an aristocratic hierarchy of consciences, for some consciences as he must say are more gifted than others. Conscience, unexamined by a reason freed of passions, is in the end but *feeling*, when there is no reference of authority other than the polemicist himself. That is a circumstance closing in upon Milton's political position, made evident in this particular treatise when he must stand against not only "popery and idolatry" but against its counter, which, as exercised by Parliament, Milton

With such lessons to the difficulty of understanding through knowing, we proceed as traditionalists, as ceremonialists, in our discursive conduct of intellect toward those circumstances which impinge upon present intellectual action. And thus we must distinguish *potency* and *act*, saying that act resolves potency into actuality. Are we dealing only with intellectual abstractions in following Thomas in this distinction? Perhaps. So then we turn to the immediacy of circumstance at hand as the test. We watch a child who is delighted with a kitten or lamb, reaching for it to "play" with it, as we suppose from our detached adult perspective that supplies the event such a term as *play*. But why should there be for us, almost without exception in our "adult" response, such a derived delight in the event? It is both immediate and personal. Nor do we need to know "personally" either the child or the creature to experience this delight. Also, our inclination to delight makes us vulnerable as "adult," as any clever advertiser of wanted or unwanted products knows all too well. A random thirty-minute program on commercial television will demonstrate this to us, whether in "situation comedy" or in the advertising supporting such programs.

And so a question: Is it that in such event, actual or media-mediated, we recognize a reality echoed in the event or in the imitation of event? In the very nature of event we recognize potency, in relation to an act becoming an actual event for the acting agent, the child. We recognize the echo of reality through an immediacy of our sensual natures, with implications ranging beyond the level of that immediacy, beyond the level of a present event as an illusion on the TV screen, as our advertisers recognize all too clearly. Of

calls an argument by the "forcing protestant." Only through the personal conviction that he is God's special envoy to the troubled times, as he avers, may he, as the principal conscience of the troubled times reconcile himself to the problem. And he does so through a typical gnostic strategy: i.e., he separates the "inward man," which is the "understanding and will," from the outer man, the "civil man." Concerned with "liberty," he must confess that there are those "who from the imbecility or derangement of . . . intellect [are] incapable of the government of another." It is hardly a coincidence that the imbeciles and decayed intellects are those who do not agree with him. Conscience, authorized as absolute only in relation to scripture, becomes as random as the number of those professing themselves a sufficient authority in the name of conscience. The inevitable extension of that position is pluralistic sectarianism: One soul constitutes one sect. That extension reaches a crisis with Roger Williams in the New World, but the rationale is largely provided by Milton.

course they may not understand what they recognize. But with the skill of dramatic manipulations of event, they are enabled to shift the proper response to an event to a false end. The shifting here is of our own intellectual response to event, though advertisers seem equally clever in shifting our sensual response to an imagined event to similar ends. The uses of the human body and its appetites is considered the proper end of our knowing in the ads. This is true of the media's uses of us, whether we consider the sexual spectacles of advertisements for drink or food or the medical concerns with the body which focus upon bodily nature as an end requiring the latest over-the-counter concoction. We may believe ourselves attractive to curvaceous women or muscular men through an automobile the ad suggests, or have restored our bodily functions as mechanically ideal through headache tablets or laxatives or unguents of various sorts. But we lose sight of the slight of mind. We are not attractive or healthy; we desire to be, and in the disparity we do not question desire in relation to the advertised end. Actuality and potency are manipulated in manipulating us, effectively because disjoined from the reality of being.

Our intent is to turn from such false ends of worldly delight in the body, or fears for that body's health, without thereby rejecting those delights or good health. We attempt to do so by reference to such a simple and common experience of event as that in which a child reaches out to some *thing* in its surrounding world. When we reflect upon our own pleasure of delight in the child's reaching, what we might discover is that the delight in us is deeper than the otherwise isolated, present event itself. What we find happening in ourselves as intellectual creatures is an imitation of the event. There is a movement out of a potency into an actuality within ourselves so that the event witnessed is not separate from our observation of it. That is, we are not "objective" in our response, but then neither are we merely "subjective" in our response, except when we are moved to mediate ends as if ultimate, in a sentimentality of feeling which distorts our intellectual action of response to things, as in diabolical advertising. Rather, what is effected in us is a recovered openness to reality itself. In ordinate response to event, let us say we *become* more appropriately in relation to the truth of things and thereby *are* more fully an intellectual being, by which term we mean to convey a unity of *person*, to which unity (let us remember) the sensual dimension of personhood is not excluded. For as *person*, actions of knowing involve that fullness, that complexity of our peculiar being which the scholastics distinguished from angelic being. The fullness of response here spoken of is an act of love toward the truth of things, a celebration through our openness as person to existential reality. In it is an answering moment of light to our response, one T. S. Eliot speaks of as occurring in a "still point" of the turning world. One knows an encounter with a light which is separate, and not a mirroring of whatever small campfire our own intellect has managed to husband against the threat of darkness. It is a beckoning lantern, encouraging us to the journey in the ways of the world toward the fullness of light, toward an opening of that fullness to light we speak of as *understanding*, and toward that eventual fulfillment by light which we speak of as *wisdom*.

Of course, under the emotional coloring which hovers in our response to event, we may move improperly or excessively so that the true nature of the event in relation to our becoming is distorted, even though we take it as understood. That is the point of our indictment of the "advertisers'" manipulations of our intellectual inclination. But the primary indictment must always be, not of any advertiser (though he may not escape blameless) but of ourselves as intellectual creatures failing in our gift. By such failure, a sentiment proper to intellectual being in its relation to reality becomes eroded to sentimentality. Consequently, it distorts our intellectual vision. It limits or shifts that vision away from the truth of things. Put metaphorically, that desire in us, whose movement is love, comes to rest upon a thing, but not properly, so that the quality of our intellectual response is that of a possessiveness, and not an action of love, whatever the thing may be. The thing is willfully enslaved to intellect, even though there may not be a sufficient power in our existential circumstances that allows us a natural enslavement of possession, to take and hold the thing as our property. The erosive effect is independent of any actuality of empowered possession of things in nature or law, for the destructiveness is not, as a *primary* abuse, of the thing in itself through our actual, virtual, natural possession by willfulness. The destructiveness is more significantly to the willful intellect itself. It is in this arena of intellectual action that sin is destructive of the soul. It is here that gluttony, lust, avarice, and the like effect our diminution of being more radically than any manifestations in the flesh, even the manifestations of bodily disease.

We are used to considering sin in its effects as if it were synonymous to the spectacle that may attend the sin. Thus the glutton is a Falstaff, excessively portly. The envious is a Cassias with lean and hungry look. In respect to the spiritual state of the soul, our dramatizing of that state through analogy occupies us with a sensual sign in the interest of our perception of a spiritual state. We lose through the modernist drift of philosophy, which encourages identity of spectacle and nature, the realization that sin is an actual circumstance of an actual soul. The necessities of drama nevertheless tend to enlargements upon the analogical dimension so that grotesque figurings without reference to spiritual actualities result in excessive distortions of the natural world. But that is a world which has denied the spiritual context which implies that the natural world is itself a *made* world. We end then inevitably with a distortion of sentiment proper to our sacramental relation to natural existence. Sentiment proper to intellectual being becomes eroded to sentimentality, so that intellectual vision is dislocated from its focus upon the truth of things, though it continues restless through a residual sense that sin is actual to the soul. We are left, that is, with an undesirable presence of guilt, which we would expiate in circumstance itself, in relation to spectacle, when it must be expiated in the soul with the support of grace.

The differentiations of *sentiment* and *sentimentality* I have considered at some length in *Possum and Other Receits for the Recovery of "Southern" Being*. (See especially "Possums in the In-Between" and "*Possum, Posse, Potui*.") By the excess effect of willfulness upon sentiment in pursuit of desire, desire itself becomes dislocated from its proper object. And so sentimentality in the final deportment becomes a deportment of will toward things as a final end, even though under the initiating impetus of love. Such an action of love abused may mistake excess as an enlargement, when it is rather a movement of atrophy of our desire to love. Our vision toward wholeness in the light of understanding is thus reduced. What is at ultimate risk is the wholeness of our own being as created intellectual creature. For we may become fascinated, in a literal sense, by our own inordinate attraction to a proximate end as the full exercise of intellectual action.

By our perception of an event within the circumstantial necessities of our intellectual response to reality, we said, we experience the wonder of immediacy.

And so we may be held arrested by that sense of wonder. To maintain the wonder becomes an *obsession*, we say, and since the proximate cause of the initial wonder is an event in existential circumstances, an encounter of intellect with a thing or things, we are tempted to maintain that wonder by arresting circumstances. But the end of such an attempt is a spiritual melancholy, since the soul is thereby denied its proper end. Intellect itself, however clever in denial, continues aware intuitively of that lost end. We know all too well the temptation, and the pathos attendant upon the false attempt to maintain our moment of being, our "still point." We know a person who is obsessed by youth as wrinkles come and hair falls out. Another is obsessed by sex, till orgy becomes a substitute for beatific vision. (John Donne understood a relation proper between our sexual and religious natures, and out of that understanding makes such daring metaphor as that in his poem in "Ecstasy." On the other hand, J. Alfred Prufrock does not understand the fullness potent in our endurance of time and so is obsessed by the bald spot in the middle of his head.)

Self-victim to obsession, we lose the enveloping impetus needed to bear us on the long journey of our becoming, the proper end of which journey is never proximate though always spoken of in relation to proximate circumstance. That is, in the present circumstances of the soul's being, the proper end is necessarily spoken of within the world as proximate to the journeying soul. The end of our being is spoken to us *through* the actualities of beings proximate to our intellectual response. In this respect our hypothetical event of the child's response to one of nature's creatures may serve as parable, the event itself in its actuality casting a light to the child's own intellect. In a detachment from the immediacy of such an experience, intellect is likely to make what we sometimes term "Romantic" assumptions about such event. Indeed those assumptions characterize philosophical and literary movements we give the grand title of "Romantic Age." Some of the assumptions, out of Rousseau or German Idealism, we observe as dominant in the rise of English Romanticism, and a considerable library is at hand which explores the point. The circumstances of our child-parable is the subject of a body of literature, from Blake and Wordsworth down to us, a body of such a considerable volume that one could make an impressive anthology of children responding to creatures selected from that literature. But it would be more difficult indeed to make such an anthology from literature before 1700.

What one would wish of such an anthology, however, is that it would include satiric or realistic correctives to the impetus of sentiment toward sentimentality which becomes evident, especially in popular literature, from the time of Wordsworth. Thus Dickens and Lewis Carroll, Henry James and James Joyce would be seen to set their made things against popular sentimentalities. But even so, one might discover, beneath the distortions, a rightness in a Blake or Wordsworth: For each is measuring, not an abstract idea against reality, borrowed from continental philosophy at the turn of their century, but rather measuring the idea by the immediacy of experience. Such is the dominant focus in Blake's famous songs, for instance. And we need only look at the brief lines of Wordsworth's "Intimations Ode," where he recognizes the actual distance from reality of his own intellect as he watches Hartley Coleridge, a child, playing at his feet.

It is important to this concern that, though we may see twentieth-century philosophy and literature as a reaction to nineteenth-century philosophy and literature – with the rise of Realism and Naturalism and Positivism, conjoined to the general deportment in intellect of this century which is termed Modernism – it is important to remember that an atrophy of intellect such as we suggest is never simply a matter of historical evolution, though it may be broad enough in effect upon intellectual community to warrant characterizing an epoch of intellectual history as the "Romantic Period." (I myself consider the so-called Romantic Period as beginning with Dante, for reasons argued elsewhere.) Sentimentality is not a characteristic in nineteenth- or twentieth-century intellect alone. What we are suggesting, rather, is that the "Romantic" inclination is a contingent possibility out of our created nature as intellectual creature, and at any moment in creation.[2] We may make the point perhaps by reflecting further upon our own immediate inclinations within existential circumstances. One in particular is an inclination which we only more or less resist, since it is a constant contingent to intellectual action this side death itself. It is that inclination we have just discussed: sentimentality.

A sign of intellect atrophied through sentimentality is a very common theme in our literature, from the temptations of Calypso to Odysseus down to our pathetic television dramas. We would arrest the moment of recognition in an experience, by an act that transforms not *some* potency into actuality but *all* potency into actuality. That is, we are much inclined to an attempted arrest of our becoming within a never-never land, a land which we might with traditional shibboleth call Eden Lost. The point is so thoroughly underlined by the art of our most intellectual poets in this century as to require only a naming of a few works to strengthen the point. See, for instance, Henry James's *American*, Joyce's *Portrait of the Artist as a Young Man*, Eliot's "Prufrock" and "Gerontion," Hemingway's *The Sun Also*

2 I have explored this "Romantic" inclination in its abiding contingency to intellect, regardless of epoch or geography, in the two works preceding this one, *Romantic Confusions of the Good: Beauty as Truth, Truth Beauty* and *Intellectual Philandering: Poets and Philosophers, Priests and Politicians*.

Rises, Fitzgerald's *The Great Gatsby*. More recently, Percy's *Moviegoer* or Robert Lowell's *Notebooks, 1967–68*. (If one chose to limit the concern to literary manifestations of the endangerment of intellect by sentimentality, he might indeed take as historical parameter to this modernist theme Joyce and Robert Lowell. Joyce's Stephen Dedalus, at the end of the *Portrait of the Artist*, represents the "Romantic" poet reduced to writing notes to himself, as is Lowell in his *Notebooks*.)

But aside from literary manifestations of this attraction of intellect to Eden Lost, we know other contemporary evidences of this dislocation of desire. Consider the modes of dress we find some parents imposing upon children, against which there was violent reaction in the 1960s by those children intent on recovering their own Lost Eden. On high occasion, at Easter perhaps, we see children frozen as innocent adults in suits and ties, like daddy's, or dresses and slippers echoing mama's world. The colors are apt to unsoiled beings, whites and pastels, residual signs tending to deny the world's realities. Parents will nevertheless be reminded of those realities, given the futile attempt to keep small children unruffled and unsoiled at least until the ceremonies of high innocence have been acted out. In Wordsworth's version of the ambiguous battle between the adult who would be a child and the child who would be an adult, there is a mutual conspiracy against reality, whereby the child as little "Actor" is busy at "A wedding or a festival,/ A mourning or a funeral," to which the child "frames his song." The adult is likely to be touched by nostalgia, as is Wordsworth, through such innocent formulations of imagined reality as the child's play.

The impulse to arrest the moment, to seize it by a violence of a will to assume power over being, is most ancient, though very modern to our experience as it is prevalent in modern literature. In our day, we take delight in the "instamatic" camera as arresting time and nature's unchanging course of weathers. In fact, recent advertisements of the virtue of these cameras emphasize this aspect. The ads play an action in progress against the camera film's arresting of that process. A moving picture is juxtaposed to the snapshot image on our TV screen. The snapshot is a permanent arrest of the fleeting moment to be tested against the "actual" moment of the actively filmed event. As if the active images were not themselves caught away from the actuality of event by a sequence of still frames only mechanically brought "alive." What awaits us when the snapshot is interred in the album, the notes in the notebook, the TV turned black and the cassette shelved? Where *are* we at such a moment of turning? That is the moment of terror always, and made more terrifying insofar as we are dependent for our peace upon arrested moments to defend us from the flow of our own being toward an actual end.

Concerning our native inclination to an arrest of a moment, which the inclination to arrest signals as already lost, need we be reminded that as subject for adult delight images of small children with small animals, or small children with large animals, is a favorite subject? The child in relation to mouse, the child in relation to giraffe or elephant, feeds a memory of our lost wonder in, and old encounter of, a green world by our green intellect. Similarly, young love at its moment of awakening is subject for comedy or pathos in our popular art. Such are the appealing advertisements of Eden Lost, catered to by technology's skill in making illusions of arrested Eden. But the fundamental catering is by our own personal inclination to such arrest through intellectual reactions that would arrest mediate ends. Thereby we become threatened with the loss of ultimate end. Given the technological marvels with imagery as a seeming control of reality, whether by words or pictures, we might even recover a new respect for those old "superstitions" in primitive people who see photography, for instance, as a species of black magic. As sophisticated, "civilized" people we take their reactions as at least quaint, but more likely as a backwardness, which we hasten to preserve in its quaintness by "anthropology" as science – an applied technology of intellectual arrest. But those supposed superstitions imply a more incisive recognition by the "primitive" intellect of the relation of intellect to reality, about the relation of action to potency in being, than we are likely to credit. An African or South Seas tribesman objecting to having his picture *taken* may express an objection more profound than our understanding as sophisticated anthropologists allows. For the picture *taken* is a *taking-from* the flow of being in the context of reality. It is a perversion, in this context, of the sacred to the profane. The ceremonies of innocence such as Eliade explores in the relation of the sacred to the profane might raise questions at last as to whether the primitive response to sophisticated intrusions is more innocent, even less sophisticated in the context of intellect's encounter of reality, than the supposedly sophisticated intrusion upon that innocence.

I do not mean to argue that such "takings" from reality are to be prohibited. I do not intend to destroy my camera. Rather, I am concerned that our "takings" be understood in their nature as "takings." For the spectacle of our common relation to reality, reflected in our making snapshots or studied portraits or films, or at a level advanced in our dramatic "takings" from reality in significant literature, speaks significantly to the reality of our nature as discursive, rational, and therefore limited, creatures. Such spectacles as we would arrest by art point toward our *reflective* nature as intellectual creatures. The technological physics of our reflective art is analogical to the reflective action of intellect itself in its relation to existence. What is of concern, as always, is the danger of arrest through reflection, the temptation to step aside from the flow of our own being within contextual creation, by analytical arrest, which in our day is an arrest served by a most formidable technology. In our earlier figure, the danger is that of a hunkering down about the moment's fire, in a retreat from the dangers of the necessary journey toward enveloping light. It may be a moment of beginning, out of which hope may grow. But only where there is the courage to abandon the arrest. That was a recognition Eliot came to, which he reflects in the concluding lines of his *Waste Land.* In those concluding lines there is the beginning of a hope which must grow through the journey, a recognition understood in his "Ash-Wednesday." Through "fragments shored against [our] ruin" by our reflective intellect we may "at least set [our] lands in order," toward a faring further, as the *Waste Land* has it. As "Ash-Wednesday" recognizes, this is itself a moment of arrest: "This is the time of tension between dying and birth," the moment of danger to being, to which an intellectual movement is the necessary agency out of the dangers of such an arrest.

What we wish to arrest, I shall be suggesting, is that wonder to intellect that stirs desire in our will. What results when we succumb, when our understanding is insufficient to the existential experience itself, is not a realization of the rest which the will properly desires, but an *arrest.* For rest in the sense of the reality that stirs our desire lies only in fullness. The end of desire, St. Thomas tells us, is a resting of the will through the fullness of our becoming. It is a rest in the Cause of all things, including our own restiveness. That is a rest St. Thomas names Beatitude. Meanwhile and meanplace, the wonder of being, actual and potential, stirs desire toward that end. And it is intellect in us that is stirred. It is intellect that wakes the will toward a prospect of that end. Will in its freedom, in its willfulness, would seize the present moment as if it were ultimate, rather than only proximate, means through which may come a showing of the light of the ultimate.

The ultimate is hinted at through things encountered in wonder as if those things might be in a timeless state. But the timeless state is yet to be realized by the person, embroiled as he is in the sorting of ends through intellectual action. Because arrested moments may be falsely oriented to the proximate circumstances of time and place as if these were the limits to the potential of person, the desire stirred in the person by his own shimmering restlessness may bring forth any variety of utopian distortions of reality out of an intellect gone astray from its proper end. Utopianism is a term widely applied to social and political manipulations of reality in relation to the community of mankind, but we need reminding often that it is a species of private worship by an arrested being, to which each person, separate from his concerns of social or political institutions, is always and in every place susceptible. It is the being of the self whose arrest is the death of that self.

III

It is through words, at last, that we begin to make those distinctions about intellect that set it and the will aright, as for instance in a reordering of proximate and ultimate ends in relation to a native – a natural – desire in intellect for a coming to rest in the fullness of the person's potential being. Words are a proximate light to intellect, let us say, whereby we focus intellect and will in an ordinate relation to the mystery of being. We have words as a specific gift to our existence. Specific, that is, in the sense that sign is significant out of the *species* of our being as created intellectual creatures. It is sign that steadies intellect's approach to reality. If at such a point it be objected that language "evolves" as man's brain enlarges, that objection ignores the mystery of potentiality *specific* to man.

The argument, which exists in various manifestations, assuming the evolution of language as an accompaniment of the evolution of the species in our post-Darwinian context, by implication or deliberation takes the argument to discount a first cause of specific being. That is, Being Itself, that *Ego sum qui sum*, the living God, is thought to be discredited by such argument. It is an assumption possible, however, only by its dependence in limited science and by avoiding the philosophical dimension of the question. That the position is untenable is made evident by many commentators, one of the most effective being Etienne Gilson, whom we here present as representative. In his "Analogy, Causality and Finality" (*The Spirit of Mediaeval Philosophy*), Gilson remarks that "our actions, or the products of our actions [in our present instance, that actions whose effect is the made thing, language] must of necessity be first of all in us before they can be in themselves what they will be when we have produced them." This is to remark our nature as *homo faber*, as opposed to *homo creator*, a distinction important to our own pursuit of this peculiar gift to man, his gift of making. It is a statement refining the nature of man in relation to causality implicit in his being itself. But, Gilson reminds us, "*homo faber* can never become *homo creator*" because man's nature as maker does not extend to the making of himself. That is, man – this specific, particular *person* – is not the first cause of his own being. Of necessity, in respect to causality, he but participates in his own being and is not his being's primary cause.

Man as maker is such out of his initiating givenness, for which he is not primary agent, however much he might will it otherwise – would will himself *to be* otherwise than by and out of the givenness. On the point, Gilson once more: "Man exerts no causality save in so far as he *is*," and this *isness* is precedently a given. "The first act is the being of the thing," in this instance the particular person. This is the "very act of existing exerted," in which formulation the passive verbal *exerted* in relation to the active verbal *existing* indicates a causal agent different from the *existing* agent, the person. That is the first action, in relation to which a second action is effected. It is in a second act that we find the person participating in his existence as *homo faber*. This "second act is the causal operation of the being, the intrinsic or extrinsic manifestation of its first actuality by the effects it produces within or without itself." (Étienne Gilson refers us at this point to St. Thomas, *Summa Theologiae* I, 45, 5 Resp.) The distinction between first and second act becomes important to any understanding of how it comes about that this inescapable distinction, repeatedly certified to us by experience itself, is set aside by ambitious pride in this creature *homo faber*, who desires to be *homo creator*.

Only in prying this second act, through which the agent participates in being, away from first act, by which first act the person *is* as effect and not cause, does it become possible to the person to assert the illusion of himself as creator. But to say a thing willfully does not make the meaning true over precedent reality. Still, by such a strategy it comes about that man, and particularly recent intellectual man, asserts language not as made in consequence of the first act of his being – a realization of potency dependent in that first act – but as created by man. To *create* in the precise sense in which Gilson defines it is to cause a being to be, a possibility open only to Being Itself.[1] We recognize this to be the Christian principle, established philosoph-

1 It is important to see here the difficulty to finite intellect in understanding the issue. For what is at issue is that Being Itself (God) creates *ex nihilo*. Gilson says cogently of this assertion: "Whatever we make we make out of something else, and therefore we can not conceive an act the term of which would be the very being of the effect produced. Nothing is easier than to repeat that God has created things and created them *ex nihilo*, but how can we prevent ourselves imagining, even while we deny it, that this *nothing* is a kind of matter from which the creative act draws its effects? We can think

ically by St. Thomas in building upon classical philosophy and revelation, which recognizes the actuality that existing things participate in being – participate in the first act. And they do so by virtue of the second act. That is why we must declare with Gilson that "*homo faber* can never become *homo creator*," as only God may be, though we must be steadily aware of our inclination through pride to assume ourselves creator in this fully *originating* sense proper only to God as Being Itself. The inclination is a "Modernist" one, centrally anchored in the assumption that language is thus *created*, the supposition being that language is a conspicuous instance of an effect of man as *homo creator*. We recall in passing that this bad seed is planted in Western intellect by Nominalism and has proliferated in Western thought with more tares than the struggling wheat can overcome.

Language, sign, is not therefore *created ex nihilo* but is consequent to that primary, that first act of being whereby man is what he is. Language is intrinsic to the nature of man and is not summoned out of nothingness by man's will, as is the pretense that underlies Nominalism. Language is therefore an effect of intellect's participation in that primary act of being itself through secondary act. Thus language becomes a significant manifestation of the actuality of that being man, who is peculiar in the orders of nature in that, as Gilson says, "In man, and in man alone, nature attains to consciousness of itself." In this light, we must consider words as a significant light on truth in consciousness.

Words, signs, are a light on the journeying of the specific being, the person. That journey is necessarily limited by the proximate limits of potency to the discrete being that *is* discretely, and therefore limited, by the first act of its being – whereby it is the specific thing it is – this specific per-

---

only of change, of transmutation, of alteration; in order to think creation, we should need the power of transcending both our degree in being and our degree of causality." In a note to the words, Gilson remarks that this is the reason Greek philosophy did not "attain to the idea of creation," a point he has effectively established earlier. Surely he is right in describing our difficulty in approaching this idea of creation, though we have intimations of the necessity of a reality beyond comprehension and have additionally the support of revelation that asserts the actuality of what escapes our finite intellect. But we must add to this that it is undeniable to us that we cannot escape knowing the truth that "Whatever we make we make out of something else." That recognition alone serves to caution us in presumptions about our own power as creators.

son. Words are thus *significant* of truth in a root sense of that term. Put metaphorically, words are that sort of campfire to a moment's respite along the intellectual way. In them, through them, truth may flow as a gift to intellect to sustain it on the necessary journey. But that light which seems to be in words may become a most certain darkening when mistaken, when presumed "enlightened" by intellect as the creator of the word. That is the corrective in the mystery of St. John's opening gospel words, "In the beginning was the Word," a word precedent to the beginning of the person who is thus an effect of the first act whereby he *is* through the act of the Word.

When we lose a focus in the world by losing our recognition of the significance of the word we utter, we lose the light we must husband in our words. What is at issue here is not fire, but the light of truth, and that light is a gift *through* our primary being, through that first act of our being. It is not a light seized from heaven by the force of will as in a Promethean violation of the gift of our being such as we may nevertheless witness exercised by some intellects. All along the way, that light of truth is to be conserved ordinately in the events of a person's becoming, his openness to the gift of potency which constitutes the second act of his being. That second act when ordinate is the suitable love of the self by the self. For only out of that ordinate self-love is it possible to *truly* love any "neighbor" – any *thing* in creation separate from the self.

It is precisely here, in relation to the light of truth conserved by words ordinately taken, that intellect encounters the darkening danger. We might put it that words themselves allow, though they do not command, a darkening of intellect when will is gone astray. Words may be easily used as a shield against the enveloping light of reality, that indwelling of being itself that sustains all things. Words may be defensively deployed by intellect in order to maintain the illusion of intellect's own light as enveloping all reality. That is the tendency we have attributed to "Modernism," one aspect of which is the dislocation in "Romanticism" of the *intuitive* intellect, whose companion error is the dislocation by certain Enlightenment thought of *rational* intellect. That is to put the point in relation to recent historical dislocations of intellect from being, about which "dissociation of sensibility" a considerable literature exists.

But we are attempting to move beyond the entrapment of historical context. We are attempting to recover the present circumstantial relation of intellect to reality in which lies an abiding truth about that relationship which is regardless of time and place. For it is only in doing so that we may come to an accommodation of the past and future in this present – escape the entrapment of history. It is in this context that words such as *making*, *habit*, *potency*, *act*, and so on become crucial to the ordering of our repeated encounters, through creation, of the true and the good and the beautiful in this present moment. For, eschewing the arrest that is tempting to intellect in such moments recovered and rather recognizing the moment as a point of departure toward a point of final rest, intellect must always return to time and place, return to the actuality of the person's existence in circumstantial reality. This is always to return to the point of intellectual departure in order to depart anew, and perhaps as renewed.

Now if we are by nature intellectual creatures as we contend, it is against our nature not to act as intellectual creatures. It is, then, a distortion of our nature, an elected atrophy, to seize the moment of our return as the point of final rest for intellect. That will be to fail as intellectual creature when all is said and done, and it would be most particularly a failure in our present attempt to enlarge our understanding of man as maker. We must return always to the proximate necessity to intellect of intellectual action. But we must always turn from that reflection on the proximate to the ensuing action whereby intellect turns outward to circumstantial reality, turns outward into the flow of time and place within which a person is *person* by the limits of circumstantial being, both his own and the world's.

When we have said the proper words, then, the question yet remains whether any act is done by the saying, since such saying is intellect's own proximate action, here and now, in which respect there follows a conclusion that such action has proximate end. That is the recognition by T. S. Eliot, who in *Little Gidding* puts it that "any action," including every phrase and every sentence, is always a "step to the block, to the fire, down the sea's throat/ Or to an illegible stone." He adds words that speak our point: "[T]hat is where we start." Repeated action, out of an end that is a beginning, is necessary to the constancy of our pursuit of the truth of things. It is to "things" in their existential actualities that intellect must return always, a return to beings, lest it be isolated in its words which it has reduced to merely its *own* words, in that possessiveness of closure against reality. That is the closure Joyce dramatizes in young Stephen's notebook conversation with himself at the close of *The Portrait of the Artist*. Eliot also dramatizes it in Prufrock's turning from reality in that "drowning" which concludes Eliot's famous poem.

The danger is that our very words may themselves become mere snapshots of the truth of things, arresting us from our proper return out of self-reflection to the continuous immediacy of actual things. However clever our arguments, unless we are turned toward actualities by them, we can but atrophy as intellectual creature. That such isolation of intellect by words has repeatedly occurred in our recent history is nowhere better certified than by the widespread suspicion of "intellectualism" in the popular mind by its common-sense recognition. If we become intellectuals in the popular, pejorative sense of the term, we shall have betrayed our *very* nature, that first act which is the gift of our being, since the end whereby intellect is empowered is suitably a rest in being itself, not in that intellectual isolation from being which gives us our age's popular term "alienation."

Now this is not simply a modern dilemma, though we tend to value it as our peculiar agony. St. Thomas speaks to the point in refuting one of his objectors in the *Summa* (I-II, Q. 3, A. 4): "The will's first object is not its act, just as the first object of sight is not the act of seeing but a visible object." The will's end is not properly itself, despite Existential attempts at such a supremacy of will over objects, a "modern" philosophy I suggest as ancient, at least as old as Euripides. For the error here made possible by the will's intent to itself has a long history among us, though its recent manifestations do not always appear ancient in origin. In another text, and again in response to a very "modern" rejection of his argument about the intellect's relation to the truth of things, St. Thomas observes that an objection raised to a point he has made "takes nature as divided against reason and will; whereas reason itself and will belong to the nature of man." The error at issue is the gnostic one which would separate will from creation through the act of will. And most specifically, though the irony is devastating, the will thereby can succeed only in a separation from creation in respect to that first act of creation relevant to it, the act whereby the willful person is the very person he is. The action is consequentially a self-reductionism. Thereby, will intends its own transcendence over nature, including a transcendence over its own given nature. If we put it in a popular aphorism adapted to the attempt, will attempts to lift itself by its own bootstraps out of creation. Or, in another formulation, the person wills to be a "self-made man."[2] What we

2 The allusion here – "self-made man" – is to Ralph Waldo Emerson and his "transcendental" version of modern gnosticism. See my chapters in *Why Hawthorne Was Melancholy* dealing with Emersonian thought, most conveniently available perhaps in *Modern Age* as "The Abandonment of Reality: Emerson's Legacy to 'Man-Thinking'" (Spring 1981) and "Emerson as

find, on sober reflection, is that such an attempt always drags creation along with it, inalienably binding its own given nature to itself despite its most radical attempts, short only of an actual suicide of the body.

In our own day the futile attempt at willed transcendence is widely dominant of our thought, as it was pervasive of that gnostic thought about reality which St. Augustine set himself to oppose after almost becoming entrapped by it himself. The difference between St. Augustine's milieu and our own is that we have abandoned the ancient gnostic belief in the actuality of the transcendent, for the ancient gnostic's attempt at self-rescue – his attempt to lift himself by his intellectual bootstraps – was in the interest of a more inclusive transcendence than that of the merely limited intellectual self. He intended to transcend creation, but intended thereby to become a part of the transcendent whole and not declare the whole of transcendence to be the self itself, as is the modernist's attempt.

The version of gnosticism dominant in our day attempts to support the intellect as autonomous, as the one transcendent. Whether that position is a cause of or an effect of the growing terrors to the isolated consciousness we need not attempt to answer. We remark instead that such a position makes inevitable the intellect's isolation from reality, an isolation in which there is neither a sense of proximate rest at its own campfire nor hope of any ultimate rest other than oblivion. It is a circumstance of intellect itself in which, in Flannery O'Connor's characterization of it, "Judgment will be separated from vision, nature from grace, and reason from imagination." The recourse to this isolated intellect is some species of violence in its response to the undeniable truth of things, whether it be the violence of self-centered thought within the isolated intellect whose effect is a reduction of its potential, or the violence of proximate actions in the world against its isolation. The latter is, incidentally, a contradictory shaking of one's fist against an unknown god, for the act of violence here is against an intentionality separate from and therefore taken to be antipathetic as well as antecedent to intellect.

The popular mind understands the impotence in such an isolated intellect, which is why that popular mind tends to use the term *intellectual* pejoratively. It realizes, however inadequately it may articulate that realization, that such "intellectual" isolation is a betrayal of the gift of intellect itself. And it knows at least tacitly that it shares with the intentionally isolated intellect a common intellectual nature. It is therefore irritated by the "treason of the clerks," though such words may be foreign to its knowledge. Cer-

Alchemist" (Winter 1984).

tainly the members constituting the popular mind are by their nature intellectual creatures, and sufficiently cognizant of that common nature that they recognize repercussions upon the community of mankind itself from the betrayal of intellect by intellectual isolationism as practiced in a deliberate manner of separation by gnostic intent. Such acts of isolationism are but willed exceptionalism from the context of being. And so the "treason of the clerks" is more widely perceived for what in truth it is than the treasonable clerk may accept, since he may easily escape his dilemma by his own use of pejorative term. That is, he may characterize his antagonist as "unsophisticated."

This intellectual, who is in truth a pseudo-intellectual, will make a defense by ridiculing the unsophisticated characterization of his position as "egghead" or the slightly more subtle charge against him that he inhabits an "ivory tower." But when the "popular spirit" charges such clerks, whom we more characteristically term the *intelligentsia*, as removed from "the real world," it is an inadequate defense at last when they declare their constructed abstraction of reality to be the real world in contrast to the shadow land of the *hoi polloi*. There is often more truth than envy in the epithet "egghead." It is especially so if the isolationist intellect manages its disjunction through its facility with sign as Nominalistic only as the strategy to his maintaining his isolation. Such is one source of the diversity of self-contained sign systems evolved by various specializations of intellect, creating a burden upon the common language that further separates community into factional elements in respect to the necessary common consent of intellect to the pre-eminence of reality over sign. The specialist of limited signs will appear "elite" in respect to those sophistications whereby he manages signs beyond the capacity of seemingly lesser intellects to call his management in question; not the signs themselves, but the purported "reality" created (as opposed to authenticated) by signs. That is the issue! It remains to be said, of course, that such "popular" denigrations of intellectualism often are accompanied by a rejection by that chiding intellect of its own responsibilities as intellect, just as it is to be recognized that another form of refusal of intellectual responsibility within the common community of mankind is to merely accept and defer to the isolated intellect through a false humility, the paid tribute to pseudo-sophistication. The combined influence of these varied intellectual refusals upon that community of mind in the end is an intellectual provincialism of an extreme pluralistic community.

With such complications of the problem of intellectual action before us, we must reserve our terms the more carefully. By *intellect* we mean to signify that which is common to humanity by virtue of the nature of personhood itself, which nature alone allows an acceptable use of such collective terms as *humanity*. It is an important concern, since it is only through intellect that we recover a community of thought. Against what is rather a pseudo-intellectualism, then, we must affirm as specific to each person's nature the powers of knowing as intellectual creature. But we shall be able to maintain this term properly only by remembering the actuality it names as common to us all, the true end to be recovered through intellect. The initial responsibility is to the truth of each person as particular being. He is made particular out of the gift of nature specific to human kind, but within the limits of his own specific being as discrete person.

The initial concern, then, is to reorient intellect to its proper end, through its response to being, both proximate being and ultimate being. I maintain that this ultimate being is the cause of all being, Being Itself. In pursuit of the proper habits of intellect, we are bound by the obligation of our own nature "to learn how the truth of things stands." The binding, we assert, is implicit in our very nature, to be discovered and certified by our acceptance of that necessity to out nature of that proper "habit of being," our intellectual nature in act. That is the beginning of a right will in relation to the gifts of our specific being which constitute our existence as discrete creatures. And through the habit of making, we recover actuality out of potentiality, a growing deportment of being in its ordinate relation to "the real world." Such preliminary extensions of our fundamental principle – that man is an intellectual creature – sets us in the way we are to go, and if my reader will not consent with full will to the principle and to our preliminary observations beyond it, perhaps he will at least accept the attempt as toward some "saving of the appearances" of our apparent existence as intellectual creatures. At the least, that might lead us to some recovery of a concern for the relation of mind to existence less disturbed by the panic of our present intellectual desperation which threatens the intellectual community at this moment of history. For what we are witness to is the collapse of the intellectual community as it at last recognizes its self-reduction through the illusion of autonomous transcendence.

To accept the argument as merely metaphorical may perhaps move us closer to accepting as well the mystery of mind's relation to its object. That is a crucial nexus not satisfactorily resolved by the latest biological sciences or the latest physics. At the level of conscious encounter of intellect with things lies the locus in which we must find, if we are to find it at all, an intellectual action bursting the closing shell of our self-induced intellectual solipsism. Solipsism is the false end which all ideology founders upon, though in a concession of false humility the particular ideologue may concede his ideology but one alternative. We here declare such attempts an evasion by intellect of reality, signifying intellect isolated through the presumption of its autonomy. It is thus that the attempt bears witness of a truth, though it is not the truth it supposes itself to witness. The other alternative is not idealism but realism. The escape from self-isolation and the despair of the collapse of the self effected by an opening of the self out of its finitudes, toward a fulfillment of the self, which is beyond its own power to accomplish precisely because of its finitudes. In moving toward the self as part of a whole, a being among beings sustained by Being Itself, lies the prospect of the self as a whole of a whole, discrete in its limits as such a "whole" person necessarily is.

Our argument involves the contention that in the course of recent intellectual history, intellect has found itself more and more confined, the irony being that its increasing limitation has been self-imposed in the name of an absolute freedom – in the name of its autonomy. In that Dantesean condition of its punishment, whereby presumption imposes its own punishment, intellect finds itself engulfed by pitiable agonies as it realizes its pretension to reality as it presumes itself its own cause. The most depressing of conclusions to its quest for that posited "freedom," which must for the conclusion set aside the realities of existence, is its isolation. We shall be concerned with this consequence to the mind, and in pursuing as desirable the alternative openness to reality we must remark consequential effects beyond the closing of the self. For such a presumption to freedom, which is the gnostic presumption of intellect, contributes to the disorder we experience of transgressions upon the world by intellect in the world: Exacerbating circumstances to our being in relation to creation and to community is the conspicuous contributions of intellect in our century. We may speak paradigmatically here: Just as we think ourselves escaped the closed Ptolemaic vision of the created world, with earth and social humanity the center of the universe, we begin to replace that center with man's individual mind itself. For the erosive assumption grows, till at last generally operative in social deportment itself out of the Renaissance, whether a tacit or implied or explicit assumption: Mind is the principle of being, as our modernism would have it. The question becomes vexing in our day. Which mind, or which minds, or which communities of minds?

Beyond question, we confuse the reality of our personal experience by the false assumption of mind as first cause of the experience, a temptation always at hand if we consult our actual experience of life, that mystery of our personhood in its response to its own existential being. If that is a present reality out of which our will engenders false principle, it is ancient as well. And it is more ancient than Descartes, who says truly, *I think, therefore I am*. The truth, as Gilson observes, is not an ontological truth, though our wonder out of the recognition of this limited truth obscures the point – as it did for Eve in the garden, we might add. For always there is the precedent. Galileo follows Ptolemy; Einstein follows Newton – each dependent not only upon precedent minds but most especially upon its own existing mind as precedent to its present action.

It is perhaps through desperation – or perhaps arrogance, or both – that intellect would save its own appearance by taking refuge in itself as its own cause, obfuscating the reality of its own existence as encompassed by a reality more complex that itself in its aloneness. Whatever the confusions and bafflements attendant upon openness of intellect – and they are always considerable – we grow to prefer them rather than the alternate terrors of isolation. For in that state of intellect when it is closed upon itself, it collapses in despair about its own being. The small star, the significant point of light called the *person*, by despair collapses to a black hole, to borrow from our modern metaphors about the enveloping space of modern physics to characterize despair.

What is in prospect, in our own view, is a balance of tensional inclinations through the will, a balance between the pull to the self and the attendant collapse of the self and the pull out of the self. The significant danger of the pull out of the self is an abandonment of the self by a dissolution into the all. Such is the tensional pull between the self as god and the all as god; between the self distinguished as the one significant existence, and the all made indiscriminate through sentimentality.[3] To submit to the one inclina-

3 Eric Voegelin speaks of this tensional complex to consciousness in a famous passage worth here recalling. "Existence," he says, "has the structure of the In-Between, of the Platonic *metaxy*." The difficulty in solving the tensional problem, which he describes in relation to Plato is that through Plato, one cannot at last reach the ground of that experience as deeper than the *metaxy* itself, as deeper than tensional poles, and for reasons Gilson presents

tion in a journey toward despair is the route taken by gnostic intellect; to submit to the other inclination in a journey toward a hope which is ungoverned by discretion about realities is to consent to the obliteration of the self. Neither is the openness we desire intuitively. If we might name recent intellects representative of the two inclinations as suggested in their works: the one inclination we find in Nietzsche in his pursuit of the superman; the other we find in Teilhard de Chardin in his pursuit of an oblivion of person at Point Omega.

Our own thought is that the desire most affecting intellect if fulfilled will not be fulfilled by the illusion of transcendence of reality in the will to power, nor by an excess of sacrifice to an oblivion of the self in the all in a refusal of our person in its potency. Rather, we must regain the awe-full recognition of the Psalmist and celebrate the most immediate miracle of existence: "I am fearfully and wonderfully made." In the delight of this recognition, so tempting of rest in the mystery of my own being, I may not restfully conclude of that fearful wonder, myself as an existing intellectual creature, indeed a holy "I," that "I" am either my own effect or end or that "I" am sufficient to the rescue of any or all other existing things through the sacrifice of my own particularity to the all. I must find an ordinate love of myself in relation to the all, and I am enabled in that journey toward an ordinate openness of my being to beings and to the Cause of beings, through the gift of intellect. It is a gift to be recovered through a will neither collapsing nor dissipating. For such willfulness must, whether that of a self elevation or a self-denial in the orders of being, in the end be declared a self-denigrating submission to the ways of the world rather than a

effectively in the opening chapters of his *Spirit of Medieval Philosophy*. If through Gilson we may discover solution to the tensional suspension, Voegelin nevertheless effectively characterizes our experience of that tensional condition to consciousness itself: "[I]f anything is constant in the history of mankind it is the language of tension between life and death, immortality and mortality, perfection and imperfection, time and timelessness, between order and disorder, truth and untruth, sense and senselessness of existence; between *amor Dei* and *amor sui*, *l'âme ouverte* and *l'âme close*; between the virtues of openness toward the ground of being such as faith, hope and love and the vices of infolding closure such as hybris and revolt; between the moods of joy and despair; and between alienation in its double meaning of alienation from the world and alienation from God." Quoted by John H. Hallowell in his "Editor's Preface" to Voegelin's *From Enlightenment to Revolution* (Durham: Duke University Press, 1975).

self-fulfilling submission to the truth of things in their existential reality. We must learn to make our growing way among the things of the world, the body of creation, by submission to reality, beginning with an acceptance of that first act of our being whereby we are and within which we participate in the second act of our being. We must accept, at our beginning, ourselves as a given, a gift to which we are responsible through the second act of our being, our intellectual act.

IV

We are concerned, we have said, with that discrete intellectual creature constituting mankind, the person, considering that in our day this creature seems as never before isolated from the community of like creatures he discovers by his intellect within the larger world. The larger world we speak of variously, attempting to name a totality of existential reality, whether we name it *creation* or *universe* or the like. If we speak of it in Thomistic terms, we mean to include the totality of created beings and by exploring the *person* in relation to this inclusive creation (mindful always that we explore from the finite creature's perspective), we tend toward an eventual discovery or recovery of *person* in its givenness as that givenness is circumscribed by circumstantial existence in general and discrete existences specifically (essentially) encountered by intellect. Person is discovered and discovers out of its actual existence at this point: *now*, and in this *place*.

By our intention of recovery of man's discrete existence, we may hope at least for some recovery of a community of mind among intellectual creatures, or at least among some of them, accompanied by a more comfortable perspective upon man's nature sufficient to dissolve somewhat the disquiet which results from our growing fear that intellect is isolated from any reality other than itself. For with this sense of isolation from existence other than its own, our creature presently begins to doubt even its own existence, a doubt which Descartes has not resolved for us by declaring the existence of intellect to be certified by the act of its doubting questioning of itself. A Cartesian doubting Edgar Allen Poe puts succinctly in its extremity of thought:

> *Is all that we see or seem*
> *But a dream within a dream?*

Always, we must start over with the Psalmist's timeless question: "What is man, that thou art mindful of him?" But if we take the question as merely an internal colloquy as does Poe, the *thou* merely a self-address, we shall be able to come only to the agitated *acedia* of a J. Alfred Prufrock. We shall come only to the despair of the self as dream.

Recovery from this disorientation of intellect from reality requires discrete intellectual actions of *making*, the habit proper to intellect by its nature. The burden upon my argument requires an exploration of those principles contingent upon the assertion, principles to be tested as firmly as possible by the habit of our being characterized in the term *homo faber*. Our acts of intellection, which constitute for us our individuality – divided unto ourself as a discrete existence, so to speak – those acts effect our experience of existence. If we were so fortunate as to already enjoy a community of mind consenting to these assertions, we might forego the present necessity, a somewhat tedious building of argument in relation to these known but largely forgotten principles. But the terms of our argument are neither generally available in our pluralistic intellectual community, nor the gist of the argument itself acceptable to large portions of that community at this point of our history, as it might have been to the intellectual community in 1300 A.D.

But in order that we may move at all in this present intellectual making, we must first require consent, a willing suspension of disbelief such as Coleridge begs of us as readers of a poem. It is a consent required in order for us to experience a poem in its internal self-containing being, as the thing it is in itself. We are more hesitant to give such consent when concepts of philosophical principles are at issue. Yet, unless we do so to some degree, we shall never move philosophical discourse beyond either a momentary entertainment of intellect or a mere description of the hypothetical that can mean in the end only an underlining of our separate isolation. My concern is that we first give a willing consent to possible being – the argument we are making – such as we afford in our response to a poem. This is to beg a consent to judgment deferred.

Now, by that consent, we may build a context within which to consider at last the reality of discrete experience of existence as actual and as suited to philosophical reflection. We may in that context discuss such a term as *discrete intellectual creature* with a presumption of faith in at least the possibility that such a creature exists. We must at last of course either give assent or withhold consent to the context of this made argument, as we do in our response to that made thing, the poem. We respond in either respect after experiencing a made thing as a consequence of a willing suspension of disbelief. There can in the end be no doubt that these things exist, though some are more perfect in being than others. The hope of some recovery of a community of mind is still sufficiently alive to warrant our attempt, especially given intellect's desperate circumstances in this moment of history. In brief, what we ask is an initial gesture of good will toward the possibility of a community of belief about man as intellectual creature, in the interest of our recovery from the intellectual malaise that threatens.

Initially then, assertion follows assertion, so that the context for intellectual response is provided rather abruptly. Assertion itself is complex, in that, if it intends to be more than hypothetical, it already implies a position of conviction dominant in the asserting mind. One might attempt to put the whole texture of assertion conditionally. One might say, and repeat with each step in the making of assertions, "let us suppose that." Let us suppose that man is intellectual creature. Let us suppose that intellectual act is an action of making, and so on. To do so conditionally would require of intellect itself, however, a dissociation from its own acceptance of principles, an exercise of intellectual action with virtues of its own no doubt, but an exercise replete with danger. For the fault lying between actual belief and rhetorical strategy – the void – yawns. By the very act of dissociation, there is a growing difficulty of making an initiating association through tentative consent. Skepticism is a habit no less than gullibility, and its erosive aspect is the tacit assumption by the skeptical intellect that it withholds consent by its dissociation, thus becoming "objective." But withholding assent, as for instance to the proposition that man is intellectual creature, carries within it an openness to contrary assent: that he is an accident of evolutionary forces, for instance. Skepticism carried to extremity becomes cynicism, in that intellect refuses consent, explicit or implied, to *any* possible truth. What underlies cynicism is therefore an assent to nihilism, though it be an assent kept secret from the cynic by himself.

Now in respect to central principles, from which intellectual actions must develop, a fictional or conditional relationship between the active intellect and the principles upon which it acts conditionally are anything but "value-free." Whether one assert intellect an accident, a summary of evolutionary accidents in a mechanistic universe, or a created intellectual creature, however contingently phrased to the protection of intellect as "objective," that action is already touched by a precedent action of assent in some degree. Even the supposition of detached objectivity by intellectual action is fraught with questions of consent to buried principle. Acknowledging assent, acknowledging the inevitability that a "pure" objectivity is already tainted, may prove in the end more nearly "objective" than the presumption of detachment which is secretly tainted by the "subjective." This is a lesson taught steadily, and often subtly, by Plato's Socrates.

The concern here is to establish a level arena to intellectual encounter, out of the belief that all serious argument about the nature of reality in relation to intellect is founded in faiths in conflict. If my mode is indicative, begging at the least a subjunctive consideration – a willing suspension of disbelief in entertaining my mode – I understand such a "subjunctive" address to be by its very nature always in some degree a fictional mode whose contingent action is an indicative consent or dissent. The issue is always the consent to a truth accepted as truth, to the openness of a "yes" by intellect. Even, let us add, if that consent be "Yes, there is no truth." From my position, of course, that is a contradictory action in that negation is necessarily founded in a positive rejection of a positive consent to truth. It is here that the pathos of intellectual despair rises, in an incompleteness of understanding by the intellect. In consenting to the "truth" that there is no truth, intellect prevents rescue to a healing openness to truth. If one requires evidence or at least suggestive illustration to the point, consider this in relation to the intellectual dead-end to which T. S. Eliot finds himself arrived in about 1920. He recognizes – understands – the contradiction, and moves out of it, beginning with *The Waste Land*'s concluding section, "What the Thunder Said."

My "subjunctive" principles are ones to which I have already given an indicative consent in some degree, then. To say this has the virtue of alerting my hearer in order for him to govern the degree of his willing suspension of his own disbelief. I trust that thereby I pay him that respect to his own power of intellect which I value highly. And so to our concern for man as an intellectual creature in a context of creatures, a being among beings, whose peculiar nature sets him apart in certain respects from other beings, while he is in certain aspects like other beings.

Being, in respect to man as a created nature, is a gift *enchanced* through a progressively sustained action, which is to say it is always at risk through its own action. From my point of view the risk is of losing that sustenance which is grace. I understand it that here we encounter a partnership in being, the prospect of a partnership through the willed actions of intellect under the auspices of will as governed by prudence. This is the true country of the second act of being which we distinguish from first act, the being of our person as given. We are speaking here, in scholastically traditional terms, of the created soul's engagement of existential reality – its engagement of its own and of all existences contingent to its existence as the second act of its being. We might here recall, in respect to the virtue of *prudence*, St. Thomas's remarks in his "Prologue," II-II of the *Summa*. "As for the intellectual virtues, one of them is prudence, which is contained by the cardinal virtues and numbered among them. . . . The other three intellectual virtues, namely wisdom, understanding, and knowledge, share their names with certain gifts of the Holy Spirit." The "enchancement" (my neologism) of intellectual being is the contingency of its fulfillment, in my view, through prudence, which discovers the ordinate practice of a relation among those other intellectual virtues. And what it discovers is an implicit hierarchy of intellectual virtues, whereby knowledge prudently taken leads to understanding and understanding to wisdom. Such intellectual action, I believe, is always under the auspices of grace, reflected in these virtues which share their names "with certain gifts of the Holy Spirit."

For the moment we may set aside this sponsorship of grace by the Holy Spirit, though one must at the last accept (so I believe) that grace as a reality is implicit in existence, in manifest being itself, whatever the intellectually perceived manifestations of being in the peculiarly existent thing. Our concern is first of all, however, with an action of intellectual being, the movement establishing a relation of the existing intellect in its response to itself or to whatever is not itself. Our naming of an *existent thing* (here, the intellectual creature) is suitably named by the present participle as a *being*. It is suitably named in that the term is suggestive of a progressively sustained action, one familiar to us in the experience of our own existence. We know our intellectual action as an effect out of the nature of this discrete existence, this *being manifest*, which is ourself, whether or not we consent to that gift of knowledge, which is both *in* us and *to* us, of our own being as effected by the Lord and Giver of Life as St. Thomas would have it. *Being* thus sustained is potential in its second action, even though that action might become confused in our understanding by an assumption of intellect that it is its own cause and therefore second action is really first action of being as intellectual creature.

The sustained action we mean is not dependent on movement or change as ordinarily understood in the field of space and time by the term *action* as thus restricted. We witness ourselves as a discrete creature through our actions of eating and growing, of moving and resting, and so conspicuous are these actions as measured by movement that we tend to limit the term *action* to such easily observed events. Indeed, a sense of action reduced to movement or change, measurable in relation to time and place, tends to an inevitable reduction of the complexity of action by the very imposition of that name through our act of intellection. There is a tendency in intellection to attach sign (our *word*) to spectacle in response to our perception of being, but the action of being is deeper in its nature than spectacle accounts for. *Spectacle* here has to do with the conspicuous, evidences of a going-on-ness in a discrete existence, the perceived manifestations of being. If we take the *person* to constitute *being embodied* and do not take that as simple first act, we incline to confuse body and being, even as when in speaking of man's soul we tend to separate soul from body in a gnostic division of the simple existence. We more properly say that the soul is the substantial form of the body. This inclination to divisiveness of being by thought, out of our finite discursiveness, tends to arrest our openness to the being we nevertheless acknowledge by sign. But insofar as the act of naming our perception allows that naming to rest sign *on* being as reduced to spectacle – to *body* as determinate of being, for instance – that action closes our intellectual act against the fullness of being.

To have said this is to have come to Gilson's concern for the dead-end from which classical philosophy could not find an exit. Plato's God, he says, is left ambiguous, a divinity who "belongs to a class of multiple beings," with "rivals in the intelligible order of Ideas." As for Aristotle and his unmoved mover, Aristotle "stopped on the way" to a recognition of God as Being and consequently leaves the unmoved mover a "separate, pure act, thought of thought" as set forth in the *Physics*. Aristotle is able to go only so far with "a natural theology," says Gilson in *The Spirit of Mediaeval Philosophy*, stopping short in his *Metaphysics* of "being as being," a necessary substance always in act. For Plato, on the other hand, the Demiurge "becomes, not Being, but the Good." If good is primary, then the perfection of being implies limitation, and "that is why the Greeks prior to the Christian era never conceived infinity save as an imperfection." St. Thomas to the contrary sees the good as an aspect of being, not the other way round.

Christian philosophy understands God as Being Itself, from which derives the recognition of an identity of essence and existence of God, as distinct from the order of nature. For the classical philosopher to the contrary, movement is the contingency of modes of being. What Plato and Aristotle "both lacked was the *Ego sum qui sum*," after which revelation in *Exodus* the "universe is no longer suspended from the necessity of a thought that thinks itself." It is rather "suspended . . . from the freedom of a will that wills." What Greek philosophy fails to provide at last, though both Plato and Aristotle move near the recognition, is that leap of thought which passes "beyond the plane of efficiency to the plane of being." The idea of creation, which is "wanting in Aristotle" is dependent upon a recognition that God as First Mover is therefore *Creator*. In the Greek thought, movement itself is not seen as ultimately requiring creation as the act of moving. What we have not arrived at, till St. Paul and the early Fathers, is a recognition of the *first act*, whereby a thing is the thing it is and in which continuous act, being itself is an action. The primacy of Being is a recognition necessary to issue from the entrapment of the closed perception of God as *thought thinking*. To St. Thomas, God is Being in perfect act, whereby finite creation consequently *is*, and *is* in relation to the action of being signified in the verb *is*.

Given such contrary argument from Gilson, who has thought long and hard on these questions, we must ourselves move cautiously with that classical term for man out of Aristotle, whereby man is declared a rational animal. The danger, since the perception of man's nature lacks the primacy of Being Itself as the initiation of the being of man (whereby we call him *spiritual*), is that we shall become entangled in the motions of things, held within a natural theology which cannot relate at last to the supernatural Being Itself. We may even suspect that Modernist thought, having rejected Being Itself, adapts the Aristotelian definition ("rational animal"), turning the borrowed concept to an increasingly reductionist, closed version of mankind. The classical concern for "motion" in both Plato and especially Aristotle is renamed "evolution" in the adaptation. By that manipulation of concepts, we find ourselves reduced in our understanding of this creature man. And if so reduced, we shall be in further danger of seeing man as dualistic in nature. Especially so if Plato becomes dominant in the attempt to salve the residual longing for some "spiritual" component to the new gnostic definition. Not that this direction does not recognize the dualistic threat, which it attempts to contain by the development of imminence, anchoring the desire for godhead in matter itself. The difficulty proves, however, a species of intellectual assumption which I have elsewhere called "inverted Platonism," whereby the specific intellect in its action of accounting for creation assumes tacitly at the least that its own actions are the first cause of creation. It little matters as a rule, in the press of the argument, to insist that such an argument is divided and may not have it both ways, with thought at once a spume of matter, while the thought of the advocate of that thought is somehow altogether transcendent of the determining matter of which it is a spume.

As for the dualistic threat in the Modernist adaptations of classical thought, that danger is subsumed by Thomistic realism. Man is spiritual creature, a position which does not deny aspects of his singular being. That is, the singularity does not deny aspects of his rational or animalistic dimensions. That is why Thomas's characterization of man as a *singular* creature, in whom the soul is the substantial form of the body, becomes crucial to our recognition of this unique nature, our personhood. Man is a singularity, dependent as image of Being Itself. Man is not by that dependent nature dualistic, though nevertheless dependent in his singular being. Additionally, this discrete *person* is called a species unto himself, in the classical sense of *species*: Each person is unique creation by God Creator. The epithet *God Creator* suggests the limited perspective possible from our intellectual finitude. God actually sustains created beings in a continuous creating present, in that first act of existential being. Thus we say existence *is*, through the grace of the "Lord and Giver of Life."

There is not, of course, any suggestion of necessity intended in this formulation of our perspective toward God Creator. Again, Gilson speaks to our point. Through the Christian distinction between *essence* and *existence*, Aristotle's "eternal world, existing outside God and without God" is changed utterly, and the change is by that devotee of Aristotle, St. Thomas. And now, with this distinction, not only does it "remain true to say that all that is, save God, might be other than it is, . . it now becomes true to say that all save God might possibly not exist." That is the truly radical vision in Christian revelation, whose philosophical formulation is given by St. Thomas. Gilson (in *The Spirit of Thomism*) summarizes that vision: Actual existence (*esse*) is "that by virtue of which a thing, which [Thomas] calls *res*, is a being, an *ens*." Essence is "the being-hood or being-ness of being." (How essence is related to created beings in distinction from essence in the Being Itself, God, is adumbrated by St. Thomas in a key treatise, his *On Being and Essence*.)

We are here touching upon an elementary and abiding difficulty which this intellectual creature man has in responding to existence, given that the limits of finite intellection impose a discursiveness upon his attempt. It is a problem remarked by a recent philosopher, a member of that plurality of our intellectual community who is not in much sympathy with the principles I would advance but who recognizes the proximate difficulties any intellect experiences in attempting to deal with being through discursive signs. Brice Parain, a philosopher with whom Albert Camus found himself most compatible, remarks in his *A Metaphysics of Language* that words "constitute a kind of reality in relation to thought," but one which is independent and corrosive of thought and of reality itself. "Language," he says, "is fertile only because it devours existence." Again, "when we name something we in fact kill it. It is no longer a tree, it is a concept," the determination of a term being a negation of that portion of the being of the thing not touched by the term. We must, he warns us, "distrust what we say, each of our words having two faces – one turned toward being that it represents, and the other toward the negation of being that it practices by not being what it represents." In the final reality of language, it "can only say that it is impossible to say anything about [being]."[1]

One recognizes in Parain's argument the desperate circumstance of

---

1 Parain, in lamenting the two faces of language, is no doubt indebted to De Saussure. Gilson responds to the complaint in his *Linguistics and Philosophy*: "De Saussure did no more than state a fact in saying . . . that 'the linguistic phenomenon constantly presents two faces.' It is necessary to add, however, that these two faces, although corresponding, are heterogeneous. . . . Since the physical face is the only one which could be measured and scientifically described [thereby excluding *meaning*], every linguistics which wants to be a science tends to reduce the transphysical or nonphysical face to the physical. [But when linguistics denies the nonphysical face, *meaning*] philosophy cannot excuse itself from intervening in order to recall the rights, not of philosophy, but of reality." It is Parain's dilemma, out of Cartesian thought, which leads him to say with sardonic irony that "What is revealed to us . . . in our moments of silence is that we are a kind of compost heap on which language germinates, grows, and flowers." He sees the "double" nature of language as "a mixture of being and nonbeing," as distinct from Gilson's way of seeing it, which is as physical and transphysical. Gilson sees the *word* analogous to the life of man, in an analogy we shall presently engage. As if responding to Parain's complaint, he says, "if the meaning is to the word what life . . . is to the body, it is natural that language should have a life of its own and that words should be born, mature, flourish, mutually fecundate each other, grow old and die as all living things do. This is why artificial language, be its inspiration mathematical or logical, is a language born dead." The issue here we shall engage further in Chapter VII.

thought as action in relation to being. His assertion is that thought or being is forever defeated by this peculiar inclination to words, which inclination we to the contrary are contending is natural and out of our very nature as intellectual creatures: this inclination to sign. It is the sign above all else that defeats intellectual being for Parain. "All difficulties of philosophy arise from the fact that we constantly have two pictures of ourselves, what we feel and what we say, and from our not immediately knowing why these must be two and not one." Once committed to words, "one no longer knows where he is, in reality or fantasy." And as if words were not themselves a sufficient enemy to our existence as discrete creatures, there is the additional enemy, thought itself. "Why not . . . invert the *cogito* and say: I think, therefore I am not. For to think is not to be, it is to wish to be. . . . To think is to struggle painfully in lies and errors, to struggle against them, to escape from them." In the context of Parain's argument, the only escape is into a thoughtlessness, an existence separate from both thought and word. He speaks with nostalgia and a touch of envy: "Nightingales have no need of poets; each of them is a poet, superbly, fittingly and with simplicity." And in that speech we hear the Romantic poet, both a John Keats who laments that the nightingale, unlike the poet, sings with "full-throated ease" because it is not cursed with the nature of thought, and Eliot's J. Alfred Prufrock, who would choose to be "a pair of ragged claws/Scuttling across the floors of silent seas" to escape thought and word.

The point of introducing Parain here is to mark the sort of end we come to through Romanticism as practiced by some of our poets, in whom a desire for a comfortable openness to being is their supreme desire, beyond the seeming reductions of that dream-state of happy nature by thought and words. One might ask Parain whether Prufrock's crab is not also superbly, fittingly, and with simplicity a poet. To grant either nightingale or crab that state, of course, is but to deny the particular nature that is Parain, for nightingales have no need of poets because they are nightingales, and we have but confused the proper object of human desire through misused language when we thus confuse the categories of being. Not that our difficulties with words in relation to being, as acknowledged with some desperation by Parain, aren't pressing difficulties. But the difficulties are such that we shall not resolve them by avoiding what we may and must come to know about thought itself in relation to being. We must do so within the limits of our finite intellectual being, and in doing so we must take recourse to words. A poet contemporary to Parain, one acutely attuned to the problems of intellect in our world, says something similar to Parain's lament, but he does so in affirming the necessity of our moving through thought, and through words out of thought, toward reestablishing a community of intellect against the desperateness of mind's isolation from being:

> Words strain,
> Crack and sometimes break, under the burden,
> Under the tension, slip, slide, perish,
> Decay with imprecision,
> Will not stay in place,
> Will not stay still. (Eliot, in *Burnt Norton*)

One need not, indeed must not, pass over that inclination to intellectual act which distorts the complexity of being by the very act of affirming being through sign, through word. Let us put this difficulty faced by intellect at an extreme of its approach to being: The material cause of an existence (the *material cause* being but a partial aspect of the "thing's" full being) is too easily and falsely concluded the essence of the thing by our intellectual action. But this inclination to distort the actual most usually results from a carelessness of thought about the material dimension of being; the material dimension is most immediate to perception through our senses. To envy nightingale or crab is to reduce by wishful thinking all being to the merely sensual. But even nightingales and crabs have as a part of their actuality a dimension beyond the merely sensual, though they do not participate in that dimension except insofar as they are creatures sustained in their being by virtue of their creatureliness. This is to say that they too *are* by that *first action* we have considered. Our response to a creature's being, if we are Keats in his poem or Prufrock in his monologue or Parain in his argument, springs from our proper but impatient (and so inadequate) desire to know. And it is an impatience that implies as much an envy of the angelic mode of knowing as envy of the assumed "pure" sensual level of a crab's or a nightingale's being.

V

One need not believe in angelic existences to recognize the attraction of the angelic mode of knowing as defined by St. Thomas. Our very impatience to know, our resistance to the limitations upon intellectual action by the burden of discursiveness, has kept alive, even in a modern thought supposed liberated from medieval conceptions of thought, the dream of a purified deportment of mind, whether described as "instinct" or as "intuition." The one term, *instinct*, commits thought as mechanistically determined as the explanation of thought, though just how that detached "scientific" evaluation of thought is justified in its assumption of its own detachment from mechanical existence is rather vague. Sufficiently authoritative in deportment to the problem, the patron of deterministic mechanism presumes to judge thought from his assumed transcendence of deterministic cause. Just why that authority is sufficient, however, is not evident.

The term *intuition* as opposed to *instinct* shares, if but residually, the view of intellect out of medieval thought, whereby intellect is active under the modes of intuitive and rational extensions toward being. Depending upon the degree of behaviorist commitment by the rationalizing intellect, especially as anchored in neurological science, thought is often in our day supposed a sort of neurological afterglow or perhaps a cumulative encodement of the history of the species activated by a present response to stimuli in the present embodying creature, or perhaps a combination of these. *Instinct* is adumbrated in sophisticated systems of its manifestation as restricted to mechanistic nature. *Intuition* is rather an act of gnostic transcendence of those mechanistic determinations of response to stimuli. The one direction in the accounting of thought seems content with the certainty of its science, though innocent of the presumption of its own transcendent platform beyond mechanistic existence itself wherefrom it declares mechanism the inclusive principle. The other – dare we say – *intuitively* resists the implication of an entrapment within the mechanistic system and its refinements of psychological sciences. It would find ground to its actuality beyond the limits of behaviorism and thereby rescue the prospect of transcendence. In both attempts lie always, through a desire not sufficiently accounted for by evolutionary determinisms of whatever species, that desire for a perfection of being. Such is the desire in this discrete creature *man thinking* for teleological fulfillment. Either the angelic mode or the animalistic mode seems the alternatives to modernist thought. Either the instantaneous thought beyond even the miracle of silicon chips, or that other elemental state of biological being whereby one is blessed with the perfection of the crab scuttling across the shores of silent seas.

But we are already knowing creatures when the problem rises, and we are disturbed by the mystery of knowing itself, impatient for some absolute assurance of knowing. Out of impatience we would either not know at all our teleological end, the intellectual state of the crab; or we would know with the purity of mathematically instantaneous inclusiveness, as with the microchip, that modernist version of angelic intellect. What breeds impatience as knowing creatures is the inescapable experience of knowing itself and the inescapable recognitions of the nature of that experience insofar as our finite instruments of knowing will reveal that nature to us. That revelation when pursued rationally is slow, is discursive. And it is most disturbingly reflective in its aspect. Reflection becomes disturbing because it emphasizes always the *not known*. The modernist defense against this disturbing sense of absence to intellect has been to put that absence as the not *yet* known, out of which defense rises various gnostic utopianisms which rest faith in science.

That we know, let us say, is a recognition through analytical action but necessarily in response to a precedent experience of knowing. Aye, there's the rub. For always, when we conclude that we know (of which conclusion one species is put negatively – *we do not know* is itself a knowing not to be denied), our conclusion always follows a precedent act of knowing. In reflecting upon the nature of thought, we do so always in a divisively analytical way in which thought is already precedent. With the act of conclusion, we are by that reflection upon it divided from the initiating thought. *I think* as an affirmation raises immediately in us the awareness of an "I" that is already thinking, revealing at once in turn a recedent "I", the new "I" aware of the "I" in the affirmation "I think." Disturbed by the absence of an inclusiveness of the "I" within affirmation of thought itself as existent, we desire that inclusiveness. And since its absence is discovered through analytical thought, we come to suppose that the fullness desired may be accomplished by the *knowing* which analytical thought allows us to order toward some end. With the paradoxical defeat of the desire to transcend the necessity of thought through thought itself, in a stasis beyond self-reflection – as in the "receding "I" – we intensify our analytical attempts at an accommodation to thought.

It is a process whereby consciousness, we might say, seeks rescue from the exile which seems decreed by thought. But in that process we become confused in consequence of our expectations that the process (which let us call the science of knowing) will rescue us from that exile. In the journey of return out of exile, we become more and more dependent upon signs as the instrument of the process of the "I's" recovery. We tend at last to rest faith in the adequacy of sign as the necessary instrument to orient us in our exile, a compass of our own designing. Put in terms more immediate to the recent history of our intellectual attempts to overcome exile, we incline to suppose that the science of signs, linguistics, will rescue us from Brice Parain's dilemma, in which conditioning of thought by the necessity of signs, as he says, "one no longer knows where he is, in reality or fantasy." Since World War II, we have become increasingly desperate as the promises of linguistics prove disappointing to our desire. The severity of that disappointment is reflected in Parain's *Metaphysics of Language*. We remember that Parain is writing his rather plaintive concern for a "metaphysics" from the international center of linguistic sciences, bubbling to the surface and washing across the academic mind out of Paris with what has proved in effect debilitating influence on the academic community. Parain was acutely aware of difficulties in this new thought, while too many academics tended to embrace that thought, usually for no better reason than because it was new. We observe here, against such provincialism, that in fact it bears in it genetic origins in Nominalism.

Another philosopher, immediately within those same circumstances and at the same time as Parain was issuing his little book, undertakes a critique of the problem which is more helpful in resolving the dilemma of *thought* to the thinking creature. In 1969 also, Etienne Gilson published his *Linguistics and Philosophy: An Essay on the Philosophical Constants of Language*, the English version translated by John Lyon and published only in 1988. Gilson begins his argument with a consideration of "The Myth of the Decomposition of Thought" and with observations helpfully restorative to that impasse Parain reaches. (Parain's disciple Camus had also reached that impasse.) The gist is that one may not expect to reconcile thought's relation to reality through a "science" of signs, but must rather recover philosophy to the task. Gilson observes along the way a failure of some linguistic scientists to discriminate between their science and philosophy, with the result that they advance a pseudo-philosophy as if it were philosophy authorized by science.

We need to notice that Gilson is quite sympathetic to the arguments of some linguists. But others, such as Condillac, receive careful dissection of their arguments, by this precise pathologist of thought, Gilson. Condillac, for instance, uses an analytical method that "treats mind as a thing composed of parts," perhaps seen by analogy as derived from the neurological sciences of the brain, an engine constituted of parts. What the method leads to, as applied to mind, is a "simultaneous decomposition of thought and language." The consequence is that "The numerous family of ideologues . . . are witnesses of a school which profited by mind's limitlessness in order unrestrainedly to attack it through all kinds of limitations." That is, they use the reality of mind they possess but do not acknowledge – its limitlessness – as the means whereby to declare mind limited. The very action denies the intentional principle, the conclusion about the nature of mind, so that the effect is a willed reductionism toward mind itself. The reductionist view, though false, is possible only through the contradictory truth about mind, its limitlessness. It is possible to manipulate the reality of thought itself thereby, Gilson says, "Because thought is not made up of parts [as opposed to language or the organ of the brain itself], it is always possible to devise a new manner of breaking [thought] down." It is possible, because mind is limitless to itself.

Gilson appreciates how one might come to such a pass in dealing analytically with thought. For, like Parain, he sees language itself seemingly caught in this duality of thought-language. The question is a delicate one whether the analyst begins with thought or with language. But, he says, "this is always why, whether the linguist wishes it or not, grammar is philosophy and all philosophy implies a certain view of language." Thought is itself, Gilson will hold, a simple "thing" without parts, but a temptation to intellectual action to divide it rises in the natural power of intellect itself. Intellect as discursive in relation to the limits of finite existence is affected by its own existence as incorporated soul. "This natural power to break things down belongs to the realm of sensation as the point of immediate origin to discursiveness of intellect [in its response to reality], for the diversity of the data pertaining to sight, hearing, touch, etc., puts us in the presence of distinct data." But what must not be overlooked is that the presence of distinct data to thought is not thought itself. Thought "is not truly composed of units."

In order to support that position, Gilson turns to language as distinct from thought, remarking in doing so that "The concept of the soul has been brought into disrepute by modern positivist psychology to such an extent that when today a person looks for an explanation of the status of thought itself outside of language, one does not find anymore anything either inside or outside himself to respond to the question." What Gilson attempts is a recovery of the actuality of our experience of thought, in relation to intellectual encounter with reality. It is such encounter that we attempt to articulate as our experience, witnessed through sign. He begins with an elementary observation about signs as delivered through the body from mind: "It is evident that the written letter depends upon the spoken word. There are no spoken letters. Spoken words are not composed of letters but of sounds." But when we attempt to deal with the word either as spoken or written in a "scientific," as opposed to "philosophical," manner, we encounter immediate obstacle. It is "practically impossible to come to know a word isolated from a phrase, because, taken by itself every word is susceptible of many different senses." In addition, though "sentences are made up of words which determine their meaning, . . it is almost as true to say that it is the sentence that determines the meaning of the words of which it is composed" so that one may even say "that language is not composed of words but of what the poet called quite appropriately 'understandable mouthfuls.'" Spoken words are not composed of letters but of sounds, though the analysis of sounds, like the analysis of letters of the engraphed signs, does not take us very much nearer the mystery of thought itself as an existing cause to secondary manifestations of thought, the sounds or engraphed letters. Communication requires language, requires the sign, wherein "every signifier and signified" is, in its turn, at one and the same time signifier and signified. That is a proposition oriented by our realization of a reality about signs: "The sign post is not the route which it points out." And so we return to the proximity of Parain's concern, to which Gilson speaks in saying that "Between [speech and thought] there seems to be interposed a kind of creative liberty which is called mind," through which created liberty mind attempts to mediate the *simplicity* of thought itself beyond itself through the *complexity* of sign.

It is perhaps appropriate here to consider those beguiling terms to which we have had recourse already and to which we must appeal subsequently: *simplicity* and *complexity*, as those terms are applied to existential realities, here the reality of simple thought in its relation to the reality of any complex sign of thought. In doing so, we shall bear in mind cogent observations Gilson raises against the pretense of linguistics to decompose thought itself. The insurmountable obstacle to such deconstruction which "thwarts the striving of linguistics toward the ideal of perfect scientific rigor is the fact that words have meaning," but only through active thought, not in themselves. "In order to disembarrass itself of this intruder [*meaning* upon the *instrumental* language as proposed to be objectively scientific], the belief has been devised, or it is at least spoken of as if believed, that it is the sign itself which created the meaning, and the signifier the signified." Such is the issue of Cartesian Idealism, through which intellect itself is disjoined from reality and thought as thought thus justified, but not by reality itself. Rather, with the intentional autonomy of intellect under the auspices of will, intellect attempts to declare reality. In this late work, Gilson adds what is for him a very old warning to the post-Cartesian philosopher, but adapted to the linguist as scientist: "If a linguist says to me that it is our language which first models the world that we think, I know that he is not speaking to me as a linguist but as a philosopher who, moreover, would excuse himself from giving me any philosophical justification for his opinion." In the 1930s, in a series of incisive essays, Gilson has already engaged the philosopher who might approach the relation of intellect to reality as does this latter-day descendant, the linguist who is devolved from Cartesian thought. Those essays are recently collected as *Methodical Realism*, 1990. It is a work preliminary to this later examination of linguistics as descended from Cartesian thought, in which earlier work Gilson makes clear his position as Thomistic realist.

Having thus suggested something of the philosophical context of our present concern for the word in its relation to thought, with Gilson's help, we may better undertake the distinction meant in our words *simple* and *complex*. Ordinarily when we say a thing is simple, we mean it is self-evident to the least subtle intellect. That *thing* in this sense is self-evident in its unity and thereby immediate to our perception and consequent thought "about" the thing. We suppose that we not only know it but understand it as well. Since things differ in their "thingness," however, some things are more immediately available to intellect than others, so we begin to concern ourselves with relative complexities of "thingness." We must, for instance, following St. Thomas, at last conclude that God's is a simple existence, though in attempting to approach divine simplicity with the lame aid of finite intellect we divide and divide, attempting to understand the absolute coincidence of being beyond division, glimpsed only by vision. The indivisible relation of essence and being in God is a simplicity defying finite understanding. A *thing* always *simple* in its *being*: By such a use of the term we mean to speak of essence. But in that simplicity of being we are at once moved to distinguish actual and potential when we would understand *created* things. We recognize and acknowledge here that, while the essence of a thing is not actually divisible, it is divisible by the action of analytical thought, one extension of which thought is the use of language as an instrument acknowledging the actuality – the reality – of the thing perceived in intellect and responded to by thought. Thus we say of the simple existence of the discrete person that the soul is the substantial form, substantiating form, through that first act of love initiating its being.

What we are attempting is a witness to intellectual encounter of reality, in which the intellect's *knowing* a simple existence – responding to essence of the particular thing – must then labor to articulate that knowing through signs toward understanding what it knows. At an elementary engagement of this concern, we recall that at the level of sixth-grade grammar we say (or *used* to say) that a "complete sentence" expresses a "complete thought." At that level of grammar we may note in passing that we have largely failed in our educational institutions precisely because we have forgotten what Gilson reminds us of, that "grammar is philosophy." Here an illustration of the point, from a sixth-grade workbook used to teach college freshmen: "Jesus wept." A complete thought, needing no "complements" or "modifiers" to signal the integral fulfillment of subject-predicate. But then we must also consider those elaborate "sentences" of a Henry James or William Faulkner, the bane of college sophomores. Are they also "complete sentences" expressing a complete thought, and their 200 or 500 words used toward making a reflection in signs of *a* thought?

If so, we begin to appreciate Gilson's point that the "sentence" itself affects the meaning of its words in a reciprocity to the word's contribution toward a simple thought. Indeed Henry James's attempts at a simple thought shares in its rhetorical and logical deportment of words the negative manner whereby one attempts to define God if one is a scholastic. Or there may be such an attempt toward positive attribution, as for instance when James disengages the term *romance* from *realism*. In his "Preface" to *The American*, he is concerned with "experience disengaged, disembroiled, disencumbered, exempt from the conditions that we usually know to attach to it," in the interest of an art catching a universality of experience. But the disengagement must be limited. He resorts to figurative language to make the abstract, subtle point: "The balloon of experience is in fact of course tied to the earth, and under that necessity we swing, thanks to a rope of remarkable length, in the more or less commodious car of imagination; but it is by the rope we know where we are, and from the moment that cable is cut we are at large and unrelated: we only swing apart from the globe – though remaining as exhilarated, naturally, as we like, especially when all goes well."

One might appropriate the sentence in its idea, which is still not its simple thought, and say of thought: Thought in intellect is dependent in reality, certified by experience. It follows that words out of that thought are therefore secondary and not primary to the actuality of the thought. Through words we attempt to mediate thought, whereby reality is perceived. The mediation is among intellects. Therefore, Coleridge is right in warning us of the danger of fancy as a disengagement of thought from reality through the instrumentality of words. Though something central to the Jamesean concern for realism in literature is clarified by such explication, much is sacrificed, not the least sacrificed that presence of James himself in his words. For in the original words the presence of his thought as peculiar to his person is unmistakable. One aspect of it, I suspect, is his deportment of uneasiness toward "romanticism." It is not just that romanticism, represented in his fellow novelist Hawthorne from whom he wishes to be distinguished, but in the English Romantics as well. But that aspect of the words, though not actually beside the point of our own thought about reality as related to language, does not appear to be as immediate to our concern over thought as *simple* in its presence in intellect. We must forego a temptation to its pursuit for the moment at least.

If the sentence is a complete thought when grammatically complete, then the same may be said of the paragraph – or the essay or story or poem. The thing of words, whatever its extension, when adequately formed by artfulness, is said to have "unity" as Aristotle remarked. The labor of articulation, the attempt to say "understandable mouthfuls," then, is the labor of art to limit language to the strictures of reality upon thought so that thought may be *simply* communicated, though the media of that communion be complex in another sense, as must be said of Greek tragedy's form which combines poetry and dance and so on. On one occasion I suggested that the end of our liberal-arts training is to hear, to really hear in its agonizing simplicity, Oedipus's cry of recognition in *Oedipus Rex*: "Woe! woe! woe! all cometh clear at last." But that climax of simplicity requires the complex inclusive drama of the full text to be effected. Similarly one might say that the end of our religious training is to hear in its agonizing simplicity "Jesus wept." To know the implications of that most simple thought is to know it at once as simple and to know that language is at last inadequate to that simplicity, though we are obligated as rational, discursive, created intellects to attempt to come to terms with that enveloping simplicity.

This is to say that the enormity of that simplicity caught by these two words – "Jesus wept" – is available to us as finite persons only in consequence of a long and complex enduring of intellectual growth. That is a recognition of necessity which enlightens the philosopher or poet on his journey through the dark woods – through the complexity of his being, toward a vision of ultimate simplicity of being. And it is a journey allowing no rest in any words of the moment, however tedious or repetitious the continuing labor of words and with words. If it were not so, then we should have only *a* word – one poem or one story or one philosophical discourse. Even in the saying, we move already beyond *a* word. Whether toward the silence of St. Thomas or not: That is the contingency in our making of a way through words. And when we have at last neared an end of that laboring journey, we shall discover that at the last there is, as there has always been, but the one Word necessary to the rescue of our labor as person.

If we accept as prelude to discourse, or believe as a reality, that thought is simple and not divisible, we begin to perceive something of the drama in intellectual life: It is the drama in which finite intellect must approach through its elaborate, complex structures of words, its "mouthfuls" which it strives to make understandable to itself, a simplicity of thought in which, through that simplicity, intellect lies open to reality. It seems always impossible to say just what we mean, to echo Prufrock, for whom words were rather deliberately projected as defense against encounter with reality, either simply or complexly taken. For Prufrock, words are forced as a protection of intellect isolated to itself. The subtlety in Prufrock as paradigm of the Modernist intellect is his recognition of the inadequacy of words to reality, so that his retreat into words becomes a retreat into a fortress wherein lies no simple true thought. To have said this is to recognize how apt Prufrock's envy of that "pair of claws," though even more apt would be, perhaps, that small animal protected by coral excrescences. An excrescence of words for Prufrock confines an emptiness of intellect, the obverse of Oedipus's deployment of words toward recovering the truth in reality.

The point is worth extending, since it speaks so tellingly to our Modernist pretensions. We see Henry James dramatizing his own Prufrock in "The Beast in the Jungle," in which story John Marcher counters reality with words and gestures maintaining his deportment of closure against reality, most significantly the reality of his own peculiar being. In the end, Marcher encounters another mourner as he is leaving the tomb of his Beloved, whom he had denied when she was alive. He sees himself in the context of reality at last, but himself as a pitiable (not tragic) figure. He can put his recognition only as negative indirection. The other mourner Marcher knows at once as "deeply stricken – a perception so sharp that nothing else in the picture comparatively lived, neither his dress, his age, nor his presumable character and class; nothing lived but the deep ravage of the features he showed. He *showed* them. . . ." The perception is of a ravaged person, an emptiness accomplished by denials such as Marcher has himself practiced, whose alternative has been all along the openness of love, a haunting *doppleganger* at grave's end.

That he is himself already self-victim he *knows* at last, but now he also *understands* his own agency in the self-deprivation. "The Beast had lurked indeed, and the Beast, at its hour, had sprung; it had sprung in that twilight of the cold April when, pale, ill, wasted, but all beautiful, and perhaps even then recoverable, she [his suspended Beloved, May Bartram, whose grave he now frequents] had risen from her chair to stand before him and let him imaginably guess. It had sprung as he didn't guess; it had sprung as she hopelessly turned from him, and the mark, by the time he left her, had fallen where it *was* to fall." And where now it *is* to fall, on him. For May waited his recognition of his own mortality, she herself being sick unto death, as are we all. His denial is through the subtle defense of words detached from the immediacy of reality. Though James would himself be reluctant to say it, the denial is that whereby words are directed against the Word. That is the completion of Jamesean "realism" that will follow in the poetry of T. S. Eliot, from "Prufrock" to "Gerontion," to the poet himself as present in "Ash-Wednesday." Marcher himself comes near that recognition, so we see in a complex rendering of his simple thought about himself as intellectual creature: "He was drawn there [drawn back repeatedly to May Bartram's presence, as Prufrock to the woman at the tea party] this time as irresistibly as the other, yet with a confidence, almost, that was doubtless the effect of the many months that had elapsed. He had lived, in spite of himself, into his change of feeling, and in wandering over the earth had wandered, as might be said, from the circumference to the center of his desert. He had settled to his safety and accepted perforce his extinction; figuring to himself, with some colour, in the likeness of certain little old men he remembered to have seen, of whom, all meagre and wizened as they might look, it was related that they had in their time fought twenty duels or been loved by ten princesses." That is the moment the Beast springs, the moment of refusal of openness to reality, in which moment in the story he does not see May Bartram as very near death but retreats into a pretense of having seen his own sickness unto death. It is the same moment of "depraved May" for Eliot's little old man, in which the Tiger Christ springs in "Gerontion," whose consequence by the refusal to meet openly that springing end is the emptiness of that little old man, Gerontion. (From these remarks one recognizes how closely attuned to James was the young Eliot, as a more extended explication of "Prufrock" and "Gerontion" in relation to James's "Beast in the Jungle" would certify.)

The complexity of language, we are saying, is the necessary means toward a complete, simple thought, whose completeness and simplicity is sought primarily by the intellect in its makings of thoughts. But the danger lies in language as a complex means of avoiding simple encounter of reality. Missing this aspect of the grammar of words as philosophy, of logic as philosophy, of rhetoric as philosophy, we shall fail to reorder intellect.[1] We have considered, though not exhaustively, the rich simplicity of *Jesus wept*, of Oedipus's *Woe*! *woe*! *woe*! We might add Marcher's "The Beast had sprung," and Prufrock's "But here is no great matter." The simple thought is embedded in a context of words as complex in structure as *Oedipus the King* or "The Beast in the Jungle" or "The Love Song of J. Alfred

1 It has been the bane of remedial grammar for half a century, as taught at the college level, that in its concern to supply a sort of instant vaccination of the student against abuse of thought by words it supposes the grammar of the isolated sentence the way. Sentences taken separately seem most immediate, but anyone having to deal with the problem of pronoun reference through such artificial approaches to composition knows how impossible the task once the move is made from isolated sentences to the student's composing a paragraph on a "theme" – a simple idea. If the sentence is in part determinate of the meaning of its words, the paragraph is similarly determinate of the meaning of its sentences. The attempt to appropriate "lab" techniques to the articulation of thought has done more to erode effective thought than the latest stop-gap against the common illiteracy of entering freshman, the computer lab.

Prufrock." And we find the abiding truth of such simple thought more widely encompassed as we attempt to come to terms with words. Thus "Jesus wept," we might say, has first of all its enveloping context of the New Testament, most immediately that event reported of Jesus' raising Lazarus from the grave – Jesus' weeping for the always springing tiger of man's conjuring willfulness, in response to which the Pharisees at once "from that day forth . . . took counsel . . . for to put him to death." To slay the springing tiger by denying it is that old gnostic denial of reality, very like Marcher's version of it in his imagined denial of reality – his seeing himself figured like "certain little old men" – beyond life but seemingly timelessly on this side of death.

"Jesus wept." That is the intolerable moment, caught by Dostoevski in that most remarkably complex rendering of words against those tears, Ivan's poem of the "Grand Inquisitor." It is the simple thought which William Faulkner attempts to accommodate in one of his lesser works, in part lesser because Faulkner is himself unable at last to be reconciled within conflicting simple thoughts. In *The Fable*, near its end, there is the "temptation" of the Corporal by the General, in which the virtue of man as autonomous is posed against the openness of love's sacrifice by the corporal. It is a spirited entrenchment of autonomous intellect against reality which the General establishes with the strategy of words. His is an argument out of one of those simple thoughts I suggest as a tensional pole to intellect, the thought that "I am able" of myself to order being to a simple unity by the power of my will. The General, speaking of mankind to the Corporal, who is now doomed as a sacrifice to the idea of autonomy, says: "Oh yes, he will survive it [universal collapse] because he has that in him which will endure even beyond the ultimate worthless tideless rock freezing slowly in the last red and heatless sunset, because already the next star in the blue immensity of space, will be already clamorous with the uproar of his debarkation, his puny and inexhaustible voice still talking, still planning; and there too after the last ding dong of doom has rung and died there will still be one sound more: his voice, planning still to build something higher and faster and louder; more efficient and louder and faster than ever before, yet it too inherent with the same old primordial fault since it too in the end will fail to eradicate him from the earth. I don't fear man. I do better: I respect and admire him. And pride: I am ten times prouder of that immortality which he does possess than ever he of that heavenly one of his delusion. Because man and his folly –"

"Will endure," the corporal said.

"They will do more. . . . They will prevail."

Jesus wept is thus set against *Prometheus exalted* by his own prevailing. These are the two simple thoughts held, one or the other, by faith, and around them orbit most of the words uttered by mankind, the "mouthfuls" attempting to justify our partial understandings. For on either hand, given the limits of intellect, understanding can itself be but partial, the recognition which intellect accepts when it becomes wise. Our words, then, orbit one or the other simple thought; or at once one, and then the other; or become lost in a suspense between the two poles, each of which promises order to intellectual response, promises respite to man's restless desire for fulfillment of his own reality. The simple action at issue is whether man will submit to reality in a movement of vulnerable openness or whether he will instead refuse that submission in an action of closure consequent to embracing his "primordial fault," his "pride" in his own capacity to effect his own immortality. But the immortality of the higher, faster, louder voice is divisive of simplicity, having assumed itself to be its own angelic creation, defiant of its limited understanding of the knowledge it possesses. Understanding thus lies on this side of wisdom, and so intellect becomes doomed to inhabit its discursive nature through the defense against limit: the defense of words, words, words. Its "immortality," as specific intellect, will become its own word: its poem or statue or whatever idol it makes to its own glory. And we must note the pathos attendant upon that necessity in our best "romantic" poets, including Faulkner. Through words thus taken as idol, the drama we might call that of our Original Sin is exalted, in idols that prove dead ashes at last. For the poet, the scientist dies. His made thing – the poem or the formulated thing – may last a little longer.

Our greatest poets reveal this recognition of the made thing's inadequacy to immortality to us in their several ways. Oedipus' cry of woe reveals the collapse of spirit under the inadequacy of his knowledge, out of which knowledge he has wielded power through words. His cry comes at that point where he collapses with "All cometh clear at last." But against this agonized cry, we have set the testimony to Christ's agony of spirit: *Jesus wept.* This is the moment of turning in an openness to the fulfillment of the Cross and the Resurrection which we are to emulate. In his moment of tears, Jesus accepts the burden of all history, that history before and that after the moment, in a sacrifice of tears. Not tears such as the poet is limited to, as in Virgil's "tears of things," but His tears for things, the sign of an abiding, sustaining love of our finitude. Oedipus experiences the moment of isolation in which he is separated from his own history no less than from all Thebes. But all along he has been separated from the actuality of his being up to that moment, and he becomes separated from the potential of his being thereafter, a condition incidentally which reveals a certain poverty in Greek thought. We might well note Sophocles' recognition of this separation in his attempt to recover Oedipus in *Oedipus at Colonus*. In that play there is a rudimentary anticipation of an Assumption as the only solution, but one not justified by the experience of man in and of himself. (It is one of the ironies of literary history, in this light, that Sophocles makes *Oedipus at Colonus* before he makes *Oedipus Rex*.)

Between the two cries, intellect is always suspended, between the exile of oblivion and that paradoxical surrender of the self, an exile from the self, which is answered through grace by the self's recovery. That is the recognition which Eliot, for instance, comes to in "Ash-Wednesday." At the two poles, at the center of each pole, lies the mystery of a simple thought whose countering attraction orders our orbiting words. The one pulls words to a collapse in our words' futilities. But at the center of that other pole is the attraction of the Word, which makes intellect itself pregnant with the meanings of existences. It does so through its openness to the truth of things beyond its own comprehension. The words from such an intellect are likely to reveal a spectrum of light, a varied response to the orders of truth in reality. For it is thus that finite intellect receives portions of that one Light which is refracted in the range of things in themselves, that Light which is our first act of finite being.

Intellect's refraction of that light in finite colorations called words, beyond its own absolute authority over the signs of truth in its multitudinous manifestations, shares something of that light by the necessity of its being. That is the heart of that mystery of intellectual openness to being which Eliot attempts to speak of, once he has surrendered his own jealous intellect's world to "oblivion" and consequently discovers the world itself restored, though changed to his seeing. Having accepted the lost, unspoken, unheard word as inadequate, having stilled his own word, there comes a vision of the centering Word:

> Still is the unspoken word, the Word unheard,
> The Word without a word, the Word within
> the world and for the world;
> And the light shone in darkness and

Against the Word the unstilled world still whirled
About the center of the silent Word.

This section of Eliot's "Ash-Wednesday" has been sometimes severely faulted for its prosody, but considering its burden, it proves subtle indeed, advanced over his earlier mentor Alexander Pope. For if Ajax "strives some rock's vast weight to throw," requiring of the verse that it too "labours, and the words move slow," what is the poet to manage when he would dramatize his arrest by the Cause of the cosmos encountered at last in the small things adjacent to his senses? The encounter is followed by lines Elizabeth Drew calls a "mockery of chiming syllables," a descripting not apt however since it is not mockery that is underway but the bafflement of awe, out of which wonder grows anew toward an acceptance of the encounter. For such is the vision here remembered in the dramatization as if in the present moment of the "spoken" words, that words are inadequate to the experience. Out of that encounter of the Uncaused Cause, the Word present even without the poet's own word, that poet understands what must follow: the necessity of trying once more for the true word with which to witness the vision. We have seen the alternative to this quest for "meaningful mouthfuls." It is Faulkner's General, praising the unstilled word of man, his "one sound," his human voice "planning still to build something higher and faster and louder" against the pending collapse of his *self* in "the same old primordial fault" which elicits the General's pride in man as self-sufficient.

VI

Oh, to be possessed of the angelic mode of knowing! For that angelic mode is unhampered by the conditions of material existence to the knowing creature man, conditions that seem always to encourage his primordial pride. Our finite, *embodied* being, with its multiple conditions to our actual existence (if we are to exist at all) has as the one overwhelming condition that we are hampered by this peculiar given nature from at once satisfying intellectual desire. Thus man is set apart from both angels and nightingales. One may, if he is Brice Parain, hold that language is "an instrument of mortality." He may conclude, then, "that perhaps only at the moment of death is it possible to be a new untouched sensitivity." Meanwhile, in the climate of inescapable thought, it seems equally inescapable to that thought that as intellectual creature man is agitated by a "yearning" which "never attains an end," a yearning "to live animalistically," since that longing coexists "with the uncertainty of thought."

Parain's sense of animalistic being, supposed by him to be possessed by nightingales (in which illustration we may hear echo of John Keats's great Ode), seems rather a state of unselfawareness, which is a condition of being capable of varied interpretation. To be unselfaware for Keats was to be void of thought altogether so that thought was thus denied its cruel end of turning upon the thinking self to underline that self's "loneness." Obliviousness to one's own existence. That is also the condition Prufrock longs for, the state of the "pair of ragged claws." But there is that other antipathetic possibility of escape of one's "sole self," the angelic perfection of intellect which transcends the "animalistic" conditions impinging on the freedom of thought. This intellectual creature man, this embodied spirit, is torn between a desire for release from thought's interrupted continuousness in truth which is the good of the intellect, which he imagines the happy state of animal existence, and a consummation of thought in an angelic mode whereby thought transcends its "self" to sustain itself in a perfected continuum.

If the animalistic mode of existence, which man shares with other embodied beings, interrupts his thought's continuum, then little wonder that he may dream as a desirable end that he become fully animalistic, rejecting the wholeness which thought itself reminds us we must fail to achieve intellectually in the context of creation. But on the other hand, if the dreamed angelic state would be a perfect intellectual action, transcending material existence as a dimension of the given nature of man, then animalistic nature is not to be embraced, but rather rejected. Either election through will, we observe, is a gnostic action – an attempt to deconstruct the reality of being as encountered in particular natures, in this instance the given nature of man as embodied spirit. For to elect either is possible only as an intellectual action. The one direction, unable to exorcize the spirit, will in one way or another turn toward material existence, but with the spirit still hauntingly present, though perhaps cleverly rationalized as an effect of immanence – an elevation out of material existence, upon which that "spiritual" or "intellectual" presence is nevertheless dependent and to which it is therefore subservient.

In the other direction, unable to come to terms with its aspect of material existence which is hauntingly present to the spirit, intellect may declare material existence an evil to be exorcized in relation to which death itself is the one effective exorcism of the body from spirit as Socrates argued. Either attempt to engage the given nature of man, we repeat, is a gnostic attempt whose intent is to deny the reality of human nature, and to deny it most especially as *given* human nature. For in denying the given, intellect itself becomes the agent restructuring its own being to suit its false dream. Intellect, as intellect, would will its own being as either animalistic or angelic. We are speaking here of a "puritan" reductionism by intellect, of desire idealized, though we do not as a rule recognize this intended "purity" of the gnostic bent toward intellect in the materially immanent philosophers. The "puritanism" of what we prefer as "materialism" tends to escape recognition. Most especially we miss that puritan aspect of animalistic gnosticism when we observe certain spectacles attendant upon it, aspects we find castigated by the "angelic" species of puritanism as "hedonism."

This "angelic" puritanism seems more obvious to us, especially given the recent history of "Puritanism" as it grows out of the Reformation. Indeed, the "angelic" puritan is likely to insist on disjoining man as maker from the joys of such making. The "Puritan work ethic" haunts us in its effects especially as exacerbate by the Industrial Revolution. And the coincidence here fathers the Technological Age. Our attempt to reconcile making as a necessity to human existence, but not a very agreeable necessity, separates the necessity of making from human nature through technology's ingenuity. What we *do* must be set as far as possible from what we think we *are* or what we *want to be*. That is how we come to have a *job* or a *profession*, rather than a *calling*. For a *calling* is a summons to perfect our potential through our actions as intellectual creatures. Our dominant action is that of making. One sees signs of the pathos of spirit attendant upon this separation of our deportment of being as a making action. And in those signs we may discover at least a suggestion that we are caught between the two species of gnostic temptation we have just defined. Our *vacation* time is widely separated from our *work* time, not by the accidents of time and place as defining those distinctions but by the divided spirit that establishes the separation. Perhaps the point is reflected in a bumper sticker I see on a vehicle in a university parking lot: "I'D RATHER BE FISHING!"

What we shall be arguing all along is that to accept these two tensional poles as actual in relation to the reality of existence as human persons is to accept false ends to our existence. To accept either is to suppose it desirable that man should be some other nature than man – either a "pure" animalistic nature or a "pure" angelic nature. In recognizing the poles as both false, we might at the same time better understand how each "makes the other for to win," their antipathy being out of a common sentimentality about man's nature. And let us recall here our earlier suggestion about sentimentality: It is a consent by intellect that feeling invest intellectual action with authority, thus dislocating intellect from its responsibility of discriminating among its proper ends, the ends orienting desire through the truth of things known. Thus the common temptation through intellectual sentimentality to transcend or subscend given nature encourages the "modernist" gnostic in his devotion to the theory of evolution. That is the now-common temptation which has supplanted the historically earlier "angelic" puritanism. This modern version of gnostic puritanism, dependent in evolutionary theory, posits an infinity of change to being, and thereby it disallows any prospect of rest in a perfection of being. Nevertheless, it carries in it still a whimsically embraced possibility of transcendence over one's own nature. This is to say that in evolutionary theory as a support of material, immanentist faith there is an incipient angelism.

In either of these temptations to intellect, whether to the angelic or the animalistic nature as an idol to intellectual action, it seems sufficiently clear that there is nevertheless in man's will a desire for rest in his being beyond the uncertainties of discontinuous, non-inclusive thought. Inclusive thought on the one hand or inclusive thoughtless existence on the other must leave us restless. The one would have thought subsuming the all in a simplicity of knowing. The other would have thoughtlessness consumed in the simplicity of unknowing. But underlying both dreams, such is the irony attendant upon the attempt to escape our given intellectual nature, there lies an envy of the angelic mode. To know all is to be freed of the necessity to know. To know nothing, through intellectual action that accomplishes animalism, is only another version of the refusal of our gift of existence. (That is what the young student projects as his condition of freedom in the world, once he is out of "school.")

If we need to underline the argument further that the two gnostic inclinations are akin, perhaps we might consider our fascination with "artificial intelligence" at this moment, its virtues intended to serve our pluralistic intellectual community. In our advance over nature through technology toward perfecting "artificial intelligence," two aspects of that progress seem to fascinate us: its nature as instantaneous "knowing," so that in the obliteration of time from the discursiveness of its action "AI" approaches the angelic; and its nature as disembodied, or virtually so, since the only embodiment is the silicone chip, celebrated to the popular mind as infinitesimal. Thus AI may at last not only do all our important thinking for us, but has the companion virtue of not imposing upon the material world. We shall be fully leisured in consequence, and New Eden made of earth by our own made angels. But these are made by the actions of finite intellect. Alas!

It seems antique, no doubt, to be speaking here of an angelic mode of knowing in our advanced age, an age which no longer acknowledges the possible existence of "old-fashioned" angels. But that is now qualified by AI, since what is denied is the old version of angels as created angelic intellect independent of human intellect. If man makes his own angels, that is, as we might put it, another matter. But even here, though we would thus delegate the offices of intellect, we cannot deny a rather common desire in our nature to *know*. What is not desirable is the labor of intellect in its own making, required if it is to know. What we would avoid is that tedious labor of rational intellect which is otherwise necessary to our coming to know: those labors through which we move discursively in pressing knowledge beyond the limits upon intellectual action which we associate with the body in our concern to understand. (How does the *brain* relate to *thought*?) Through thought we find the body a hindrance as well as perhaps a desired end, if a hedonistic end is posited as our anticipated Edenic condition. The fascination of AI, in this respect, is that it escapes – almost – the limits of time and space in knowing "purely." It is not exhausted in body, either by time or space, as is the struggling *official intellect* (as opposed to artificial intellect). For *official* is a suitable characterization of our deportment toward AI. By a willed flick of the finger, we shall know, and our finger is always at the switch and so therefore superior to AI.

Still, one knows what happens when the "computer is down," whether in respect to intricate patterns of air traffic or one's monthly bill or the words secreted in "hard" or "floppy" disks. The sudden necessity of intellectual action out of given nature, with all the handicaps of our discursive limits, returns – to our panic. I mean to touch the history of the term *panic*, for though the experience out of computers being "down" is not of an encounter of a god in the wood as in the old Greek sense, it is an encounter with a forgotten, neglected god in a darker wood, our *self* as created, now feared to have failed in ordering actualities of our nature toward potentiality. And a part of that panic is the exhaustion attendant upon recovery, of getting our self "up" when the computer is "down." Thought is hard, and hard upon both intellect and body alike, as any honest student will testify.

If the ancient gnostic separated soul and body intellectually in order to resist or reject the body's handicap upon knowing, our world certainly separates mind and body, even in those arguments that would hold mind to be only a sort of rarified energy immanent in material existence. We need think only of popular or scientific interests in the possibility of "subliminal" modes of knowledge to be aware of a continuing desire to be, if not like the gods, then at least like the angels, even when we dislocate such knowledge to elemental natures such as crabs or nightingales as symbolic of such a desired perfection. The student, facing tomorrow's examination in algebra, dreams of dreaming the needed formulae into the mind. Perhaps one might play a recording of those formulae, under one's pillow, throughout a night's sleep, and wake in command of the triangle at a level more fundamental than conscious thought grants. And the advertiser aims images below the level of conscious intellectual encounter to stir a desire in us for some particular cooling drink, a desire which the conscious action of mind might otherwise reject or modify. For we must require, not a glass of water, but a beer. And not simply a beer, but this particular brand. Such dreams and desires, and manipulations of appetite in recognition of our dreams and desires, speak not only a continuing hunger for power over a person through some "angelic" mode of knowing effected by technological power, but speak as well a faith that such a mode is actually part of the nature of our being, even though denied by its formal arguments. It is a faith affirmed by St. Thomas no less that by extensive research in advertising as to its potential to modify the person through psychological manipulations of mind. Modern assumptions differ very widely from St. Thomas's, of course, as to proximate and ultimate ends implied by "angelic" knowing. In both, nevertheless, there is the common principle accepted that the mind's action affects that complex being of which mind is a part, including effects on the body and its sensual response to existence.

However clouded our understanding of what is meant by *action* in relation to the *being* of the action's agent, we at least tacitly recognize that action in its human aspect is anchored in intellect. But here we must recall a larger and more inclusive sense to *action* than our immediate concern for intellect, so that we may come to a more precise consideration of intellectual action as peculiar to man – that created creature who is by the gifts of his nature himself a would be "creator," a maker. We may speak of action initially as manifest in any being – a stone, a tree, an animal. Action in this sense intends to express a degree of resolution of potency in the creature (stone or tree or animal). Here we name a "being-in-act" so to speak, as opposed to a "being-in-potency." We mark such action in our perception of a thing. If the thing perceived is a plant, we recognize well enough both its present act of being and its movement toward a fullness of being. Thus we recognize a relation between act and potency when we speak of the oak that is in the acorn. If we are poet, we may lament the stone in its full potential being as not eternal. It is subject to a ceasing to be, whereby "Not marble nor the gilded monuments/Of princes" seem as impregnable as our own word.

In this sense of action, we intend to speak of the sustained, but not thereby immortal, being of discrete creatures. And if we follow St. Thomas on the point, we understand that such creatures are actively sustained in an initial, a first, action of their being. They are, *actively*, but not in the usual sense of such a term as *activity*, a sense that has long lost its immediacy to us as our wonder that *anything* is at all, a meaning lingering still in the roots of words like *act*, *activity*, *species*, *spy*. This first act whereby a thing *is* gives us a faint recognition of its originating and continuous actuality, which does not say that it may not fall from actuality. By this first *act*, we may say, a thing is actualized *specifically*; that is in *species*. If we speak of this act as one of grace, we call it perhaps substantiating grace, the grace whereby any and every created thing is.

Our first response of wonder and awe to this first act of being, which is at once first and continuing, is through the senses, and through that response wonder becomes a part of our intellectual encounter.[1] It is a wonder mediate to our knowing the reality of the Lord and Giver of Life, the sustaining cause of existence, that Love that proceeds from the Father and Son, the Holy Ghost. Whether or not one accedes to this declaration, he will nevertheless have experienced the wonder of the first act of being, however fleetingly. The experience of encounter of being, and its effect on intellect as wonder, is the point G. K. Chesterton remarks in "The Ethics of Elfland": "A child of seven is excited by being told that Tommy opened a door and saw a dragon. But a child of three is excited by being told that Tommy opened a door." In our turn, as adults in the 1990s, we are highly excited to be told the wondrous prospects in "AI" or in gene theory, although we are likely to be far removed from recognizing our wonder as a response to *first action*. Our poets again and again attempt to recall us to that wonder.

In respect to this first act of which we are speaking, it is an effect upon intellect of a perception of existent creatures. Its course to intellect is through the senses. We might put it that through the mediate means to intellect of this wondrous act – that is, through our senses as means – there is present to intellect initially the spectacle of this first *being-act*.

Spectacle in art is our response as makers to a necessary reduction of the fullness of that first act of being. Thus we say that art is an imitation of the action of nature. The action of nature existentially is the reduction perceived through second act as consequent upon the first act of being, a response of particularity to that first action. Art, through spectacle, imitates this reduction, this specificity of being to particularity, lest we be overwhelmed by our own necessary finitude. For, as we might say, man cannot stand too much truth – that is, he cannot endure a fullness of truth given his

1 Elsewhere, I have suggested a distinction between *awe* and *wonder* in relation to the intuitive and rational dimensions of intellect. *Awe* is an emotional effect consequent upon an intuitive encounter of being. *Wonder* is an emotional effect of rational intellect's engagement of its intuitive encounter. *Wonder* reflects a movement whereby reason explores the encounter of being whose first effect is *awe*. *Wonder* thus reflects a more controlled response to intellect's encounter of being.

finitudes, short of his achievement of perfection of his finitude called Beatitude. Put yet another way, so disproportionate is the fullness of that first act of being to our possible perception of that act in our temporal estate that we are shielded, except in those mysterious instances of blinding vision such as St. Paul experienced on the road to Damascus, or Dante in the inception of his great poem. Or, to shift the arena of our experience of reality from the witness of art to the witness of science, we see an implicit recognition of this disproportion in the "Big Bang Theory" of the creation of the universe, in which phrase there is a whimsical dimension to both *big* and *bang*. But whatever the degree or province of our intellectual attunement to this first *being-act*, what seems certain to us to be recognized by our intellect is this act's unwavering constancy, however apocalyptic our speculations may become about the end of the universe or the end of history or the end of the self itself.

We have introduced this distinction between first and second act of being earlier, as adumbrated by Gilson out of St. Thomas. But it is of such importance to our exploration that we must return to it. Our intent is to return to it as a common experience, testified to by our poets no less than by a philosopher such as St. Thomas or Gilson. And since in the history of the relation of poet to philosopher it is a recurring pattern that philosopher follows poet (as Wordsworth suggests in his famous "Preface"), the dependence is significant. Indeed, a philosopher like Plato or Aristotle acknowledges the poet as precedent in the journey of intellect, and so recent a philosopher as Gilson repeatedly turns to the poet as witness of the validity of the rational exposition of concept which philosophy provides. And so here, we remind ourselves of Gilson's exposition of the Thomistic principle of being in relation to act, which prompted our melded term, *being-act*. From the position we must occupy as created intellectual creatures, we find ourselves always in that in-between whose limits as the arena of our being are between "*first* act" and "*second* act." We explored Gilson's designation of the first act: It is "the being of the thing, of that which is called being in virtue of the very act of existing." It is an "exertion" by a cause which is not in the discrete being, which *is* by that first act. Here we must make clear that this exertion is not in the created being by its nature as this specific being, though it is nevertheless within that being in its initiating and sustaining action of a very existence. It is a necessary distinction, lest we confuse the "second act" as the primal cause of being.

Now the "*second* act" differs in that it is "the causal operation of this being," and we recognize this causal operation as "the intrinsic manifestation of its first actuality," its recipiency of that "*first* act" by the effects this second causal action produces, both within itself and outside itself. St. Thomas distinguishes the first and second act (*Summa* I, Q. 48, A. 5): "The first act is the form and integrity of a thing; the second act is its operation." We might put it that the first act bears fruit as the beingness of the created entity. By the operation of that created thing, *consequent* to the first act and so designated as second act, we are made aware of the existence of the thing. By its "fruits" we know it. Thus is established the arena of the being of the thing itself, and when that thing is the person, whose nature is intellectual, it "finds itself" within the arena of its givenness as reflected by its operation of response to that knowledge. What it seeks thereby is the good of itself, the good of intellect. And so we say the locus of man as person is *being-act*. Whether or not we have succeeded in clarifying the distinction by exposition, we may have at least prepared by the effort to recognize the witness paid the distinction by the poet in his use of words. And we begin with a poet rather far removed from any formal pursuit of philosophy, though we recognize him as a philosophical poet. As such, he is especially far removed from the influence of St. Thomas Aquinas so that his testimony from the experience of his own intellectual action in his own in-between may be of special interest. We shall then introduce another poet, more deliberate in his dependence on the scholastics, especially upon Duns Scotus and Thomas Aquinas. Neither poet will be a surprising presence to my reader.

William Wordsworth declares a recognition of encounter between first and second action manifested in particular existing things. He speaks of a "motion and a spirit, that impels/ All thinking things, all objects of all thought,/ And rolls through all things." Wordsworth is not expressing some simplified pantheism here, though he_is_often charged as doing so. It is a charge perhaps because the critic knows on the one hand Wordsworth's independence from Christian philosophy as established by the scholastics and on the other hand his coming to a refuge in a Platonism after such testimony as that we have just quoted, from his "Tintern Abbey." But at the time of "Tintern Abbey," he is rather testifying to an encounter through intellect with being in things.

I suggest that Thomas would call this a creative effect of Being Itself, the cause of that manifested existential things encountered, the "Motion" sustaining existence. That is a threshold of encounter which Wordsworth subsequently does not cross. But his is a recognition nevertheless of that first movement, that first act, and he responds with his second act, initiated through the senses given to this singular creature, the human person William Wordsworth, as an aspect of his own given nature. His initial inclination is toward an ultimate rest in Being Itself, the proper end of a second action which is peculiar to man as intellectual creature. This is the action of the soul toward its Cause, and as such is a causal orientation in itself. Such, then, is Wordsworth's threshold experience, his moment of an in-between prescribed by first and second act as recognized by St. Thomas. Let us turn to the poet who advances, as Wordsworth could not, over that threshold to a vision of being as dynamic.

Gerard Manley Hopkins concentrates Wordsworth's visionary moment witnessed in "Tintern Abbey." He does so in speaking of the "instress" of every specific being. To that recognition of instress, finite intellect when properly oriented by its recognition responds through an action of making which attempts an "inscape" commensurate to its vision of the "instress." Hopkins's "Pied Beauty" attempts a witness of his experience, his effected inscape from actual encounter through words. The words would imitate the action of intellect in its nature, as responding to encounter. And again, the words would bear witness to the first act of being (recognized as "instress") as adumbrated by Gilson out of St. Thomas in our version of instress. What intellect has experienced is the "father[ing] forth" of all things. All things "whatever . . . fickle, freckled . . ./ With swift, slow; sweet, sour; adazle, dim." Such a phrase as "father-forth" attempts that simplicity of action which Wordsworth might put as "rolls through all things."

Now this "fathering-forth" of being *effects* what is first encountered by intellect as the spectacle of creation, a spectacle suited to our sensual perception, the necessary modulation of the first act of being as required by our limited intellectual knowing. On this point we shall have more to say later in respect to Dante's understanding of symbol in his own great tribute to the First Cause of Hopkins's "pied beauty," in Dante's *The Divine Comedy*. Here we rest content to recall, much more immediately available to us perhaps, the clear distinction Aristotle makes between *action* and *spectacle* in tragedy. The significant action of *Oedipus Rex* is beyond sensual response, except through the aid of the spectacle of the staging action of the play. The reminder recalls us to the difficulties of *actualities* beyond *perception*, which nevertheless are necessarily approached by intellect through perceptions, the necessity to our finitudes. But these actualities beyond our perception are independent of spectacle in respect to their essence.

When we examine reflectively our particular experience of existence, when we contemplate the effect of perception upon intellect, we may begin to realize that such encounter is a constant, however far removed we may ordinarily be from a continuous wonder of encounter. Reminding us of the appropriateness of wonder is surely one of the offices in service to the common good performed by a poet like Wordsworth or Hopkins. Wordsworth, for instance, recatches, recaptures if but fleetingly the wonder of present experience in his "Tintern Abbey." He recalls as actual in the past and continuing in the present as a present effect of his own encounter of being long ago in an English countryside. There had been the sense beyond the body's senses of a "presence" that "disturbs" with a sudden "joy of elevated thought." That elevation rises above the rational. It is a sense of a presence intrinsic to the being of a variety of creatures perceived in a moment of his exultation, and it leads him to declare "a sense sublime/ Of something far more deeply interfused" in the world than sensual perception alone can account for by the resources of his merely rational faculty. Even though he has come to that encounter through sense perceptions and must at last attempt to deal with the encounter as rationally as his mind will allow, neither the senses nor rational response are sufficient to the experience. Wordsworth, let us say, is a poet committed to an intuition of being, attempting to remain open to encounter through the senses but not confident of the rational intellect's power to accommodate such experience as thought. Indeed, "Tintern Abbey" is (as Wordsworth himself remarks) an elegy to the loss of intuitive vision, a vision seemingly displaced in him by the intrusion of thought. Or so he fears at the time of the poem.

Let us summon our other poet to this most difficult topic. Gerard Manley Hopkins is less suspicious of thought, having been schooled in the scholastics. Hopkins praises a glory melding his own ordered will and intellect to its being through discrete creatures. His is a visionary moment, opened to him through the first action of will toward the *very* being of discrete creatures. In his "Windhover," so homely an encounter as that of watching a plow turn dirt in a furrow speaks a "shine" in the turned soil that is not simply that of sunlight reflected from moisture-glazed soil. There is a deeper embering of being out of soil itself. His arresting words of celebration conclude in praise of Christ as Lord of being: "sheer plod makes plough down sillion/ Shine." And, as if countering one of Shakespeare's bleak nihilistic moments, in which Shakespeare laments the voiding of being when fire is "Consumed with that which it was nourished by," the ember ceasing along with the exhaustion of its fuel, Hopkins rather cries joyfully that "blue-bleak embers . . . / Fall, gall themselves, and gash gold-vermilion" in praise of being itself.

Our concern here is centrally, of course, with the intellect's approach to and understanding of this first action of our being through which we are allowed to respond to particular creation. But we must also deal with *action* in a different sense from that just discussed, and specifically with that action of intellect whereby it encounters a first action which is not caused by the finite will itself. Here is the initiation of the second act of being, dependent in the first act which is pure gift because the giver is pure Love. It is through the second act that intellect must itself strive for a purity of response, in imitation of that initiating Love, that first act whereby the respondent *is*. *That* it *is* is its first act which is not its own. Through this second act, however, there occurs the beginning of the exercise of a habit of being toward a possible encounter *with*, and a rest *in*, Being Itself. We are thereby reminded once more that intellect is the essential differentia of man, as distinct from other creatures constituting creation in its orders of being.

Here man differs from stone or dying fire, from corn or nightingale. What is special to this existence is discovered in the concept of analogy. The analogy may be generalized, as Gilson does, in saying that "since the effect in question [the effect of creation as the first act of a particular creatures being] is one which all [other effects] presuppose – that is, being – it is precisely in its existence and substantially that the creature is an analogue of its Creator." It is thus that the thing "receives its *existence* from God simultaneously with the existence of its forms." In respect to man as such a created thing, the significant form received. Through that form it exists in a way analogous to its Creator, as no other time-bound creature exists. That is its intellectual form. And because the significant habit of being to this creature is intellectual action, in echo of its Cause, it is important that we keep firmly in mind the distinction introduced earlier between action and spectacle. We recall, for instance, that Oedipus as a figuring of intellectual man has as his decisive *action* his recognition of the truth of things impinging upon him. The action is not the signs of that action, the words and gestures accompanying the action, and not even the cry of woe. For that is a cry "fathered-forth" by his act of recognition and so is more nearly present as spectacle of the actual action. Such is one poet's making signifying an action.

To come closer to this action of being – this second act exemplary in man – we may say that a gift of intellectual nature is the nature's conscious recognition of that act, though the recognition is of an act which is immaterial and so not an essence *in* the spectacle of act itself – the words or gestures. Still, it is through spectacle that we approach act in its naked – that is, its immaterial – actuality. Let us observe, in this connection, what happens as our intellectual act when we speak of *a* man, rather than of a *being*. We may be misled by the spectacle of language itself, through its inclination to sever accidents adhering to particular being from particular being itself. Thus in speaking of "a man" the term may suggest a static entity. The term *man* seems less truly reflective of that *going-on-ness* of the entity we would name. (It is this *going-on-ness* that we would designate as first act.) As we struggle to acknowledge the being of this peculiar act of being – this *thing* experienced by intellect – the struggle of naming it seemingly arrests it. That is a concern that troubled Brice Parain, as we saw, but it does so principally because Parain does not distinguish the arrest in its locus, which is not the thing itself. We do not "kill" a tree by naming it. The arrest is in the effect of the naming action upon the actor doing the naming, not in the creature named. Our engagement of open encounter with the thing itself is affected. Thus it is the acting intellect that is endangered by its own act, not the thing. For no thing can be endangered by this "killing" arrest *significantly. Essential* effect upon a thing is possible only by the withdrawing of the first act of its being, and that is a possibility only to God, the Lord and Giver of the life of that thing, its initiated being whereby it is essentially itself. The intellectual arrest effected by the name imposed upon a being, as if the imposition were the action of its formal being, is but a partial arrest of that perverse intellect, though it may be of sufficient partiality as to disturb such a presumptuous intellect with a sense of its alienation from being.

In speaking of the endangerment consequent upon misguided intellectual action, we must make a distinction quite clear. We mean here by the term *endanger* to name the reality of an attempted distortion of the being of a thing. But it is not the object of the intended intellectual action (the thing in itself) that suffers distortion in its essence, though accidents attendant upon essence may be affected. Such is the misunderstanding attendant upon gnosticism in its desire for power over being. The point at issue, then, is quite separate from the conspicuous spectacles of destruction of specific beings, though such destructions are nevertheless effects out of gnostic intent. When one chops down a tree, there is an effect upon the tree. But this is an aspect of action differing from the attempt upon the tree through conceptual manipulations of it. It may well be that manipulations with the instrument of conception seem to justify the manipulator in chopping down the tree, for such is a "window of opportunity" through which intellect may escape its responsibility of stewardship in relation to creation. (It must be added that proper stewardship does not exclude those actions such as chopping down trees.)

A considerable range of endangerment to specific beings within the realm we engage through spectacle is conspicuous in our century, of course, whether focused upon trees or upon whole peoples. Indeed, our century is littered with the debris of violations of the world's body. But here we are concerned to distinguish the helplessness of finite intellect turned gnostic rebel through its intent to effect essential being. It is a point of concern important to our address to genetic engineering at this moment, for instance. So that, though the distinction may at first appear insignificant in relation to the spectacles of destruction of the world's body, we should make a crucial error were we to divorce those actions from the more subtle ground of action in intellect itself. This is to say that the most profound action is the movement of thought in consciousness under the agency of individual will. And that action, which is decisive, may seem only tenuously related to its effects upon the world's body. Intellectual action may be at once primal and unspectacular, though we may rest some comfort in the belief that by the fruits of those actions we may know trees whence they spring. As for the problem from the perspective of our "tree," figuratively taken, primal action of intellect may appear remote. As an event, this movement of intellect whereby it *mis-takes* the tree is not easily related to spectacular event. Nevertheless, there is an intuitive recognition by the forest of trees walking so to speak, by the commonality in relation to spectacular disruptions in the social and political arena for instance, whereby there grows a suspicion of "intellect" itself.

To recognize and come to terms with the distinction at issue, we are suggesting, makes possible a recovery of intellect in relation to the spectacles of destruction or construction of which it is primal cause. For such effects, while they do not transform the nature of things in themselves – do not transform essence – nevertheless affect the world's body consequentially though not essentially. To recover from such a mis-taking of things is to recover the proper accord of intellect with the limits of being. It is to recover from violations by "second acts" of that being which is the first act of things whereby not only intellect itself, but all things, *are* in themselves. That is the level at which the orientation of intellect to its proper stewardship of the world's body must be regained. To do so will make possible an ordinate response to intellect's ordering actions of stewardship – to its making of things, as of houses from trees, or social order from consort of person to persons.

The burden of Brice Parain's indictment of language, we recall, is that the word kills the thing. Our point differs radically. Indeed, if Parain were right about this power of language over being as absolute, we would conclude that a single intellect by language would hold power over all being. Though the gnostic intellect might desire it to be a truth of its own power, we hold to the contrary that will and intellect in relation to being (and ultimately the significant relation is always to its *own* being) is not a pursuit of trophies of being, to be hung on intellect's walls in sign of conquest of being.

The gnostic hunter may, in one aspect, stalk being with poisoned arrows of will as it were. But more usually, that intellect justifies the hunt in the name of the common good. The pretense of weaponry in Parain's position is rather analogous to that dart-gun veterinarians and animal-control specialists use when creatures rupture their cages at the circus or zoo and are suddenly at large in community.

There is that other way toward being, however wild it may seem in its threatening actuality – that of an open intellectual patronage of being. In this right-willed address to being, intellect may indeed be given moments of respite, accomplished with the mediating services of sign neither supposed as poisoned arrow nor drug-bearing dart. Through its word there may occur a still point, to intellect's health but with no actual essentializing effect upon the creature encountered by intellect. That is the moment of grace Eliot speaks of, as we have observed, in which there is a sense of the Word within the word, mediating intellect and thing in a moment's respite beyond the measure of time or place. We are here attempting to distinguish that attitude toward the use of language for power over being on the one hand and the use of language to accomplish St. Thomas's "union" of intellect and thing, a union which we are calling the encounter of intellect with some other. The use of language toward certifying the reality of that union is not only through a mere prudence as the proper intellectual virtue, but that deepest meaning of St. Thomas's "union" which is the sacramental conduct of intellect in nature out of intellect's given nature. It is the proper deportment of intellect, the action of our intellectual being.

Having said this, we may add that in some moments there is a seeming rest, but it is a pause to intellect whereby it savors the good of intellect, delights in the food of being as it were. But alas, the sense of rest, if not seen for what it is, becomes transformed to an arrest. The vision in an event becomes transformed to *idea*, to which intellect shifts its desire as if idea were an object promising a continuous rest, a respite from the seeming jungle of being in which the tiger is always set to spring as an event. Such is the birth of "ideology." And that is why we must be often if not steadily reminded that idea so taken has deleterious consequence upon the taking intellect itself. Even so there remains always that disturbing hope, a desire for rest short of Beatitude. For in the actuality of intellect's encounter with being, action is unwaveringly circumscribed to the weariness of intellect. Only with great difficulty may it shield itself from the insistence of a return to truth consequent upon its multitudinous encounters with being in time and place.

Intellect is always vulnerable to the good, we say. That does not mean that it is incapable of resisting that good, and its resistance most commonly is by retreating behind the spectacle of its own action. That is, it would isolate itself within its own spectacle, those ready masks of its being. Such an attempt takes advantage of language's tendency to attach as spectacle. The most decisive word of defensive attachment, one suspects, is "I." To use "We" in the name of the common good only somewhat alleviates the danger, and may indeed be treacherously used, as I take Prufrock to do in the concluding lines of Eliot's poem, in a suicide-murder whereby the *you* and *I* of that poem become a "We" and drown into the spectacle of the tea party. (I have explored this treachery in the speaking voice of the poem in *T. S. Eliot: The American Magus* and elsewhere.)

And so our signs, which are necessary if intellect is to acknowledge its actions as beyond the self-encasement possible in the "I," require close and careful attention always. This we must be constant in saying, in the hope that thereby we may see the truth signified. For our word as mediator of intellectual action tends not only to become a tranquilizing dart but a poisoned arrow, given intellect's inclination to a comprehension of being through the will's hunger for dominance over being, its will to be "as the gods." *We* are required to remind ourselves therefore – *I* am required to remind myself – that comprehension by finite intellect is impossible in its fullest sense precisely because intellect in this creature man is finite. That is why St. Thomas makes a careful distinction between two senses of *comprehend*: first, "as including what is comprehended in the one comprehending," but in another way as "nothing other than grasping of something now directly possessed." This second sense names the dangerous one to intellect, in that intellect would consume the comprehended object by intellection, when will is inordinate. This is the sort of aggression against being by intellect which is so largely the curse of, and in, intellect in our present world.

The second sense of *comprehend* is, we say, analogous to a literal description of an action in its material aspect, as when an actual, sensual thing is taken in hand and possessed by the force of physical restraint. It is from this older sense in the term that we come to apply it to the consensual – to an idea taken and held in mind. It is through metaphorical extension that we come to that first meaning given, as usually understood. But it is a meaning dangerous to intellect insofar as intellect is tempted to a devouring possession of the thing "comprehended." For if the thing comprehended is possessed as a prisoner of intellect under the wardenship of will, the violence of command over the nonmaterial thing is such that it is enslaved. Or we should rather say that the intent is to enslave by possession, while the actuality is that intellect itself becomes possessed by idea. That seems apt characterization of that intellect we term *ideologue*. Put another way: When will is thus inordinate to its responsibility to move intellect in a touching of, a stroking of, an embracing of the existent thing (whether corporeal or other), that is when will would devour the existent to digest the thing's being under the illusion that intellect is its own ultimate end only as fed by being. It is then that intellect and will become progressively ravenous. Like Dante's figure of the wolf encountered near Hell's gate, willful intellect is starved by its very feasting upon being. It is deconstructed by its actions. This is the progress of intellect in its Faustean aspect, its doomed pursuit of its own autonomous happiness as if complete happiness might be attained by man's natural powers.

It is to this confusion of the objects and the ends of intellectual act, in relation to the desire of intellect for happiness, that St. Augustine speaks when he says that happiness lies in our "adhering lovingly to something for itself." (See *On Christian Doctrine* I, 4; *On the Trinity* X, 10, 11). "Adhering lovingly to" moves the understanding quite differently from the impulse to enslave the object when will would stir a hope of happiness in and of the will itself in a false rest resistant to circumstantial pressures. One is rather made happy by participating in the gift of being common to creation, not in commanding being to the willed end of one's own happiness. Happiness willed proves to be only an arrest in alienation. The encreatured being that stirs desire in our will must be held lightly, then, like a wild bird resting a moment on the opened, upturned palm. When fingers curl to cage about it, the hand no longer "adheres lovingly to something for itself." Instead, one holds something merely for the holding self's escape of panic.

We dwell on the point in a homiletic way because the aggression of intellect upon being is a habit so widely established in our common understanding of the relation of intellect to existence. As a gnostic habit of making, it controls our actions of mind impulsively rather than thoughtfully. It seizes upon things, grasping creaturely existences. Such is that bad habit of intellect, willfulness, for which we seek remedy. But so pervasive is it as bad habit that sermon seems almost a necessity precedent to any intellectual attempt to the recovery of a right will through steady argument. To recognize the ravishing wolf, itself ravished by its actions, is prelude to Dante's encounter with Virgil, we might observe. Virgil is a figuring of right-willed intellect as suited to leading the pilgrim soul Dante through the bowels of the beast of perverse intellect, presented as Hell in the great poem. The wolf as we encounter it just outside the Inferno is seemingly a milder creature than the horror at Hell's center, and its subtlety is thus the more deceiving.

Consider a species of this wolf nearer home, the general assumption of the relation of the person to the common good as advanced in a mild seeming, a just civil doctrine: One has an inalienable right to the pursuit of life, liberty, and happiness. Those abstract shibboleths justify a range of intellectual actions of self-destruction from lowest to highest, their very abstraction from created existence allowing us to deny the limits of finitude in ourselves as created creatures. By our actions, the life we save may be our own. Our common slogans tell us this, the words long since expunged of intellect's knowing the abiding light cast in intellect as the truth of existential reality: He who would save his life must lose it. Suppositions about the self and its potential when governed by those shibboleths are but fancy's images of light and shadow. When thus removed from the anchor of image in the actuality of existences, a darkness of mind is a seeming light.

We make this disconnection from reality through the magic of abstractionism, the manipulation of an assumed possession – a comprehension – of actuality as possessed by the willful intellect. The abstractions of *life*, *liberty*, *happiness* are thus freed of the anchors imposed by reality. We might better say *life* in relation to *property*, the actual level of the particular incarnate intellect's struggle with the realities of its existence, the being of itself. The struggle in intellectual life with the actualities of creation, the struggle of this discrete life with the *properties* of its own being – that is the arena within which happiness appears or does not appear. And happiness appears or fails to appear in a direct relation to the discrete intellect's manner of holding existence by the specific properties of being. Held lightly in the opened hand or grasped tenaciously by fingers turned in upon the closed territory of the palm? Right-willed, or willful?

Happiness, says St. Augustine, is "joy in truth," and there is joy in the truth of finitude itself, despite the hesitancy to believe it so. The relation of life to "property," a relationship of metaphorical extension here (though with deliberate implications to social and political confusions besetting us) – this relationship yields to our understanding the truth of the limits of being, without which limits our recognition of and understanding of the gift of happiness may not descend to us or burgeon in us. Happiness is an effect of an end perceived or accomplished, not an end in itself. It is an effect following an understanding of the limits of being that governs our adhering lovingly to existences for themselves, which is to say: a holding of things lovingly in their limited being. Thus happiness is a false idol when raised as the end object of actions, as if happiness were a *thing* to be possessed by an act of will. One has, in moments of happiness (as our reflection on the actualities of happy moments will remind us), a sense that happiness is a gratuitous gift, a something *supra*, and not an end achieved through our actions. One is properly grateful and thankful for that gift, so long as a restlessness does not intrude. The restlessness is will's attempt to clutch happiness as a possession, a property in being with unencumbered title.

A poignant emotional residue is so conspicuous an effect of our mistaking happiness as a thing possessed that it becomes a thematic category in our literature from ancient times to our own: *carpe diem*. By will, seize this moment's happiness. But the same residue gives rise as well to darker dramas of a bargaining over happiness with the devil, as in Marlowe and Goethe. The poignancy is an inevitable consequence of the will's shifting in its relation to existence from an openness beyond itself to itself as end, an end which can be but vaguely described as a state of happiness. It is an ancient difficulty to intellect. Gilson might even find in it an aftermath of that Platonic distinction whereby good holds primacy over being. Similarly, happiness may be taken as the cause of being, or of any state of being worth having to the self. The intellectual process involved, managed by the will, establishes mediate ends as sufficient to the happiness of the intellect. For an *effect* called happiness seems caused by the mediate end as embraced. Thus comes that turning, whereby an effect is embraced as if the final end of desire. In the event, however, what is arrested is desire as it turns from its proper object, Being Itself. In the experience, or so we seem to learn from reflection upon it, we are left with a memory of the effect of a moment, which we recognize as a moment already decaying at its zenith of "happiness." Thus Keats's advice that we seek melancholy at the moment of the April rose, not in decaying autumn.

To seek happiness as the end, out of a memory of a moment about which we conclude ourselves to have been "happy" – that is a procedure which must prevent happiness altogether. To close fingers upon illusive happiness is to find it seeping through that active grasping. The effect upon intellect is not the cause of that effect, a most illusive distinction when we would articulate it out of actual experience. And so we depend upon our poets to speak to the circumstance. It is the circumstance central to Goethe's Faust, we said, in his pursuit of that moment he would stay because of its "fairness." His desire to embrace illusion is so intense as to cause him to risk his soul to seize it. It is as well the moment lamented by that unhappy poet Keats. His great "Ode to a Nightingale" is one of the touchstones to our pursuit of an understanding of making as the proper habit of our intellectual being. It turns in its drama on the attempt through making to arrest the happy moment. It is poignantly effective art, in part because we know intuitively, as we join its action of the words with our own finite capacities, that the "thing" that fades is not simply the nightingale's song, but the moment of openness to the song and through that song, a moment of openness in which there occurs St. Thomas's union of intellect and thing. Our own intuitive intellect recognizes it as such, through our consent to the poem as an imitation of the action of peculiar human nature, our intellectual nature. The moment fading, before the poem's words even begin, is that of a self-forgetfulness in which there is no concern for happiness at all, only a union with the thing perceived in an enveloping context of things: the nightingale's song. The poem echoes an open, self-unawareness, which is misnamed happiness in retrospection. It is so named by the words begun at the edge of the decaying moment itself. Misunderstanding the nature of that visionary moment, the voice sings lament, having settled under the supposed oppression of a "thought": the self as inescapably and always a "sole self." Thus this "Ode" might well be called an "Elegy to Ever-Fading Happiness."

Such, then, is the most constant theme of our literature, high or low: the failure of the soul when through will it sets about gaining as the only world of the soul its moment of happiness. It mistakes the merely local as an eternal moment of openness through perfection, the moment St. Augustine or St. Thomas would call the state of Beatitude. To will a direct purchase of happiness proves foredoomed, since that is a turning from the potential fullness of being to a provincialism of the moment. And because the temptation is a constant to the will, through the grace of moments remembered as happy, pathos and tragedy are the consequent moods of our singing of the soul, the makings by intellect which we call art. Alexander having conquered the moment's world, must weep as the "sole self" returns, dissolving the visionary moment of his world all conquered. That is the lyric moment, embedded again and again in the tragedy or the epic, in which we join weeping our fallen nature through art. That is the moment we already considered when Oedipus cries "Woe! woe! woe!" It is the moment to be transcended at last, perhaps, in the understanding of that other all-embracing moment of tears we discussed: "Jesus wept."

And so we here remind ourselves: When the will in pursuit of the life and liberty of the soul mistakes as final end a life and liberty established by intellect – a rest of intellect in happiness – the will has succeeded thereby in orienting the soul to a chimera. Thus one would seize a false dream in an action which prevents vision. And having so turned from vision, how else may the soul respond than to ask Keats's weeping question: "Do I wake or sleep?" Because such chimeras are the illusional ends so prevalent to disturbed souls in our day, though most variously disguised, our obligation as intellectual creatures is to recover the truth of things in their stead. Truth, we must emphasize, is the good of the intellect. That is why we must revisit as carefully as good reason allows the truth of the nature of man as intellectual creature. Thus it may prove possible to recover our intellect as committed to truth by its nature. Not to happiness as instant fulfillment of desire, but to a pursuit of the truth of things, a cumulative good of intellect in its becoming. An effect along the way of that recovery may be, through grace, some moments of happiness to intellect. But a moment of rest sustained by truth, when the steadiness of our understanding returns us to the necessity of our setting forth from that moment always. At least that is the necessity this side of Beatitude. If the poet reminds us of the intuitive response to being which speaks by indirection of the end possible to desire, it is the philosopher who complements that intuited truth. Hence we shall turn now to the philosopher, to his concern for the nature of intellect itself in its encounter with truth. The relation of thought to truth as signifying intellectual action in response to encounter with being: That is the philosopher's theme. Let us as poet go as we may along with the philosopher and rest if we may at the small fire he provides for a moment on our long journey.

VII

Brice Parain sees man's mind as a compost heap, on which words feed, flourish, and die. It is a desperate message he bears about language, a bodiless vampire turned loose on existence, or perhaps a fungus on being, which survives past its having been generated by the uttering man. We have with us for a while the words of our fathers' fathers, and that gives to language itself an appearance of immortality. Neither marble nor the gilded monuments of kings, Shakespeare suggests, last so long as our words. For being bodiless, they are less victim to time's decay. In that mood, Parain says: "That which lasts best, apart from the sun, . . . is words. The first words that were collected have succeeded in preserving their meaning even after the fall of empires in which their language was spoken. What is revealed to us then in our moments of silence is that we are a kind of compost heap on which language germinates, grow, and flowers."

One can only come to such a dark version of the word from a faith in principles not at last acceptable, however. For Parain is committed to an immanentist view of existence, to the "birth of thought beginning with the amoeba," though he finds it "as difficult to conceive as the creation of the world by God." Thought moves toward contemplation of the condition of itself so that the "natural continuation of contemplation would be silence." But then silence seems possible to man only when he ceases to be. "The ridiculous thing about life is that only death delivers us up to true solitude, and hence, to true freedom." Meanwhile, this side of death, the moment of our silence reveals only "our dependence." The nearest solution short of death itself seems to be our "capacity to live animalistically, so to speak." Which is to say, a capacity to escape thought by regression toward amoebic existence. For to think, as John Keats puts it hauntingly, is to be filled with sorrow and leaden-eyed despair, to be alienated and separated from desired happiness. "Why not," says Parain, "invert the *cogito* and say: I think, therefore I am not. For to think is not to be, it is to wish to be. . . . To think is to struggle painfully in lies and error, to struggle against them, to escape from them." Little wonder that a Prufrock, burdened by such thought about thought, will declare he'd rather "be a pair of ragged claws/ Scuttling across the shores of silent seas," a considerable devolution toward the amoebic condition of dividing cells in nature.

We find Parain's argument convenient, as a summary of that train of thought out of Descartes, leading to the agony of alienation which Parain captures rather effectively. And we see in his argument that he is trapped by the immanentist burden of Cartesian thought which at last can allow no transcendence. Indeed, thought is the only transcendent, effected by intellect itself, which becomes by its continuing dependence an intolerable burden. And it is in this never-never land of thought about thought that language rises, mocking thought itself. It is at this impasse that Parain finds his two faces to words, one turned toward being, the other toward nonbeing. And for Parain thought itself is a species of nonbeing. It is in his premise of an immanentist limit to being that the difficulty rises, which position Gilson opposes by a counter-premise in his own view of the nature of language as it relates to thought. Gilson rejects Cartesian Idealism, not because it may not say a limited truth, but because it presumes its limited truth the final, absolute truth about thought possible to human intellect. As he says, in *Methodical Realism*, "*I think therefore I am* is a truth but it is not a starting point." There is a precedent choice to be made: "Either one begins with being, in which thought is included . . . or one starts from thought, in which being is included." Cartesian Idealism has made the choice by rejecting the alternative. It is a temptation difficult to resist, but the "fact that everything is given me in thought in no way permits me to assert that everything is reducible to thought."

What experience teaches us, if we observe our own intellectual action here and now, is that "thought is only possible where there is first of all knowledge." It must follow that "rather than the subject [i.e. mind] finding its object through an analysis of knowledge, it discovers its knowledge, and itself, in the analysis of the object." Which is to say that the truth of things measures knowledge, and consequently justifies thought, rather than the other way round. Gilson puts the difference by distinguishing the realist from the idealist: "*Res sunt, ergo cognosco, ergo sum res cognoscens.*" I know because things exist (*including* my own thinking). Therefore, I am a knowing subject. "What distinguishes the realist from the idealist is not that one refuses to undertake this analysis whereas the other is willing to, but that the realist refuses to take the final term of his analysis [*I am a thinking subject*] for a principle generating the thing to be analyzed."

Gilson's *Linguistics and Philosophy*, as we noted, appeared the same year as Parain's *A Metaphysics of Language*, in 1969. Parain's is a sort of last-ditch defense of Idealism, in which defense his heart no longer hopes for any happy issue. In taking the impasse with language at the surface of the dilemma, on a principle not reexamined, Parain allows to language its two faces: a mixture of being and nonbeing, insofar as any meaning might be ascribed to language. And he concludes that nonbeing devours being. Instead of a view of being as continuously sustained, he sees it as continuously decayed. To the contrary, Gilson finds two faces as well, but quite differently designated. In considering the word, he first separates the physical dimension (sound, written letters) as quite distinct from the word alive as *meaning*. The locus of the word's life is intellect itself. In this approach words are sustained in their being in part by intellectual action. An analogy, not precise but suggestive, is that of God in relation to his creature man as compared to man in relation to his creature the word.

The analogy is limited, given the distinction that, whereas God *is* being, man only *has* being as recipient of the first act of being. That is why we must say that the word is sustained in the being we confer only in part by our action. For in addition, the word is sustained by the truth of things, independent of but mediated by our act of making the word. It is in the *meaning* of the word that we find either a convergence with or divergence from the truth of things – either a coincidence with or a violation of the truth of the thing as held by intellect. That truth depends from the relative fullness of "union" (to recall St. Thomas here) of intellect and the thing in itself, the consequence of truth in intellect precedent to the eventual word as memorial of the encounter of union. That encounter is also precedent to the concept, the presence of thought in intellect which signifies the precedent union, from which the meaning of the word derives. Given this complex of relations between the word and truth, one sees how it may be that some words are true and some false in the meaning they bear. This said, we must also say with Gilson that it is the nature of the word to bear meaning, whether true or false. That is the point Gilson raises in faulting modern linguistics, which cannot maintain itself as a science, he says, unless it reject meaning from the word. It is a necessity to that science, lest it be required to defer at last to metaphysics. We now turn to that difficulty as Gilson addresses it.

If man is created in the image of God, man's words are created in the image of man's thought as centered by knowledge, with limits to the analogy as just presented. Language is thus art, in Dante's sense: The word is nature formed by intellectual action. Now the underlying nature thus formed by the act of making is in one aspect the intellect itself through its actions of making. Words are, in this respect, things "made" by intellect as an effect of its own becoming, in its fulfillment of its potential being. Now any made thing is constituted of form-body, from man's perspective upon essential realities, and especially evident in his made things, echoing by analogy man's own nature as in the image of God. In respect to this proposition as we put it, we may see Gilson sustains the nature of words as dependent upon meaning, whose mediate cause in the making of meaning-full words is intellect. It is in this way that he defends meaning against the Cartesian deconstruction of reality whose roots lie in Nominalism's disjunction of words from reality. For meaning in words, despite Nominalist pretense to the contrary, is not a creation *ex nihilo* by intellect through a process of making words. Meaning is sustained by being itself, and insofar as the word bears true meaning, it does so because it is ultimately dependent on being. Meaning, a knowledge of the truth of things, is in intellect as a knowledge intuitively held by intellect and not commanded by intellect. This is to say that an initial intellectual openness to being necessarily precedes thought itself, since when we think, we discover intellect already possessed of some knowledge which may not be attributed to the action of intellect, the action which St. Thomas would call the "second act of being." There is an initiating acceptance by intellect following upon its encounter with existential reality.

The modern linguist's adaptation of Nominalist thought does not help matters, Gilson says in *Linguistics and Philosophy* (quoting De Saussure), when it declares "the name" as "significant and understood." That is the direction to thought about language which will in the end make language that vampire of being which so troubles Parain. Gilson to the contrary observes that a *word* for one person is but a *noise* for another intellect. Concept is not in the word itself as may be proposed by the linguist. "The meaning that is attributed to it does not partake in any way in the nature of the noise, and inversely. It is in the hearer, not in the sound, that the metamorphosis of meaning from noise, of sign from sound, is made." Therefore it is necessary to conclude that "with the word a person has already left the purely physical."

It is at this point that Parain would declare that thought itself, leaving the physical, enters that oblivion of nonbeing, whereby to think is not to be, as he says. But it is here that Gilson argues a distinction between two realities, or rather between two aspects of inclusive reality: that of the physical and that of the nonphysical. It is in the nonphysical arena that one finds the necessity of a metaphysics, for one is dealing with a reality, though not with that aspect of reality that submits to characterization in terms derived from physics. The difficulty – the error – in that climate of thought exhibited by Parain is that his words attempt to treat the accidents of being as essence. If the word is not its letters, which are only representational of the "mouthfuls" of the spoken, neither is the spoken itself the word. On either hand, the word measured by physics instead of approached as truly existing in the realm proper to metaphysics, will miss the essence, the meaning. That meaning is *in* mind, not in the accidental manifestations of the word as registered by the brain. The creation of language by intellect is marvelous precisely because it overcomes this difficulty whereby the physical is a handicap to the metaphysical deportment proper to mind. It is a difficulty overcome by the strategy of indirection within the physical realm, in which realm it is necessary to maintain language *through* that realm but *toward* the intellect as receptive to meaning in the word in quite another realm. In considering this aspect of language, Gilson, in "Language as a Human Achievement," observes: "One sees with the eyes, one smells with the nose, one hears with the ear, one walks with the legs, but one speaks with the mouth, teeth, nose, and many another organ no one of which has as its specific function to speak." Thus man has employed organs that are incidental and not specific to the action of speech, organs within the physical realm of his being that nevertheless make words possible by their incidental adaptations. By this indirection a community of mind becomes established as a reality transcendent of the material reality within which these organs have their primary function. The metaphysician, says Gilson, is "naturally persuaded that language is exercised by an incorporeal intellect." In this recognition, one could "truly say that a transcendental power 'uses' the body for ends of a transcendent order akin to itself."

C. S. Lewis in his "Transposition" (*The Weight of Glory*, 1949) develops an interesting argument supportive of Gilson's point. He is concerned with our experience of reality beyond the limits of physics, and especially in relation to the limits of our physical perceptions of meaning. So disproportionate are those metaphysical experiences to the capacity of sensual response, he argues, that in our sensual response to varied experiences we have the same sensual reaction to experiences different in radical ways. Speaking of aesthetic rapture, Lewis remarks: "I find that this kick or flutter [of sensual response] is exactly the same sensation which, in me, [also] accompanies great and sudden anguish. Introspection can discover no difference at all between my neural response to very bad news and my neural response to the overture of *The Magic Flute*. If I were to judge simply by sensations I should come to the absurd conclusion that joy and anguish are the same thing, that what I most dread is the same with what I most desire." Socrates, we remember, remarks the similar relation between pain and happiness in the *Phaedo* at the point where the irons are removed from his body.

A further point by Lewis, in speaking of the limits of signs by their restricted physical presentation: "The very same shape which you must draw to give the illusion of a straight road receding from the spectator is also the shape you draw for a dunce's cap." The distinction, then, is not in the sign, but in the intellect. After further examples he concludes: "All our examples suggest that the brain can respond . . . to the seemingly infinite variety of consciousness without providing one single modification for each single modification of consciousness." The brain, as distinguished by actions of thought, is limited to a necessity of representing the variety of thought in limited, physical responses since it is a physical organ limited in its sensual responses. That recognition signifies a quite different dimension to the existence of consciousness from its physical locale, the brain.

An error in approaching this mystery of mind as distinguished from the brain, from below – from the realm of physics – leads to the error of supposing the lower adequate to the higher. Thus the very mystery at issue, intellect itself, "sees all the facts but not the meaning." And so Lewis concludes of that error: "The extreme limit of this self-blinding is seen in those who, like the rest of us, have consciousness, yet go about to study the human organism as if they did not know it was conscious. . . . The critique of every experience from below, the voluntary ignoring of meaning and concentration on fact, will always have the same plausibility." Thus trapped by its own act of reductionism of reality, intellect dooms itself to the lower level, that of fact retrieved from material existence, overlooking the point we have already made: It is only possible to intellect to establish itself as atrophied, as fallen from its position higher than the material end it would establish as its limit. Its own being is thus atrophied to a merely material existence. It thus accepts the lower as ultimate. Little surprise then that, as Lewis says, "There will always be evidence, and every month fresh evidence, to show that religion is only psychology, justice only self-protection, politics only economics, love only lust, and thought itself only cerebral biochemistry."

For Gilson the "transcendent power" that uses the body is intellect itself, and by transcendent he means that it exists in a realm trans-physical. In distinguishing the power that uses and that which is used, as for instance the organs of the body in the projection of words, Gilson is concerned that we make a careful distinction between *thought* and *language*. Thus he argues that at a point the physical and metaphysical adjoin – the one actual in terms of the material the other actual in terms of the immaterial, but both of them realities. Thought "begins to descend into language" at this point. But we *know* (rather than *think toward*) that thought is antecedent to this point. It already exists. It is a something we may call "x." Now this "x," says Gilson, "which has not yet been spoken, ought to be in some fashion present to my thought, for otherwise I could not try to say it." One might put it that thought exists "about" a presence in thought. This x would seem to be a presence *in* thought, but not thought itself – a something whose manifestation in the realm of physics is through words articulated.

Such is the genesis of language, at a point where careful distinctions must be made if we are to avoid the cul de sac of Cartesian Idealism.

What we come to in identifying this initiating presence to thought, which is itself (as is also true of thought) antecedent to language, is *knowledge already possessed by intellect*. It is a presence in intellect consequent to direct encounter with being. It is a present effect of the *essence* of a thing, St. Thomas says, that is made immediate to intuitive intellect. In its presence in intellect it is called truth, a knowledge of being precedent to thought and without which thought would be impossible. On the point, Gilson observes that "infants think before speaking. Every parent knows this, and moreover, no linguist contests the issue." But the point being granted, where does that leave thought itself on the question. Can we, he asks, "imagine thought devoid of words. . .?" And yet we know such as an actuality in the "*in-fans*, the nonspeaking." Thought existing before language thus speaks, though not in *words*, "the experience of a presence whose nature escapes us and whose reality is attested to only by its effects, which are however material, audible, visible, and objects of a particular science, phonology." We cannot certify with science this distinction, since "thought becoming language is already language."

One cannot account for the *transposition* of thought to words, the higher to the lower, to borrow again the term C. S. Lewis uses in his argument supportive of the position at issue. One cannot, because the instrument of this accounting is inadequate to the reality of the thing for which it would account. That is the point Lewis makes: "Our problem [is] that in what claims to be our spiritual life all the elements of our natural life recur: And, what is worse, it looks at first glance as if no other elements were present." But we see, in the light of the necessity of transposition – the accommodation of the higher by the limited mode of the lower, of the spiritual through the material dimension of spiritual existence – that "the spiritual is richer than the natural. [But] then this is exactly what we should expect." If instead we reduce the spiritual to the natural, the realm of the soul to the limits of the amoeba, then a reduction of reality proves inevitable, to the denigration of human nature as spiritual creature. Hence it is that the "brutal man never can by analysis find anything but lust in love; the Flatlander never can find anything but flat shapes in a picture; physiology never can find anything in thought except the twitchings of the grey matter."

Thus Lewis argues the difficulties in the transposition through intellectual action between the transcendent and immanent realms of our being. Thus we discover the conditions of the Platonic In-Between which holds man by his very nature as spiritual creature engaged in both material and immaterial reality. Of this impasse to the critique of thought from the physical dimension of our being, Gilson says that the linguist cannot allow meaning to the word, since meaning immediately requires the metaphysical address toward that transcendent, toward extra-material being. That is, toward thought itself as the locus to intellectual movement toward truth. There is, he says, a "venerable tradition" that takes it for granted that language owes its intelligibility to the immateriality of the human soul, but its most illustrious representatives have some difficulty in saying what an 'immaterial being' could be and how it comes about, if it exists, that such a being could be connected to a body." The key word here, spoken in relation to the arguments of Aristotle and St. Thomas, is *saying*. For it is one thing to know a truth, to hold a good as a good in the intellect, and to truly say that good in signs.

Such is the difficulty to finite intellect, which by its nature is in that In-Between, partaking of a complex reality that is both material and immaterial. As finite, embodied spirit, ours is the mode of discursive intellect. Therefore, "language is possible only on the condition of proceeding by means of a sort of parcelling out of thought. . . . But the thought that speech expresses, the very meaning of speech, does not lend itself to any division." That is the point we made earlier, in relation to the "mouthful" of speech called the sentence, which the grammarian says "expresses a complete thought." The complete thought is itself indivisible, so that we must, as best we are able, attempt to convey that undivided "thing" through our only means, language, with the inevitable consequence that articulation violates its simple existence. But that we cannot *simply say* does not discredit the simple thing itself. It is in attempting to overcome this difficulty that intellect devises strategies more and more sophisticated, whereby language grows – not in its own existence as separate from intellect, but through intellect's struggle to capture the simplicity of thought with the widening, increasingly complex, net of language. If Parain or Prufrock envy the amoeba or lowly crab their animalism, other sophisticated intellects may as easily grow to envy the angelic mode of intellection, even as such an intellect seeks to supplant the angelic creature through its own self-elevation by gnostic manipulations of reality.

What we have been wrestling with is the impossibility of ever adequately saying just what we mean. It is an impossibility effected, not by an absence of meaning in that thing we would say, but by the handicap to finite intellect of its limits of articulation. The struggle to articulate meaning is always necessary, though ultimately doomed. Such is the prospect of our labors on the journey toward conclusion. We thus repeatedly find ourselves in a present moment, required to make a new attempt to say just what we know, so that by the saying perhaps the true meaning itself may become more accessible because understood by another intellect. That is the progress we pray for, from knowledge, to understanding, to wisdom. It is the part of wisdom at the last to recognize and accept that we have not been able to say meaning adequately, since the complexity of being itself contains us and we do not contain that complexity. The additional aspect of wisdom, without which it would not be sustaining as the most desirable deportment of intellect to reality, is the continuing knowledge that the thing which we know and are unable to articulate is nevertheless a thing, is a reality, despite all our failure of language in relation to thought to adequately praise it as the thing it is. Always, we discover, there is yet something more to be said of it.

With that recognition of the limits of our saying we may come to say, at least, that intellectual action is the making of an order to intellect's deportment toward that which it is inadequate to comprehend. It does so in relation to the presence in it, beyond scientific demonstration of that presence, of thought. For thought has – in terms understandable even to language limited by our material existence – thought has no beginning whereby it might dictate its own expression structurally. On this difficulty, Gilson reminds us of

"The well-known embarrassment of the writer who 'does not know where to begin.'" That embarrassment occurs because "thought has no beginning which one could cause to coincide with that of the written word." It is for this reason that our speech is always uttered *in medium res*, a circumstance which T. S. Eliot, that philosopher turned poet, in an attempt to find an accommodation of language to thought, at last cries out against somewhat desperately, though afterward Eliot came to accept the reality of intellect's constriction in its present moment. In *Burnt Norton*, he laments that "words strain." They "slip, slide, perish, decay" under the tension of our intellectual pursuit of an ordered journey toward an acceptable silence beyond any inadequacy of language – toward a silence in the immaterial realm of truth. What has to be acknowledged is the continuing circumstance to intellect, requiring its using words in as precise, as purified, a manner as can be managed, knowing in advance that words fail of perfection. It is a continuing necessity to finite intellect, because we are not only at this singular, present moment in "the middle of the way." Dante, required by language to a beginning of thought which has no beginning, used such *a* beginning to initiate his own middle of the way at the outset of the *Divine Comedy*. But intellect, Eliot recognizes, is all along its way always in such a middle. It is "in a dark wood, in a bramble,/ On the edge of a grimpen, where is no secure foothold,/ And menaced by monsters, fancy lights,/ Risking enchantment." In those circumstances, always attendant upon intellect, "The only wisdom we can hope to acquire/ Is the wisdom of humility: humility is endless."

Our task as intellectual creature then? To say in an acceptable way something justifying our presumption in attempting to say the truth. And that acceptable way is determined, not by the unaided power of intellect itself, but by a grace whereby intellect responds to reality. The reward of that response is a unity with things through the truth of things. Such a term as *word*, seen in this light, seems to become a most formidable obstacle to the sharing of the meaning of truth which the word would carry. The *word*, so simple a mouthful that we become arrested by its simplicity in defying our saying, after which more mouthfuls follow. But thus it shall be so to the last syllable of recorded time as we may anticipate. We *know* what a word is. "Say the word only and my soul shall be healed." But for us to say what it is justly, in relation to its *isness*: There's the rub of physics against metaphysics that sparks wars and conflagrations among intellectual creatures. Little wonder that we find ourselves, under the necessity of our circumstantial existence of the In-Between, alternately poet and philosopher. What we may come to consider, further along, is that the necessity is prepared for the good of intellect itself. It is prepared by grace as suited to its nature. We know this true, even though we cannot fully demonstrate that knowledge scientifically. We know it to be both intuitive and rational in its nature. And thus we would persevere in thought, both openly passive and restrictedly active in our pursuit of the truth of things through that most significant action of all actions, the movement of and in intellect in its response to the gift of its own existence.

VIII

In the interest of our pursuit of the truth of things – the proper occupation of this intellectual creature man – we discover that whenever two or three are gathered together it becomes necessary that we agree on certain terms, certain words, as carrying meaning from one mind to another. The complication is considerable, since the problem is to make the word, which exists in the material realm, convey a meaning whose existence is in the immaterial realm. The difficulty is not so formidable in our imagination as that whereby being *is ex nihilo* through the grace of God. But nevertheless it is formidable enough: We must attempt a sufficiency of a material existence as a medium bearing on immaterial existence; a sufficiency of the lower to the higher; a sufficiency of the physics of language to the metaphysics of language. The margin of imperfection to such a making is, or should be, sufficiently apparent to make us careful, and more careful, with our words. In an age little concerned with responsibility to words, we appreciate even more the undertaking of the poet, who must (as Eliot says) be devoted to "purifying the dialect of the tribe."

The poet's help comes in the light of an impossible responsibility to the word. On the one hand, the sign must be established in its limit, lest it violate the reality which its meaning depends upon. A word may attempt to say more than it can. And in this aspect of the problem, we discover words proliferating as a corrective of themselves. Such an aspect of our signs reveals our attempt to convey thought through words as we have already used, in this essay, an instance being when we say, "put another way. . . ." That is to attempt the same meaning "in other words," in recognition of the limited power of our words in relation not only to reality but to our own concepts. In the reaction to that tendency to excessive discursiveness, we may on the other hand concentrate in the word as limited, resisting proliferation of words, as when we attempt the compactness of meaning in "symbolism" if we are a poet in the post-Cartesian world. That is, with rational intent we would make the word pulse from within itself with "meaning" multiple. (That is a complaint against the poet typical in our century, registered against him again and again, and against no poet more often perhaps than against our sometime-Virgil to the present journey, T. S. Eliot.) Caught by the circumstantial impasse, whereby simple meaning is forced within the incommensurate medium of sign, we do what we can, knowing how words decay under the pressure of simple meaning. For we would mean this, and mean it precisely, without other meanings attracted to the accidents of word in its transmission to another intellect by our materially governed sign through his senses. Somehow, other meanings float in the immaterial dimension of that other intellect as in our own, becoming confused, through the accidents of the word, with the meaning we would transmit. A considerable publishing industry serves to rectify this problem, with dictionaries and encyclopedias of an infinite range of special concentrations. The confusions attaching to transmissions of meaning is trouble enough in our attempt to say a just thing about meaning, to say "just what we mean." But it is further complicated by a more fundamental difficulty, namely, rectifying the meaning we ourselves intend to be conveyed by the word we utter as true to the reality which gives rise to it before we hazard utterance, recognizing the precedence of truth's effect in our own immaterial realm, our own "mind." That is a level of concern antecedent to our attempt to witness any truth we hold by uttering the word of all words suited to that truth so that it may be received as bearing that truth by another mind.

If a justification of established terms is needed, these continuing difficulties do so. Not that we are not, in the interest of truth's good, obligated as intellects to consider and reconsider terms once established in our confidence. It is rather that (with that caution always operative) we find an advantage to our support of intellectual action through terms long examined as they have been long used. What Gilson says of the term *immaterial being*, for instance, applies to a whole class of terms that we shall be using: There is a "venerable tradition" supporting that term. What we must attempt is to bring to that venerable usage our own judgment of whether the term continues viable, in relation to our experience of reality. For through this balanced concern for the terms as viable *now* we may the better protect thought from a reduction to cliché.

We find ourselves using certain terms, then, out of a long tradition of the intellect's attempt to recover and understand, by deliberate thought, intellect's own experience of its actuality – its given life in the context of whatever accidents of its particular being, its life as effected by its dependence in the created world, the first act of its being. Some of our terms might require a more considerable justification in present intellectual circumstances of our decayed intellectual community, as perhaps they would not have done in fifth-century Greece or thirteenth-century Paris. But none are strange or esoteric, only long neglected. Indeed, most are very common, which may be a condition best characterizing the problem. The question may well be whether the very common aspect in any sign is evidence of an overlay of imprecisions which require recovering its center. I mean such words as *word* itself. Or *knowledge*, *understanding*, *wisdom*. Or *individual*, *person*. There are of course less usual terms: *practical intellect*, *speculative intellect*, *intuitive* or *rational intellect*, and the like. But above all are those terms that are at once most common and most wrapped in mystery – *be*, *being*, *existence*.

Words is a term whose meaning is (more or less) available to us, with which and against which we must attempt to bring the actual experience of our intellectual life as a test of its continuing viability wherever two or three attempt to understand the mystery of complex existence through words. Now the particular intellect is the final determinant of the appropriateness of a word to the mystery of existence itself. We know that our own intellect exists at a point of time and a point in place, though of itself it has no dimension of time or place. We know that it is hemmed round by conditions to its being that require its engaging circumstance so that it may the more fully *be*. If it be demanded that we *prove* this assertion, the demand itself is a sufficient proof. In this realization, what is actually realized is my own existence as intellectual creature at this moment. I find myself in a certain way located in this place, for which I can give precise coordinates of time and place upon demand. It is a point at which most immediately I myself engage these temporal signs set down somewhat awkwardly with a rather ancient machine, an old Remington typewriter. Concrete enough, though what is evident beyond this contingent time and place of my intellect as it sets down letters is an existence of my intellect reflected in temporal and spatial limits. Still, what is reflected is my intellect's *immaterial being*.

The common-sense acceptance of coordinates to the manifestation of this immaterial but existing creature, the intellect – the temporal and spatial coordinates of intellect – is undeniable. I exist in this body, in this house, in this town, and so on. That is the knowledge in wonder of which young Stephen Dedalus scribbles his own coordinates on the fly-leaf of his school text. What is required in the face of such mystery is common-sense acceptance, which speaks not only a communal consent to the meaning carried by words, but affirms as a knowledge in the intellect using those words the reality of both itself and of other things, including the reality of words as existing. Words exist both actually according to their immaterial nature and secondarily through the accidents of their material manifestation – their sounds and visual inscriptions and the like. Meaning in words derives from that immaterial knowledge possessed by intellect, which derives from actual experience of things. That there is a communal acceptance of such an immaterial reality of words is evident: I should receive your letter to me if you addressed it in my name to Box 115, Crawford, Georgia, U.S.A. There might well be a delay. The words would not be instant to me, though we are obsessed at the moment with the instantaneity of "faxing" words. Always there is a degree of fallibility in the actions of intellect, more or less exacerbate by its necessity to operate through and from within material reality. Complaints to the U.S. Postal Service about mail delivery certifies such possibility in the contingencies of intellect's material context. But all this activity in the material dimension certifies our faith in words as bearing meaning separate from the material limitations upon meaning with which we always contend. And that certification further justifies what we know as personal experience of complex reality to which words would stand witness.

This is the immediate arena in which language exists perpetually in a present, which is adjacent to my presently active intellect. By its existence, language also gives some suggestion, not only of a *present* to my intellect, since by such a term intellect might appear too simply designated at a point of time and place as if determined by them, as if the temporal and spatial were determinate of its nature. Rather, if we look at our father's looking at this phenomenon of language in relation to the *numen* of intellect, we begin to see – if but darkly – into the mysterious relation of a physics and a metaphysics coincident in language itself. Gilson reminds us, for instance, that "classical grammars define the present of the verb to be as that of actual time," meaning the actual time of the utterance of the words. Anyone who has struggled to teach, as rational exercise, the grammar of tense sequence to students who are not naturally imbued with their own language will know how difficult it is to orient such a student to this present actual time orienting the verb. In such intellectual exercise, one is always dealing with a "historical present," which the student finds it difficult to submit himself to, since it requires a submission of his own actual, present moment of his wrestling to a condition of intellect in the immaterial dimension of intellect.

He will turn longingly to the relief of an academic period's conclusion, to a drink and random chatter. He may submit to that flow of language in an engaging novel with a sense of his own presence in the language – a present presence. But the experience is easily destroyed if he looks too closely at the temporal accidents of the language as registered on the page in verbs of the narration which has otherwise swept him up and away into imagined events.

We very nearly rob the unsophisticated reader if we call attention to the past tense verbs of the historical novel. That they are *formally* past (i.e., past time in their form) does not formally correspond to the experience he has in the present of his reading. But more than conventional formality seems at work and it is of further interest that this willing suspension seems best effected, not by the logic of argument demonstrating that necessity to an imaginative experience, but by the virtues of art whereby there is no overt consent, only a tacit, covert consent of the will. We know from experience and from testimony of others the problem of "getting into" a book. What occurs we might describe as a willing suspension of our actual time and place, this actuality of circumstances in which the reader exists. Those are the circumstances which, presently, will require his closing the book and going to dinner or to sleep. We are dealing with (in Gilson's words) "the intelligible borne by the material and sensible." We are acting at a locus in which physics and metaphysics engage toward melding with each other in a vision to intellect, and Gilson remarks this, in relation to his discussion of the "customs of Language," as the locus in which we must explore the mystery of existence itself. The challenge here is to our understanding along the slow way to wisdom.

If we say that language happens in the actual present of our discrete being, in respect to temporal and spatial circumstances, we may easily understand the point. We measure it by experience. As I write these words, and as you read them, there is our experience of a present, though they are not the same present. In consideration of this point, Gilson quotes Emile Benveniste: "The only tense inherent in language is the axial present of the discourse." The point in time and place of the saying of words, at which they stand in time and place as intersected by intellect. In this respect, we may distinguish my present *as I say* these words to your present *as you receive* them, though both are a present in relation to the words themselves as existing things. The calendar times of the two "events" may vary from seconds to hours to days to years, but still language itself carries as its point of reference "one single temporal expression, the present," in relation to which present the words are ordered in our pursuit of articulation of a thought as representing a truth. Benveniste remarks of this aspect of language, of his own relation to any interlocutor: "My 'today' becomes his 'today,' although he may not have found it himself in his own discourse, and my 'yesterday' becomes his 'yesterday.' Reciprocally,. . . I, becoming the hearer, convert his temporality into mine . . . . [The temporality] of the speaker, literally foreign and inaccessible to the hearer, is identified by the [hearer] as that temporality which informs his own speech when he in turn becomes the speaker." And from this observation of our customs of language, Benveniste adds, "The condition of intersubjectivity alone allows linguistic communication." (Quoted by Gilson from "Le langage et l'experience humaine," *Problemes de langage* [Paris: Gallimard, 1966].)

We may recognize here our own experience in discourse, and it is an experience not limited solely to a temporal presence of speaker and interlocutor in a commonly present place. It is an experience upon which one depends in projecting words beyond speech into letters, through which this customary consent allows a presence of the past to us through language. It is an encounter of intellects made possible through a consent of intellect to reality as non-temporal and non-spatial, the reality of intellectual immateriality. What is required, and we are more accustomed to the requirement than we realize, is a faith in that immaterial reality; in brief a faith in the meaning of words beyond the accidents of words, whether the accidents of speech or letter. It is largely the accidents that doom words. Meanwhile, we *know* that meaning has an actual existence, and we know that meaning's existence is insubstantial in respect to material existence. It is, Gilson says, a "spiritual" existence, but we remain "impotent to conceive the spiritual other than as the material with zero dimensions. One cannot represent to oneself that of which one speaks. Nevertheless, without an intelligible reality of this sort words would not have meaning; one could not speak." The key word is *intelligible*: We know that we know this reality called *meaning*, as represented to others through *words*, although we cannot represent that thing, known in material aspects, though the long history of "symbolism" shows our continuing attempt to do so. Thus it is that we stand in helpless awe and wonder in response to Dante's multifoliate rose.

We are arrested by what we know, then. Gilson says to this point that "the meaning of the word escapes servitude to space, for it is an act of thought, and thought exists, but in a literal sense *it has no place*." And in the light of this realization out of experience, it is "inevitable that language should lead us back once more to the threshold of the immaterial and of the meta-physical. Everything leads to it: biology as soon as it admits that there are living forms; noetics and epistemology as soon as they reflect upon the conditions required . . . in order that science might be possible; linguistics itself as soon as one accepts language in its relations with the understanding. . . ." It is in our return to this threshold that we become most aware of the necessity of precision in the saying, or attempting to say, true things about the truth of things. For it is only through *saying true things* that community may be established and maintained, wherever two or three are gathered together under the auspices of language.

It is at this point worth our saying: The necessity of precision in our saying is the ground common to intellects characterized as philosophers, whatever vision of the truth of things the particular intellect within that community may advance. This is the community of the *spoudaioi*, the mature intellects. But those intellects whose calling is to a service in the precision of articulation of the realities of intellection very easily are made to appear isolated from a concern for the common good by the requisite discipline of their calling. One effect upon the common mind from this perceived isolation of the philosopher is the easy cliché that leaves the philosopher pinned and wriggling on the wall, pierced by cliché. Thus that popular conception of the Medieval philosopher as one concerned to argue over the absurdity of how many angels might stand on the head of a pin. What is at issue in such argument, ultimately, is the relation of the material reality to immaterial reality, and whenever that "angel controversy" is unresolved, it surfaces again, as in the modern concern for *meaning* in relation to the *word*.

It is in part his recognition of this burden upon the philosopher in his obligation to the precision of words, an obligation that tends to make him appear at odds with community, that leads Plato at last to locate his highest philosopher in the hierarchy of soul (in the *Phaedrus*) beyond the usual anchor of souls in community. As Gilson says, "common sense is, in the order of the intelligible, philosophy in the unworked state," but the distance between the unworked foundation and the worked structure upon it appears greater than it is and too easily serves to estrange the philosopher from community, as Socrates witnesses most dramatically in 399 B.C. What concerns us in our present meditations upon man's common nature as maker is the common ground to that making that exists for common sense and for formal philosophical structuring of common sense, to be recovered in language itself as binding community in the common good of reality. A part of the difficulty to this task is perhaps the rather deliberate cultivation of the estrangement among "higher" intellects themselves, whereby false philosophy flourishes in this latter day. The inclinations to estrangement are nevertheless not only real but also ancient. They persist in the long history of community, so Plato's concern may be of some help to us to show that the problem is not peculiarly our own at the close of the twentieth century.

In the *Phaedrus*, then, we find Plato distinguishing the *philosophos* and the *philokalos* the lover of knowing and the lover of beauty. And he would establish them as proconsuls to the order of souls in community. If they are "above" other souls in the hierarchy as he suggests, they are not so much at an apex of the pyramid of social and political community as at a tangent to both the apex and the foundation of that structure, and related to its whole. This lover of beauty and this lover of wisdom serve beauty and wisdom first of all, through a purity of intellect purged and made pure by the precisions of intellection. Thus their service to the *polis* – or perhaps *his* service, since the terms as Plato uses them separately seem intended to apply as aspects of a single intellect – is ancillary, not direct. Their ultimate concern, though in the name of community, is for the truth of things, in which truth lies the beauty of existence itself. The possession of truth through its beauty (as a limit upon finite intellect's possible relation to simple truth) is the good of the intellect. In possessing that good, the lover of the "beautiful truth" serves community, though in appearance it is an indirect service, since the love of the truth of things is primary.[1]

1 Let us remember once more the point of significant difference between Plato and St. Thomas in relation to *good* and *being*. Gilson, in *The Spirit of Mediaeval Philosophy*, observes that Plato is so resolute in his pursuit of the *good* as ultimate that he overlooks the significance of *being*. Insofar as he is concerned with *being*, it is relative to and subordinate to *good*. St. Thomas, anchored in Being Itself as ultimate, takes *good* as an aspect of that *being*. Thus God is perfectly *good* because he perfectly *is*, and not the other way round. Plato's is a philosophy striving to the transcendent, but in that striving it loses the crucial import of being, with the result that the mutability of moving things, the decay in nature so to speak, obscures the vision of perfect being as ultimate. In understanding being at best as dependent in good, and at worst as a hindrance to the good, Plato proves precursor to a modernist error that perversely uses his position. Act is good, in this error, and being dependent upon act. Since act is reserved to finite intellect (though without

And so we underline a point: The "philosopher" as citizen, even as with the "poet" as citizen, is by appearance seemingly removed from the minutiae of actions necessary to the common good, seemingly removed from the "nitty-gritty" of life, though in the event neither the poet nor the philosopher is actually so removed. That he is not removed is registered over the course of Western intellectual history in the perennial concern for the poet as "vatic" poet and for the king as "philosopher" king. Such is the popular expectation of poet or king. There is no way that in the end we may avoid, whatever our calling, the nitty-gritty dimensions of the order of nature, most pressingly evident in the hierarchy of human nature, evident as hierarchy *in each person.* And so the realities of the orders of being always present circumstances that may be used to denigrate the variety of gifts of being within creation. Doctrinaire egalitarianism in our age attempts to deny order as established through particular acts of being whereby particular things exist, *each in its own nature* (and with a structure of its own nature of a relative complexity, as well). What is perverse in this denial is a false suggestion about the moral consequences to this undeniable order, whereby the exceptionally gifted either suppose themselves or are supposed by others as *morally* exceptional by the virtue of discrete, exceptional gift. But if we set aside as morally determinate of a being, that being's undeniable aspect as discretely differing in particular persons and see this *discriminately* as the reality of our gifts of being, we may somewhat recover intellect to perceptions of the orders of being without distorting the moral implication. For specific existence of specific creatures is not an egalitarian gift in respect to their particularities as discrete beings. The complex nature of existence requires as a consequence of existing *at all* differences of particularity. And differentiation is the principle of hierarchy in orders of existence. Thus we may know, and accept as separate from moral judgment, that just as some animals are superior in animal gifts to others *in certain respects*, so too are some intellects different from other intellects. It is in recognizing, by intellectual action, this distinction that the orders of community may be recovered to a harmony of love. Even the philosopher and poet may at last be recovered to community and thus to service in the common good. And inso-

---

the searching questions implicit in the acceptance of finite intellect in act) the transcendent is relocated to the locus of finite intellect as the only "transcendent." This is the Modernist perversion of Platonism which I have on occasion termed inverted Platonism.

far as community is thus recovered, the conditions to the moral worth of discrete souls will be supported by community itself, beyond envy and pride.

If the philosopher is concerned with the truth of things for the sake of the good of his own intellect, it does not follow therefore that he is not concerned, though properly at a secondary level of concern, for the good of the community. It is in his balance, his proportionate intellectual concern for ultimate and mediate ends, that he practices his gifts. To speak of a secondary concern is not thereby to denigrate that concern, for it is not an accidental concern. But to find the proportion – that is the challenge to intellect. It must be emphasized, however, that it is a challenge common and not peculiar to the philosopher. That is the recognition implicit in the prayer of our general epigraph, "teach us to care and not to care," as we have already suggested. And so for the philosopher, as for any intellect intent on its proper end, there continues the necessity of precision in attempts to maintain a common ground of intellectual acts in pursuit of that viable community, which community exists wherever two or three are gathered together in the name of the truth in reality and under the auspices of words. Those intellectual acts are independent of the accidents of time and place, though not indifferent to those accidents.

Now this is to say that intellect's primary movement is toward knowing and understanding "how the truth of things stands." And we are not talking here only of the philosopher, but of every person. In relation to its immaterial existence, though affected by the accidents of time and place, intellect's essential nature is not determined by those accidents, except as it may willingly yield its nature to accidents and thus refuse its own given nature. It is this special nature of intellectual being which distinguishes the *person* in the orders of creation. Anchored in this specialty as *person*, there follows a common availability in intellectual actions of a mutual support in the common good of the intellectual creature man as community of persons. That is the support of community when the term *community* is rightly taken, aspects of which we designate as social or political orders in which and through which the specific person is supported as person. The support is not of the individual member in its mere relation to such an order, but of him as person in pursuit of the perfection of discrete gifts that are implicitly created, recognized when we say of the person that he is spiritual creature. Within the scheme of things, within creation's orders, there is an economy to spirit in its circumstantial aspect which must be served by community as established in the concept of the common good. Thus the commerce of intellectual action must be founded on acceptable principles of intellection that are healthful to the community of intellect in the world. But its foundation and ultimate cause as community must be understood in relation to ultimate and not mediate ends of community, and that means the ultimate concern is the good of the discrete person.

That is the point Jacques Maritain is making, in his *The Person and the Common Good*: "As an individual, each of us is a fragment of a species, a part of the universe, a unique point in the immense web of cosmic, ethical, historical forces and influences – and bound by their laws. . . . Nonetheless, each of us is also a person and, as such, is not controlled by the stars. Our whole being subsists in virtue of the spiritual soul." In that distinction of *individual* and *person* lies further explanation of our point concerning the philosopher as primarily concerned for the good of his own intellect and only secondarily concerned for the good of community. Hence Maritain adds,

> It is the human *person* who enters society; as an individual, it enters society as a part whose proper good is inferior to the good of the whole [which is constituted of persons.] . . . [B]ecause of the highest requirements of personality as such, the human person, as a spiritual totality referred to the transcendent whole, surpasses and is superior to all temporal societies. . . . With respect to the eternal destiny of the soul, society exists for each person and is subordinate to it.

And that, too, is a point dramatized by Socrates' death at Athens. It is a delicate point, learned and relearned in the course of human "history." Maritain puts that point succinctly: "Man finds himself by subordinating himself to the group, and the group attains its goal only by serving man and by realizing that man [as discrete *person*] has secrets which escape the group and a vocation which the group does not encompass." As group and as person, then, we must learn to care and not to care.

Such is the healthful ground to the commerce of community through intellectual action, the foundation to intellectual principles healthful to the community of intellect in the world and to the person in community. The establishment of caring and not caring as ordinate to our gifts of being as *person* is a considerable office of responsibility, not restricted to the philosopher. For by our very existence, each is a person – each is an intellectual, spiritual creature. In consideration of this office of responsibility to the self as peculiar to each of us, we learn that our concern is not primarily to make an "originality" of articulation of truth, a making whose ultimate end we suppose to be the uniqueness of the thing made – aphorism or poem, picture or garden. What is required is the mutual caring through shared visions of truth, signified by the virtue of charity.

That commits us in considerable degree to the traditions of intellectual action. For it is in those shared actions that we discover at last that community is not a concept limited to this present point of history but to the gathering of persons within intellectual actions independent of temporal or spatial limitations upon community. It is thus that we discover ourselves gathered with Socrates or Dante no less than with our immediate neighbor, through the mystery of language – of sign – in which a reality unyielding to any science of time or place, any material dimension of reality, is discovered to be actual by intellect itself. The concern for "originality" as an end *to* and *in* the thing we make – the poem as well-wrought, the argument as effectively put – is a concern for the action as an end and not as toward an end transcendent of all action in its finite limits. It is to take a lesser good as the greater good. It is here that the illusion of immortality through art will prove embittering, for instance, out of that disorder of the good. To have originality as an end is like having the eye as an end, rather than having seeing. *Seeing* is an action in the realm of the metaphysical as opposed to the physical.

Putting aside originality as an end of intellectual action, we may then depend less fretfully upon authority as tested through the accidents of time and place and not found wanting, though authority may be more generally acceptable at some points of time and place than at others, by specific minds in any time or place. Such is the prelude to an ordinate concern for necessary terms.

For we must rest a confidence of some degree out of an affection of our own intellect for the *philosophos* and the *philokalos*. Because removed by the accidents of time and place, we are not required to abandon their present witness to us of the truth of things, whether the witness of Plato or Aristotle; or of St. Augustine or St. Thomas; or of Dante or Eliot. Theirs is a continuing practice of responsibility to precision in seeing the truth of things. Insofar as that precision helps our own blurred seeing, we must make them welcomed to our company in this present. But in doing so, we must not make a dangerous mistake. Precision is welcomed, not for its own sake, but for the sake of our seeing. Precision in articulation is not the end we must seek, any more than happiness or originality is an end to be sought. Such are effects of intellect's pursuit of truth, not the object of that pursuit. That is why St. Thomas's words of caution need often recalling, in our concern for the validity of the present witness to truth by past intellects. Our concern for the importance of "tradition" to present circumstantial confusions of intellect must be governed by the proper end: "The purpose of the study of philosophy," St. Thomas says, "is not to learn what others have thought, but to learn how the truth of things stands."

IX

If we have such difficulty in establishing the meaning of the word *word* in our thought, how much more difficult the meaning of *truth*. We are concerned, not with *a* meaning, but *the* meaning: We are discontent with anything less, though in the agony of failure to possess that meaning we may turn from the object bearing the good of truth to intellect. To know the truth is to be made free, but we grasp purported "truths" only to have them collapse as mere "thought" turned into ashes by the very grasping. We become desperate. It is with this desperation that the fictional character Haze Motes, in Flannery O'Connor's *Wise Blood*, declares that "the only truth is that there is no truth." His denial must be made positive, as a *something* to believe in, even when there is (so far as his intellect can convince itself) nothing to believe in. Haze Motes is, as a figuring of the Modernist spirit, somewhat exceptional, in that he openly displays the agony of spiritual displacement, the condition of spirit in which the truth is not simply relative, but nonexistent, so in his desperation he will insist that Jesus is "a trick on niggers."

It is G. K. Chesterton who characterizes the more usual display of our spiritual displacement by Modernism. Chesterton says that "those who have lost their faith in God do not believe in nothing, they believe in anything." But to believe in anything and everything, indiscriminately, is in effect to believe in nothing, though that pretense is often with the façade of a residual Christian virtue, tolerance. To believe in everything indiscriminately is to conduct ourself with a general indifference to all things, as if there were no discrete truth suited to the nature of discrete things in themselves. Among the conveniences to the denial is a foregoing of intellectual labor, the substitute for which labor is an easy assumption of a spiritual largess toward the *all* that is indistinguishable from consent to nothing. One "feels" good about nothing, in an antithetic imaging of ourselves as God brooding over chaos. Thus the illusion of being freed by our feeling from the responsibility implicit in the nature called personhood. That responsibility, an openness to the truth of things in themselves, requires respect for discrete being by our acts of intellectual discrimination of one thing from another.

What then of this illusive truth to be found in things? And in its pursuit, what comfort may be given to one intellect by other intellects? St. Thomas in his reminder of the central concern for truth as regardless of what men have said does not mean that we may ignore "what others have thought" about truth, only that such a knowledge is at best a beginning toward truth. To pass the comprehensive examination for the doctorate in philosophy does not make one a philosopher. It only provides a grammar supportive of the ensuing journey through words to truth. And it is only truly supportive when that grammar *intends* intellect to the truth. As for the meaning of *truth*, St. Thomas attempts an understanding of that meaning through a consort of intellects summoned to his support.

A principal one is St. Augustine, a venerable, though not an infallible, presence to Thomas's thought. Thomas summons St. Augustine's words as acceptable: "Truth is that whereby is made manifest that which is." And again, "Truth is a supreme likeness, without any unlikeness, to its source." Thus a sort of colloquy with St. Augustine in the present moment of articulation by St. Thomas, who adds to St. Augustine's meaning of *truth*, "Truth is the equation of thought and thing." *Equation* suggests a con-forming, in which truth is the enactment of intellectual being through intellect's consent to the encountered thing. The truth that is thereby the good of the intellect is the necessary mediation to intellect of immaterial existence of disparate things. In this event, this conforming of intellect and the object, the essential nature of the two things exist in an accord. It is an accord in the elemental ground to immaterial existence, *being itself*, whose actualization of accord is through essences related out of being, an act of grace.

Such is the *simple complexity* (a necessary paradox in terms) of truth that much must be said of it. Truth's nature and intellect's possession of that nature are the most central desire to intellect. The extensive history of mankind clearly shows this in the record of mind, in our words. Beside this concern for truth, our sexual drive, our worldly materialisms – all the usual themes of concern out of the restricted material limits to human existence – become as nothing. To be or not to be. But what is it to be – what is the truth signified by *being*? Hamlet, Ophelia are not soap-opera figures, precisely because the roiling concern for truth consumes their moment's blossoming as "romantic" presences. And so intellect presses on. In the very midst of a bacchanalia at the King's Court, we are told, St. Thomas slams his ham of a fist against the table and shouts a conclusion to his meditative argument: "[T]hus I refute the Manichaean." Or, in quieter circumstances of our reading a book, in a certain presence of Aristotle and St. Augustine and a gathering of the *spoudaioi* whose concern in common is not what they have said or might say or what others might say, though that is a necessary deportment of intellect to its desired end. Rather we join them in desiring what the truth of things is, quietly and meditatively.

And so St. Thomas says that the "true resides in things and in the intellect," but resides in different ways. The recognition of this distinction is necessary if intellect is to order itself to being. To know a thing, to know the truth of a thing, is not to *be* a thing, though the sentiment of openness to things may so easily become sentimentalized by feeling as to tempt false words whose false meaning appears to assert an identity of subject and object. The modern abuse of the term *empathy* is heavy with this distortion. Instead, intellect open to the truth of things is *fed* by the truth of things. That truth is an *aspect* of how and ultimately why *things stand.* Things stand separate from identity of intellect and thing in the melding which "truth" effects.

We are speaking here against a species of confusion available to intellect. It is a confusion whereby intellect engages in a pseudo-mysticism. It is the conditions of intellect's relation to things out of which so easily rise cults, when not clearly understood. We know such recent cults, centered in crystals or in single syllables uttered repetitively toward an obliteration of thought, are instances from the popular press. Thomas argues against this inclination to a "oneness" which attempts the obliteration of all identity – the Cheshire cat species of philosophy or religion. For Thomas there is "the true that is in the intellect" which "is convertible with being," but "the true which is in things is *substantially* convertible with being." (My italics.)

The issue here to be clarified is in respect to epistemology, regarding which the distinction between *substantially convertible* and *convertible* is crucial to understanding the intellect's actions. In pursuit of this delicate distinction, Thomas adds that "truth is primarily in the intellect, while being is primarily in things. This is so because truth and being differ in idea." *Idea* as used here is for Thomas an actual being, though immaterial, whose source as cause is God but whose locus of manifestation is the finite intellect. What seems at issue is the actuality of truth itself as a "presence" in intellect. It is that "x" we heard Gilson discussing earlier: "[T]his x, which has not yet been spoken" must be "in some fashion present to my thought, for otherwise I could not try to say it." It is "truth" that one thinks "about," truth metaphorically the seed nurturing thought whose proximate effect is the good of the intellect. Truth as a presence *in* intellect, a presence deeply at the heart of thought, is to be distinguished from *phantasm* or *image* or *word* and, at last, also from the *meaning* the word carries as well. It is an actuality, and not a sign, which is why the term *presence* seems necessary to the attempt to articulate that actuality.

This would appear almost to suggest that truth is palpable to intellect within itself, as it seems similarly to stand in the act of the thing that is: that *stands* – thus spoken of as *substantially convertible*. And if we recall the recent attempt at this reality, say by John Locke or David Hartley, we will observe how easily a figurative articulation anchored as metaphorical term in material reality decays toward literalness, as in speaking of the mind as a *tabula rasa*. But the presence of truth in intellect as *actual* or as *palpable* are quite distinct in meaning, though the mystery of images to thought confuses the distinction. Certainly for a time it confused many of the Romantic poets, Wordsworth and Coleridge, for instance. But reflection suggests that we *know* the presence of this x – this truth – as a reality in mind in a way separate from knowing a presence of images in the mind. Indeed, we find ourselves employing images in the attempt to capture that impalpable presence, a projection of which images is in our words. Our creative action of intellect – as the poet will be quick to recognize perhaps – is to make the truth in intellect *substantially convertible* by attempting an incarnational action of language. It is through the material dimension of existence that we would convey truth, toward its eventual presence in another intellect also within an immaterial world of thought, that other intellect. We intend to convey it unscathed by the necessity of a *body* to our words. For our difficulty is that words must be transmitted *through* material limitations upon finite intellect. We must *say* words or inscribe signs of words. And thus we put our words at risk in the circumscribing materialities to our finite intellects. This is the condition to our intellect which makes us "a little lower" than the angels.

Such, then, is our initial encounter with the abiding intellectual concern for *truth*, and with the difficulties to that concern. We begin now a pursuit of the intellect's knowing of truth through its actions, actions decisive to the life of person. Of those actions, recognized in consequence of the truth received into intellect when it is open to reality, we move on to other of the terms which we introduced. The necessity of *naming* is implicit from what we have said, though naming risks an arrest of perception of the going-on-ness of the singular creature about which we attempt to say the salient *word*, to name the beingness of the thing standing to our intellectual action and in some mysterious way thereby standing *in* intellect itself as that unnamable "x" in thought itself. Though we must say that thing in its beingness is not at actual risk from our intellect's encounter with it, since its going-on-ness is not an effect of that encounter, the danger of arrest to our own intellectual action itself is present to the attempt. It is the danger, through a *mis-taking* of this encounter, which led Brice Parain to complain that to think is not to be but to wish to be. That is the dark Cartesian end for Parain, who complains, "I think, therefore I am not."

The desperation of witnessing by words the actuality of encounter with being, such as we discover in Parain, speaks the always proximate danger of an arrest of the perception whereby truth comes to reside in intellect. We know intuitively that the actuality to which we struggle to give a name is not essentially affected by the possible arrest of our intellectual act itself, through which arrest we fear the loss of the self. The desperation of words may nevertheless occasion an attempt at a self-willed life, whose cause is supposed the will freed of grace. For there is a fear of losing self-awareness in visionary action, a fear transformed by pride, whereby we would *be*, but by our own action. In the sequence of effect out of pride, not actual to things but accepted as if actual by intellect, the being of things – things as they stand – is taken as the effect of intellect's act. Thus that which is not is taken as actual by intellect. It supposes itself possessed of a truth, when it is rather possessed by the false. This is the gnostic danger to intellect, whose actual effect proves at last only the separation of the soul from the truth of things and the consequent diminution of that soul itself. The recognition of this effect of willful pride we have made popular under such terms as *alienation* and *angst* in our day, as if that were a peculiar condition to our existence in the modern world.

The creature, the thing that stands to intellect as distinct from the action of our encounter of the thing by intellect, continues in its own habit of being – the habit intrinsic to its nature through its going-on-ness. It is sustained in a contingency of its actuality to its potentiality so that its essence is not radically affected by our intellectual action toward it. Even when aggressions out of intellect intrude upon the creature in material ways, so that in ways measurable to physics that creature is modified, we have not thereby transmuted that creature's essence, the given nature of its own thingness. For there continues as its complex of essence the relation of its actuality and its potentiality, beyond the accidents of our modifications imposed upon it. Though mutated, as we would put it in our modernist intents upon being, there continues its beingness, for which intrusive intellect may make no claim itself as the "originator," the God of a new being. Nevertheless, at this moment of our scientific advance upon material existence by biotechnology, there grows the supposition in some eager wills that essence may be transmogrified by the will's intent focused upon the actualities of a creature. The supposition intoxicates intellect with assumptions of its own infinitudes. But those suppositions are out of a confusion of the modes of thought termed *science* and *philosophy*, the difference between which is knowledge held and knowledge understood. The confusion has been a hundred-year burden, sometimes characterized pejoratively as "scientism." The attempt of "scientism" is a species of alchemy, pursued with religious fervor. (To recover somewhat from that latest seduction to alchemy, one might begin with the work of thought about science and its relation to religion as advanced by Stanley Jaki in a number of works, beginning with *The Road of Science and the Ways to God*.)

A suitable attempt at the rational exploration of our intuitive perception of being, the act of intellect's first knowing the truth of a thing, requires of the rational intellect the proper habits of its own being, habits by means of which intellect participates in but is not the first cause of its own being. It is a participation, a habit, of being in a different sense from what might be said of the stone's or the tree's participation in its specific habit of being. In this complex field of intellectual being, one must account for a variety of aspects of that unique being, intellect, aspects experienced by intellect before its attempt to rationalize itself. The range is from the region of its immaterial realities down to its material realities. Given our experiences of this range of encounter we come to name this unique creature as characteristically intellectual. And from that accounting we pursue our understanding of the intellect's complex nature, toward the possibility of understanding the peculiar, discrete existing thing as a *person*.

The most troublesome burden upon intellect is the necessity of moving toward this understanding of itself as the proximate agent to its knowing action, though agent and not First Cause of action. That is a necessity not imperative to any other creature in creation, this action of the self knowing itself intentionally. It is not at once a necessity freely acceptable to some selves, or to all selves at some points of journeying. We notice, in John Donne's protest in one of his Holy Sonnets, an objection to this unwanted necessity. The speaker arraigns God as unjust: "Why should intent or reason, born in me,/ Make sins, else equal [with all creatures], in me more heinous?" In the history of intellectual decline from responsibility of intellect to an accommodation of its nature as distinct, and known to be distinct, we come in these latter days to a whimper that had been in Donne a shout of protest. We come to Prufrock's weak "I should have been a pair of ragged claws/ Scuttling across the floors of silent seas."

What we here affirm, against these dramatizations of anger and defeat, as we have against Parain's indictment of action through language as doomed to fail in the attempt, is that an accounting *for* our own intellectual acts *by* our own intellectual acts – with the recognition that such accounting is never comprehensive – is the proper habit of intellect whereby it participates in sustaining the being which is proper to its own nature as that intellectual creature, man. Thus we participate through intention in the making of ourselves as the person, that being which is possible within our gifts of being. The one prohibition: a false supposition of ourself as the principal cause of our being. It is in the balance founded in this ordinate recognition of the "self" that we exercise responsibility for our gifts. And we recognize a truth already present in intellect thereby: The action of intellect is the habit necessary to the gift of our particular nature. That is, in the constancy of intellectual action, this particular intellectual creature by the action comes more and more into its fullness as an existence.

The point we wish to emphasize, since it is of concern to our argument that a "making" is the proper habit of our being, is that by intellectual acts of knowing and understanding the fullness of the being of this active agent of making, this person, we effect our being under the auspices of grace. There is, in this respect, as consequent to intellectual action or inaction, either a certain *making* or *unmaking* of the self, regardless of the accidental good or bad external effects of that making or unmaking. Whether the made thing, the poem or argument or garden, is good, that is a separate question. But antecedent to such a question is a reality: We *are*, through grace. We become more fully through our participation in being through action, and the action proper to *person* is *intellectual action*. It is in this sense that we contend that making is the proper habit of our being, by which we mean the making of a thing through the practical intellect, the poem or garden or house. But as an overplus of that making is the realization of the potential nature of the active agent himself. Or we should better say, as an *underplus*, for the realization of the potency of person underlies and is more important than anything else the person can make.

Should we require scripture to the argument, we might say that here we speak of that proper love of the self required if love is to be properly oriented to existences other than the self. It is a self-love precedent to that movement of intellect outward from the self, though we do not mean thereby any sequential ordering, whereby one *first* loves oneself properly and *then* some other thing. The becoming of the self as a consequence of the action of love turned toward being moves the fulfillment of the soul. The commandment is put that one loves one's neighbor as oneself, a commandment suggestive of coincidental movements of the soul by and through love. For we recognize that an inevitable consequence of the proper love of one's neighbor is the ordinate love of oneself. Thus intellectual action under the auspices of ordinate will is the exercise of the proper stewardship of things in themselves, one of which things in this responsibility of our stewardship is our self. The primary effect of intellectual actions of making, of an active participation in the complexity of creation out of being, is the coming to be or the fall from being of the intellectual creature so acting. Whether that "making" creature fall out of its makings or rise through them is dependent upon right will.

X

Having made such a claim about intellectual action as a cause of our coming to be out of potential being, we need to clarify a point. For our general argument is that making is the proper habit of intellectual being, and we must make clear our own sense of *making* in this context. As we have applied it to the agent's *making himself,* we must recall that St. Thomas makes a distinction between *making* and *doing*, which distinction we here appropriate for comment. We turn to the *Summa* I-II, Q. 57, Art. 3. There he distinguishes in setting prudence apart from art. Art, he says, with recourse to Aristotle, "is the *right reason of things to be made*, whereas prudence is the *right reason of things to be done*. Now *making* and *doing* differ . . . in that *making* is an action passing into external matter . . . whereas *doing* is an action abiding in the agent, *e. g., to see, to will.*"

Our own argument, at first sight in an apparent conflict with Thomas, holds that, since *doing* constitutes an act which *makes* an actual of a potential in the external world, an analogous *making* of the actual of his own potential occurs in the agent. It is a *making* in an order differing from that making with external effect, but a making nevertheless, since by an act of will something is now actual which was before only potential. The making of art, for instance, has as its end a thing made whose being is confined to the limits of time and place in various restrictions of the made thing's own being. But the *making* of the intellectual creature that is consequent to its own *doing* is a making of a thing beyond the restrictions of time and place. Indeed, intellect recognizes that its *doing* involves a making of the self. In that recognition, and when the will is not a right will, there rises the danger of intellect's disorientation of its being, both actual and potential. It risks dislocating its *being* as *maker* from its proper end. In that disorientation its primary concern as maker may turn inward to a making of the self as the proximate (as opposed to ultimate) object of its actions as maker. Such is that destruction of the self which is an effect of that sin we call pride. Thus when the self becomes the primary object, the effect of this turning is a closing by intellectual action upon the world being made, the world of the self as possessive of itself – as the cause of its own self making. It is a turning from *being*, to which our proper act must be an openness. This is the "shadow of turning" in intellect which scripture reminds us is absent from God's open love of the being He "makes" by virtue of that supreme reality: *that he is*.

The point at issue here will prove crucial later as we come to deal once more with the intellectual creature's actions for the common good in relation to its own proper end which is transcendent of the common good. And it is on this point that we shall need to clarify our use of the terms *practical intellect* and *speculative intellect*. We do so now, with a reminder: Just as one endangers his gift of happiness by turning to happiness as an object, so does he endanger his own coming to be by turning to that effect as a primary object of intention. *Caritas*, the open love toward being, may thereby turn into pride, the inversion of *caritas*. That is the turning we speak of as the sin of pride, occasioned in some degree at the slightest turning of intellect away from Being Itself. As for this making of the self implicit in the making of some thing, let us turn to a helpful illustration.

We observe the gymnast or ballet dancer in a moment of perfection, in which the sensitive powers and intellectual powers of a single soul are one, simple and indivisible. We know at once the particular action of being of a person, all of whose members and faculties are ordinately accommodated to each other, but accommodated by an intention beyond mere accommodation, in one flowing action. And though we are quite aware, out of our cumulative habits of knowing, that in this oneness there is nevertheless a considerable diversity when we consider the simple action, we are at the moment ourselves arrested. We are held because of that very knowledge itself, but we are held *beyond* knowledge as well, in an act of consent to the marvel of singleness in so complex a creature. And in our falling away from that moment of recognition, we cry with Yeats, not with words but by our breath caught and held in our own singleness through awe with the dancer:

> O body swayed to music, O brightening glance,
> How can we know the dancer from the dance?

Ours is a moment in which we know we have experienced the reality of a perfection, in which the material and immaterial natures of this creature are reconciled, though only for the moment. The intrusive question comes, dissolving our suspense in awe, and there follows question upon question out of our experience. But the questions rise from a knowledge already in us, which we hold from the experience, though it is not a knowledge available to intellect simply by its power to know or its desire to know. There has occurred a moment of grace to us, through an encounter beyond any determination to an encounter that is possible to intellect as intentional under its lone auspices. It is not an encounter exclusive of such determination, but beyond the power of determination, even as the dancer or gymnast might testify to having acted *beyond* the limits of the self: "I outdid myself!" For, in a sense, we have sought encounter of event in time which gives some earnest of perfection, somc justification of hope that transformation may be possible, wherein the material and immaterial dimensions of our discrete natures may be reconciled. And for a moment we have found what we sought. But we conclude that we have been "graced" beyond our own intention. (What a falling away, then, when the judges flash their scorecards from 1 to 10!)

And so we carry the moment with us in memory, and because we do, we visit and revisit it. What we come to accept about that event is, first, that we now know something quite beyond the powers of our rational accommodation of that knowledge. We have encountered a simplicity of being which we can only describe as a perfection of being. It is a knowledge raised in us – a knowledge we possess – witnessed by our weak words. That knowledge is more likely to be best raised through words in the keep of the poet than of the philosopher. (But also better by the philosopher than by the judges of the event.) That is why we turned here to Yeats's famous lines. The poet's response is closer to the moment itself, in that the poet's is a celebration of the climate of awe engulfing our knowing in the moment of the event. Even so, there is already the falling away, and as we fall from *awe*, the climate to the knowing becomes that of *wonder*. It is in this climate of wonder that the philosopher must succeed the poet.

In putting it this way, in putting Yeats as poet, St. Thomas as philosopher, we are moving by analogy. For what we are suggesting is that, in each person there is that experience we tend to associate with the poet on the one hand and with the philosopher on the other. We are saying, in effect, that Plato's concern in elevating the *philosophos* and the *philokalos* in the order of souls constituting community – the lover of knowing and the lover of beauty – is paradigmatic of any *person* taken separately from or rather taken beyond community. We are in such high moment not simply of the order of the *polis* as projected by that poet-philosopher, Plato. The poet in us, so to speak, may yield to the philosopher in us, a possibility inherent in our intellectual nature. But we do so because knowing a moment beyond the philosopher's reach. It is a possibility of our nature answering a necessity of our nature, already provided by God's providence. We move from awe to the region of wonder. We enact it necessarily because we are falling always from timeless moments of perfection as we may encounter them from time to time, and so forced to the level of reflection.

What this means is that Yeats's concluding lines from "Among School Children," a poem whose concern is very much with the mystery of knowledge in relation to desire, is the poet's concluding surrender to the philosopher. "How can we know the dancer from the dance?" That is at once two kinds of question: first, a rhetorical one, implying that we *cannot* know that distinction in the event encountered, for there is that simplicity of perfection in the event preventing distinctions at the immediate level of visionary encounter. But second, given the fallen nature of intellect through its finitudes, the rhetorical question turns insistently into an empirical question, as if to know rationally the answer were somehow to regain the level of a rhetorical transport to the threshold of the experience in its immediacy. As if through *wonder* one might regain *awe*, and in that progress even perhaps pass on beyond our awareness of the self as held by either awe or wonder into a timeless moment. That is the moment, we may realize, that William Butler Yeats pursued always through his art.

I am suggesting that through this example of Yeats's dancer in whom we may experience a moment of perfection, and the explication of the consequences to us of that experience, we have a limited paradigm of the reality of our continuing existence as intellectual creature. As finite, we move from moment to moment, through *encounters* with reality as possible to finite intellect according to the potential which is resident in its given nature. We do not mean, certainly, that such a paradigm is precise in its formal nature, as if we have drawn a pattern unvarying to each event which we might pursue as the builder does his blueprint. Always, the gifts of specific personhood affect the appropriateness of paradigm. Yeats as poet or St. Thomas as philosopher are gifted beyond myself as poet or philosopher. And yet there are affinities in our natures and in our desires suggesting kinships more fundamental than we would allow were we to define poet or philosopher as exceptional to human nature, or were we to deny fundamental kinship on our distance by degree from such gifted presences to us as Yeats or St. Thomas. Yeats recognizes as much, in the poem we cite, turning in the moment of a falling from his visionary recovery of his own past moment to the comfort of the philosopher. And to whom else but to Plato, Aristotle, Pythagoras? His old beloved (Maude Gonne), as he looks at the school child before him, is suddenly present, in an illusion of his having somehow summoned the past into a present, while it is recognized as still a past. (For this "sixty-year-old public man," this inspector of Irish schools, knows Maude Gonne to have aged as well.) Who but philosopher can riddle for us such presences of the past?

As for the inadequacy of our paradigm to suit every encounter, we recall as well that by paradigm we find ourselves committed to the sequential, a necessity to our nature as discursive intellect. But one may not say that awe is succeeded by wonder as the sequential necessity to intellectual nature, that the poet necessarily precedes the philosopher. (One nevertheless remembers Wordsworth arguing that the poet's is the first and last of knowledge, that the poet precedes the man of science and follows after him.) The rational exploration of aspects of our encounter, as we have undertaken it, is however necessarily analytic; we are committed in some degree to the artificiality of sequentiality, since our words are themselves so handicapped, in evidence of intellect's handicap of discursiveness (oh, to be angelic intellect!). That procedure even simplifies St. Thomas as *person* when we concentrate on him as philosopher. In actuality, we might suspect that he is rather more a mystical poet than sometimes recognized. But his words, too, are governed by the precision of his wonder to such a degree as to obscure the climate of awe in him.

In analytic, discursive explication, we have been trying to remake event – recover encounter in a moment remembered by intellect as an experience of a truth in intellect's true nature. We have been trying to make acceptably real that moment as a perfection of being possible through intellectual action. In that action a diversity of powers in *person* become raised beyond self-conscious intentionality. The sensitive powers, diverse in themselves, the intellectual powers, equally diverse – the dimensions of being in relation to material and immaterial reality of personhood – all these and more we would transform in a present moment of simple being. But it is a moment we cannot sustain, whatever word we speak in that attempt, whether as poet or philosopher. And what we are left with, in the event remembered, is a sense of loss, which stirs desire anew. Desire so stirred in turn raises the problem of temporal intrusions upon that desire for a simple existence maintained by desire itself. The old haunting presence of Eden Lost stirs the philosopher to action beyond the futile attempt by the poet (a Keats or a Yeats) to stay the moment.

As for the reality of that moment of experience, we do not require the ratings of several professional judges of gymnastic event, though we may know an added exhilaration if in some especially rare moment the event is officially rated a "ten" on the scale of official judgment. Nor do we need a Yeats or a St. Thomas, necessarily, though there is that added sense of a community of consent when, given our like experiences, the responses appear as like, witnessed by the exemplary deployment of meaning in their ordered words in tribute to experience. We burst into applause – literally or figuratively, as we say – in the shared acceptance of a rating of judgment at the level of perfection, 10. But we do so not simply to honor the agent receiving the judgment, nor simply to second the judges as judges. Within the response there is as well our honoring ourselves as a part of the action witnessed, an action in which we participate by our consent to possibility. And we observe, as a sort of "trickle-down" effect into the material dimension of our being, that we "feel" much better about our *very* selves through this participatory act of knowing a perfection in another being. As spectator, whether of dance or music or tragedy, we are enlarged in community.

After that moment on the stage or in the arena, the ballerina or gymnast departed and the lights turned down or up for our departure, after applause has raggedly died, we discover that we do not require the stuttering conversation in the lobby nor tomorrow's review of the event in the local paper nor the weekly critique of aesthetic event in the journal to convince us of the reality of that moment. We do not even require the studied reflection of a book on the art of such event to be persuaded of having known, for a moment, a perfection of being beyond rational justifications of that knowledge. We have known, in ourselves, our own body swayed to music, our own brightening glance, a perfection of oneness of the sensitive and intellectual powers through the openness of encounter with being. We possess a truth in our own soul, made manifest in the soul by that which is truly known for the moment. And what we know is the reality of *is*.

The reality of our own existence among existences. That actual moment remembered, and by the remembering, we seem somehow to hear an echo of Eden. It is echo that calls forth the philosopher to consider the significance of memory in relation to desire.

And we know as well that it is not possible to rest in recognitions of truth as possessed in intellect. We cannot, because of circumstances to intellect. Those moments of encounter of being lead us to anticipate such moments, and the anticipation becomes more immediate in relation to our own being. Most constant to us is the desire for a perfection of being in ourselves as intellectual creatures. But the desire, stilled fleetingly in the visionary moment in a realization of potentiality, is not sufficiently answered by that moment, for that moment is already past. We consider that our nature fallen allows us only the moment, however strongly we desire beatitude in the world: that is, however strongly we desire a continuous perfection of being to the instant of desire.

There follows, then, a very practical necessity, stirred by wonder. We must pursue that object which desire has known but fleetingly, and in that necessity rises the temptation of our turning, of our taking-amiss the desired end by confusing its causes as anchored in objects affected by material limitations of our being. We may, for instance, in that turning see ourselves as an object dissolving from high moments of encounter, in that illusion: the self entrapment of the self in "nature" or "history." It is thus that we may mistake the relation of memory to desire, as if desire could be only a backward wishful thinking occasioned by remembered moments of encounter as determined by time and place. Because now past and in some other place, we begin to be suspicious of desire itself. Desire for a moment of youth made eternal is the intellectual decay we term *nostalgia*. We know ourselves thereby entrapped, and the consequence of that knowing is a growing despair. That is the condition of that spiritual state which T. S. Eliot experiences, reflected in his poetry up to *The Waste Land*. And we note to our point that the *Waste Land* sets out explicitly from a necessity of solving the enigma of desire's relation to memory. It is to that enigma that the philosopher turns. Eliot as philosopher does so, no less than as poet, witnessed in his poetry from *The Waste Land* on, but increasingly evident in his criticism as well. For ourselves at this point of our concern, let us turn once more from the philosopher-poet Eliot, to the guidance of the philosopher St. Thomas.

Our rational nature, St. Thomas suggests, wishes to know about such an encounter as the one Yeats dramatizes not only *what is done* in the moment, but also *why that act was done*. Such is the necessary address by rational intellect of the circumstances of being in its remembered moment of perfection. Otherwise, we shall not recover to our will nor to intellect those habits proper to them in the soul's pursuit of that continuous perfection of being which St. Thomas calls beatitude. St. Thomas, quoting Gregory of Nyssa, affirms that "the two most important circumstances are *why an act is done* and *what is done*." The first, the *why*, raises questions of ends. The second, the *what*, raises questions of means. It is in these questions that we begin to concentrate upon intellect in its disparate powers, those powers we speak of as *speculative* and *practical*. As St. Thomas puts this point (*Summa* I-II, Q. III, A. 8): "The object of intellect is *what* a thing is, the essence of a thing." Though in a moment of perfect action by intellect we may experience essence intuitively, we are not able to rest content. For "[w]hen man knows an effect and knows that it has a cause [that is, knows intuitively], he still has a natural desire to know the cause as to *what it is*." That is the impetus of desire to formulate concept, whose outward effect is language. "That desire," St. Thomas adds, "is one of wonder, and is a cause of inquiry."

This is to say that finite intellect cannot be content to rest with its knowledge *that a thing is*, but compels itself by desire to inquire *why a thing is*. The first is a gift to intellect to its good, a good whose consequence is the action of, the life of, intellectual being. In this respect, we might suggest that the initial gift to intellect by grace is a pure "science," a knowledge of truth, out of which gift intellect becomes ravenous for an understanding. It is moved by a desire for a knowing fulfillment of its love of being. We should remark at least in passing that intellect's propensity for error easily leads at such a turning point to a confusion of "science" and "philosophy." That was the heart of Gilson's objection, we recall, to the "science" of linguistics, as it would be to the "science" of biology when the one refuses *meaning* and the other *life* as the mystery in which linguistics or biology are founded. *Meaning* and *life*, without which the special sciences could not exist, requires a metaphysical openness toward the founding mysteries.

If we propose a distinction between the speculative and practical intellect, or between the intuitive and rational intellect, we must emphasize at the outset that we are not dealing with separate powers of intellect, nor with separate intellects. We are addressing an existent simplicity as best we may – discursively – knowing beyond absolutely persuasive articulation that intellect is flexible in its simplicity and thereby suited in its potential actions to the disparateness of ends upon which intellect depends in its pursuit of the perfection of its simplicity. We recall St. Thomas's warning (*Summa* I, Q. 79, A. 11): "The speculative intellect by extension becomes practical. But one power is not changed into another. Therefore the speculative and practical intellects are not distinct powers." Insofar as I perfect my habit of intellectual being (we say) my intellect is a simple oneness in act, analogous to that simple oneness of act we celebrate in the ballerina. How can we tell the speculative from the practical? That such a question is either possible or pertinent suggests a truth we already know: We are not born perfect intellectual creatures. We are rather created potentially perfect in intellectual action, each according to the limits of the gift from Being Itself which is our nature as a specific rational creature. We must remember here, therefore, that *intellectual action* sums and assumes our total being, since as intellectual creatures we are incarnate and so limited as a sum of potentiality so to speak. Within that totality we distinguish the actual and potential, but neither is without limit, since either may exist at all only as dependent in the limit-enveloping gift of our actual-potential being – the particular gift of existence itself, whereby one is *this* particular *person*.

The point needs emphasizing, in respect to the limit whereby we *are* at all: The body is intricate to the perfection of intellect. It is in this knowledge that we may the better understand what it means to say that the "speculative intellect *by extension* becomes practical." The direction of that extension of speculative to practical is toward actual being, toward existing things as immediate to intellect's own finite being, and the most immediate instrument to that extension is through the senses. Thus we consider that the practical intellect has *proximate* ends which are means to an *ultimate* end. The ultimate being of the self is the province of our being touched upon by speculative intellect. It is the practical movement of intellect that engages most of Cicero's categories of circumstances which St. Thomas accepts to his point: *who*, *what*, *where*, *by what aids*, *how*, *when* (Cicero's *On Rhetoric*, I, 24). But this practical action of intellect comes to center at last upon the question *why*, which though relevant at the level of the practical, as reason comes to understand the other answers, becomes at last a question in a dimension of being beyond those accidents of circumstances – beyond the limits of intellect's worldly vicissitude as addressed by practical intellect. The *why* restores to desire the prospect toward our higher end, restores the speculative inclination toward the higher end proper to our intellectual being.

The relation of intellect to object, in relation to object as a proximate end of intellection, is of such importance and complexity that we summon St. Thomas once more (*Summa* I-II, Q. 7, A. 3):

> A circumstance is said to exist outside the substance of the act though affecting it in some way. This happens in three ways: first, as the circumstance touches the act itself; second, as it affects the cause of the act; and third, as it touches the effect. A circumstance affects the act itself either by way of a measure, as *time* and *place*, or by qualifying the act, as does the *manner of acting*. It touches the effect of the act when we consider *what* someone has done. It affects the cause of the act insofar as the circumstance *why* is referred to the final cause, *about what*

to the material cause or object, *who* to the principle efficient cause, and *by what aids* to the instrumental efficient cause.

Accepting what we know of man without the necessity of a rational justification of that knowledge – namely that he is as intellectual creature imperfect – we are thereby prepared to pursue the possibilities in his intellectual being. To do so we need not affirm intellect fallen as a consequence of Original Sin, though I so contend. One need only acknowledge as self-evident to present experience that through actions of intellection the intellect comes closer to its potential. The prospect of our maturing is spoken at every level of our experience of life. We know it in the blossom turning fruit, and we know it in our own mind moving beyond its blossom stage, however longingly one might wish to arrest the blossom, to keep it from falling into the fruit. We are born *potentially* knowing. Our science of biological conception, gestation, birth is sufficient to show that at birth we bring an already established knowing into the light, for which reason mothers sing to their unborn child. But we are not born in any perfection of potentiality, even as the ballerina is born only potential to the dance of being, though not yet a dancer. Life in the world is desire for actuality, the anticipation of potentialities becoming actual, and our desire for this life is fed by the actualities of encounter along the way.

In the light of this proposal about the nature of our life, let us say that the action of intellectual being is a habit fed from within the discrete soul by prudential virtue when that soul is governed by a right will in relation to its foreknowing of desire. That is the anticipation of its becoming which is suited to the nature of the soul through grace. Prudential virtue accepts the actualities of nature toward the limits of our possible – our potential – being. A right will is a will which both desires and directs intellect toward that end. The will is "the name for rational appetite." (*Summa* I-II, Q. 6, A. 2, Reply Obj. 1) It is a *right* will when it is prudential in accepting intellect and the limits of intellect as under the general auspices of the limits of its own being. It is "rational desire": that is, it is an active inclination governed by reason, even as it governs reason. It is deliberate (that is, intentionally reasonable) toward a good the intellect perceives. As St. Thomas puts it, the right will in act is "simply a kind of inclination proceeding from the interior knowing principle, just as the natural appetite [such as that for food or water] is a kind of inclination proceeding from an interior principle without knowledge." (*Summa* I-II, Q. 6, A. 4) It governs by its inclination the whole complex we call the discrete intellectual creature, and guides it toward a high moment of simple existence as a perfection of a discrete, created being. That such governance is arduous and repeatedly imperfect requires only our remembering the long hours our ballerina spends at her bar, or before a mirror, alone in her labors toward a perfection yet far off.

The action of intellectual being, then, is a habit fed from within the discrete soul by prudential virtue when that soul is governed by right will. And that habit of being is dependent upon intellect in its practical and speculative capacities. The aspect of intellectual being most crucial to good habits of being is, of course, the will, in which lies the cause of agonies of lost moments of perfection. For, given our fallen nature, will is easily self-besieged. Its temptation, given that it may command both the practical and speculative actions of intellect, is to succumb to the illusion that will itself is the primary formal agent of an autonomous, discrete being – *this* soul in which *this* will is resident, *this* "self." Will is tempted to dominate the being of which it is *member* and not formal cause. In reality, the will has limits of action in its participation in the discrete soul's vital being, as the repeated frustrations of our will demonstrate to us. Its limits are those of its actively *allowing* an *in*-forming. It has the power in relation to being to remove obstacles to the *full*-filling of the soul's potential.

Here let us be reminded once more that *potential* is used to designate the created limit of the discrete soul's created being. It is by the act of creation that a discrete being is granted its *going-on-ness*, but within limits, without which limits it would not be the thing it is. Limit of being *explicitly* makes an existence of a discrete creature. A created thing is by its creation finite, and so it can in no sense be infinite in potential, a fundamental and self-evident aspect of being denied only by gnostic deconstructions of being whereby the will would establish its own particular existence as autonomous. We know how pervasive such gnostic thought is, and we know its effects at the most common level of intellectual action in community. We need recall only the illusional slogan that "*anyone* can be president" of the United States and look honestly at ourselves and at those about us in the shadow of that false rubric. For even those who do not acknowledge creatures as created admit under pressure the limits of potency, however decayed our language under gnostic manipulations of community intellect. Of itself, one creature does not become another: A stone does not digest, nor does it grow by photosynthesis. Though certain minerals transmogrify to marble, they do not become diamond. In respect to discrete intellectual beings, the potential in separate instances differ so conspicuously that only through a false saying – by false witness – can one affirm as an absolute that *anyone* can do or be *anything*. What becomes so readily lost in such perversions is that dignity appropriate to the discrete being. For it is the thing it is because it is *a* being, not *any* being. As a popular principle, then, this perverse assertion (that anyone may be president) is a false one designed to rob discrete beings of that whereby they are what they are, both actually and potentially.

Any being, we must insist (if a right will is to serve its intellectual host) is limited by the necessities contingent in its existence as a created being. Properly, will's office to that created being (man) must be governed by an active consent to limit, most immediately an active consent to the limited gift of this soul, its own, to which as member it owes allegiance and service as does the ruler to the citizens he rules. That is, the will is member finally in a simplicity of discrete existence, in a person, concerning which simplicity we shall speak more presently. And because of the created nature of this intellectual creature, man it follows that the will is required to give consent to the nature of all existent creatures.

The intellect on the other hand, in contributing to a proper governance of the soul by the will, requires for its operation a division by categories of being itself. For only through that action is it possible to come to terms with *what is done* in relation to *what is*. This is but to say an old proposition: Created intellect is discursive by its created nature. Its finite nature does not allow intellect an immediate and full understanding of the being it perceives, however demanding the will upon it for such immediacy. For the will, in willing to be "as the gods" in respect to possessing understanding, can but violate the actuality of its finitude thereby, coloring its desire with the illusion of absolute autonomy. Meanwhile, intellect in its practical extension willy-nilly must deal with *category* through acts divisive of simple being, acts signaled to itself and other intellects by signs, gestures toward being, and most conspicuously those gestures we call words. Sign is a special necessity insofar as intellect would come to understand its own existence, in that by its finitude it cannot know its own being instantly and simply. If we say that an *idea* is an aspect of a thing known, we are already aware that the idea is not comprehensive of the thing known. If, in respect to the signs necessary to even such a limited knowing, we declare the *sentence* to constitute (at its best) an *idea* or a *single thought*, we know with what labor of intellect, through the structure of words in a sentence, we approach that simple, single idea.

We are nevertheless reminded, by the very acknowledgment we make of the limits of intellectual finitude, that intellect's discursiveness serves its own finitude. But its seeming divisiveness of being as intellectual act does not necessarily speak an actuality of division in the existential creature which the discursive intellect addresses by its action. In speaking of the *person*, for instance, we use such divisive terms as *will*, *soul*, *intellect*, *body*, and the like. But one may not therefore assume an actuality of *parts* in the person, not even in the most common division whereby we distinguish *body* from *soul*. We are speaking of aspects of a being as perceived by finite intellect focused in a limited way by the necessities of its nature. There is consequent to its nature the divisiveness in the intellect itself that follows upon its focus – its extension to an object. That is why we are so arrested by awe, no doubt, in those moments when we acknowledge a perfection of being by turning toward finite intellect's limits: When we cry out that in that moment we cannot tell the dancer from the dance. It is, we must say at last, a mystical moment, such as those our great artifacts of mystical literature attempt to witness.

Finite intellect in its practical necessities then, necessarily acts divisively because of its created nature. But it "knows" as well a prospect beyond such necessity in which there is promise of a resting of the desire to know.

It is that state of beatitude which St. Augustine and St. Thomas speak of. Meanwhile, however, short of the perfection of beatitude, one must deal with finitudes. And so the will's consent must be first of all to *this* simple being's actual and potential existence. It is a consent to a recognition by intellect. For intellect moves the will in one aspect rather than the other way round: Intellect responds to principles, bringing itself from potency to act (Thomas says) "with regard to knowledge of conclusions." (*Summa* I-II, Q. 9, A. 3) That is what we experience of ourselves through the ballerina's high moment, a recognition of a high simplicity of being to which the will gives spontaneous consent, though on the morrow it may modify its consent. Through a right will, governed by prudence, the soul responds openly to being – in the first place to its own being, but also to beings encountered in the existential matrix of creation that constitutes the circumstances of its existence. The intellect, we are saying, perceives through intuition that its perceiving self, and the inclusive matrix of the self as well, is nourished by beingness, is dependent in being. It must perceive this mystery of existence through active encounter, a discursive encounter, with particularities. That is, intellect encounters being through the spectacle of being that speaks to perception and so to intellect out of the limits of discrete existences – stones or trees or man or the perceiving self. Thus intellect knows intuitively the general dependence of existential reality upon beingness.

But such intuitive – angelic – knowledge is always a partial knowledge, given the nature of the intellect. Put in scholastic mode, the intellect knows through that aspect of its nature spoken of as *intellectus*. Then it pursues that partial knowing through the *ratio*. Once more we divide the indivisible action of intellect so that the simple nature of intellect may be *pointed toward* by our signs. In this habit of knowing through *intellectus* and *ratio* in concert, prudence grows as a virtue of the soul.

It is well in this conclusion, to recall St. Thomas's distinctions of the *intellectus* and *ratio*: "Although human knowing really takes place in the mode of *ratio*, nevertheless it is a kind of participation in that simple knowing which takes place in higher natures, and we can thus conclude that human beings possess a power of intellectual vision."[1]

1 This excerpt from St. Thomas's *Quaestiones disputatae de veritate* Q.XV.1, is quoted by Josef Pieper, *Leisure, the Basis of Culture,* trans. By Gerald Malsbary (South Bend, Ind.: St. Augustine's Press, 1998, p. 12.I'm indebted to John Hittinger's "Reason and Intellect in Two Texts of St. Thomas Aquinas," a thesis submitted to the School of Philosophy, Catholic University of America, 1978, in my exposition of the distinction.

XI

Prudence, St. Thomas says, is "a right method of conduct." And again, prudence is "a virtue especially necessary to human life." That special necessity is our present concern, in respect to which we remember that "human life" by its nature is the going-on-ness of an intellectual creature. If prudence is "contained by the cardinal virtues and numbered among them" (*Summa* II-II, Prologue), we remember that "[a]ll other moral virtues are traced back in some way to the cardinal virtues." What is thereby suggested is that the cardinal virtues are those primarily associated with the given rational nature, and therefore pertinent to the special province of intellectual act in relation to rational desire – which is to say, in relation to the will. For we make a distinction between rational desire, the will, and natural inclination called appetite. (*Summa* I-II, Q. 1, A. 2)

What is of immediate concern to us is that prudence is the virtue appropriate to both rational desire and to appetite, governing the pursuit of fulfillment by rational intellect. If appropriate to appetite, it is especially so to intellectual actions peculiar to this knowing creature, man.

And so St. Thomas is careful to insist on the relation of prudence as an intellectual virtue to those other intellectual virtues, knowledge, understanding, and wisdom. The relation of prudence as a habit of intellect becomes especially pertinent to our concern with the continuing argument that making is the "proper habit of our being." And we may note of prudence a certain detachment, as it were, in its relation to the other intellectual virtues. The concern which Thomas develops in the opening questions of the *Summa* II-II is for the primacy of faith over all virtues in the end, but to arrive at that realization requires the action of intellect in support of faith. And that means a careful distinction by intellectual analysis of the special relation of the soul through its faith to its proper end, beatitude, and the participation in support of that relation by the active intellect. In making this distinction then, whereby he establishes the relation within his earlier distinction between rational desire and natural inclination, the immediacy of prudence to intellectual action must be carefully established.

Concerning natural desire, then, there is a distinction to be made from either rational or sense appetite. Natural desire is the inclination of the soul out of its given nature, an inclination to the suitable in respect to that given nature, and it is separate from any dependence in knowledge. It is distinguished from sense desire and rational desire, both of which are dependent upon knowledge, for in these a certain knowledge is an aspect of the desire. Thus we *know* that we desire *water* when thirsty, in distinction from irrational creatures, whose desire for water is rather related to natural desire. Thomas puts this matter thus: "[E]very inclination arises from some form." Thus "natural appetite arises from the form that is present in the natural thing, whereas sense appetite as well as rational appetite – the will – arises from a form known. Hence just as natural appetite tends to a good that is in fact good [in itself], so sense appetite as well as the will tends to the good as known. Consequently for the will to tend to something, it is not required that it be in truth good, but that it be apprehended as good." (*Summa* I-II, Q. 8) We might put it that the teleological impetus of a being is its natural appetite, and since the end of human being is the perfection of its being, its beatitude, because also given intellect it is capable of taking a lesser good for a greater good. It may mistake its proper "joy in truth," as St. Augustine puts it.

Another point is here relevant. St. Thomas argues (*Summa* I-II, Q. 4, A. 4, Repl 2) that in every instance save one, an act of intellect precedes the act of will, the act of rational desire. That exception is the act whereby there is movement toward the final act of intellect, namely its beatitude. It is that act precedent to will that is out of natural desire, as distinguished from rational desire. And it is in this juncture of action that will, to the expense of the soul, may set itself against the greater good in a pursuit of a lesser good as if it were the greater – as if the lesser good were in fact an *unqualified* good rather than a *useful* good. And it is in respect to this inclination to error on the part of the rational desire – of will – that prudence becomes most centrally important. It does so as if in a certain way it were detached and superior in its virtue to the will.

It is here that we may remind ourselves once more of what constitutes a "right will." St. Thomas says that it is an action of love toward things "under the common notion of the good which [intellect *knows* as common]." But to know the good and not distinguish lesser from greater good, under the supposition that the good is the good? Is that the end to the concern? Here is where trouble lies for will. In truth, St. Thomas says (*Summa* II-II, Q. 9, A.

4, Reply 3) the "blessedness of man consists in due use of creatures and an ordered affection for them," whereby the useful good is not confused with unqualified good, the end of blessedness. And the necessity of governing rational desire by prudence affects intellectual action here, suggesting a certain elevation of the soul by prudence over its gift of intellectual power. It is here, for instance, that the soul clings to its recognition that faith begins with divine truth, that knowledge, understanding, and even wisdom are related, not to divine truth, but to human reason. And, because nothing is more certain than the word of God, "knowledge is not more certain than faith, nor is anything else." (*Summa* II-II, Q. 4, A. 8) It is prudence which will require at that impasse between faith and knowledge that one maintain faith, lest all be lost through despair.

It is faith, then, under the support of prudence, that reaches an accommodation at last between natural desire and rational desire, in that act whereby there occurs a movement of the soul toward the final act of intellect, beatitude. And it is here, in a sense, that prudence in support of faith suggests a sort of elevated detachment of the soul above, or perhaps inclusive of and greater than, its intellectual faculty. St. Thomas, concerned with the relation of prudence as an intellectual virtue in relation to knowledge, understanding, and wisdom, remarks of this prudence that it is concerned with contingent things – in our present point, the contingency of the soul to its own beatitude. (We should remember that art as a virtue is also concerned with contingent things.) On the other hand, knowledge, understanding, wisdom are concerned, not with contingent things, but with necessary things. They are gifts of the Holy Ghost, and as particular gifts are operative in a relation to the soul's final end and so stand in a different relation to the soul from that of prudence.

This general discussion of prudence leads us to a figurative suggestion about its relation to the soul: In relation to the other virtues, prudence is a sort of older and wiser counsel to those virtues, in that it has always had as its concern the ultimate end to which the soul is directed by its natural inclination. But if it is older and wiser, we must be careful in our deference to it among the virtues, as is clear in our saying that faith, for instance, bears a precedence. We would also say that love is itself the consuming virtue, in that it is the drawing force of the soul's perfection, whereas prudence is an enabler. Having become so heavily involved in distinctions here, we might also say that the virtues informing the speculative intellect, in anticipation of the final end of the soul's blessedness, suggests that in that perfection, all the virtues will have dissolved from intellect's necessities of providing the will with a complex knowledge of virtue whereby the will in its earthly limits is required to establish those habits as distinctly related by intellect to the several virtues. In the beatific state, perhaps, the soul is beyond concern for virtues, cardinal or theological, as well as beyond a concern for the intricate effect of those virtues as habits of our being. But that will be to have gone beyond evil in having gone beyond useful good. It is the *meanwhile* that always confronts the soul. Meanwhile, then, the soul in its journey toward beatitude must explore the useful good, in the light of Being Itself, of Whom the useful good is an aspect. The soul perfected is the soul simple at last in its being. But so long as good is under construction in the soul, through its encounters with the accidents of its circumstantial existence, good is anything but a simple being to intellect and will.

Anciently, the cardinal virtues have contributed to the building of the perfection of intellect, the *hinge* (from *cardo*, a hinge) swinging the *person* toward the good. Insofar as prudence is the measure of justice, fortitude, and temperance, it orders those virtues. And in doing so, the habit of prudence steadily reveals to the intellect the necessity of an ordinate movement of the soul through faith, hope, and charity. Prudence is an enabler of the other virtues, practiced most immediately in relation to the other intellectual virtues – knowledge, understanding, wisdom. And though it is most evident as a virtue in relation to offices of practical intellect, its ultimate responsibility concerns the soul's movement toward unqualified good. In its evident service as a virtue, it is through prudence that proximate means in relation to proximate ends are ordered to that higher good. Though philosophy untouched by revelation does not recognize the importance of this larger context to prudence, it is clear enough that the classical mind, Plato's and Aristotle's, for instance, exercise prudence *toward* that end which their intellect never quite discovers, as Gilson makes evident in his *Spirit of Mediaeval Philosophy*.

That is why we can say that Plato and Aristotle, as does St. Thomas, recognize prudence as enabler of the good of the soul, affirmed as the necessary habit of "a right method of conduct" in the exercise of all virtues as those virtues are peculiar to ordinate will. In the light of revelation, the classical philosopher's concern for the good of the soul seems relative because in relation to a proximate end, in contrast to St. Thomas's unqualified end, St. Thomas's Good which is Being Itself. To come to this recognition is at once to appreciate the appropriateness of classical philosophy to the pursuit of truth out of a faith that accepts divine truth through revelation. It is also, incidentally, to recognize in those great classicist some evidence of the truth St. Thomas names in distinguishing rational desire and natural inclination. For there is, surely in Plato and Aristotle at least, that natural inclination to the soul's proper end, although rational desire does not fully succeed in establishing the true end of that natural desire, the soul's beatitude. It is a difficulty to them which Gilson has considered as their failure to locate Being Itself as the necessary, precedent reality upon which all else depends. Not making that discovery by understanding, there is possible to their systematic thought only an aspect of that Being Itself, the posited unqualified good, which for Plato (for instance) is the Idea. It is in this light that one honors such great minds, while recognizing that something more is necessary to the resolution of the intellectual journey they have advanced so considerably.

Through prudence, the soul discovers the other virtues necessary to its journey, though it is through revelation that one knows the proper end of that journey. It is here, however, that another cautionary note is in order. For though faith responds to revelation with a certitude about the ultimate end to the soul's journey, faith is not sufficient in itself to accommodate the mediate concerns of intellect on the journey's way. Not to recognize this is to be susceptible to false revelations, as it were. For what faith desires may become confused by the very aspect of the soul's given nature as intellectual creature. Lesser goods, mistaken by intellect as greater goods, may in the mistake allow faith to rest in a lesser as if a greater. That is why the reminder always that one must be cautious in response to apparent acts of grace, for the visionary moment in which grace is taken to be primary may rather be an illusionary moment. The subtle evil that proceeds from the Adversary is sufficiently able to manipulate illusion till it may be taken as vision. That is why the Church, for instance, is so careful in its evaluation of miracles.

Prudence, and the virtues discovered under the auspices of prudence as valid virtues, then, are necessary to the soul's journey to its proper end. Otherwise we may discover that what we have taken by faith is not truly by faith, but through wishful thinking, which can appear to the imprudent soul as faith. Thus our hope will lack the proper coordinates to its transcendent desire, and in its failure at last succumb to despair. Similarly, charity may become a concession to worldliness, become submerged in worldliness through the circumstances to charity. Thus the charitable act may become an end in itself and not an act out of love of God, an act in the name of God.

Compare, for instance, St. Thomas's remark (*Summa* I-II, Q. 13, A. 1) that "if an act of fortitude is done out of love of God, it is materially an act of fortitude but formally an act of charity" – i.e., an act from within our love of God. It is prudence, we are saying, which orients the several virtues to that end whereby as temporal acts, the acts are *materially* separate but are *formally* one in charity. That is why charity is the greatest of the virtues, as it is also the reason that charity when not formally resting in the love of God becomes an act out of pride, not love.

In this distinction lies the meaning of St. Augustine's saying that "enjoyment is to adhere lovingly to something for itself." This "enjoyment" or "delight" is wonder understood at last, the principle of which understanding (again St. Augustine) is to know that our joy in, and love of, something for itself is not the final resting end of joy and love. "Not because they are, does God know all creatures spiritual and temporal, but because He knows them, therefore they are," St. Augustine says (*De Trinitate*). When the long habits of prudence lead at last to this recognition, one may love creatures spiritual and temporal for themselves because they are creatures of a loving God. Such is that condition of "blessedness" in which man at last is able to make a "due use of creatures" and maintain "an ordered affection for them."

Prudence is thus "especially necessary to human life" as Thomas says of the temporal circumstances of human life. Therefore when we speak of prudence, we shall understand as a complement to it, as necessarily consequential to the habit of prudence, those other virtues of the soul implied in prudence's "right method of conduct." For it is out of prudence that the soul's pursuit of a fullness of its discrete being, a proper "self love," flows through the operations of the practical intellect because ordinately desired by the will.

Now to put the matter more properly in respect to this intellectual creature man, and closer to our theme of *making* as our proper habit: The discrete soul acts toward its fulfillment through art. That is, the means to that habit of being which is proper to the discrete soul is that action of the practical intellect which we call *making*, whether our concern is the action of making by a president or a poet or a priest. It is most specific to the order of man's being that he is by virtue of the limited order of his possible action a *maker*. It is in this respect most particularly that he is created in the image of God. He is so *through* the special mode of intellectual act we call the *practical*, in distinction from the *speculative*. For as image of God, he participates by similitude but not in an absolute simplicity of his being as maker. He participates, we have said, under the principle of proper proportionality. One does not speak divisively of God as *practical* or *speculative* or the like, since it is necessarily posited of God that discursive division is not an actuality *in* God, but rather a necessity to finite intellect. This relation of man as participatory image of God, indeed, is the central burden of St. Augustine's and St. Thomas's full arguments of the soul's relation to God in respect to the mystery of being.

Now the terms *practical* and *speculative*, as applied to intellect, are scholastic terms of very precise meaning to St. Thomas, and it might be well to recall his presentation of them, in the *Summa* I, Q. 79, A. 11. He develops them out of Aristotle's *De Anima*, with the concern for the ultimate intellectual end of beatitude, which means that he must see them in relation to the special nature of man as created in God's image. These are not two powers of the soul, he begins, though a certain deference of order is accorded the speculative. "The speculative intellect by extension becomes practical." The pre-eminence of the speculative aspect lies in its special relation to its Cause at last. The speculative intellect "directs what it apprehends, not to operation, but to the consideration of truth; while the practical intellect is that which directs what it apprehends to operation." Again, the "object of the practical intellect is good directed to operation, and under the aspect of truth." Later (*Summa* I-II, Q. 3, A. 4), the argument is made that the contemplative life, which is more desirable, is through the speculative intellect, and is aimed at the divine good. "The act of the practical intellect, on the other hand, is sought not for its own sake but for the sake of action; and these actions too are for the sake of some end." It is in this article that a distinction of these aspects of created intellect in relation to their creator is defined.

"The likeness of the practical intellect to God," says St. Thomas, "is according to proportionality, that is, the practical intellect is related to what it knows as God to what He knows." Now what God knows is by his knowing what he creates, so that the practical intellect's likeness as image is through the limited, proportionate act of knowing things to be what they are. The "operation" of intellect under the aspect of its practical movement is in relation to the truth of things, initially of the truth of itself as a discrete thing. The good of the intellect perfects intellect insofar as it knows things to be themselves. The operation of practical intellect, therefore, is within an arena of existing things, in relation to its existing nature as finite intellect. But the speculative intellect bears itself as image of its creator in another manner. Thus Thomas says, "the likening of the speculative intellect to God is according to union or representation, which is a much greater likeness." The practical intellect "is ordered [by right will] to a good outside of itself," namely to the good of what God knows, which "knowing" is through the first act of created being. On the other hand, "speculative intellect has a good within it, the contemplation of truth." In this contemplative mode there occurs an accord with, a "union or representation" to, God, in St. Thomas's phrase. One might say that it is through contemplation that the gift of one's being is returned to the giver through the given potency actualized, an act of the proper love of the self. If the practical intellect "does not have such a good" it nevertheless "directs man to it."

St. Thomas, in making these distinctions in relation to our existence in the image of God, says that "with respect to the principal thing known, which is His essence, God has only speculative knowledge, not practical." Such a statement reminds us that our own intellect is committed by its givenness to a movement, which is a necessity to the execution of potency, and that movement is made at a rudimentary level through the *making up* of intellect, as it were, through a *coming to* itself, which is an awakening of the self through movement toward good outside itself. One may, as Dante dramatizes – or Wordsworth and Eliot as well – come to oneself in a dark wood, isolated from that sustaining good outside intellect. But one may also come to oneself in a vibrant wood, where the good of things made pulse in response to intellect's knowing of things in themselves, which experience is the vindication of the speculative self, the speculative intellect. The speculative intellect is thus sustained by faith beyond the limited reason of science, whose arena is the limits of the practical intellect's journeying. Two intellects, we discover, may respond quite differently to the "wood of the world." Or one intellect moved to understanding responds differently at different moments. The pilgrim Dante, at the end of the *Divine Comedy*, though in the same wood whence he set out, no longer finds it a *dark* wood.

And this is to return to an important point: The speculative intellect by extension becomes practical. The intuitive intellect by extension becomes rational. The imaginative intellect by extension moves to an execution of a thing. We are at a point where language is difficult to suit to the reality known, in relation to intellectual being. *Extension*, for instance, is suggestive of those antennae collapsed upon themselves which by "extension" become receptive of radio waves. But the orientation of such a figure is misleading, since the extension is not outward from the centering self as if to embrace the all. It is rather more nearly a concentration, which in turn suggests a reduction, a delimiting. There is a further confusing ambiance in our figures and the terms of our figures, our shifting from telescope to microscope as it were, and especially as perceived from a distance, as when the plowman observes the contemplative. It is the contemplative who seems from that point given to extensions of intellect, which from the practical immediacy of the plowman seems rather a dissipation. On the other hand, from the contemplative's position (if he is less than truly contemplative) the plowman seems bogged in the mundane. Thus a view from the "ivory tower" in contrast to a view of that occupant of what seems an "ivory tower" from the elemental level of earth by the plowman.

But this foray has been by way of reminding us that, in speaking of the practical and speculative intellects, we are speaking of one thing. That divisiveness of discursive language which we may not escape tends to obscure a truth about intellect: That its practical and speculative aspects are always intimately engaged, so much so that it requires an aggressive operation of the will to disengage them, sometimes so aggressive that the effect becomes more general in community itself then is healthy to community. It is in such aggressive disengagement that we have, in the history of Western thought, the Age of Reason, followed by the Romantic Age. And I would contend that at the root of the attempts characterized as "movements" is this deliberate dissection of intellect, whereby it is prevented its simple wholeness, as I have done at some length in *Romantic Confusions of the Good*. It is at last the office of prudence to prevent such distortions of the nature of created intellect so that we may recover that simplicity of intellect in which speculative and practical actions are not only complementary but unified in themselves, capable of separation only by the dividing of the self which sets speculative against practical. That dividing is a phenomena observable in individual persons and in groups and ages of persons, as our long history reveals again and again.

St. Thomas speaks to our concern in speaking of the relation of science to happiness, of our knowing as related to our proper end. (*Summa* I-II, Q. 3, A. 6) Man's ultimate happiness, he says, "which is his ultimate fulfillment, cannot consist in the knowledge of perceptible things [which knowledge is our age's curse of specialization] for a thing is not perfected by something lower except insofar as the lower participates in something higher." His concern here is for that participation of the lower intellect in the higher, in Being Itself, but the course of his argument is through the "science" whereby finite intellects know things beneath the level of intellectual nature. "Now it is clear that the form of a stone or of any perceptible thing is lower than man. Hence the intellect is not perfected by the form of the stone insofar as it is the form of a stone, but insofar as the form shares a likeness of something above the human intellect, namely, the intelligible light." We need only recall the pathos in that specialist who supposes that he is "perfected" by specialization. He takes his minute knowledge of a species or of an operation as a transcendence of his nature.

Again, we must be careful here not to reject such specialization. The necessity is rather to put it in its proper perspective in relation to the perfection of intellect itself. It is to this point that St. Thomas speaks, in words following immediately from his last quoted ones. In forms, he says, there "can be sensed there is shared a certain likeness to higher substances, so that knowledge of theoretical science is a certain participation in true and perfect happiness." It is here that, remembering Wordsworth's assertion, we may appreciate how the poet accompanies the man of science. It is even more to be realized that we are not concerned with separate persons but with the singular person, and with the accompanying action of practical and speculative intellect in a person, whereby a thing is seen and known to be the thing it is, its *truth* thus possessed by an intellect. For it is thus recognized as a thing sharing a certain likeness to the seer and knower, namely a likeness in being and as *caused*. For stone and person are creatures of God, sharing connaturality. The "intelligible light" effects a union of intellect and thing in ways that prevent the excesses of extension or contraction in worldly distortions of our intellectual nature.

The mystic speaks to this effect, but it is an experience common to us in instances in which there is awe followed by wonder, whether one be plowman or contemplative. It is, for instance, in Dame Julian of Norwich's experience of the chestnut on her outstretched palm, through which she recognizes the sustaining grace in being. It is, more recently, in Gerard Manley Hopkins's vision, to which he turns the offices of the practical intellect in an attempt to "make" tribute to that vision: his recognition of the *instress* of existing things to which he would make an *inscape* of words, seeing even the plowman's immediacy to the mundane as providing vision such as the contemplative seeks. For, as we observed earlier,

> sheer plod makes plough down sillion
> Shine, and blue-black embers . . .
> Fall, gall themselves, and gash gold-vermilion.

And it is in this deportment of intellect toward being, and so toward Being Itself, that Flannery O'Connor says of her making of stories through the practical intellect, concentrating on the small thing she would make, "The longer you look at one object, the more of the world you see in it." The *long look*, the speculative-practical response to existence, a simplicity which we speak of as if divided, whereby an aspect is an extension or a concentration. If we are Julian of Norwich we say, ". . . he shewed [me] a little thing, the quality of an hazel-nut, in the palm of my hand; and it was round as a ball." We might see in that small quality that "[i]t is all that is made." The moment of fear, that it might cease to be, that it "might suddenly have fallen to naught for little-ness," is answered by, "It lasteth, and ever shall for that God loveth it." And therefore the conclusion – "all thing hath the Being by the love of God."

There speaks the mystic. But so heavy this hazelnut of creation, like a large coconut perhaps, that most of us must hold it with both hands. If seen however as does St. Julian, one does not think, "I hold it with both hands." One *is* through the holding a singleness, through the visionary moment, within the "intelligible light." Not left hand and right hand, not speculative and practical, not right lobe and left lobe: One *is* in a simplicity. It is only with that reflective leverage, as with the *Summa Theologiae*, that we begin our pursuit of *why* with the virtues of the practical intellect. The mystery of that vision lies in "the likening of the practical intellect to God . . . [which] is according to proportionality." That is, the practical intellect is related to *what it knows* as God to *what He knows*. But the likening of the speculative intellect to God is according to union or representation, which is a much greater likeness than that of the practical intellect's likeness.

"With respect to the principle thing known, which is His essence, God has only speculative knowledge, not practical." With respect to the most proximate thing we know, our own intellect as an existing thing, our initiating knowledge, out of the gift of anterior knowing of things in themselves which is already present to the initiating knowing, our speculative movement devolves as a practical movement, dissolves into the wonder we know *that anything is at all.*

One is struck by a certain parallel between St. Thomas's distinction of the practical and speculative intellect in relation to Being Itself and Coleridge's distinction of the Primary and Secondary Imagination. Coleridge puts it: "The primary Imagination I hold to be the living power and prime agent of all human perception, and as a repetition in the finite mind of the eternal act of creation in the infinite I AM. The secondary Imagination I consider as an echo of the former, co-existing with the conscious will, yet still as identical with the primary in the *kind* of its agency, and differing only in *degree*, and in the *mode* of its operation." There is not the same precision in Coleridge, but one sees the shadow of Thomas's speculative intellect in Coleridge's Primary Imagination and the shadow of the practical intellect in his Secondary Imagination. The differences Coleridge limits to degree recalls St. Thomas's speaking of the practical as an extension of the speculative. And his concern for the likeness of God as differing between speculative and practical might be considered as echoed in Coleridge's difference of mode. The Secondary Imagination, he says, "dissolves, diffuses, dissipates, in order to recreate." It struggles to "idealize and to unify." He concludes that the Secondary is "*vital*, even as all objects (*as* objects) are essentially fixed and dead."

It is in this concluding distinction that Coleridge departs radically from Thomas, overlooking as it were the union of intellect and thing which bears analogy to the union of intellect and "object," the effect of which to intellect is the truth of that essence of the thing which remains in the thing, the object. The "likening of the speculative intellect to God is according to union or representation," differing in likeness from the practical intellect's likeness to God, which "is according to proportionality" of knowing the thing proportionately to God's (incommensurate) knowing of the thing. Practical intellect experiences a sort of union with the thing, then, while the speculative experiences a union with God, the intellect's necessity following from that difference, the commensurate relation of itself to things whereby it loves creation in relation to its proper love of the cause of creation. It is as if, with the intrusion upon Western thought following from Ockham and Nominalism, reaching confusions of detachment through Descartes and Rationalism, detachment reacted to by "Romantic" philosophy, especially German, as the immediate influence on Coleridge, Coleridge is struggling to recover a pre-Ockham mode of thought about the experience of his own mind.

XII

We have emphasized that the immediate locus of this concern for the "self" as image of God is oriented to the fullness of Being Itself through St. Thomas's "principle of proper proportionality," inherent in the discrete creature. The argument is developed in his treatise *On Being and Essence*, and spoken to by his distinction in the relation of created intellect, as practical and as speculative, to Being Itself, the relation we have just considered. One pursues that principle as limited by the discrete, specific existence of intellect as in the image of God, and within time and place. For it is there that we come to understand the nature of the discrete soul in its "proper proportionality" as a being. It is in relation to this limit of being through proportionality that the soul responds to the limiting circumstances of its being. It moves from the experience of being, accompanied by awe, to the wonder of being which it experiences as a rational desire for perfection of its own being. But it can do so only within its limited circumstances of being whereby it is *particular*. It moves from within the gifts of its particularities as circumscribed by that whole which we call creation. Such is the proximate ground to the soul's action of becoming its limit of being, its *be*atitude. This proximate ground to the particular soul is a point in time and place at which it responds to the accidents of its being, the conditions to its being, and its response is through intellectual action. A possible consequence of this necessary action is always contingent. It may by its actions orient itself to the benefit of that "intelligible light" out of its union of truth in intellect to essence in the thing itself. But it may also suffer misapprehension of that light, taking it to be caused by itself as the center of creation. From this misapprehension, it becomes but a short step to the lively, waking intellect to conclude itself creation's cause. The duration of the soul's response as a being to other beings is in the circumstances of its "ground" of being, to which we supply accidents – time, place in several respects of those collective terms. That duration we speak of metaphorically as our allotted "three score and ten," an allotment symbolic and not contractual, though protests against the Lord and Giver of Life by some souls at some points on the way are as if there were such a contract assuring temporal, spatial durations. And indeed, such have been the advances upon the accidents of circumstance in our day as to constitute attempt at an overriding contract, reducing beings in their created proportionalities toward temporal and spatial eternities. I think of medical advances, devoted increasingly to our material immortality. Such are inevitable to the concern of practical intellect when it is disjoined from its speculative nature. The abiding truth of immaterial existence, used by practical intellect within its own immaterial arena, would deny that immaterial arena as resonant with transcendence to the intellect.

In this proximate ground, within the durational limits, there are effects of intellectual action in that ground. The effects are not radical to being itself, though they are of circumstantial effect upon discrete beings. Such effect is often evident through the changed *spectacle* of particularity to the intellect as perceived through the senses, though such effect is not necessarily apparent in a literal sense. That is, there may be no palpable effect of intellectual action, since the country of the soul is a state peculiar within the largesse of material creation within which the "making-man" partakes through his actions as both of the immanent and the transcendent. Effect may be actual, though actual only as immaterial reality. Certainly, the effect of the soul's action upon that acting soul is not always evident to other souls within the common ground – to other beings in the existential world. The action of contemplation through the speculative intellect, for instance, is unlikely to register in immediate consequence of that action in the spectacles of particularity associated with that soul as we encounter it in temporal and spatial presence. The contemplative man may seem to have no strong presence in a given community. We speak aphorism to the point: Still waters run deep even if unfathomed. Hence on occasion, our readings of the signs of other souls require revision: Fathomed, we may also discover that stagnant shallow water is also still. Material evidence of immaterial actualities tend to be uncertain, and in some ages of community more than at others.

Effect, whether registered through our perceptions of other souls or not, nevertheless speaks the truth of a discrete particularity of the acting soul, as we learn to read action more perceptively. But often enough the soul's particularity is witnessed in the existential world by the secondary effects of its acts of making upon that world. Such evident effect of the action of soul in the matrix of its contingent ground we may illustrate: Here is a poem or a garden or a formula – temporal fruits of intellectual action good or bad when that action is either in concert with or counter to the existential matrix. Such temporal fruits, as we must repeat, are always dependent in immaterial and material ways upon the existential matrix – upon the diversity of being – whether we speak of garden or poem. That is because man as maker is a maker through proportionalities in being and is not absolutely a maker.

As creature, man cannot be the absolute cause of the creatures of his making. Our point nevertheless is that our finite understanding of the state of the soul – the degree of established being of the soul which we have spoken of as its *going-on-ness* – when witnessed by its effect as being (the fruits of any making) is at best a limited understanding. Its fruits are not an exhaustive, full measure of that making soul to the finite intellect attempting a measure. That is why in the community of man the relation of justice to mercy is so difficult a principle of community. We know the soul through its fruits, but only in a limited way since our knowing is finite and only proportional to the absolute knowing of God. The *going-on-ness* of a discrete soul does affect its circumstantial world, though not radically at the level of the essence of the things affected. Indeed, proper habits of being are desirable in that soul primarily for its own good only. Only at a secondary level, in the light of eternity, are those habits for the common good. Through such habits, there are good effects upon the circumstantial matrix of the soul's existence in its conjunction with the created world. That relation signifies the proximate effect, which is secondary in that the primary issue is the being of the acting soul. *This* being, and not the ground of existence which we call *being*, is at risk. Therefore we say that the primary issue of action of the soul is its proper habit of being in the interest of its own becoming.

A proper habit made actual has the continuing effect in the soul of strengthening it through that disciplined repetition which is the nature of habit in relation to the intellectual creature. We commonly put it that the "character" of a person is strengthened by good habit. Such a habit is realized when the will, through the intellect's actions, practices the disposition to that good which is appropriate to the nature of person, to the intellectual creature. Thus one establishes proper habits of diet or exercise or rest and the like, insofar as appropriate to the sensitive powers of the particular person whose sensitive gifts are themselves particular. (For which reason regimes differ between person and person.) This is to observe that a particular person whose sensitive gifts are not those proper to a calling as athlete would establish improper habit, counter to his discrete nature, in pursuing improper proximate ends as if his calling were to be athlete. Similarly, proper habits of study or contemplation and the like are established as appropriate to the intellectual power of that person, in whom because of the particularity of his discrete existence there are limits differentiating persons one from another in respect to the explicit gifts of intellectual particularity of each person. The gift of a unique nature to each person establishes the limits within which habit becomes either properly or improperly established.

It is one thing to recognize the relation of proper habit to unique gift of personhood, of soulhood. It is quite another to accomplish out of that recognition those proper and ordinate actions of being which we name as proper habits. For the first mystery to the discrete soul is that the country of its potential is to be possessed by actions of intellect limited in the range of intellect's knowing, not only in that all persons are finite in this respect but have also different gifts of potentiality. It would be rather obvious to common sense that a blind man as navigator of a ship risks ship and all its burden. It is equally obvious that a blind man might serve that ship and its company (called a community) as a seer, as we accept out of the stories of Teiresias or the legends about Homer or the history of John Milton.

What makes the problem difficult to the individual soul, of course, is the difficulty it has in comprehending particular gifts of its own being. For the potential of a perfection of a being is relative within the matrix of circumstances that includes each unique intellectual creature differently. It is a relativity, in our concern, that exists under the auspices of that absolute cause of particularity, the cause of our unique, i.e., varied particular existences. And it is through proper habit that the discrete, unique member in the created matrix of the soul discovers that relative "absolute" which is proper to it, the perfection of its own being designated beatitude. Meanwhile, that member pursues habits of being in respect to particular sensitive powers and to its intellectual powers that are particular to that member as it seeks to discover whether its potential powers call it to its being as philosopher or ballet dancer as technician or machine operator.

We summarize our point thus: Habit is a necessity to the becoming of a person, to the actualizing of the potential being unique to a person. When we speak of "the habit of being," then, we mean to include within the phrase those multiple actions necessary to the completeness of the being of a person as limited by his potential – that is, a potential circumscribed by the circumstances of his discrete being. Habits are intended perfections of actions toward the perfection of being, and are established under the agency of the will-directed intellect. When we understand this argument fully, we will not suppose that habit is so simple as when we think of it as automatic routine, a common misunderstanding of the true nature of habit in our own world. (One suspects the misunderstanding has its cause in the association of habit with the concept out of psychology of the "conditioned reflex.")

Significant to the establishment of good habits of being, we have said, is a continuing practice of acts proper to the nature of the agent. When that agent remains alert intellectually to the responsibility of those habits that are truly proper to its given nature, habit will never be simply a conditioned reflex, though one might speak metaphorically of it as if it were. That is, intellectual habits, strengthened by attentive use, become a part of one's active knowing, which is not necessarily an analytic knowing. That is why in an encounter with circumstances that are repeated, it becomes less necessary to intellect in its encounter with the same circumstances to act with the same degree of discursiveness of intellectual action. Out of experience, prudential virtue as a governing habit is established in the soul. In this regard, St. Thomas remarks that "a habit of opinion needs to be caused by many acts of reason, even on the part of the possible intellect." (*Summa* I, Q. 51, A. 3)

We ought, in relation to this last point, remember that, as habit is the deliberate exercise of a disposition in the unique soul, so too are habits in that body of community of which the discrete soul is said to be a member. By analogy, that body of community is caused "by many acts of reason" (good and bad) in the temporal circumstances of the discrete soul, though community is incomparable in duration. A community (our popular term is a "society") extends in time and space beyond the limits possible to the particular person. But similarly such communities rise, flourish, decay, while the soul is immortal. Because they do so through a complex of intellectual actions of that body we call community, the habits established by many acts of community reason remain potentially operative in a continuing community of souls in time beyond the actual presence of all the members constituting that community. Our recent concern for the relation of *tradition* to the *individual talent*, a concern on which a considerable library is written in this century, is essentially a concern for the proper relation of the discrete soul to a community taken more largely than the society of the moment. That concern too often fails to consider, however, the relation of the discrete immortal soul to the exigencies of history, of "traditional" community.

There is stirred in us an intuitive recognition of a principle of community, largely because we have so generally lost a deliberated understanding of that principle: The body of community is nourished by a proper habit of the being of community beyond its temporal and spatial determinates. That nourishing effect becomes reduced, and sometimes even poisonous in the body of community, when we lose the governing principle implied: that the habit of being of community must be proper to the nature of community itself. The "traditional" is often either superficially maligned by gnostic interests or superficially elevated by an intuition unsupported by reason. But so long as a traditionalist is a traditionalist through more than a "conditioned reflex" of intellect, he will serve community as a conscience, rescuing the viable in those proper habits of opinion that have been established and maintained in community independent of those accidents of time and place that affect community, the accidents of circumstance. One does not embrace *all* of Western civilization. Nor do any of the fathers (living or dead) of that civilization accept all, if they maintain proper habits of being in community. Intellect in service to being, whether of the discretely existing soul or of the community, is devoted to the principle that the action whereby a being (soul or community) approaches perfection is governed by that habit of being proper to the nature of that being, not by the mere history of that being. The nourished tree flourishes the more as husbandman intellect distinguishes dead wood from dormant. The difficulty lies in knowing the one from the other, as well as knowing the relation to the seasons of circumstance to the tree.

In respect to the desirable habits of being in the discrete soul, one might put it that the will removes obstacles to grace's largesse. To be in a state of *right will* is an enabling act, though not a cause of grace. And that act is, most fundamentally, the will's consent to being. This consent is an open acceptance of being, made through a response to the particularities which are encountered by means of the senses, an operation of the given nature of the intellectual creature. Encounter with being is pursued by the will through the discursive actions of intellect, explicitly those actions of intellect characterized as practical. One begins to understand increasingly thereby, through such an openness in the pursuit of being, that all things are *enabled to* being and *sustained in* being by grace, by the Abiding Causing of being. Such is the transcendent agency of being we acknowledge as "the Lord and Giver of Life," an agency recognized in thought *through* particularities. For particularities are suited to intellectual thought and discursiveness as they are engaged by the sensitive power. This is to say that it is *through* embodied creation that intellect is opened to being, which is why St. Thomas affirms that our necessary progress toward the transcendent is first through the body and its senses in relation to the body of the world. Our senses open intellect to the transcendent. And we might here observe, since some of our argument about making as the proper habit of our being depends upon the witness of the poet, that poets in particular celebrate this progress of intellect through the sensual world. Not that the poet always bears witness to the "Lord and Giver of Life" under this aspect of an understanding, a point we remark in considering the poet's response to particular, elected creatures as a present *omphalos*.

In an ordinate openness to created existences – to individual creatures, whether stone or kestrel or person – the open soul "sees" discreteness, which is another way of saying that the open soul "loves" particular existent things in themselves. Such a response to being, we remember, is necessarily singular, since the actions of intellect are necessarily singular. For as St. Thomas observes in respect to intellectual action, including the refinements of action by the will, those actions "are about singular contingent things, which because of their variety are uncertain." Thus are we reminded of the nature of finite intellect: It cannot possess – comprehend – being but nevertheless pursues comprehension through that limit upon intellectual nature that makes necessary the singular encounter with "singular contingent things." This pursuit of comprehension of singularities we have defined as the proper habit of intellectual being.

Now the intellect is properly ordinate in its openness to being through particularity insofar as it recognizes the existing thing it encounters as depending from the Causing of all existence. (I have used *Causing*, rather than the usual *Cause* here, to emphasize once more the *going-on-ness* of an abiding active Cause, just as we used *being* earlier to emphasize the *going-on-ness* of the caused thing.) In this recognition of dependence, what is disallowed is our worship of any particular thing as an end in itself, though the sense of awe accompanying the recognition of being in a particular thing sometimes tempts to such a worship. Considerable doctrinal controversy results from this confusion, whether we look to the question of nature worship in pagan thought or the relation of art (as in icons) to worship of the transcendent Causing Agent of nature and of art. When nature or art becomes an end in itself, it ceases to be that necessary *omphalos* to the soul which leads the soul *through* the created toward the Creating Agent. In such an arrest, the soul becomes entrapped by closure.

A false worship *of*, rather than *through*, the thing as *omphalos* results because, in valuing a lesser good which is a means as if it were the greater good of an end, the soul comes to center its love in the lesser good, thus entrapped in a closed world of the self. It is in respect to such premature assumptions of happiness that St. Thomas speaks so often to alert us to the *proximate* in relation to the *ultimate* good, lest the proximate good which is a means to an end become an object in which intellect anticipates a rest which must prove illusional. It is when the soul is opened *through* the existing thing to the Causing Presence that it delights in an ordinate love of creation for itself – that is, with a proper love of a lesser good. That is what St. Augustine speaks of, in defining the ordinate love of creation as "enjoyment," which is an action of adhering "lovingly to something for itself." Thomas speaks of this adhering to the thing in itself as the will's love of actual existent things insofar as that love is to be related to the soul's ultimate end. For "ultimate happiness [beatitude] consists in the vision of divine essence." One ordinately loves the created creature "in subordination to God" and "this is precisely what makes the will right." (*Summa* I-II, Q. 4, A. 4)

We love the created thing as it is *species* of an Absolute Good, *species* in its technical sense. That is the effect of love whereby the *omphalos* opens the soul beyond the actuality of the thing and allows the soul to move toward its proper end in relation to the Causing Agent of all things. Insofar as the thing becomes an end to the soul's movement toward an ultimate end, the intellect has taken a first step toward a reduction of the existent thing to an image of the worshiping intellectual creature itself. The end of this dislocation must be therefore a worship of the worshiping self. We have already touched on this point in relation to the poet in distinguishing symbol as understood by Dante and symbol as understood by the French Symbolist poets of the nineteenth century: Dante's symbol is a window, but symbol becomes mirror in Mallarmé or Rimbaud. The concern for an ordinate love of the created thing as itself, as a sort of window to Being, is a crucial corrective in a love of the poem or painting as icon, or love of the nightingale as incarnate being. That concern establishes the proximate object as a means to the soul for its progress to final end. It is this concern for an ordinate love of created things that we pray for when we say, "Teach us to care and not to care."

XIII

Through ordinate love of creaturely existences, one attempts to participate in that partnership of will and grace through which the soul moves toward a perfection of its specific grant in being. This condition of the soul's openness to being is the condition we speak of as piety toward being, and when in that state of pious address to being the soul is properly spoken of as possessed of a right-willed intellect. For the state of piety which is required of the soul's becoming is out of the fundamental gifts to its becoming, the special gifts of its nature, namely will and intellect. Thus only may this discrete being (this *specific* soul named sacramentally through baptism as both *in* nature and *beyond* nature – John or Mary or Matthew) become *grace-full* rather than *will-full*. The *will-full* action, on the other hand, is most consequentially an action toward the soul's un-being.

This is so since the principle of action in willfulness is a withholding of consent to being, through an inordinate appetite for self-being. Dante would make appropriate imagistic account of an ironic paradox of cause and effect upon the acting soul, its insatiable self-consumption through willfulness. For the proximate effect upon the soul of this perversion of its being is the un-being of the acting soul itself. There is a deconstruction of its being, an actual decline from actuality out of willfulness. Not that such a willful soul may not mistake this diminution as self-construction, self-creation.

The concern to be recovered in respect to this denigration of soul through its own agency is one anciently recognized, though a concern largely ignored by our world. For, since the willful soul through its willfulness may cause extensive, if not ultimately radical, effect within the existential matrix and that effect appear arrestingly as spectacle, still the most cataclysmic effect is the un-being of the soul through its separation from being. We do not ordinarily realize the magnitude of this cataclysm to the soul because we less and less believe the soul itself exists. We may grant to Socrates, as an argument in the exercise of intellect, that no decisive evil can be done to the good man. We may grant at the level of argument that since the discrete "soul" is immortal (theoretically at least), that same soul if in a state of piety described as proper to a right-willed intellectual creature cannot be radically destroyed by the world. But in our actions of intellect engaging existential reality, we nevertheless have difficulty dealing with proximate effects of willfulness upon existential creation. We have difficulty precisely because we do not believe in the soul as an actual existence separate from its mere name in a construct of argument advanced for the exercise of, or entertainment of, the intellect. This is to say that we continue amenable to intellectual curiosity about what men have thought about ideas (Socrates or Aristotle or St. Augustine or St. Thomas) but do not engage that thought in the high cause of the truth of things in relation to that thought. But only by such engagement can mere curiosity be transformed in the hope of the soul's salvation. To come to that change is to understand that it is intellect which makes possible that salvation, though it may not earn it. That is, intellect is the gift to us which allows us to remove obstacles to grace.

It is in thus failing that we lose our sense of the magnitude implicit in saying that it is the willful soul itself that is most profoundly at risk in its evil acts. And thus the spectacle of evil effects in the existential world becomes arresting, as if those effects were the final end of the evil act. Of course, though the murderer's destructions of his own soul must be the final effect to be recognized if one believe in the reality of the soul, the victim nevertheless requires our prudential pursuit of justice. But this is not in response to spectacle, properly speaking: It is properly in response to the reality of both the evil soul and the victimized soul in relation to the reality of that body of souls we call community. In a world held by secular intellect and not held sacramentally, a civil war between those bearing the standard of justice and those under the standard of mercy must eventually divide community against itself. In such a community our concern is reduced finally to proximate ends of justice and mercy, as if final ends. The banners of justice and mercy borne in such a strife must prove opaque, since they are but abstractions idolized. And so concerns for the orders of being in community are reduced to ideologies, each with accompanying idols about which to rally secular energies.

In respect to the *common good*, a shibboleth pronounced by disparate voices in conflict, we have here described the arena within which the claims of justice and the claims of mercy are always in contention. The arguments between these contentions hinge on a different understanding of the discrete creature, whether murderer or victim as creature. A belief in the reality of the particular soul has been so largely removed from the arena of creation as perceived by gnostic thought that the relation of justice to mercy is increasingly reduced to merely pragmatic contingencies of willful desires within the arena. It is as if social order, which is but a temporal convenience to the individual member, were the final end of the intellectual creature. What we come to realize is that the *pragmatic* has become the modern mind's substitute for the *prudential*, under which new principle it attempts to justify the intellectual creature's existence as merely temporal.

Accepting temporal limits, an intellectual creature must find the cause of its being within that limit. In such a relocation of the final end of *person*, what must result is a dominance of power within the temporal arena, a power purged of love, though the residual emotional effects of that term *love* still make the term seem suitable, and even acceptable, to manipulative purposes held by gnostic intellect. *Power* dubbed *love* becomes the instrument in resolving social contentions, a tendency that has been rising since the Renaissance. It is a tendency reflected most evidently in the community of man as the doctrine of *nationalism*, a concept not limited to ethnic nor geographical delineations, though so often through spectacle revealed in ethnic or geographical symbolizations. For the doctrine centers in a symbol, a local banner necessary to the community of power needed to advance the doctrine. That is why the sign becomes a necessary idol, whether a flag or a verbal catch phrase: whether the French tricolor or the American stars and stripes; whether the business logo or the athletic team logo. As we reflect on this transference of the ultimate to proximate end, from transcendence to temporal, we may realize a deconstruction in symbol itself, whereby symbol not only becomes opaque, but desirably so from the point of view of the gnostic manipulator of symbol. It is in this species of Nominalism that he discovers the most economical means of ordering his limited power out of collective intellect. In the opaque symbol, the discrete intellect, accepting the opacity without rational exploration of its inadequacy, will at once see itself in the symbol and further assume that what it sees is also common to humanity. The symbol as idol at once reflects the singular and the disparate. But it does so, not actually, but only apparently. And it is an apparent coincidence only in the discrete intellect. At that point of temporal tension, at the point of crisis in history, the falseness of the presumption of discrete intellect will break out in collapses of order, sometimes very violent exhibitions of disorder. One easily supplies specific instances, so that suggestive summary is sufficient here. In Eastern Europe, for instance, as the Marxist idol shatters from the singular opacity maintained on its surface by the force of ideological argument for nearly a century, we see emerging ethnic and geographic disorders, justified in their violence by appeal to racial and historical orientations as substitute symbols making collective antagonisms plausible. Almost any of the Soviet Republics illustrate the point, or the civil disorder in Yugoslavia at the moment. One begins to detect signs of the same emerging reorientations in Hungary, Romania, Czech Republic. Or closer to home, the same species of unrest and returning struggle to discover an end justifying discrete intellectual existence is at the heart of the "inner city" revolutions. It is the vaguely perceived disease which gives rise to "multicultural" agendas in the academy.

What we here speak of as effects in the world external to individual intellect has as cause the dying of spirit, and a dying of spirit not only in relation to discrete intellect but consequentially in the body of community itself. That is why we hear the alarm raised in defense of the family, of local community, an alarmed concern which we may notice as not centered in ethnic nor historical justifications initially, though it rapidly comes to that justification under the pressures of collective action in defense of family or community. We are besieged by external effects consequent upon the prolonged unmaking of the soul in our recent history, but lack the truth in our symbols to locate that cause and recover from that unmaking.

Now this unmaking of the soul through its willfulness, with consequent effect upon community, is a necessary effect of willfulness, however much the willful intellect may delude itself by projecting an illusion of its own autonomy. It is self-deluded so that it may deny any partnership with grace in respect to the life that is its own being or the life of the community of which it is a part. The illusion projected is a dream-imaging of the self, a phantasm of discrete being as unsupported by being, self-created *esse* independent of cause other than itself. Not that there isn't a certain actuality as witnessed by effect upon the presumptuous soul. The perversion of the true self, made precedently in the image of God, is an action dependent upon the prior existence of that true self, as evil is dependent upon good. We mean here to name the self actual and potential as precedent in being to its *action*. As Thomas says, an "evil that constitutes a difference of habits" – a willed inclination to bad habits of being – "is not a pure privation, but something determinate repugnant to a determinate nature." (*Summa* I-II, Q. 54, Reply Obj. 2) Evil actions of a willful intellect, then, are against its determinate nature, but so long as that nature is capable of intellectual action, its power to act remains always contingent to a possible good. In pure privation, potency of being does not exist and so action itself is an impossibility. It is the dim, attenuated sense of this truth which prompts those secular solutions to the mystery of mercy in relation to justice. They tend to be solutions that make social action in its secular dimension most regardless of the possibilities that justice itself is a mercy to the discrete soul. The alternative error lies in a regardless blindness to a dimension of justice in mercy. I have explored this paradox at greater length in *Possum*, pages 121 ff.)

The phantasm of the self projected by the will's illusion of autonomy is a creation by aberrant will, an icon of the self, between which two poles – the self and its iconographic phantasm – a pale ambiance of being hovers, but never with any prospect of that rest for the will's desire which we have heard Augustine and Thomas speak for. Thomas would say of this projected phantasm that only through the willful rejection of reality (the principle of its own being which is immediate to the intellect) may the illusion be sustained for a restless moment. The illusion of delight in such projections of the self is doomed, since true "delight is in the will as a result of the end being present." The thing *seems* to become present "because the will delights in it" but it is a chimera and not a thing. There must be, Thomas concludes, "something other than an act of will by which the end becomes present to the one willing it." This argument by Thomas intends to deny that action is the cause of being, which is the pervasively popular assumption at our juncture of history. (*Summa* I-II, Q. 3, A. 4)

It is from such perversions of the will in response to inescapable reality that will is led to conclude itself the "primary thing desired, which is its end," namely, "the act itself of willing," as if the "primary thing seen" were the act of seeing rather than an object. (*Summa* I-II, Q. I, A. 1) We are attempting, with Thomas's help, to deal with the pervasive confusion in Modernist thought, out of long-established bad habits, a dislocation of intellect from reality. It is, in its most radical effect upon the discrete intellectual creature, a dislocation of the soul's transcendent inclination in the interest of a self-engendered illusion of the intellect's transcendence of being by its unaided power – an elevation of the self to its own godhead by the presumption of autonomy. One is tempted to observe ruefully that this is an attempt at self-alchemy, an attempt at willed self-transubstantiation. It is an intellectual action by an agent who, if questioned on the point, would reject out of hand the mystery of the transubstantiation of bread and wine into the body and blood of Christ, though its practice as intellect is a pseudo-mystery, a perversion of the central mystery in which Thomas establishes his argument for the reality of person. It must reject Thomas's mystery, lest its intention be otherwise refuted. For what is afoot is an attempted magic: It presumes its own power to transubstantiate its "self" into the god of its own material and intellectual existence, having rejected the immaterial reality of its own soul. The formula operative in that intellect is *non servium*, the Satanic great refusal. One should not expect to encounter this refusal explicitly as in Satanic or pagan or other cults, we hasten to add. And we may observe as well that we find it incipiently active within the Church, whenever there is an attempt to reduce mystery to the level of sign. In such deconstruction the attempt is to make the complex relation of intellect to reality "merely metaphorical." Thereby intellect escapes that proper openness through reality to the Cause of reality in the transformation of the "self" made possible through grace, a transformation toward a perfection of the self. When the Church takes sign as "merely symbolic," the intent (tacit or overt) is the reduction of symbol to material signification, removing sign from its dimensions of meaning in immaterial reality.

It is a move toward making sign opaque, a necessary strategy to establishing the temporal over the transcendent. And it is a strategy widely afoot in the Church we must recognize. One of the indications of this intellectual disease, operative at the heart of spiritual community, is the disorder within the Church exhibited in those battles between the orthodox remnant and the various new theologies, especially those represented as "liberation theology."

Having made such a challenging observation, it is perhaps appropriate to remark further on the pivotal term in the observation, the term *symbol*. We will here remember what we have so far said of the relation of sign to meaning under the auspices of Gilson's *Linguistics and Philosophy*. Here we add further support, not by a philosopher or theologian, but by a literary mind concerned with philosophy and theology. We referred earlier to C. S. Lewis's essay "Transposition," in which he is concerned with *transposition* as the intellectual mode whereby the poorer medium responds to the richer medium, as intellect (a poorer medium), encumbered as it were by its material manifestation as intellect, must struggle to reach the richer, immaterial medium within which the soul is founded. *Symbolism* is a mode of linguistic "transposition" to intellect, and Lewis makes a telling observation out of his own experiences as poet and as a teacher of poetry. We quote a passage from his essay:

> It is of some importance to notice that the word *symbolism* is not ade-

> quate in all cases to cover the relation between the higher medium and its transposition in the lower.... Thus the relation between speech and writing is one of symbolism. The written characters exist solely for the eye, the spoken words solely for the ear. There is complete discontinuity between them.... The one is simply a *sign* of the other and signifies it by convention. But a picture is not related to the visible world in just that way.... The sunlight in a picture is ... not related to real sunlight simply as written words are to spoken. It is a sign, but also something more than a sign: and only a sign because it is also more than a sign, because in it the thing signified is really in a certain mode present.

One might, at this point, be reminded of the way in which the poet sometimes attempts this incorporation of the actual in the sign, as in the onomatopoeia of a word, or of words in relation to their voiced natures. We remember, for instance, Keats's "murmurous haunt of flies on summer eves." Or we recall Ezra Pound's arguments about the relation of the actual to the symbolic in the ideogram which partakes of the pictorial, or of his association of sculpture with the chiseled line of the poem. But Lewis is concerned, more than Pound, with a relation of sign to thing signified at a spiritual level, whereby *symbol* needs enlarging toward the visionary, albeit necessarily through the sensual. Of the relation of the painting's sunlight to "real sunlight," finding *symbol* inadequate to express the relationship, he adds, "If I had to name the relation I should call it not symbolical but sacramental. But in the case ... of emotion and sensation ... we are even further beyond mere symbolism.... The emotion descends bodily, as it were, into the sensation and digests, transforms, transubstantiates it, so that the same thrill along the nerves *is* delight or *is* agony." The *is* here is in the arena of the sensual temporal. What has been experienced by effect is sensual and subsequently emotional, but it is an effect through vision beyond the capacity of our full response by intellect, given its material limits. The "eye" is not sufficient to account for what one has "seen." One knows nevertheless a material effect of transcendent affection. One's senses respond, though intellect must identify the experience as an ecstacy rather than an agony.[1]

1 Lewis's sign as it relates sacramentally to our experience of the immaterial world echoes that world through the sign as raised out of sensual experiences of things by intellect. Though his terms are not the same, he is rather certainly concerned with that aspect of our experience which St. Thomas talks of, through which we experience a presence deeper than the thing itself and to which the speculative intellect attaches itself in a sort of unity, as an experience of "intelligible light," in Thomas's phrase. That light effects a

One knows as well, upon reflection, that it is through an encounter in the material medium. Here is the arena of the In-Between in which the soul exists toward its potentialities. In this recognition, one as intellectual soul may orient intellect toward this arena of creation in that mode Lewis calls *sacramental.* That is the mode of address as poet which is so effectively caught in poetry by Gerard Manley Hopkins. It is the mode Eliot, in his early poetry, resists by his ironic detachment, about which he remarks in defense of this willful detachment that the poet's mind is but "the shred of platinum," the "catalyst" liberating feelings "to enter into new combinations" thereby freed of the "personality" of the poet. Eliot's concern at this point of his journey, as he later sees in rejecting this position, is to dissociate his intellect from the dimensions of its existence in his *person*, in order to dominate as "artist" the being of the poem. But he is, by that procedure, increasingly dislocated from reality, and it leads him to a spiritual crisis, and to a subsequent conversion, for which Modernist critics have not yet forgiven him. (I have explicated this position, its consequences, and Eliot's recovery in a work on his poetry and criticism to be called *T.S. Eliot and the Still Point of Consciousness.*) The sacramental dimension of symbol, in distinction from the symbol secularized: We may appreciate the distinction most economically in juxtaposing the uses of symbol by the French Symbolists (an important influence on the early Eliot) and by Dante, the point made earlier. The dead end of French Symbolism is the opacity of the sign, which results in a subjectivity lamented as alienation. The sign for Dante, we urged, is a window upon the transcendent.

The recovery of a vision of reality, from intellect's entrapment of the self by a closing of the world, engineered by the closing of sign to opacity, reveals that closing to have been an illusional action, since it denies the reality of intellect's own given nature. Only by a resolute denial by the will that

---

level of union, Thomas says, whereby the essence of the thing is a participatory presence to practical intellect as the truth of the thing. That is the visionary relation of intellect to the thing, in which relation intellect knows that the "intelligible light" is not the light of intellect itself and that neither is it in the thing as a part of that thing's own nature. It is the coincidence through experience of things which Gerard Manley Hopkins might say effects a recognition of the "instress" of things, in response to which he would make his own sacrament of sign, insofar as his made sign can respond to "instress" with the sign's "inscape." Such is the union celebrated by his making.

its "self" is a discrete and therefore finite being, one created and not made by and of itself – only by such denial is intellect able to assert its illusion. But then it is able to do so only fleetingly. For the reality of the "self" though willfully rejected in its actual nature remains nevertheless a reality, so long as the "self" retains any degree of being beyond its own self-deconstructions. That is why we say that truism, deeper than we may suppose: While there's life, there is hope.

When we begin to see this relationship between grace and will as a partnership in the *going-on-ness* of the particular soul, we gain in our understanding of the relation between those aspects of intellect, the *practical* and the *speculative*. We do so in recognizing a dramatic tension in intellect when intellect is governed by a right will. Out of that tensional activity in intellect, the discrete soul (always at risk in its being because of its fallen nature) tends toward a contention with its partner grace, an added tensional field of its becoming. For only in visionary moments does the soul experience that saintly estate of being in which contentions are stilled through a sacrificial openness of the soul. Through that openness made possible by a right will, intellect engages (through singular acts) particular existences, in keeping with its created nature. It is a condition to the action of intellect in which, as Thomas says, obstacles to grace are removed, though grace is not thereby commanded into a partnership.

We are speaking here of such visionary moments as those the mystic attempts to bear witness to, experiences beyond any effective articulation of what it means to say that beatitude is "the ultimate perfection of . . . intellectual nature," a perfection in which desire is at rest. (*Summa* I-II, Q. 62, A. 1) The desire is natural, in that it is an inclination to the end proper to the desiring nature, but such are the circumstances of action to that proper end that it may be anticipated only by hope, save for the gifts of a still moment of vision on occasion. Meanwhile there is that constancy of tensional activity by intellect in response to created things, a response always singular in that the intellect acts "about singular contingent things." (*Summa* I-II, Q, 14, A. 1) It is within this limited arena of the soul's tensional state – this country of the soul's being – that will and intellect struggle to maintain a sustained and sustaining habit of being. In recognizing that this country of the discrete soul is sovereign in creation but not absolute over being, we begin to unravel a necessary relation of intellect to the common good of creation, the office of the soul as steward of being. The actions of the practical intellect, through the habit of prudence, are seen to be properly directed to the common good, but as a means to the ultimate fulfillment of the soul's own being. The perfection of the discrete soul is paramount in all actions of the will, and that perfection requires the orienting offices of the speculative intellect – of the singular, the simple, intellect in its speculative mode.

But there is once more a delicate point at this juncture of our thought: While we may understand this relationship of practical to speculative intellect as modal actions, we must recognize as well that actions for the common good are not directly and at once and immediately and explicitly willed to the soul's self-interest. For where such is the intent of action, the danger becomes that the self once more is in danger of becoming its own final end, the illusional state we have just considered. A proximate good to the intellect, always properly a means to a greater good, is substituted for that greater good, that rest of perfection of the soul in the Perfect Good.

Except for the actual nature of the soul, such a concern for the self by the self as its own end might appear valid, which is one reason it is so convenient to deny the existence of the soul. A present good of the acting soul can thus be accepted as the final end of the acts of making. When pressed as exhibiting an apparent selfishness, the concession may be to an indulgence in acts for the "common good" defined in libertarian context. It might then seem to follow that the will would experience that delight which is its rest in a proper end. But this could be only, as Thomas might put it, "if man were his own ultimate end." Only then would such "consideration and ordering of his actions and passions be his happiness." (*Summa* I-II, Q. 3, A. 5, Reply Obj. 3) We note here the positing of those conditions assumed of intellect by Modernist thought as long ago anticipated and rejected by Thomas. The *intention* of will in such thought posits a lesser good as the greater good, but more often than not the accidental effects in the contingent existential world blossom as evil effects. We make this point to be reminded that willfulness does not necessarily intend evil. It more often only oversimplifies the complexity of good in its own self-interest. Intention is an act of the will regarding an end, a movement toward an ultimate end, but it cannot intend an evil to itself. Even Milton's Satan knows this, commanding therefore, "Evil, be thou my good." Evil effect upon the body of being, things in themselves, is an inevitable but not decisive consequence to being itself.

Modernist thought, what we have argued as have others to be a secular gnosticism, assumes that a proper right will is exclusively the self-centered concern for the immediate good of the self. Again and again this proves the true intent when the elaborate camouflage of that assumption is reduced out of the forest of the arguments that shield the assumption. It is, nevertheless, an assumption about an ultimate good, even though we witness disturbing means to that good as they unfold in actions toward it. Such an instance is Hobbes's assumption of the natural right of self-preservation, which only serves to advance human nature as mechanistic. That this is so is evident as well in certain strains of physics and psychology that follow in Hobbes's train of thought. And Hegel will explore, out of such beginnings, the mechanisms of being as machine. (For him Absolute Idea is the truth of being as a closed system established by the articulation of facts by intellect.) Trapped within such Modernist inclinations intent upon separating idea and intellect, increasingly entrapped by a closed world, one arrives at a secularized Platonism we have said. That becomes the principle of intellect justifying a violent possession of the world through idea as system. Even Kant, struggling to escape that closing world, posits his categorical imperative within that ambiance of thought beginning to pervade Western intellect: the first principle of Modernism – that man is autonomous through the power of his intellect. Thus one wills the good: "Act on maxims which at the same time have for their object themselves as universal laws of nature."

Those principles that were understood as self-evident to intellect through the gift of being, as Thomas holds, are replaced by intellect itself as the supreme principle unanchored beyond the accidents of its being. Kant's *ought* as imperative, uttered by reason, has the meaning of a universal law, but it is a law decreed by reason, and so we are left in the closed world of circular argument. All such attempts must fail at last, since intellect cannot make an end for itself suitable to the delight of rest in it as if it were an ultimate end. The attempt contradicts the limits of man's *given* nature as created intellect. The assumptions out of which such entrapments of intellect proceed include the assumption that intellect itself is both angelic and animalistic, though such a presuming soul is not likely to admit that such a term as *angelism* is applicable to it.

This entrapment of intellect as hostage to idea, while it supposes itself the sovereign of idea (we are contending) must be avoided through the virtue of piety toward being. That is the necessary deportment of intellect in its own proximate ground, namely the soul – the deportment we have named as the habit of being. We have said that this habit is properly an ordinate openness to existential reality, including the reality of the self. Through such a deportment of intellect governed by will, existing creatures are neither rejected by the presumption that intellect is angelic in its mode nor submitted to the tyranny of intellect. Not when piety is the bearing of intellect toward reality. But a tyranny of intellect toward being closes intellect against being when its response to all existence other than the closing intellect itself is as if creation were an uncaused arena within which the soul alone defines the limits and ends of actions. On the other hand, as we have been saying, a proper openness to being allows the movement of the soul toward its fulfillment, a movement which is not self-centered. It is in knowing this truth that the soul is made truly free.

Let us add to this point that we do not mean here to argue for an indifference of the soul to itself in its movement, for selflessness such as we describe is not indifference to self. Indifference to self is at best a species of false humility, in which the potentially full existence of the self is impiously denigrated. What one recognizes in a proper address to existence, through the habits of our being which we have called *making*, is an acceptance of existences as mediate ends to transcendence through *making*. It requires of us, that is, that we adhere lovingly to existing things for themselves, our *making* thereby a praising of their existence in the name of God. That is why St. Thomas is at such pains to remind us often that the road to God is through our senses and so through the existential reality which is the matrix of finitudes. Such is the consort of circumstances within which the discrete soul *becomes*. The existing soul is in this respect itself mediate in its transformation by grace. The habit of being, in this regard, is a repeated putting off of the old man and the putting on of the new. And in such a participation of will to becoming lies the true and proper self-love.

XIV

We have been attempting to speak of an openness of the soul to being as the deportment suited to its fulfillment. Though it is no simple matter to be certain, on the evidence possible to my own intellect, to conclude that another person's deportment unquestionably reveals such an openness by his actions, we may nevertheless hold the principle as valid, since we know instances of such deportment in ourselves, from our own experience. It is not a deportment out of a necessary, imposed imperative, although we may judge after long reflection that it is imperative to the soul itself that it practice the habit of that openness in its own interest. That is, the soul must will that deportment for itself as steadily as possible. Still, we know how uncertain is our assurance that what we speak of as proper motive in action, either in the actions of others or of ourselves, is a speaking of the truth.

This seems an awkward putting of the difficulty, by defining and redefining and resaying the nature of the deportment we know to be that which is proper to the soul. It is tedious to consider. And it is even more difficult to bear ourselves with that deportment. No wonder that we take refuge in clichés: Life is a challenge; motive is never pure; even, the road to Hell is paved with good intentions. Such is the embroilment of my will in its attempt to move my soul toward a proper end that I require a supporting grace in the attempt, for which I pray after confessing. I have left undone those things which I ought to have done, and I have done those things which I ought not to have done, and there is no health in me. There follows a plea for restoration of the penitent. The restoration, in relation to intellectual action, is possible when the obstacle to restoration, the will itself, is righted. For it is will which is the actual obstacle and not circumstances, however formidable those circumstances. That is a principle to hold, if we believe that not only the evils of the day are sufficient to the day, but that we are made adequate by our nature to overcome each day's evil.

The more we consider the problem of good's engagement of the will, the more complicated the problem appears, so we might well spend ourselves in volume upon volume, attempting to order the difficulty to intellect. The literature is formidable in its volume, those works devoted to ethics by desperate intellects ancient and modern. One might be so overwhelmed by that offering that, with Eliot, one prays relief from "These matters that with myself I too much discuss/ Too much explain." We find that relief, I propose, signaled to us by an actual experience to ourselves as person. And we discover it in a memory of actual experience as person. It is that experience we know rationally by its consequence. And in that rational reflection upon experience we understand the peculiar gift in that experience as preceding our understanding. We mean, once more, our recognition that, separate from any intellectual intentionality, we discover intellect already possessed of some truth of things as effect of intellectual encounter. It is in this recognition that intellect is set upon the arduous journey in an attempt to recover such a primal openness of intellect to existence. Encounter is intentionally pursued, through a habit more or less established according to an intentionality to the good of the intellect. That habit in its ordinate effect on intellectual deportment we have already named: an openness of the soul to being, an openness toward creation in general. That is a deportment which is properly both sacral and sacrificial of the self.

Not that such deportment will free us of the danger in our intentional good. Far from it. But through that openness we may the better discover the nature of the good itself which is beyond intentionality. If we speak of the nature of that deportment we should desire, as we "feel" compelled to do, we might do so in the words of Father Smith, from Walker Percy's *Thanatos Syndrome*: He speaks of a spiritual deportment in which we "keep hope and have a loving heart and do not secretly wish for the death of others." That is a deportment approachable, but only through the trying and failing and trying again to achieve the habit of openness. It involves saying what is true, insofar as words may say what is true, with the realization always underlying that habit that our *saying*, like our seeing, can only be partial. We might put it another way: The deportment required is that of a witness to the reality of our own person, not as a person intended by its own will, but as intended by the gift of its own nature to be this specific person. Such is the proper, proximate object of desire of the soul in its relation to creation. It is, as Walker Percy among others might declare or Francis of Assisi represent, the deportment of the saint.

This habit of being which we affirm as the saint's is most unlikely to be acquired through direct intention to become a saint. The history of Percy's Father Smith is intricate and telling to this seemingly simplistic assertion.

Father Smith has had to travel through the subtle deserts of Modernism to arrive in that Louisiana firetower. The stages of his journey into his latest desert retreat make him a figure of the Modernist intellectual. But his journey in the cumulative habit of his being increasingly sustains Father Smith. However recognizable in its contemporary manifestations, his is not a spiritual state peculiar to him. That is, the accidents of his journey locate it in a time and place, but those are accidents of the journey and not the journey in its true nature in regard to his soul. This is to say that impinging accidents differ, and through those differences locate events in peculiar times and places. But the soul's journeying is always significantly within an immaterial reality independent of circumstantial accidents. The locus of its own peculiarity as a created spiritual being in no way determines the soul, though signs of that specificity of immaterial being break into the material sphere as spectacle to others – as details of event occurring in *this* time and in *this* place. Such are the accidents we associate with the "biography" of any journeying soul.

We share at our juncture of history, which is the coincidence of soul to time and place, common accidents impinging upon our attempts at a safe journey toward a community in being. But that is the common circumstance to any soul, whatever the century date of its coincidence in history. Still, we may speak of the history of this particular generation, as opposed to that of the preceding or succeeding generation. Hence we tend to characterize a generation, such as Father Smith's, by reference to common circumstances. For unavoidably circumstances lend concrete designations, memorialized by our signs. And so we speak of the history of this soul or the history of this generation of souls, the indirection of "history" through which we attempt to engage the realities of the soul. But in respect to the journey of any soul toward its proper end, whatever the inclusive dates on its memorial headstone, we must at last see these particularities of its history designated by time and place as at best illustrative of the deeper reality of its journey.

Our difficulty is that we are limited to remembering a soul first by the material sphere of being that is circumstantial to it.

Having said as much, we see that Father Smith's journey is signified in his reflections on the doctors of the Weimar Republic, moving through to his account of the horrors of Nazi concentration camps, to the horrors of these latter-day practices in the name of the common good that the novel's immediate actions display in a local Louisiana parish. What he sees beneath the circumstantial differences, however, is the common danger in the soul itself independent of the actual, historical circumstances that seem always to trammel the truth in our words. He finds the same danger reflected in the mental institution he has known as patient and in the current institutionalization of the "good" of society through gnostic signs manipulating his present community through medical science as the new god of being. But he knows that history is not sufficient to explain the dark reality beneath the historical phenomena at hand. His concern is for the danger to the soul through intellect's commitment to good intentions. The ends of this "good" intention are not seen in their essence precisely because the accidental surface of history, rather than the essence of action affecting history, is taken as the ultimate end. The violations of being by the particular soul may not be blamed on history. That is the hardest lesson our century has not yet learned. Father Smith sees the underlying horror when abortion and euthanasia as processes practiced upon humanity are supposed as justified by the circumstantial pressures of the material sphere, accepted as salvific of mankind in history. In that view of human actuality, to kill persons is to strengthen society, so that society, the gnostic idol version of it, becomes the ultimate icon commanding intellectual action. Specific creatures, then, are destroyed, with the justification that the act is for "our" own good in response to the necessities of circumstance. Thus moral action is what "history" decrees as necessary.

We are distinguishing the accidents of actions as displayed by the spectacle of events, whose cumulative nature we call history. And we are attempting to set these aside from the essence of the soul which is caught up by accidents, caught up by "history." The distinction is necessary because again and again we are turned by our own words to the particulars of this present complex of circumstances as faced by a present "generation" of citizens, not souls, illustrated by their temporal actions in peculiar circumstances as citizens. And we observe that in those actions, good intention is always dominant as justification of actions. What we do to the material sphere of creation we purport to do for the common good of humanity as it exists circumscribed by that sphere. We are concerned, for instance, to solve any major – i.e., general – medical problem affecting us. But the problem itself is declared a major priority in relation to its statistical designations derived from the accidents of history, so that the center of our agitated concern seems always the accidents of our existence as persons.

The inclination in such good intention will become, in consequence of definitions askew, the obliteration of diseases affecting "humanity." It will be so whether we speak of AIDS or Alzheimer's. In the pursuit of the "good" thus generalized, the good comes to be defined for us at last as perfections to be effected upon the *accidents* of the soul's existence. The tacit supposition is that if nature's or history's diseases, physical or psychological, can be eradicated, we shall then all be as happy as kings. It is an assumption of thought about the nature of human existence as the sum of its accidents, when all is said and the saying of that climate of thought acted upon in the material realm. The assumption itself will thus continue unexamined, and the accidents of human existence will increasingly redound upon the hapless person, the disoriented soul.

What Percy's Father Smith has come to understand about our nature is most radically different from what we have just asserted as our age's common assumption about that nature. In that difference he knows that, despite the immediate horrors perpetuated in the circumstantial arena of human society by gnostic thought, the realities of the soul in its sojourning of the world are both common and a constant to the soul in any arena at any time. Those realities are to be recognized by the soul through the offices of intellectual action's explorations of the nature of reality itself. The journeying is a constant to any soul in any historical moment because of the created nature of the soul. For the created soul is not *essentially* affected by circumstantial actions, though Modernist thought – like some ancient thought (that out of Democritus which culminates in Stoicism, for instance) – assumes the contrary. If we are what we eat, to speak metaphorically of the Modernist position, then by controlling what others eat, we may make them what we will. Father Smith comes at last to see the inadequacy of that supposition by the gnostic soul. The modern gnostic intends a deconstruction of the limits of being through its own assumption about the limits of being as the material sphere of existence. In that reductionism, accident necessarily replaces essence, so a control of accident becomes the ultimate end of intellectual action. And the most disturbing contradiction in that thought, making it a horror of horrors, is the presumption that such action is in the name of the ultimate good of the community which is thus manipulated. That is the horror Father Smith sets himself against.

It is from this recovered perspective that Father Smith considers illustrative actions, spectacles out of discrete intellectual souls as they engage the material limits of their being. He laments the destructions by those good intentions that are indifferent to the realities of being and are therefore indifferent to Being Itself. At the conclusion of *Thanatos Syndrome*, Father

Smith speaks to those who have, for a variety of reasons, sought him out, summoning him down from his firetower. He sees before him faces, but sees in none of those faces evidence of self-recognition of the discrete person's spiritual condition. That is the horror most disturbing to him, not the spectacles of events in the community. He sees "not a sinner in sight." There is no sense of "guilt," and he concludes from that evidence that "the Great Prince has pulled off his masterpiece." Speaking before this gathering of lost souls, as the TV camera from a local station records the event, he names our "strange times" as divided between two kinds of people. "One are decent, tenderhearted, unbelieving, philanthropic people." The other kind: "[S]ome preachers who tell the truth about the Lord but are themselves often rascals if not thieves." And in shock at the truth he has named, he adds, "What a generation! Believing thieves and decent unbelievers!"

But it is the decent unbelievers who are the more horrifying to him. Father Smith, echoing Flannery O'Connor's shrewd observation about the dangers of sentimentality, asks, "Don't you know where tenderness leads? . . . To the gas chambers." These "civilized tenderhearted souls" before him are signs of the central horror in the disoriented soul, which horror has been spoken to most arrestingly by general spectacle in our century, from the extermination of the Kulaks, to the destruction of the Jews in gas chambers, to the slaughter of Cambodians. "More people have been killed in this century by tenderhearted souls than by cruel barbarians in all other centuries put together."

One anticipates an objection here at once, namely that a Stalin or a Hitler are exceptional. But insofar as one can know good intention, it is not evident that Hitler and Stalin lacked good intention in their sacrifice of some persons to their dreams of a general good. That is Father Smith's and Percy's point. The advocates of seemingly less spectacular destructions by abortion or euthanasia are arresting, when we realize that perhaps 6 million abortions occur each year. And indeed, the statistical evidence increasingly raises these modern good intentions to spectacular horror, as opposed to what might seem otherwise less arresting when left dispersed around the world and not collected statistically. We can but be reminded of Father Smith's sermon to decent Godless people about the destructions out of tenderheartedness when we are told that as of the 1990s there are over a million and a half abortions performed in the United States annually. Percy cries out against this, in his fictions and essays, with our general response being as if he commits a *faux pas* at dinner in polite society.

From this diversion into the thought of a fictional character over the dangers of tenderheartedness, we may return more confidently to our concern that the accidents of history be set aside from the essential nature of the soul's experiences of its own nature. That experience occurs within what we call history, but history is not the significant issue. Through our words we are recalled again and again to a concern for present common actions that purport a common good. But it is in this juncture of the actual soul with accidental circumstances to that actual soul that we discover our own soul's journey as properly made *through* those circumstances. That is the significant commonality to mankind witnessed by the saints. It is made a constant by the nature of the soul as created by God and not by nature or history. It is this commonality which makes us members one of another, and makes us by that membership independent of time or place. We recognize that the nature of the soul is not radically *effected* by the world, because of the gift of its making.

Thus strengthened, the separate soul may develop its open habit of being within the prescribing arena of creation despite circumstances. It does so in the contingent ground to its habit of being, its circumstantial arena. Within that ground lies the occasion to it whereby it may fail to develop its proper habit of being. It may dislocate its sacrificial openness toward its final end as person, beatitude, by *mistaking* mediate ends as ultimate, as we keep insisting in alarm over our acceptance of circumstance as determinate. That is a failure possible particularly when tenderheartedness grows, ungoverned by intellect. But it is not this tenderheartedness that is the problem. It is rather the failure of intellect to govern that intuitive inclination which is not in itself wrong, but only susceptible to disorder when not governed by prudence. In a consequent dislocation of ultimate to mediate end, "feeling" becomes the determining principle, so that one "feels" justified by his good intention. The good intention is declared justified by the "feeling" as if self-evident.

Here let us consider the relation of *knowledge* held by intellect and the *feeling* about that knowledge as experienced. One knows a thing to be true, says that realism out of St. Thomas. And out of that knowing comes a sense of well-being effected by the knowing. The *feeling* is rather a motion by intellect outward, away from itself as possessed of a truth. Feeling is a consent to what is known. One cannot "feel" toward something not known, but rather feels outward from something known, and the known is the truth possessed by intellect. This is to say that one is disposed outward by knowledge held, in a movement of intellect consequent to knowledge. It is a movement opening to understanding of the known. The ambiance of this climate of thought is effected by a consent to the truth known, which is to say that the will is initiated toward an ordinate acceptance of the known in relation to the whole of what might be known. Thus intellect is *dis-posed*, is turned around from an interior obsession with the truth possessed. It is turned outward by virtue of that inner good of intellect because it recognizes that good to be caused by some outer, some other, and not simply by the action of intellect itself. This is to say that its concern turns to a desired "union" with a thing and thus away from a concern with the advantage of the truth known by intellect as the consequence of encounter. We are here attempting to discover the ordinate relation of feeling to truth.

So far, we seem well-spirited in our journey. But we might reflect upon a possible illusion of openness which may subvert the action consequent to a "union" with a thing through encounter. The intellect, as we have said already, may impose an idea it holds of that outer cause, built by its manipulation of the truth held from encounter, and may even find a collective support of the imposition among other intellects. We remarked on that contemporary inclination in respect to our piety toward "Nature," which in a present collective consent imposes idea upon complex reality out of a tenderheartedness unexamined by intellect. It is a pass we seem to have come to, and it becomes daily more pervasive, as a reaction to our recently failed attempt to impose idea on reality in the social sphere, our attempt to deify the State as icon commanding our collective worship. If not the state, then nature must serve desire. In both attempts, there is an underlying validity to good intention, but it becomes perverted through the failure of intellect to order that intention by the truth of reality, most decisively that truth that comes to intellect through reality speaking to intellect of a cause larger than "nature." It is in recognition of that larger cause that we must order our devotion to nature, to creation. But given the general failure to recognize this truth, given the recent attempt to make "Nature" succeed the "State" as a substitute for God, we must consider this present danger somewhat further.

A disturbing complication of our tenderheartedness about "Nature" in the 1990s is the increasing support by science of this latest ideology. In that support, we come to worship the created world through a new religion of *panpsychism*. It develops in response to such generalized concerns as that for over-population. By this approach, over-population is reduced to a problem of a rash on the face of Nature needing cosmetic treatment. In this relation, we might well recall C. S. Lewis's *Discarded Image*. Lewis reminds us that though Nature "may be the oldest of things, . . . *Natura* is the youngest of deities." Our view of the ancient "pagan" world from our twenty-centuries advantage confuses the view held by our own neo-paganism with that ancient version. Lewis says that "what we call 'nature-worship' [then] has never heard of what we call 'Nature.'" For ours is a personification of an abstraction, and so it has not risen "in a genuinely mythopoeic" way. Meanwhile, we are introduced to increasingly sophisticated versions of Nature, through the scientist's authority over the "mythopoeticizing" poet. One might, indeed, follow a development from Teilhard's *Phenomenon of Man*, to James Lovelock's *The Ages of Gaia: A Biography of Our Living Earth*, discovering that as the detailed evidence of scientific knowledge is increasingly turned toward the making of a new myth of creation as an organic whole, the First Cause is increasingly denied. One is tempted to suggest that we are arrived now at a point, metaphysically, which is virtually the same as in the ancient Egyptian cosmology which Eric Voegelin explores in *Israel and Revelation*, that of a closed universe, precedent to the later paganism we associate with the Greco-Roman world or with Northern Europe. It becomes necessary, then, to examine more critically the closure in science itself and its meta-science as practiced by Lovelock or Edward O. Wilson. What is developing from this turning outward to worship *creation*, abstracted to *nature* and then personified as *Natura* through good intentions to a common theology, is a dislocation of the orders of being as opening upon the transcendent.

There comes to hand, as illustration of my concern, Danah Zohar's *The Quantum Self: Human Nature and Consciousness Defined by the New Physics* (Wm. Morrow, 1990). Zohar intends a reconciliation of quantum mechanics and biology, and turns to *panpsychism* in doing so, since that doctrine, which "in one form or another has developed a subcultural modern tradition," is justified in the names of "many modern philosophers and psychologists." "By raising matter to the level of consciousness, or at least by seeing some nascent conscious properties in all matter," these thinkers "have made contact with an underlying reality not wholly alien to their own experiences." Danah Zohar names here Spinoza, Leibniz, William James, Teilhard de Chardin, Whitehead, and will later necessarily introduce Bergson. What she does not do is consider the intense critique of this aspect of their thought which one finds in Maritain or Gilson or Voegelin or others. One of the questions these examiners raise against the solution of these philosophers and psychologists in finding "nascent conscious properties in all matter": How does the lower become acceptable to thought as the first cause of that higher; how does sheer matter yield consciousness? And that question advanced, there lies the more formidable one: Why?

Zohar cites Karl Popper's remark: "Dead matter seems to have more potentialities than merely to produce dead matter." The speculative pursuit here finds in sub-material physics a sub-physics as a substitute for meta-physics. In her Preface, Zohar recalls the inadequacy of answers given the "big" questions in her childhood. "Where my parents' rather set-piece answers and the simple Methodism of my grandparents failed to offer any light, the new physics seemed to hold out to me a kind of poetic vision." Thus "quantum theory seems to serve as a useful metaphor that helps to draw these reflections [on birth, death, empathy, and telepathy] into a new and sharper focus, while at others it seems to promise at least a partial explanation for how consciousness, and hence daily experience, might actually work." The book sets out as "an exercise in metaphor," but ends (she feels) in metaphor's giving way "to evidence, or to what is at least well-grounded speculation about the actual physics of human psychology and its moral and spiritual implications."

Zohar's sense of metaphor is that of attribution, in which there arises a confusion of evidence and speculation. The good intention shifts from a determined concern for the truth of things to a justification of Lovelock's Gaia hypothesis, in which creation is seen as a unified body-spirit. It is as if her vision through intuition, in which a truth is perceived, is increasingly enveloped by an articulation of that vision careless of rational control of that articulation. The new cosmology issuing from the attempt implies an analogy between the atom as microcosm to the universe as macrocosm, to which analogy a speculation is attached: "nascent conscious properties in all matter." It is this species of "properties" which determine "nature" as a being to whose presence all particular things are subordinate. It is thus not very difficult to reduce intellectual man to a surface blemish, from which reduction all manner of gnostic manipulations of man become possible through biotechnology as the new theology whose object is the worship of Gaia.

In the 1990s, we are increasingly caught up in a civil intellectual war. Lacking a vision capable of reconciling "society" and "nature," we discover at the center of the difficulty a failure first of all to reconcile the nature of community itself to the temporal conditions of community existence. The civil war results from a conflict of ideologies which posit uncompromising idols, each commanding as an imperative the concentration of collective power in the name of an idea. At the base of the confusion lies the confusion of symbols. It is through symbols that the concentration of intellectual power is effected, but when these symbols lack a sufficient grounding in reality, when they become thereby Nominalistic, they lose orderly articulation. The most fundamental symbol, whose proper signification has been lost through ideological manipulations, is that of community itself, so that we are no longer comfortable with our intuited necessity as persons to be members one of another in a community of persons. The symptoms of this radical dislocation of community are daily evident, in pitched battles of one sort or another. A present instance sufficient to our point: the current battle between ranchers and environmentalists in the West, over the reintroduction of the timber world in the Southwest and in Yosemite National Park. Meanwhile, the lowly snail-darter in Tennessee waters and the spotted owl in the Northwest still affect policy, though largely forgotten creatures by the popular spirit. On either hand lies a confusion of ultimate and proximate ends.

We may choose this contention between environmentalist and industrialist as illustrative of the problems of "nature" worship. Their pitched battles dramatize the dislocation of community from reality in a sort of allegory of modernist confusions. The confusion exhibited on either hand is out of a sentimentality born of a valid but insufficiently understood sentiment, with the "environment" the abstracted arena of conflict. Perceptions of things in themselves dissolve to an imagined perception of an abstraction as engineered by intellect, which is then taken as if that abstraction were ultimate reality. The transcendent Cause of being is thereby lost.

The dislocation of the environmentalist appears less conspicuous than the more obvious, because measurably, destructions of "nature" by those who appropriate the world's "body" through technology for ends misnamed material ends. For society as "materialistic" is misnomer, even though "materialism" is used on either hand, whether by the immanentist who finds intellect inherent in material existence or the exploiter who denies being to the created existence he exploits. On either side, ideological motive out of abstraction denies the realities of material existence. Thus such a shibboleth as "wealth" may be used on either hand: By the environmentalist in relation to the Edenic existence he would establish by not cutting a tree; by the corporatist technician in relation to his version of Eden as the "bottom line." Neither is a materialist in the deepest sense appropriate to the term. Neither engages the complex reality of existential being in which there are recognized both material and immaterial dimensions to existing things.

Thus emerges, in the intellectual attempts to control the social body, a civil war in which *laissez-faire* as the tacit policy on either hand is in contention for control of the social body. On the one hand, in the name of "nature" as the cause and end of intellectual action, the state is enlisted as executive agent of the policy. On the other, man as the exploiter of "nature" contends as well for the state as executive agent of the alternative policy. The impassioned doctrines such as "natural" goods, untouched by technology, has been a conspicuous symptom of one position, in which doctrine the implication is that those made things such as fertilizer or insecticides are not "real" things and are therefore evil in almost the orthodox sense of evil – i.e., as an absence of good. That means that the reductionist doctrine will not be prepared to deal with botulism or cancer, except as caused by man-made perversions of nature. Nature itself cannot be a cause, since evil is not in it. Meanwhile, the impassioned doctrine of corporatism would command primacy over the world's body to its own opposing ends. The contention comes more and more to be reflected in the besieging of state offices by lobbyists of these antagonistic factions. The intention is to command the structure of the state in order to impose doctrine by political power.

If one reads Paul H. Weaver's *The Suicidal Corporation* (Simon and Schuster, 1988), he is likely to conclude that these principles in contention are indeed but factions out of the same reductionist abstractionism, and Edith Efron, in an extended essay on the book (*American Spectator*, June 1988), catches the point of dislocation. She observes, out of Weaver's accumulated evidence, that the founding fathers of corporatism (Rockefeller, Vanderbilt, Carnegie, Mellon, and so on) manipulated reality in such a way as to prepare the ground for both the economic liberal and economic conservative forces that have wrestled to a draw in the twentieth century. "With their left hands, they gouged out special favors from the state (cartels, trusts, monopolies, tariffs, subsidies, land grants) and ruled over their 'scientifically' organized fiefdoms. And with their right hands, they were altruists. They granted that profits were necessary, but ceaselessly proclaimed themselves . . . to be dedicated, above all else, to society, to their communities and to the welfare of others." What Weaver himself concludes of these corporate founding fathers, who are a radical departure from those earlier political fathers at the time of our national founding, is that they are visionaries but that their vision is singularly Modernist in our sense of that term.

Efron summarized: "[T]hey were revolutionary-scientific-collectivists who saw great uses for the state, had no use whatsoever for the free market, and wanted to organize and control their own markets." It is an important historical fact that they established as necessary to the program envisioned the institution of "public relations," which intended to serve (as one of its founders, Edward L. Bernays put it) an "invisible government." Our concern for the subversion of elected representatives at the federal and state levels of government by "public relations" lobbyists reveals how late we react against this invisible government "as formalized agencies of special interests."

The address to existential reality by either environmentalist or corporatist is that each distorts a mediate end into an illusion of a final end by reductionism and then celebrates the dream thus established as in the public interest. It may not be said without considerable modification that a deliberate evil is intentional in the body of doctrine advanced on either side. More certainly, however, we may say that a "good" is intended whose reality is not an actual but a putative good. In the name of the common good, accepted as ultimate, either faction in their contentions for our soul may become entrapped in history and in nature by their strategy. The proximate effect, at the level of the "rank and file" participants, is the necessity of a commitment of the soul to a position as enlistee in a temporal civil war. What may eventually occur to us is the realization that this civil war, apparently engaged in the circumstances of community as if in its interest, is more fundamentally a war within the separate soul itself. For by its commitment to a reduction, which it makes to appear an enlargement – its own mediate end projected as ultimate – that soul succeeds in reducing itself from its proper movement toward fulfillment. We are speaking here of the soul of the disoriented environmentalist and of the disoriented corporatist.

We have urged that desirable fulfillment results when mediate ends are ordered proportionately to an ultimate end. What is required is that balance we have considered, whose prayer for its steady maintenance is, "Teach us to care and not to care." This is to say an obvious truth, from St. Thomas's perspective, which because obvious on one hand or because rejected on the other may be either carelessly presumed or not entertained at all by intellect. That is why the simple and the obvious must be so often repeated. The obvious truth is that intellect is responsible for an orientation of the soul's inclinations to the good that allows its actions of good intention to avoid the evil effects of a good mistaken in its proper proportionality upon ultimate good.

XV

The philosophy supporting orthodoxy, out of St. Thomas Aquinas, holds that an ordinate movement of the soul toward its end is possible through ordered habits of the practical intellect. The practical intellect as an extension of the speculative intellect turns the soul outward. Consequently, the movement is through the proximate other that it addresses in its actions of making, and since that larger end is seen as the significant end, its makings are appropriate to the limits of the common good without foreclosing the soul from its ultimate good. It will not ignore the lesser good, but neither will it mistake the lesser for the greater. It cares, and does not care.

Let us consider, speculatively, that it is through actions of the practical intellect, with its intent to the common good as a proximate end, that this discrete agent of the action of making is enjourneyed beyond the immediate proximate good upon which it is intent. The discretely existing person, we say, may thereby be habitually recovered toward transcendent end, an end which it *naturally* desires, since that desire befits its given nature. The will's rest in a perfection of the discrete person's unique being is the ultimate end, but when examined from the intellect's point of view within circumstantial limits to knowing, there rather appears an indirection at work to accomplish that ultimate end. One might put it figuratively in relation to the sailing ship's necessity to tack into the wind. And it is in such proximate necessity of tacking that intellect becomes endangered. It may take the proximate leg of the journey for the whole of the journey, and especially when the intellect, operating as practical, mistakes that operation as the full dimension of its operation rather than as an *extension*. Practical intellect thus becomes dominant. In this direction of its extension, the practical intellect may well end up with pragmatism as its ultimate range. The speculative will thus be reduced to residual. In the issue, the end of a new "pragmatic" intellect will take its well-being as limited to proximate circumstances.

On the other hand, when the practical intellect and speculative intellect are in accord, they are more singularly related than suggested by our terming them separately. By our separate naming it is as if they were "members one of another" rather than they are the same undivided property of the soul seen under separate aspects by the necessity to our finite discursive intellect itself as it attempts to understand its own operation. It is in a simplicity of action, through an openness to being, that intellect becomes self-forgetting, the mystery of which self-forgetfulness is the person's movement, his action of self-fulfillment. We must recognize the paradox of indirection of our action as a direction through cumulative actions of the legs of the journey constituting the course of the larger journey toward ultimate end. Thus recognition within the keep of intellect as speculative sees the practical intellect may be tempted to the confines of proximate created beings and thus fall short of its transcendent end. The repeated tacking necessary may become simplified into a steady tangent from the true course without the offices of the speculative to the navigation of the soul. In such failing lies the prospect of proximate ends as idol, through which the soul at last worships itself as an end. For there are many alluring islands along the way of our seeking the continent of our true country, and none more alluring than that temptation to become sole proprietor of the self as islanded.

In contending that man, by his actions as maker, makes himself, we are following Thomistic thought, though the assertion may at first appear somewhat irregular. I find support in Gilson's exposition of the relation of the potential in the creatures of nature in respect to the glory of God. ("The Glory of God," *The Spirit of Mediaeval Philosophy*.) In exploring the scholastic extension upon classical thought, as clarified by revelation for St. Thomas, Gilson reminds us (out of Aristotle) that an "effect always bears a likeness to its cause." It follows that made creatures, which are the effect of creation by Being Itself, are analogous to God "merely by force of existing." Creatures do so proportionate to their given natures, but are not bearers of resemblance as if begotten rather than as made.

The difference most conspicuous here is the distinction between causation in Being Itself and causation as bequeathed proportionately to made things as likenesses by effect. In respect to creatures, causality in things differs between the Greek and the Christian perspective upon the question. For Aristotle, existing creatures (such is his understanding of a general principle in nature) "move themselves in order to acquire their own proper substantiality and to imitate . . . the divine perfection of the unmoved mover." (Gilson's summary.) But St. Thomas holds that things move themselves "in order to acquire the fullness of being." It is an important difference, in that in moving from the *degree* of an initial realized being as made to a *perfec-*

tion of potential being, they thereby "perfect their likeness to God." Christian causality, therefore, is "a sequel and an analogue of creation," though it is not actually *creative*. That is, its becoming is not out of nothing, anymore than its causal acts as effecting eternal things is capable of bringing any *thing* out of *nothing*. God as Being is perfect. Made creatures as beings in consequence of the effect of creation by God are "open to further possibilities" of being that have to be acquired by action. Creatures "attain to the perfection of their being" by the exercise of "their proper operations." And by that exercise, they consequently bear likeness to God both by their actual existence and by their causality, which is the operation of their becoming.

So far, the argument has been in regard to created things in general. (Gilson gives us the texts for the argument out of several treatises by Thomas, especially the *Summa*, *De Potentia*, and *Contra Gentiles*.) When we turn more specifically to man as a made creature, we recall that his likeness to God is according to his nature, and that the nature as peculiar to man is his intellectual being. In realizing the full potential of that being according to the proper operation of his nature, he does so insofar as he is proportionately like God as creator, as maker. It is in this respect that man is called by St. Paul "God's coadjutor" or, says Gilson, in the "high words of Dionysus" man is in the world "to become a co-operator with God."

This aspect of his nature commits man as steward of being in a particular way, differing from the responsibility to being of any other made thing. For man recognizes that responsibility and comes to know it as shared by other things, but by each according to its own nature. His knowing, then, is a special burden as it were (as he may see that gift of knowing in opposition to the limits of other made things). He is committed by this knowing to the realizing of his own potentiality, but also to the potentiality of other things as steward of other things of nature. It is thus that he is "co-operator with God." Each existing thing serves "as an instrument for the creative work of God," but man serves particularly in relation to the coming-to-be of things, not only of himself, but of other things. That is an operation of his special nature as an image of God.

Now if we say that man realizes perfection through operating according to his special nature, as coadjutor or co-operator, the object of his making is to enable the incomplete thing to its completeness. That is why Thomas, for instance, says that the poet as maker has as his first responsibility the good of the thing he makes, for in making it good in itself he perfects it insofar as it ultimately depends as a likeness from the creator God, not from man the maker. The action of this making is the office of stewardship attendant upon the operation of man's given nature, the realization of created possibilities and among those possibilities to things realized one instance is the poem. The poet does not create the *possibility*; he executes the possibility toward its perfection.

Now, since as steward man is most directly concerned with the realization of his own perfection, whereby he fulfills his peculiar likeness to God, and since that requires the operation of his nature to its fullest, the fullness of his operation corresponds necessarily to the fullness of his potential being. It is in this sense, then, that in making, man may be said to make himself. Thus it is that his making is the proper habit of his being. By acting according to his nature, a making is effected. And furthermore he shares, by analogy, another aspect with his creator. For since an effect always bears a likeness to its cause, and since man shares thereby in causality, the thing he makes bears a likeness to him insofar as he may be said to be its cause. We know, for this reason, the made thing to be born out of a particular person. Knowing Yeats or Eliot, we recognize this unidentified poem as "by" Yeats or Eliot.

If we speak of this inevitability of effect as bearing upon man himself as maker, we do so remembering that in *making* himself he does not *create* himself, though pride may tempt him to that supposition. Nor do we mean that in his participation in his own becoming, which is dependent in his created and already existing possibilities as person, he necessarily does so by his own deliberate, rational intent. By intent he considers his own being as primary to the exclusion of all other responsibilities of his stewardship. But the self as object of an intent of self-fulfillment easily loses orientation, loses the more fundamental concern of that fulfillment, which is a perfection of itself *as a likeness of God*. A reduction of the complexity of self-fulfillment, whereby rational intellect cares only for its own becoming, will end in an unbecoming – will end in an isolation at last through the diminution of the self.

We must make it clear, however, that an ordinate concern for self-perfection is not only desirable but necessary. For that reason, for instance, there is that necessary attention of intellect to itself, its making of itself as rationally perfected through its concentrated, deliberative attention to its gifts as intellect. That is, after all, the nature of that self-discipline we call "education." At the same time we will recognize that the operation of the virtues of rational intellect is but one of the operations proper to the nature of man as steward of being in service to his own beatitude. *Caritas*, for instance, is a virtue whose action is outward from the self. One loves all created things, in that they are created; in that each thing is by virtue of its very existence through proportionality a bearer of some likeness of its creator, to be held by intellect in that respect. The complex responsibility of man's created nature is aptly summed in saying he *is*, by his analogous likeness to his creator, *steward* of being. It will follow from that recognition that his beatitude is through the perfection of his stewardship under the auspices of his practical intellect. The perfected action of his created nature, which in its perfected state is continuous perfection, is a created possibility in which alone hope rests at last.

We will recognize, out of such speculation, that the selfless action for the common good through the offices of stewardship, whereby through a seeming indirection that soul becomes ordinate to its own proper end, is fraught with dangers of selfishness at every moment. Selfless action may be neither absolutely unself-reflecting nor solely self-reflecting without damage to the person underway, the person in the making. The balance in self-love is that which is maintained between the practical intellect's necessity to care for the common good and the speculative intellect's necessity to care for the soul's proper end. The paradoxical assurance that "he who would save his life must lose it" speaks to this delicate balance of the soul's deportment in the world through intellectual action. It is, then, action at once responsive to the proximate circumstances of the soul's becoming in the conditions of time and place and to that progressive motion toward its perfection.

We may know this condition to our journeying, without understanding what we know. And in attempting to understand what we know, as we must do, we find it necessary to come to words, another of those very dangerous islands along the journey's way. Thus in speaking of this balanced action of intellect in its effect upon the agent soul, we reflect upon that reality through divisive terms, while recognizing intuitively that such diverse terms as *practical* and *speculative* point toward a being simple in its actuality. That is why we must be constantly mindful in our meditation that the intellect which allows meditation is not a composite, anymore than the person is a composite of body and soul.

What we begin to uncover is that, through such terms, we attempt to speak of an active disposition of intellect toward its object of knowing; from there, we recognize that objects of intellection are of two species – those of mediate ends and those of ultimate end. The first moves the will to act out of a principle perceived intuitively, the principle of being itself. But the movement of the will is both toward a proximate object and, often with less certainty of knowing, toward an ultimate object. In the first, the will acts proximately to the common good; in the second toward the ultimate good of the soul's perfection, which is beatitude. In the first movement of will, the will centers its desire in the mediate object, in an action which is properly a means toward a final end. In the second movement, the object achieved having been joined in understanding, desire in the will is replaced by a happiness of being which stills desire. That at its ultimate extent is the state of perfection of the discrete soul which is called beatitude.

Following St. Thomas, then, let us say that there is a drawing of a being (the intellectual creature) toward a perfection of its being which is its final end. It is a drawing responded to out of that being's given nature as *intellectual* creature, a response of the will which is complicated for the will since its response is discursively singular. That is, intellect encounters singulars, not the whole of being. In addition, its response is to objects often differing in their place in the orders of being, and that is a complication to understanding. Response is out of the intellect's nature, a knowing response which is limited by the intellect's finitude as knowing creature. The will's acts of knowing are of objects, first, in the proximate arena of its circumstance. But second those acts are *toward* an object transcending all circumstance. In the first, the will is moved by desire in an action of knowing, but the created object drawing that action is suited to intellect's knowing it as a means. Nevertheless, the accomplishment through that action has a certain aspect of an end, requiring an accomplishment of that mediate end as an actuality of knowing, out of the will's movement from desire. Because it is a mediate end, however, a possible consequence is that the will is easily tempted to a rest in the mediate end, taking it not only as a good, but as a sufficient good. That is a direction taken toward "worldliness," which is not in and of itself evil. For mediate ends are not by their nature evil. The evil lies in the taking, in the elevation of the mediate end to ultimate by intellect, the procedure of the will toward an idolatry of the mediate, as we suggested.

The means to the intellectual creature's proper end are so various and so multiple in complexity that the labor of choice under the realization that the intellect is imperfect exacerbates the will's desire for rest. It may, in attempting to escape despair in the pressure of the complexity of circumstances confronting choice, submit to a proximate comfort in a moment, though so long as it is not dead it will not rest happily there. We recall Prufrock's desire to retreat to the surface of social intercourse, through the wit of words, drowning his "self" in the chambers of the ebb and flow of social chit-chat. But we do not escape the pathos enveloping his words, which speaks anything but his expectation of happiness in such suicide. Certainly the will grows weary as the intellect grows perplexed by the disparity between its knowing and its understanding. What a relief it would be, what pressures removed from practical labors, could one but rest in the object, however limited as merely proximate. But St. Thomas reminds us, "[I]t is the object which specifies the act [i.e., determines the species of the act], but the manner of acting depends upon the agent, and hence is perfect or imperfect according to the condition of the agent." (*Summa* I-II, Q. 11, A. 4)

Proximate ends, even when rightly chosen in relation to the unique nature of the intellectual creature, are diverse. Not only are means multiple but quite unequal to one soul's proximate circumstances as compared to another soul's, even though the circumstances are seen as common. What would *I* have done in the same circumstances? That is a question asked to prevent a rush to judgment in response to the spectacle of event as centering on another soul. Thus it may be that the calling proper to one soul may lead it to active martyrdom, while the calling of another would in similar circumstances lead it to its proper end through endurance of its circumstantial world in ways quite removed from the apparent activism of the martyr. It is not only difficult for the particular soul to discover its true calling through intellectual action within its circumstantial limits. It is also sometimes most difficult to accept that calling under the world's temptations to rest, which we have said are not actually the world's but in the soul itself. The calling to endure often appears to lack the heroic coloring which we may superficially see in martyrdom. We may long for arrows or stones, and thus betray our proper calling.

Given such confusing circumstances, in which a resolution to the soul through an action of martyrdom seems desirable, it is quite possible for the will to succumb to pride, thus compromising the soul at a high moment of drama in the world as it makes supreme sacrifice in pursuit of martyrdom. We remember a dramatic rendering of this moment of high drama in T. S. Eliot's *Murder in the Cathedral*, in which Thomas à Becket very nearly embraces martyrdom out of pride. At the last moment he resists the tempter, declaring that, "This is the greatest treason:/ To do the right thing for the wrong reason." But it is no less compromising of the soul's beatitude to refuse its mundane labors, its day-to-day unspectacular offices of stewardship which remain uncelebrated by the world because spectacle does not attach to them. The *enduring* of circumstances may be heroic action toward beatitude, even though such action may not be remembered in our obituary. What we are saying then is this: At any level of the will's action, whether in the routine exercise of daily offices or on large dramatic stages of the world, in the most "mundane" of actions or in moments of high drama suited to spectacle, the will is susceptible to this greatest treason: a great refusal whereby it becomes in the end the object of its own desire. That is the true nature of spiritual suicide.

Dramatic moments captivate us. We elevate and revere such witnesses to us of our possibly heroic end as we see in Oedipus or Othello. And we may take Eliot's Becket as heroic. But the attempt Eliot makes is to move the question of action beyond the heroic, beyond that limited arena Prufrock is capable of perceiving in which the poles of possibility appear to him limited. We see Prufrock's recognition of an antipathy between his own spiritual state and that of the hero. "I am not Prince Hamlet, nor was meant to be." What he does not see – nor Eliot himself clearly till much later in his own journeying, I believe – is that Prufrock or Hamlet as person is *meant to be* beyond the reduced arena defined by Prufrock at one extreme and by Hamlet at the other. The distinction at last is between heroic action and saintly action, which though not mutually exclusive nevertheless appear more appealing in a worldly perspective when heroic. The heroic admits of spectacle as accident of action, a concern foreign to the actualities of sainthood. To put the point suggestively, we are likely to feel more sympathy for a hero than for a saint because the hero appears more "interesting" through the spectacle attached to his actions in the world. We mistakenly see spectacle as true sign, without recognizing the likelihood that we rest in spectacle as accident, rather than moving through it to essence. The intent here is not to denigrate our inclination to "hero worship," which is important to our mediate concerns, but to put the heroic in perspective relative to the saintly.

We happen at this moment of mankind's history to be very much confused in our civil deportment largely because we fail to make this distinction between hero and saint. We are an age which has, more or less, abandoned the saint in favor of the hero, but we carry residually expectations of sainthood in our heroes. When the hero fails, as in some respects he is bound to do since the nature of the hero's act is that he must act beyond the fullness of knowing (consider Oedipus), we turn from him, and increasingly we turn into cynicism. But if we do not see speculatively the hero against the larger perspective suited to the saint, we will inevitably see him in a reduced dimension in relation to the traitor. And here our judgment, we recall once more from St. Thomas, is in our own manner of acting as agent – that is, according to our condition in reality as we judge the hero.

Within the body of community, several and lesser members than hero or saint sustain that body by their own actions toward the common good. And so we value, or must learn to value, actions more simply in relation to the spectacle attendant upon the heroic. We tend to measure ourselves against the hero as ultimate measure of human potentiality, rather than the saint. In ordinary deportment to the common good, however, there are seldom moments promising high drama, in evidence of which the occasional event lifts an anonymous person to celebrity status. Here, a passing stranger rescues a child. There, a citizen calls "city hall" to account and loses his job thereby. But opportunity for such actions are seldom, and when they come, the spectacle itself obscures the reality to be pursued by our understanding: Our deportment in the common good is essential in nature, whether raised to spectacle in a moment's event or forever obscure in history's confusing moments. In addition, for most of us a continuing labor of intellect in act such as required of our several callings seems hardly to promise that glory we think we see in a Thomas à Becket. But such a glory, though we sometimes may see it contrasted to our own intellectual actions in the circumstantial world, is glory taken amiss when we would require that it be certified by spectacle. The prospect of Beatitude, save occasionally as with Mother Teresa, is hardly matter for the daily press.

We must recover a recognition: The sacrificial openness to the world, such as is required of the discrete soul in its journey toward beatitude, differs widely in respect to the greater or lesser spectacle that may attend it. Not to see this leads to our romanticizing sainthood, thereby reducing it to the level of the heroic only. The effect of our distortion will be our self-temptation to cynicism because mere heroes must fail as saints. We become victim, therefore, to sardonic self-denigration, since in the failed hero we see ourselves as having failed. Meanwhile, the courage of an open sacrifice to one's calling, if we attempt that calling as a teacher or farmer or whatever, involves at every moment the danger of a treason of intellect to the soul as we struggle to join the company of the saints. Our emulation of a St. Augustine or St. Stephen, a St. Thomas or St. Becket, is most likely and properly to be through mediate actions quite distinct from theirs. But the routines of life, transformed by proper habits of being, may become something quite other than merely routine to the life of the soul.

We may even discover that the habits of being properly pursued are lively and enlivening habits, a point Eliot recognizes at the turning point of his own life. His recognition, given us indirectly through his gift as poet, we find set down at that turning point of that journey reflected in the body of his poetry, after which point the earlier sardonic irony of his poetry dissolves and the ambiguity of paradox succeeds. Paradox is a complex truth known, but not fully understood. After *The Waste Land* that is the nature of the truth to which Eliot bears witness in his poetry. There is an acceptance of the paradoxical truth made possible to him when he sees a larger reality of the soul than can be accorded it by our spectacle of words. And he expresses this recognition in those lines characterizing the nature of the openness to being which is required of the soul on its journey:

> The awful daring of a moment's surrender
> Which an age of prudence can never retract. . . .

And *prudence*, here, is a use of the term as commonly understood, not in St. Thomas's sense of *prudence*. Prudence here is the fear of making a fool of oneself. That had been Prufrock's great fear. What appears to Eliot's understanding now (at the time of his *Waste Land*) is that this moment of awful daring, this openness of the soul to a vulnerability in the world, is a moment not likely to be "found in our obituaries" nor in memories of any spectacle caught by word or statue. Even in the event of word or statue, those must be inherited by the "beneficent spider." In this view, one may be called to beatitude *through* the most menial task for the common good that one may name, no less than through more heroic or more glorious-seeming actions. In the light of eternity, we must struggle to accept and value whatever our own gift of potential action in the world within the circumstances to our discretely created natures which allow us a prospect of perfection as participating agent in that potential. That is the virtue of hope.

Thus we may come to see, however inadequate the articulation of our seeing, that there are relative and various means to the perfection of soul. The means are as relative and various as the uniqueness of each created soul. The particularities of discrete existences in the world that constitute the circumstances of actual existences, God's plenty, give the discrete intellectual creature great difficulty in any attempt to respond with a habitual, simple, direct action suited to its own proper end, suited to its own perfection. Always, choice of action is necessary, but unless ordered to the acting soul's ultimate end, such actions can only leave that soul in a continuing unrest in the world. For mediate ends can but frustrate that desiring inclination to the ultimate when themselves mistaken as ultimate. As Thomas says, "the will rests absolutely only in what is ultimate." To seize the mediate as an ultimate is, of course, most common. We need only remember the multitude of those who, in the world's eyes, appear "successful" but who exist in a miserable spiritual state. On the other hand, we may name some at least whom we recognize as happily restless, as it were, anticipating perfection but content in the interval in their actions for the common good. It is not uncommon to these that, to the world, they seem most "unsuccessful."

XVI

Through the actions of the practical intellect as an extension of the intuitive, and in consort with the intuitive, in which action there is a losing of the self as the primary object in existence, the self is gained in an openness of its nature beyond self-centeredness. It is an argument that eludes full rational explication, though we need only remember instances of self-forgetfulness when we are turned to some proximate end. In such memory we *know* what we cannot *comprehend* rationally. We forget ourselves in reading a great poem, for instance. We are aware of having forgotten ourselves in the physical labor of putting a plant in the earth. We forget ourselves in our gestures of friendship and love toward another person, or in a spectrum of such gestures toward things other than ourselves. On occasion, indeed, we may so much forget our self as to risk it for some other.

Stories of selfless acts of rescue from fire or flood or wreck are carried in the evening papers, alongside the misdeeds of political or religious or social agents in community, which misdeeds are of course given larger media "play."

This self-forgetfulness, through which we have a knowledge – a "sense" – of our own recovery, is a gain in being which we credit through the speculative intellect. For the speculative intellect may acknowledge grace as operative in such transformation of the self, even if we may continue baffled that neither the speculative nor practical intellect is confident of a full knowledge of this mystery, which is our loving participation in existence. It is, however, by that participation that we become ourselves – act fittingly in relation to our potential. It is not that we necessarily have, antecedently, a conscious intent, whereby we say, if I do this act, I shall fulfill my essential potential, realize my being. Of course, within the proximate conditions wherein the practical intellect functions, mediate goals are consciously perceived and consciously pursued. In respect to that fullness we call beatitude, we do not measure an action against the accomplishment of that effect upon the self. For to attempt that approach to spiritual fulfillment is to assure a continuing attention to the self which prevents that selflessness necessary to the openness of intellect. There is requisite a losing of one's life if it is to be gained, but the sense of life here is more inclusive of our nature than as categorized by safety slogans on the literal highways we travel. That is why we welcome such figures as St. Francis of Assisi, who gives some witness of what is meant by this "losing" of one's life in an open love of existing things.

These actions of intellect, the one we call selfless and the other selfishness, we know in ourselves. And we know them radically different, the one reflecting an open response to circumstantial context, the other a retreat from that context, an attempt to shut it out. The difference lies in our own "manner of acting," a manner not to be charged to the context as the primary determinate cause of our action. In attempting to understand the radical difference in our manners as agent of action, we may well consider intellectual action itself in degrees of its simplicity, giving it the analysis of our reflection. We do so cautiously, aware of the dangers of intellect's dividing the simple, an intellectual action never more dangerous than when turned upon intellect itself. Nevertheless, we venture that in the circumstances to the existence of our intellect, the arena of intellectual action, both modes of our intellect, practical and speculative, if considered as *partial*, help us accept at last that fullness when the rational and intuitive are in mutual balance and concert. That must surely be the condition necessary to our self-forgetfulness.

Finite intellect, for all the strategies of analysis, cannot comprehend *being* in that sense of *comprehend* which means *contain*. The part cannot comprehend the whole. But we nevertheless know though we cannot comprehend ourselves as a whole. And then we also know this whole as part of a larger whole which we cannot comprehend, creation. And we know that this knowledge is valid. We know out of these several knowings the desirable manner toward truth, whose absoluteness we also know we cannot comprehend. In these recognitions, we find ourselves already anticipating aspects of intellect in action, for we are setting a part from whole, while by speculative intuition placing the *what* and *how* of such action in relation to the larger *why*, knowing that *why* to be real but elusive. In this fundamental stage of intellectual action, wherein intellect considers itself, handicapped though it is as a partial being, what it posits is its actions as *practical*. That is the movement of extension of the simple intellect.

We might recognize in this attempt a particular aspect of the practical extension: It is a single action toward a particular object, in a movement by intellect to command a means toward a recognized but not comprehended ultimate reality. In this always-present movement in response to circumstantial contingencies, the single object as the limited necessity to the limited operative principle of practical intellect is perceived by intellect. That much we may understand of intellectual action itself.

It is here that intellect struggles most, in that it seems to be required to lift itself by its own bootstraps. For it is heavily burdened through these encounters of its individual objects by an awareness of itself as an object as well, and the attempt is to escape that awareness of the intellect as its own agent. The attempt lies through a simplicity of action. The simplicity of action toward which we struggle, this self-forgetfulness, we believe consequent to virtues if to be achieved at all. But it is initially and particularly consequent to that virtue of prudence in our ordinate habit of being, supported and sustained by the several virtues, cardinal and theological. It is in this point of our refraction of the simple intellect that we recognize the importance of that virtue called prudence. For through prudence it seems possible to recover the necessary actions of the rational intellect to a support by the intuitive. If the practical intellect in its action is restricted to a single action toward a particular object, that means it is restricted to a discursiveness, requiring by reflection an accommodation of these multiple singular actions to a simplicity of direction under the influence of intuitive intellect. That influence governs toward the soul's larger end.

We have touched on this point to suggest that the actions of the practical intellect are analogous to that tacking in the face of the winds of the world, the always-circumstantial necessities to intellectual action. The larger parameters of the journey at issue is on a line beyond those worldly winds, and to be recovered by a visionary compass reading guiding the journey, a reading made by the speculative intellect. And so we consider: In the actions of the practical intellect, singular actions toward disparate objects within existential circumstances – those circumstances whereby each proximate attainment involves contingencies – present contingent difficulties beyond the practical intellect's full foresight of these consequences. The local island beckoning, the sudden local gale, the unexpected reef – all these are steadily intrusive upon the larger perspective of our journey. At each moment, on each leg of the journey, we are threatened since tempted to a reduction of the means – the tacking against the prevailing winds of the world – to a comfortable end.

Mediate ends thus become final ends to intellect when thus dislocated in its journeying. One must struggle on nevertheless, knowing, though not knowing with full comprehension, the distractions of contingency that are so seductive to our intellectual desire for an end. It is the burden, we might suggest, that is the most significant evidence of that continuing mark of Adam, the burden of a presumption that through intellect we may be as the gods, knowing (i.e., comprehending) both good and evil. The sweat of the brow, in this perspective, is most fundamentally an intellectual sweat, not that simple one of the muscles delving the earth. Despite the limited conditions to its action, the practical intellect must achieve proximate ends. That is the labor whereby it may exercise its stewardship in creation. The larger necessity is a liberation beyond its stewardship of creation, to the adoration of the cause of all creation. But that intellect is incapable of this accomplishment by its own power, despite whatever pretensions by intellect to the contrary, is the reality feeding the virtue of humility, the most difficult virtue of all to our intellectual action.

The recognition that intellect is insufficient to its own rescue, to the lifting of itself above circumstantial limitations, is most ancient. The recognition, indeed, provides the limited arena to the poet within which the tragic hero emerges in our literature. Oedipus, for instance, lacking full knowledge of the circumstances of and the contingencies to his actions, lacking the dimension of a consent to grace in his circumscribed actions, must nevertheless act. His responsibilities to his calling as king demand that he act for the common good, and the ironic complication is that he acts out of what are recognized as good intentions for the common good. We hear the lesser members of that social body, the residents of Thebes, resisting his action, fearing unknown consequences. The difference between Oedipus' necessity to act in the common good and the fear among his subjects of the contingent, proximate effect of such action establishes the tensional ground. These poles help focus not simply a tragedy governed by dark fate out of fated action, but a tragedy of person (Oedipus) out of heroic action.

When we have put aside the element of rashness and the weakness of rational intellect in Oedipus, aspects of his "character" that ally him with ourselves, we value beyond those limits his bearing as hero. Oedipus fallen at the end of *Oedipus the King* is somehow greater than Oedipus at the height of his power and respect as King of Thebes. He moves us through his actions (which are, let us not forget, actions of intellect) beyond the lesser effects of pathos, and perhaps even beyond the country of tragedy itself. For when pity and fear are overcome in that purging that is the effect of tragedy, we are indeed on the verge of a new country. There is a recognition of that new country, though beyond the possibility of Sophocles' understanding, in the conclusion of *Oedipus at Colonus*. We might consider to this point that *Oedipus at Colonus* reveals its protagonist as moved more by intuitive intellect than by rational intellect, and though he is formally the play's protagonist he seems removed from the events dramatized. For a hero governed by the intuitive is less amenable to spectacle, a necessity to drama. One begins to understand through such reflections how it is that dramatic tragedy emerges from religious rituals, rituals through which man attempts to come to terms with the mystery of his being in the circumstantial world. For ritual moves us intellectually beyond the limits of intellect itself, into that country of mind in which a mystery draws us beyond our intellectual finitude. (On the spiritual nature of tragedy in relation to catharsis, see my *Reflective Journey toward Order*, especially in Dante's advance beyond Greek tragedy in relation to catharsis.)

Such then is the communal drama designated tragedy, as opposed to Dante's *Comedy*. We might say for our immediate purposes that tragedy engages the limits of the practical intellect and thereby wakens the speculative in us. We turn to the proximate world after dramatic rituals, such as *Oedipus the King*. We turn to the existential world, knowing that the hero is a hero precisely because he accepts the necessity of intellectual action, which being restricted to the world of circumstantial reality proves consequential beyond the limits of our knowing. The practical intellect must act in the contingent world, within a disquiet to that intellect that results from its knowing the contingency to be beyond its power to control.

That we have largely lost both this awareness of the limits of knowing in relation to contingency and the sense of obligation to action despite the limits explains much of the disarray of Modernist thought in relation to communal action in the world. For with the Modernist assumption of intellect's autonomy, consequential effects are easily discounted. Indeed, the presumption follows from the elected autonomy that contingency is inconsequential, since autonomous intellect assumes a power suited to unforseen consequences. We will solve the resulting "problems" as we come to them. At the point of future necessity, intellect will prove equal to the problem, since intellect, unlike the consequential problem, is independent of the finitudes prescribing the problem as a problem. Such is at least the tacit presumption of intellectual transcendence of reality. And nowhere is the point more generally pressing upon our existence as community than in our current attempts to deal with the technology loosed upon the world by practical intellect once it is freed of its visionary ordination toward a transcendent end through its speculative mode.

If we read that darkly pessimistic analysis of our enslavement to technology, Jacques Ellul's *The Technological Society*, we are tempted to despair. Or we are at least disturbed by the emerging effects upon our *person* by the un-personal dictator of our social world, technology as the new god of being. We begin, slowly and haltingly, to attempt a recovery of the older wisdom which recognizes the limits of autonomous intellect. Intellect disjoined from reality and at play in the field of contingency for some hundreds of years now at last begins to trouble us, though with that uneasiness rises the temptation to a collapse in "anti-Intellectualism." We feel a growing dis-ease with biotechnology as an immediate instance. Increasingly, we are inclined to introduce ethics into science, somewhat desperately. But increasingly we discover ethics possible only if we recover a metaphysical vision that might reorient science itself. Still, in this moment that is ours, in which presumptions by the practical intellect gone astray have effected dislocations of actions in being, we find ourselves with fewer and fewer heroes. And we must seek long before we come upon ordered intellects. The ordered intellect we require is one aware at once of the dangers of intellectual action contingent in intellect itself, resident in "the manner of acting" by the intellectual agent and not in the object of the action as St. Thomas reminds us.

If the intellect must act by extension in its practical power (such is the lesson to be relearned), it must do so in respect to a recovered speculative action. The field of practical intellection is of an order separate from that of the speculative. For the object of the speculative intellect is not the multiple means encountered through discrete and separable objects. It has a singular end, discerned if but faintly through metaphysical vision. The object of the practical intellect is the *useful good.* The object of the speculative intellect is the *unqualified good.* The difficulty which finite intellect has with unqualified good, consequent upon its finiteness, might be described in antithesis to the practical intellect's assumption of autonomy: The speculative temptation is to an assertion of power over being in the interest of its own power to establish unqualified good. That is an assumption by the intellect that it is God. The gnostic error, then, lies in the perversion of the speculative intellect.

In another possibility of failure by intellect, out of intimations of the absolute good, intellect may at first assume a prophetic role, whereby it reduces the contingent existential world in favor of a more direct access to unqualified good. It may then assume the unqualified to be possessed by its own actions, supposed larger than the limited action of its *intimations* of that absolute, of that unqualified good. Such an assumption may effect a suspension of action by the practical intellect. We might observe that Sophocles dramatizes this possibility in Teiresias, who through his visionary powers presumes to transcend Oedipus' contingency. He argues in consequence that any action is obviated by the prophecy itself. His argument rightly infuriates Oedipus, we recall, who is intent on executing a good for Thebes through the powers of action reserved to the king, actions toward the useful good, which good he takes, alas, as unqualified and not as useful good.

In our terms, we might say that *Oedipus the King* dramatizes a contest between the practical and speculative intellect, each projected at a disengaged extreme, the one represented in Oedipus and the other in Teiresias. In the argument over action, both king and seer lose control of practical reason, lacking the virtue of prudence, though both insist on prudence as the special virtue to the position he maintains. In the event, the drama decays to frustrated name-calling as each supposes himself alone committed to the complex truth of things. They lose control, Oedipus because he rejects the balancing of the practical by the speculative, Teiresias because he rejects the balancing of the speculative by the practical. The danger in Oedipus' position is conspicuous, and the consequences of his willfulness are immediate, radically destructive of the common good. The danger in Teiresias is more subtle, as Dante will remind us in his pilgrim's encounter with Teiresias in Hell. There the seer is on an endless treadmill journey in a timeless, placeless dimension, his head turned backward so that he is trapped by the diverse singular objects as phenomena, suited to the practical intellect. He is denied the larger vision of the necessary journey whose singular object is the unqualified good. Dante rebukes the presumption of finite knowledge as adequate to its contingencies, including false prophecy which presumes itself transcendent of the finite.

It is false, since to read contingency as if an event actual in time future, as does Teiresias, is to presume an unqualified seeing of contingency, the tacit assumption of which is the absoluteness of vision in the finite agent.

Put another way, that is the error of focusing the speculative upon the mediate as if the mediate were ultimate. Though Sophocles' seer in fact sees accurately through the maze of contingency, what he sees lacks the saving perspective needed, a perspective Sophocles as maker recognizes as necessary to true vision and which he has already attempted to point toward in *Oedipus at Colonus*. That play is actually made before *Oedipus the King*, a consideration if we suppose Sophocles himself to have reached the limit of his pursuit of mystery through his own speculative intellect, so he returns to the immediate ground out of which the mystery rises speculatively, the ground in which Oedipus and Teiresias contend in that futile contest between the practical and the speculative intellect. Of course Sophocles is not addressing the problem of action for his hero in the terms we are using. But if the terms we are using speak to the truth of the nature of intellect in action, independent of the accidents of time and place, then they are appropriate to Sophocles no less than to St. Thomas. Insofar as a concern for the truth of how things stand is the poet's, both poet and philosopher – both Sophocles and St. Thomas – are concerned with the same reality of experience though their experiences are differently named and within differing circumstantial constrictions to their naming, differing social and political contingencies, the accidents of "history." That is a discovery St. Thomas makes in reading Aristotle, embracing him as *the* Philosopher, though Aristotle never reaches a discovery of Being Itself as the sure ground to philosophy, as Thomas does.

Thomas (*Summa* I-II,Q. 8, A. 3, Reply to 3) remarks that "a useful good and an absolute good are not species equally dividing the good, but are related as that which is for the sake of another and that which is for its own sake." Such is the problem of *means* in relation to *end*, always a complex problem to the will's action since it requires a judgment of the contingent effects of an action of means toward an end. What this means is that my action in this present moment (the only moment possible to action) requires a reasoned judgment of contingent consequences to the context of means in relation to an end intended. That is why, knowledge being finite, the hero acts at last beyond the reach of intellect. The alternative is to assume a position in the chorus, merely reflecting upon possible action, as in a Greek play, or as in Prufrock's long chorus lamenting his own inaction, a chorus that is really an inordinate self-love song.

We have argued that the proper deportment of intellect is an openness to being. It is a principle of action in intellect as moved by will, but an action precedent to the intellect's movement toward an object, either proximate or ultimate, either toward a useful good or toward the unqualified good. It is in this principle of action that we discover something about the modes of the practical and speculative intellect. We may do so, whether we address that reality of action, known by our experience, with a care for a precision of terms such as is the case of an Aristotle or Thomas, or through the poet's care for precision in his imitation of actions related to actuality, such as those celebrated in Aeschylus or Sophocles or Dante. St. Thomas gives us an initiating way, through his distinction between *assent* and *consent* in relation to intellectual action. "To assent," he says, "is as it were, *to agree with something else*, and thus it implies some sort of distance from that to which assent is given." Although the distinction underway is subtle, so that in a gradual loss of precision of language the names *assent* and *consent* "are often used interchangeably," we may recover a point of difference: "[T]o consent is *to sense along with*, and this implies a certain union with the object consented to."

Now in the immediate context of the distinction, Thomas is establishing a relation between *will* and *intellect*. The will, he says, "to which it belongs to tend to the thing itself, is more properly said to *consent* whereas the intellect, whose act does not consist in movement toward the thing, but rather the reverse, is more properly said to *assent*." (*Summa* I-II, Q. 15, A. 1, Reply Obj. 3) What Thomas is concerned to make clear is an aspect of intellect which, by its nature, receives principle into itself in what we might call a passive state of intellect. In this respect, intellect is the object of truth, which in the event becomes a part of its knowing. This is the perspective of the intuitive understanding of truth, the reception of that truth at first marking "some sort of distance from that to which assent is given." Thus intellect, by intuitive assent to being which provides it "knowledge of a principle, brings itself to act with regard to knowledge of conclusions." The will, through willing the end implied by such conclusions, "moves itself to will the means to the end." (*Summa* I-II, Q. 9, A. 3) Intellect through *assent* accepts universal being and truth, stirring the will to action. But will is stirred either to will an end or not will an end. For "[the will is not moved by the intellect and by itself in the same way. It is moved by the intellect with regard to its object, but is moved by itself as to the exercise of its act in respect to the end." (I-II, Q. 9, A. 3, Reply Obj. 3)

Since the will may either will the end perceived through the intellect's assent to being or reject that end, it is in a position of power over its own being sufficient to modify the means to that end. The sort of will-full action we have spoken of as the unmaking of the intellectual creature is thus made possible. What is proper to it is a movement out of the intellect's *assent* to the will's own *consent*. In this movement it wills its own end by its consent. It does not merely *agree with something else* (assent); it actively *senses along with something else* (consent). That *something else*, which will senses *along with,* is being, and the movement implied in *along with* is a proper orientation of will to the cause of being in concert with being, in consent of *being* to *cause*. For, if we say that being depends from the Cause of being, we thereby say as well that being is necessarily oriented both *to* and (through grace) *by* its cause. The right will, then, by its consent, is ordered to its ultimate end, recognizing through that ordering the necessity of proximate actions in the contingent world. Thus by "willing the end," it moves itself "to will the means to the end." (*Summa* I-II, Q. 9, A. 3) In short, will moves itself to the necessity of actions determined by intellect in intellect's practical mode.

We are intent upon some distinction of the modes of the practical and the speculative intellect, toward our concern with action in the common good as a necessary means to the proper end of the discrete soul. In the circumstances of existence, both practical and speculative modes of the intellect are partial in their powers, given the finitude of intellect. We have affirmed that intellect cannot *comprehend* being in that sense of *comprehend* which means to *contain*, though the will would sometimes force the attempt. That is why, in the end, the will must consent along with all being to the one Comprehensive Cause of being, in a movement of will toward that Cause as its final end. Meanwhile, will must not confuse the powers of intellect, forcing the speculative into a role as mover. This is the distortion effecting an illusion of autonomy. Thomas remarks that "the speculative intellect is not a mover, but the practical intellect is." (*Summa* I-II, Q. 9, A. 1, Reply Obj. 2)

In this respect Thomas associates the speculative with a superior reason requiring the consent of the will through that higher mode and not the will's manipulation of that mode. (*Summa* I-II, Q. 15, A. 4) Superior reason is the action of judgment based on divine law, discovered intuitively through the speculative intellect. Inferior reason has as its province, not divine but natural law, and so is committed to the power of its own intellect in that more limited arena, the arena of means to the superior end. It enters that arena through an "extension" of intellect, the practical mode. This, then, is the province of practical reason. And the will's challenge lies in its proper engagement of the practical and speculative so that its own initial *assent* to the conditions of the contingent world (the arena of natural law) moves toward that *consent* required of will when properly oriented to its superior end by its proper uses of inferior means. (See *Summa* I, Q. 79, A. 9; I-II, Q. 74, A. 7)

The knowing that is designated the superior is under the auspices of the speculative intellect; the knowing (and commanding) of the inferior is under the auspices of the practical intellect. In remarking the proper address by will to superior and inferior reason, St. Thomas puts an analogy: "Just as in science we know conclusions through principles, although the knowledge of the principles themselves is not science but something greater, namely, an intuitive understanding, so we consent to the means because of the end, although there is not a consent about the end but something greater, namely, a simple volition." It is this simple volition of the will we have in mind in speaking the necessity of an openness to being proper to intellectual will. (*Summa* I-II, Q. 15, A. 3, Reply Obj. 1) Thus a proper consent to the act of the will belongs ultimately to superior reason (to the speculative intellect) when reason is employed by a right will. And thus the will may escape a confusion of the useful good with that unqualified good which is the soul's proper end, seeing good ordinately in relation to the action of the will.

That escape of confusion is easier pronounced than accomplished. For even given an ordinate role of the practical and speculative intellect, within the conditions of the contingent world, the final end of the soul may seem at particular moments lost – to be submerged by attention to proximate ends because overcome by concerns for the useful good. The actions of intellect in pursuit of useful good is in that realm within which we speak of our suitable actions as to the "common good," actions always tempting us as if to an ultimate end of the soul. For we are inclined by our nature to be "do-gooders." Thus the mediate actions of our calling in the world so easily become an end in themselves, given that the soul by its nature is intent upon accomplishing good. We know the pejorative meaning of that term *do-gooder* as given to members of our community, a meaning which implies an excessiveness that distorts the realities of the existential world through a dislocation of a proper end in the do-gooder. Still, we may not forget that an action for the common good, through a right will and ordinate practical intellect, involves a mystery beyond comprehension and certainly beyond full articulation. For if the soul through actions for the common good may be primarily in act toward its ultimate end, our judgment out of limited comprehension of the relation of useful good to unqualified good is limited, and so we may mistake, misjudge the do-gooder. That is why the epithet do-gooder is such a dangerous one when we presume to use it against another person.

As to that mystery, the speculative intellect suggests to us that the significant over-riding effect of a pursuit of useful good is the rescue, not of a useful good to the common health of the existential world, in our responsibilities as stewards of existential reality, but the rescue through grace of the acting soul itself. Such, once more, is that mystery of our individual becoming, hinted at but not formulated by the directive that we must die to the old man so that the new may be born. That is the necessity in our pursuit of the good which requires of us the constant prayer which is our epigraph, governing our concern for making: "Teach us to care and not to care." For in immanent action to temporal ends lies our transcendent beginning. It is this relation of action to our being through useful good, toward unqualified good, that Jacques Maritain speaks of, out of St. Thomas, when he says in *The Person and the Common Good*: "The person as person insists on serving the community and the common good freely, . . while tending to its own fullness, while transcending itself and the community in a movement toward the transcendent Whole. The person as individual is necessarily bound. . . to serve the community and the common good since it is excelled by them as the part by a whole." It is by the individual, acting through the practical intellect, that the common good is served. It is by the person, receptive through speculative intellect to the order of the common good as dependent upon the unqualified good, that the discrete soul is raised toward the transcendent Whole.

XVII

The gift of intellect, with its powers of engaging reality under the mode of practical or speculative action, is a mystery of our being about which our words seem both endless and indefinite. We shall at last cease from words, but whether with some sense of definiteness is at best problematic. Even so, it is the most fascinating of all subjects because so immediate and constant to our experience of existence. That the fascination breeds tediousness is recognized, even by the most lively intellects, leading Eliot, as we remember, to pray surcease from this concern which we "too much discuss/ Too much explain." And at about the time of Eliot's "Ash-Wednesday" plea, Gilson remarks modern philosophy's "obsession with epistemology" as the problem whose solution is "the necessary pre-condition for philosophy." (*Methodical Realism*, p. 34) For some rescue from our own struggle, then, let us pursue the topic as it is articulated by St. Thomas before we surrender it to the moment's silence. The risk is in preparation for our present consideration of the poet's attempt upon the mystery of intellect as separate from the philosopher's or theologian's.

St. Thomas says that intuition moves intellect, since it is by intuition that we apprehend principles "such . . . as are naturally knowable, both in speculative and in practical matters." (*Summa* I-II, Q. 58, A. 4) Our first concern is to distinguish not only intuition from rational acts of intellect, but even more important, given the decay of terms in our day, *intuition* from *instinct*. *Instinct*, which we are highly practiced in associating with animal behavior, we tend to use interchangeably with *intuition* if careless in our designations. But intuition is an aspect of knowing which we intend to associate with intellect in relation to its action of knowing, an action quite different from animal nature as taken at the level of biological and physiological existence. We assert that intellect *knows* its proper offices, and that this knowing differs from the chemical or neurological relation of animal existence in encounters measurable in material terms and characterized as instinctive behavior. We are concerned to maintain an immaterial dimension to intellectual action, although we do not intend thereby to establish a duality, whereby *person* exists in a divided nature, in an animal and an intellectual-spiritual dichotomy.

In this approach, speculative intellect has as its principal office our growth beyond knowing to an understanding of what is known. The practical intellect is concerned with rational action to this end. Practical reason, Thomas says, "judges and passes sentence on things to be understood." (*Summa* Q. 74, A. 7) We may speak of the action of practical intellect in its relation to speculative understanding: Practical reasoning "may be compared with understanding [by the speculative intellect] as motion with rest." (I, Q. 79, A. 8) But *rest* here is more nearly a wise passiveness than the neutral state the term seems to suggest. It implies, as we have suggested already, an openness to reality beyond the mind's own reality. Thomas declares that the speculative intellect is "directed solely by understanding, the practical intellect solely to action." (*Summa* I, Q79, A. 11) It is the practical intellect that "uses truth (and falsity)" in its action. (*Summa* I, Q. 79, A. 11) The "goal of the speculative intellect is the comprehension of truth," not the use of truth. (*Summa* I, Q. 12, A. 4)

What seems to emerge from Thomas's reflections on the nature of intellect is a suggestion of hierarchical relation between the practical and speculative intellect, though it would be dangerous to the understanding of his argument no doubt to separate the two and assign supremacy to one, a warning we have already made. For such a separation would seem to imply a reduction of what one might call the complementary undivisiveness in the thing itself, the intellect, in its being – as opposed to a necessary practical discursive engagement of its nature through the offices of the rational intellect. The will is nevertheless inclined toward an authority to be gained by such divisiveness. Will, commanding practical intellect, may divide and separate. One remembers William Wordsworth's complaint against empirical science to the point: Science (cf. knowledge, truth) commanded by will may "murder to dissect." The end of that dissection when concentrated upon the intellect itself is the soul divided from the simplicity of its discrete, particular existence; in one aspect of the division, *individual* is divided from *person* through will's perverse intrusion upon being.

The necessary corrective is an understanding larger than the practical intellect's attempt upon the mystery of intellect: the understanding that the practical and speculative are a continuous *one*, out of which arises a vitality of intellect that is indivisible except by the action of intellect turned upon itself. The "vitality" is thereby maimed or killed by a ruthless separation of practical and speculative. One might speak of this delicate engagement of the intellect's nature by an analogy: Dante witnesses, in a visionary moment at the end of the *Divine Comedy*, the mystery of the Godhead, and with an understanding which must then resort to the practical intellect to speak of that moment if at all – if it is to bear witness to the vision. He sees the Triune God, at once indivisible and in a community of simple Oneness. The "limitless light" thus beheld leaves the poet almost dejected by the limited power he possesses as poet to represent it to finite minds. He is nevertheless cast back upon the necessity of using images in order to give some hint of the experience in which he was subsumed for a moment by vision.

What is required, we are saying, is intellectual piety which as least embraces gladly the very limits of intellect, since only through intellect may one approach the ineffable. Put another way: What is required is the will's consent to a mystery of simple existence that is beyond any *full* grasp by either the practical or the speculative intellect, insofar as that grasp would anchor mystery in creation by a possessiveness. But despite the dangers of distortion in exploring a relation of the practical to the speculative intellect, or of the individual to the person, we are still moved by a necessity of intellect itself to partake both rationally and speculatively of intellect's own diverse operations. The intellect may not refuse an attempt at understanding and ordering itself in a proper orientation toward both the created world and the transcendent world. And that is why our intellectual actions must be those of the hero as we struggle to become saint.

In so struggling, given discursiveness as an aspect of finite intellect, one necessarily speaks discursively of the reality of intellect. For in order to speak at all of intellect in its complementary, complex undivisiveness, one speaks divisively. Thus Thomas says, for instance, that the practical intellect "intends the fulfillment of spiritual values." (*Summa* I, Q. 12, A. 4) Not one, but two, intellects seem thus named, the speculative seemingly a second. If we do not hazard the attempt, by a discursive approach to the mystery of the simplicity of intellect, despite the difficulties and dangers, we shall likely abandon that intent of the practical intellect to fulfill spiritual values through actions whereby truth and falsity are nevertheless inescapable possibilities to practical intellectual action. We should cease to be intellectual creatures; or rather, we should fall from becoming the intellectual creature that it is our nature to be.

Unless the intellectual attempt is made to understand the gift of our intellectual being, that being may become inordinately anchored in the ground of origin to intellect, in which it struggles with the true and the false. In the first place, creation itself is the most narrow ground. The particular created intellect which makes the great refusal, a refusal to sort truth and falsity, becomes subdued by a diminution of intellectual actions to the limited offices of merely practical intellect entrapped by the world, struggling to survive the exigencies of the moment. But the full, particular intellect must, through both a consort of openness to being and an action in response to being, become itself by what St. Thomas speaks of as the deportment of both *assent* and *consent*. That is to enter the arena within which its potential fullness is possible.

If any light accrues from what has just been said, by it we may surmise that it is the speculative intellect that may be said to allow a visionary perspective upon the actions of the practical intellect – as for instance the action of making a poem. We must consider both the ends of the practical and of the speculative intellect as if separate, by a divisiveness of terms. The practical intellect's end is action in response to being; the speculative intellect's end is understanding in response to being. (*Summa* I, Q. 79, A. 11) We remember that Thomas puts the point further: "The practical reason judges and passes sentence on things to be done, as the speculative reason judges and passes sentence on things to be understood." (*Summa* I-II, Q. 74, A. 7) Now to these remarks, let us add a final text: "The intellectual nature arrives by inquiry of reason; and therefore what intellect apprehends, reason attains by a process of making its way thither." (I-II, Q. 5, A. 1)

These last words engage a crucial point for any intellect, but perhaps especially for the poet. The "intellectual nature" is distinguished from the "rational nature"; but both are aspects of intellect only as discursively pursued. The first is that aspect of intellect whose movement Thomas speaks of as the *intellectus* in his *Quaestiones disputatae de veritate* (1,1); the second is the *ratio*. "Although the knowledge which is most characteristic of the human soul occurs in the mode of the *ratio* [which I here associate with the practical intellect], nevertheless there is in it a sort of participation in the simple knowledge which is proper to higher beings, of whom it is therefore said that they possess the faculty of spiritual vision [which capacity for participation I associate here with the speculative intellect]." This mode of "participation in simple knowledge" is angel-like in its nature. The angelic nature is intuitive, immediate, full since its operation is unhampered by material existence.

The implication of this complex capacity of human intellect is that through the ordinate relation of *intellectus* and *ratio*, intellect serves our given nature as spiritual creature. The conjunction serves intellect as both practical and speculative. If in the Aristotelian characterization, man is considered *rational animal*, the advance upon that view of man through St. Thomas's exposition of the nature of intellect raises that characterization to *spiritual animal*. By his given nature, in which intellect is exceptional to the rest of creation, man is spiritual creature. That is the intention in the term *person*.

An additional remark here on this full nature of man in relation to his actions out of that nature, as accounted for by the observer's practical intellect. This nature, and the actions out of this nature (given man as spiritual creature), is common to all. But a recognition of and concern for distinctions may be of especial concern to the poet, whose specific calling is to a making through words. The poet especially struggles with intimations of being through the gifts of his spiritual nature, insofar as his "calling" is truly that of the poet. Since the time of St. Thomas, we have struggled with the relation of the imagination to the reason in attempting to understand the nature of the poet's seemingly peculiar calling. Both imagination and reason, says Thomas (I-II, Q. 46, A. 8) are in man's nature. They are not simply in the poet's nature as poet, as we sometimes would have it. In respect to the calling of the poet to make things of words out of an imagination governed by the practical intellect, it is necessary that he exercise reason in his making, a necessity to art in Thomas's view which is not a characteristic concern of the poet since the Renaissance. As for the imagination, it is (says Thomas) the "storehouse of sensible things received through the senses." (*Summa* I, Q. 103, A. 4) In response to that presence of sensible things in the mind's storehouse, actions of mind within creation occur. It is in this respect that *man*, and not simply the *poet*, is properly said to be a "maker." That the poet sometimes recognizes this aspect of mind is demonstrated by Wordsworth in "Tintern Abbey," let us recall, in which poem he declares that, out of his experiences of the world through his senses, his mind has become "a mansion for all lovely forms" and his memory "a dwelling place/ For all sweet sounds and harmonies." The exhilaration of this assertion is out of Wordsworth's recognition that he is not set aside as poet by this capacity of mind but by that capacity he is made one with mankind. His testimony in the poem is that of the vatic poet at last realizing his office.

What is awry in Wordsworth's recognition, however, is a failure to recognize that through the will's involvement in the actions of the practical intellect, more than lovely forms and sweet sounds and harmonies are likely to take up a presence in our minds. Wordsworth, through a sort of kind intent toward mankind and creation in general as perceived by his own senses and stored in his own memory, nevertheless overlooks the possibility of an aberrant will. He is left with no sufficient response to evil. Nor will it prove a sufficient answer to this deficiency to declare by an act of the will that the power of imagination assures a maintenance of the mind as a mansion reserved to all lovely form. The imagination cannot control unwanted sound and disharmony. Wallace Stevens will declare its power to do so from his argument that the mind is autonomous and the imagination supreme in its manipulation of image and thereby the final arbiter of reality so that by that elevation mind is superior to either harmony or disharmony, the creator of order out of the amalgam residual in intellect. But he will in the end abandon that pretense.

In connection with these "things" in the mind's storehouse, "received through the senses," we turn to the role of intuition in its response to them. "By the aid of intuition," says Thomas, "principles are apprehended, such principles as are naturally knowable, both in speculative and in practical matters." (*Summa* I-II, Q. 5, A. 4) This intuition is most signally an intuition of being, of *esse* – a recognition of something seemingly beneath or within or suffusing both the storehouse at imagination's disposal and the things themselves in their separate being in the part of reality external to mind. It is this very recognition of intellect's "knowing" by intuition which prompts Wordsworth to celebrate "spots of time," moments of a seeming arrest of his own being in a spiritual openness whereby the "beauteous forms" already in his mind are restored through memory to the first moment of their in-gathering. (Cf. Eliot's "still point.") The event remembered and relived, the moment of "recollection in tranquility," Wordsworth says in "Tintern Abbey," is one recalling an actual experienced in nature

> In which the affections gently lead us on —
> Until, the breath of this corporeal frame
> And even the motion of our human blood
> Almost suspended, we are laid asleep
> In body, and become a living soul;
> While with an eye made quiet by the power
> Of harmony, and the deep power of joy,
> We see into the life of things.

It is the same intuitive response to being that leads Gerard Manley

Hopkins to explore a relation between what he calls the "instress" of his made thing, the poem, and the "inscape" of particular existences separate from mind and from mind's images, as we have already explored.

Such is the intuition that stirs man to a habit of intellectual existence proper to his given – his created – nature. It is when man confuses this intuition of being in its relation to the imagination, by assuming intuition an action out of the autonomous will, that difficulty arises. For the autonomous will would operate the power of imagination in an illusion of an act of creation that denies the givenness of its own nature. In the confusion, one may mistake the intuition. He may fail to recognize intuition's origin in the mind as being through the agency of that especial gift to the mind, the *intellectus* (and mistake as well the givenness of other dimensions of mind). Thus may the poet conclude his autonomy as creator, when in point of actuality he is but a maker. He mistakes the true office of intuition as being exercised intellectually in the mode of the *intellectus*.

Consequent upon this false assumption may be a reduction of the mind's stored images by the instrument of concept, images thus collectively becoming merged in concept as an idol raised to the "self," as ultimate end of the action. In the aftermath of such reductions of reality, both the reality of the acting and of the understanding mind are at risk. And through these distorting exercises of intellect there also occurs a reduction of realities separate from the mind, insofar as its perceptions of that reality exist in the mind. What is likely is an accompanying disjoining of *individual* and *person*, for instance. The perversive actions of the practical intellect appropriated to the new-found and autonomous *individual* allow an assumption of its own power of a self-transcendence of existence. It becomes displaced from its proper citizenship in existence by this specialization of *individual*. What is most rapidly lost is the proper office of the practical intellect – its desire for the "fulfillment of spiritual values" whose reference is the transcendent. The values declared on behalf of this new "individual" are often enough declared to be spiritual, but they are not properly so since they lack the orientation of *person* through virtue to a transcendent which is independent of the assumed powers of the "individual." What is lost is an understanding of the gift of being. In the end, one has the alienated self. That is, one has the intellect "secularized."

Ironies proliferate whenever we begin to lose control of terms or manipulate terms toward ends deceptively presented by distorted terms, as has increasingly occurred with the use of *individual*. In its root sense, it is a term sufficiently scholastic in precision: The thing named is *in-dividable.* But such has been the exercise of power over the term that it now largely serves a reductionist purpose. It becomes a term for an entity within a cumulative accounting system, political usually, whereby *identity* of individual in relation to individual becomes the egalitarian intent. From the view of the person who accepts the ambiance of reductionism attracted to *individual*, there rises the attraction of autonomy. The individual as autonomous, easily numbered in the abstractionism of gnostic order, holds isolated sovereignty from his own position. What is lost is the fullness as member in relation to the larger body, a relation still somewhat maintained through the term *person*, at least so long as that term clarifies the special limitation implied in the Modernist uses of *individual.*

Perhaps it would be well to recover something of the metaphysical origins once informing the terms, and we might do so economically by summoning Gilson to our concern. He explores with great care the terms *individual* and *person* as they serve a developing Christian philosophy from the early Fathers down to the medieval scholastic uses of the terms, with a special concern for St. Thomas's uses. In his chapters on "Christian Anthropology" and "Christian Personalism" in *The Spirit of Mediaeval Philosophy*, Gilson's emphasis is upon *man* as the specific and indivisible term, out of Genesis. In relation to it, he explores the speculative arguments of St. Augustine, Duns Scotus, and St. Thomas in their response to the position of Plato and Aristotle. Something of the complexity of the concern we may suggest as resting in the significance of *man* as an incorruptible substance by its nature. Against the dualism of body and soul, which would involve an accounting for two substances out of which a third – man – must be derived, the scholastic solution to the enigma argues that the substance *man* is not a combination of two substances but a complex substance which owes its substantiality to one only of its two constitutive principles. "[Man] is the unity of a soul which substantializes his body and of the body in which this soul subsists." What is underway in the argument is the attempt to understand what is already believed through revelation, through Christ: The immortality of man as an immortality of the whole, not simply of the soul, as in Platonic thought.

In this light, man as incorruptible substance is peculiar in that "not only the species . . . permanently endures, but also the individuals." We say formally that the angel as creature exists individually, each its own species. Animal creatures individually conform to the species, which alone endures, which is why the individual animal is corruptible substance. Man is most remarkably gifted in distinction from either. The angel is specific because created as immaterial existence. The animal is specific only by virtue of conformity to "species." Man is specific in respect to both material and immaterial natures inseparable in his nature so that without both he would not be at all. To this end, despite certain differences in their understanding of the ways of this principle of man's nature, the principle is itself held in common by St. Augustine, Duns Scotus, St. Thomas, and the principal scholastics. It is formulated by Boethius: The human person is "an individual substance of a rational nature." The substantiality of intellect includes both material and immaterial aspects. It is, then, as person that this creature subsists.

The development of this concept of *man* as peculiar in the orders of being leaves us, Gilson concludes, with a fundamental position on the nature of man: Because firmly based

> on the substantiality of the intellect and the immortality it carries with it [including the immortality of the body], the Christian individual is invested with all the dignity of a permanent being, indestructibly distinct from every other in his very permanence, and an original source of rational activity responsibly deciding his own future destiny. . . [H]ere we stand at the source of the whole life of the spirit in its two-fold activity, theoretical and practical, since it is precisely as rational, and therefore also as a person, that the individual is able to discern the true from the false, that is to say acquire science, and to distinguish good from evil, and achieve morality. (*Spirit of Mediaeval Philosophy*, 203)

It is here that we establish the relation of those actions of *caring* in relation to *not caring*, of practical immediacy of intellect to speculative enlargements upon that immediacy. It is a distinction which Jacques Maritain develops in relation to the terms *individual* and *person*, and since the center here is so decisive, we pursue the concern somewhat further.

XVIII

In the interest of maintaining the sign *person* as viable, we shall presently consider the uses made of it by Jacques Maritain, in relation to *individual*. His argument in *The Person and the Common Good* proved somewhat controversial among Thomists themselves, perhaps largely because his use of the terms might seem to suggest a dualism which he did not intend. Let us begin our dependence on Maritain here by recalling an earlier point: Given the difficulties to finite intellect whereby out of its given nature it must proceed discursively, that very necessity involves a seeming divisiveness of simple being by intellectual action. We also suggested that such seeming divisiveness bears no essential effect in the thing so approached, though it may have the consequence of dividing the active intellect from being itself. Always, we insisted, this is the danger attending intellectual discourse, through which discursiveness may mistake its own limited necessity as unlimited comprehension – a full possession by intellectual action of actualities. It is as if intellect were to mistake the truth of a thing as thus received for the essence of the thing – as if intellect by conquest surrounded and possessed all essences of things. In attempting some safeguard against this difficulty, we may first address ourselves further to this danger.

In speaking discursively, and so with an apparent divisiveness of things through discourse itself, intellect may assume consequences insupportable, taking intellectual means as a formal end to being itself. It is thus that formulaic reductionism of being is the continuing burden overweighing truth as held by intellect again and again, and never more pervasively of the intellectual community than in our day. Truth as held by intellect is not the same as idea projected by a term. This is an old difficulty to Western philosophy, at least as old as when Plato raised the question in the *Parmenides*: whether existence is one or many. The resolution is formally possible only if the questioner were God, in whom it is resolved by his existence as Being Itself. It is not a question Plato can resolve, as he concedes at last, his spokesman having proved that, on the one hand, existence is many but, on the other, that it is one, and seeing no resolution possible to the dilemma. That is an inevitable impasse (Gilson would say) since Being Itself is not a revelation present to Plato. Meanwhile, the necessity of terms in pursuit of oneness proves insurmountable obstacle. (When we came down to Brice Parain in our day, we found him despairing over language as destructive of the mind's desire for oneness, and he harkens back to the *Parmenides* as the beginning of the endless circling of the problem.) In accepting our use of the terms *individual* and *person*, then, toward our concern for the relation of intellect to the useful good and the unqualified good, we continue mindful of the problem whereby intellect by the necessities of its action seems to commit itself to an insoluble dualism. To come to the distinction in our terms, however, we must make a preliminary foray into the vexed question of idea itself as borne by term.

There is a fundamental question at issue in Western philosophy, our best intellects dwelling upon it as fundamental. The question: whether idea is in intellect or separate from it. It is the question lying between Plato and Aristotle most conspicuously, and it haunts our thought ever after. St. Thomas points to this problem when he sides with Aristotle, remarking that Aristotle "rejects the opinion of Plato, who held that Ideas existed of themselves and not in the intellect." (*Summa* I, Q. 15, Reply Obj. 1) In exploring the difficulty, Thomas in the body of Question XV of the *Summa* begins with Augustine, who affirms the importance of ideas: "Such is the power inherent in ideas, that no one can be wise unless they be understood." In looking to the root meaning of the term *idea*, Thomas concludes that "by ideas are understood the forms of things, existing apart from the things themselves." But this is not a Platonic proposition in Thomas as it might at first appear to be. The crucial issue is the sense in which idea may be said to exist *apart from the thing itself.* Thomas rejects Plato's understanding, in the light of Augustine's own rejection of Plato on the point. Augustine's rejection, undertaken as a necessity for his own new beginning as Christian, is at the opening of the *City of God*. St. Augustine proceeds through arguments whereby he modifies Plato in such a way that he does not reject out of hand certain insights Plato has in respect to the relation of finite intellect to idea. Thus Augustine comes to put the point in *Lib* 83, *Quaest.*, 6 46 (PL 40, 30):

> Ideas are certain original forms or permanent and immutable models of things which are contained by the divine intelligence. They are immutable because they themselves have not been formed; and that is why they are eternal and always the same. But though they themselves neither come to be nor perish, yet it is according to them that everything,

which can come to be or pass away or which actually comes to be and passes away, is said to be formed.

What is at issue in the argument between Plato and Aristotle is dualism, as St. Thomas recognized, even as he recognized Aristotle's solution as inconclusive. For if idea is itself permanent and immutable in itself, then the agency whereby anything comes to be from idea or ceases to be in respect to idea as separate from agency sets a separate pole of contention between any first mover of the idea, the agent, and the idea itself. It is against a necessary logical conclusion of dualism that first Aristotle and then Augustine and Thomas set themselves. Now the problem in their counter-argument lies with the limits of finite argument, for finite argument can but point *toward* transcendent absolutes – toward idea and agent and the relation between idea and agent at a level of the absolute where finite mind can but approach vision through the rigors of logic commanded by practical intellect and at last supported by speculative intellect out of faith. The attempt is always complicated as well by the limit of sign, of word, in pointing toward the believed but ineffable. This is but to say that, whichever position one takes, one must in the end, as an act of faith, accept the one position or the other. Rational intellect cannot in the end avoid the conditions of Pascal's wager.

A position accepted, one then must account for the problems raised by that acceptance, engaged at the level of finite intellect. And this is where St. Thomas introduces the fundamental position which underlies his metaphysics, the *principle of proportionality*, to explain the inadequacy of intellect to the problem and the necessity of faith. For it is readily evident, in the proximate sphere of the idea's relation to intellect, that "idea" can be shown again and again to exist prior to finite intellectual agency. The ideas of geometry precede the making of a table or chair, to choose a favorite Platonic gambit, so that idea clearly is precedent to the actuality of the table or chair. That argument Thomas accepts, but he holds that the argument at this level is the reduction of a necessary principle to the capacities of intellectual finitude. Idea in relation to human intelligence is, in its nature, different from idea in relation to divine intelligence, even as Augustine declares. In *Being and Essence*, therefore, St. Thomas is concerned to establish the principle of proportionality as fundamental to the resolution of the question whether idea is separate from or in intellect. At issue is the nature of *participation* of created things to the divine essence whereby any thing *is* at all.

To understand this problem of the ideas' relation to finite intellect, it becomes necessary to consider the relation of idea to the Cause of that finite intellect, and we must consider that problem first. Gilson gives us a helpful redaction of St. Augustine's doctrine of ideas as a stage in the development of Christian philosophy, a fundamental change of the classical philosopher's conception, to which St. Thomas and the medieval scholastics will make additional contribution. "Subsisting eternally in the Word," says Gilson of St. Augustine's doctrines, the ideas are "the expression of the possible participations of God," that is, of "participations" as a term for possible things. These expressions are, "like God, uncreated, immutable, and necessary with the necessity of His being. These are the Ideas." It follows from this that for St. Augustine the "divine ideas are thus the initial forms in which things have their principle." St. Thomas will modify this doctrine of idea, but not reject it. For St. Thomas, in Gilson's words, "the ideas are in God as forms to the likeness of which all things were made." But, as with our attempts to distinguish among aspects of absolute perfection, of Being Itself, under the burden of finite rationality, we must at last conclude that the ideas are identical with God since they are *in* Him and not separate from Him, as Idea is conceived as independent existence in Platonism. The distinction between Demiurge and Idea in Plato commits Platonism to an insoluble dualism. For Thomas, "inasmuch as God knows His own essence as *imitable* by a creature, He knows it as the model and idea of this creature." And, says Gilson in an observation significant to our distinction between God as creator and man as maker, "This multiplicity of ideas within the divine unity constitutes precisely the divine art," an art which is *one,* since God Himself is one.

God's art is the creature's cause as a possible participation. Now by participation, man shares as causal agent in creation, but only as St. Paul's "coadjutor." We have put this sharing in relation to the term *steward* in setting the relation of man as a peculiar nature to the rest of creation. As stewards, man is responsible to the coming-to-be of created things that are under his limited providence, not only of himself but of all created things. His providence is to the limit of his specific gifts. And the relationship turns on participation, the relation of man to God as a created being. The relation of created intellect to idea differs from the relation of idea in God. Now, as Gilson shows, medieval philosophers are in common agreement that ideas are *in* God, though they differ in their rationalizations of this commonly accepted principle. Those differences tend to obscure what they hold in common, and Gilson is concerned to restore our recognition of the common principle. For St. Thomas, "The idea is essentially God's knowledge of His own essence as capable of being participated; this knowledge is an emanation of the divine essence which includes the relation of the possible beings to God." But to St. Bonaventure, idea is "rather an *expression* of the divine truth." Duns Scotus, between whom and St. Thomas there are contentions still at issue among their followers, is less contrary to Thomas than an intensifier of the principle. As Gilson presents the point: "Instead of reducing ideas, like St. Thomas, to God's knowledge of his essence, and, like St. Bonaventure, to the expression of this essence considered in its possible participations, Duns Scotus now takes them as the creatures themselves as creatable by God, and existing in Him in virtue of their concepts as possibles." Scotus, as Gilson suggests, moves toward idea as more nearly palpable in God through participation of existing ideas.

There are, clearly, subtle and perhaps even consequential distinctions among these medieval Christian philosophers, but there is to be rescued what is common. Again, in Gilson's words: "God knows individuals, and . . . He knows them in their very individuality." This is a radical difference setting Christian philosophy apart from both Plato and Aristotle. As for the consequences of God's knowing the individual perfectly, though the individual is not in itself perfectible independent of the grace of this knowing: "It is . . . insufficient to say that God watches over the human species in general, or even over each man in particular – He watches over each particular free action of each particular man." It is this completeness of God's knowing of the existing individual that constitutes the possibility to that creature of its participation in being as person. Regarding this point Gilson remarks in concluding his exploration of the concept of *idea*, "To say everything in one word, each human being is a *person*; his acts are *personal* acts, because they arise from the free decision of a reasonable being, and depend only on his initiative. . . . If it is because he is a person that each man, instead of simply submitting to the law of the world, collaborates in making that law weigh in the world, the Christian conception of 'person' must be something very different from the Aristotelian and Platonic conception of 'man.'" Man is thus a causal agent by participation, and as such is exceptional in the orders of being.

That difference is revealed in the relation of the Christian person to the whole of creation. For as person, man is like his creator, being created in the image of God in a way distinguished from the participation of other created creatures through their own discrete existences as created. Man, as intellectual creature, is thus necessarily central to the orders of nature in respect to his existence as coadjutor. Gilson remarks this arresting distinction in saying that "Things . . . are ordained to man as to their end, not man to things, and that amounts to saying that the rest of the universe is directed towards its end by man and through man. Reasonable beings [man, persons] are there, in a sense, for their own sake, the rest are there for the sake of reasonable beings."

It is a circumstance to human existence borne out by the uses man makes of all other creatures, seldom a happy usage. When we lament what man has made of the earth or of other men, we are lamenting man's failure of stewardship. We are insisting that the recovery of a proper stewardship lies in a recovery of the significance of personhood, and further, that such a recovery lies through the regaining of a metaphysical perspective on existence itself. Otherwise, we shall continue our *ad hoc* conflicts over the body of existence. This condition of the conflict as *ad hoc* is always advantageous to the gnostic's attempt at power. His is a rejection of the full implications of man's stewardship of being, required of us as the principle of fulfillment of our intellectual being by participation.

In the light of these asides on finite intellect's divisive approach to actualities and the relation of idea to agency, we return to a concern for the relation of the *individual* and the *person* as terms divisive of an actuality. In speaking of *individual* we would denominate a mode of being in the intellectual creature whereby actions of practical intellect are directed to the common good under the conditions of time and place. In speaking of *person*, we denominate a mode of orientation to being, whereby this undivided intellectual creature through speculative intellect is the more inclined to an undivided good as its appropriate end, an end that is quite independent of the common good, except insofar as actions in the common good are means mediate to transcendent end. The intellectual creature is specifically as a *formed being* of a particular nature a single creature, limited by a potency determinate of its creation. The determination is an effect of its Creator's willing its existence. It is thus *specifically* singular. That is, it is thus specified by species, to emphasize the point by a redundancy. We are here to be mindful once more of the formal difference between man in relation to the concept of species and any other created thing in relation to species. For, given his nature as man, as person, species is dependent in the particular person, in contrast to other created things. A cat, for instance, is dependent *upon* species as separate from the existence of this particular cat in the Thomistic understanding. And just as with the *practical* and *speculative*, which are not names for two powers but a naming of aspects of a simple one, so too must we understand *individual* and *person* as a one and not a two. For we are concerned with characterizing inclinations in a single entity, the intellectual creature.

The lesson from Thomas about the nature of intellect is applicable to the nature we mean to indicate in speaking of *person*. "The speculative intellect by extension becomes practical," we have quoted him as saying. And we made the point that the *extension* of speculative to practical indicates an inclination, a *leaning to* through action, toward the created world. It is by this leaning of practical action that intellect engages contingency. "But," Thomas continues, "one power is not changed into another. Therefore the speculative and practical intellects are not distinct powers." (I-II, Q. 79, A. 11) Thus we intend, in an analogous way, that *individual* is a term designating an extension of *person*. It is an orientation of person to the created world through the actions of the practical intellect. And it is in this extension that person finds himself member of a "whole" of which person is subordinate as a part in the necessity of active stewardship of creation. At the same time he must not surrender the person's proper inclination to a final end. For person is destined to a membership in that larger "Whole" which Dante gives symbolic recognition of at the close of the *Divine Comedy*, in that complex image of the multifoliate rose.

We speak of the cartography of the soul as significantly distinct, in a capital difference from the individual. T. S. Eliot in his poetry engages this concern, resolving it at last when he speaks of the Word within the word, of the Word within the desert. Indeed, the central theme of Eliot's poetry from its beginning is his concern for the relation of *individual* to person. If these are inclinations in a singular intellectual creature which we may distinguish, they did not at first seem to him such. We discover his changed understanding of person if we contrast "The Love Song of J. Alfred Prufrock" and "Gerontion" on the one hand to the later poems "Ash-Wednesday" and the *Four Quartets* on the other. The resolution of the concern we find in "Ash-Wednesday." The poem's speaker engages here the struggle between caring and not caring, between participation in the world under the aspect of individual while yet maintaining the larger dimensions of his possible being as person. One cares for the "whole," while the vision toward the larger "Whole" keeps that care in its proper, limited orbit in relation to creation. Because a single entity, by its very singleness which cannot be inclusive of being and so not in itself a Divine Simplicity (the singleness, associated with *individual*), is by that limitation inclined beyond its limited singleness as individual, toward the possible fullness of *person*, in relation to the transcendent, the proper end of its participation in Absolute Being. That is the secret in that *desire* in us which will not be stilled by the presumption of our intellectual autonomy, a presumption which characterizes Eliot's early thought. We depend on Eliot here, since he so effectively dramatized the intellect's dilemma in its Modernist attempt at autonomy.

Though singular, this intellectual creature's operations are limited by its limited nature. Its actions are therefore relative to the proximate and transcendent circumstances to its singularity. And those inclinations, being disparate, may well have an appearance of a multiplicity of ends. These are not merely multiple within proximate ends, but between the proximate and the ultimate as well, insofar as one does not understand the nature of one's participation in being as a *person*. That circumstance to its unity, its very singleness, threatens a divisiveness in the soul itself. It therefore struggles through multiple inclinations to establish proportionate response to proximate and ultimate good. Always, its struggle is for that simplicity through which it is a member within the finitudes of creation, yet member beyond those finitudes in relation to an ultimate good wherein it may rest at last in the fullness of the Oneness it calls God. It prays, therefore, for grace whereby it may resolve the paradoxical necessity of at once caring and not caring.

We need but turn to our experience of such inclination to discover this to be a truth about our own being, however difficult to articulate. Though aware of our existence as a singular creature, there is in that awareness a recognition of complexity whereby our sense of our own oneness – of a discreteness of our being which we name with "I" – appears divisible. That is, we know ourselves complex, though one. Perhaps we might put it that we know ourselves in respect to an inclusive potency manifested variously through our intellectual actions. In act, because our act is not the same as, nor co-extensive with, our completed being, we begin to discover that our act, because it is always a single act toward a discrete end, is a reduction of potential fullness. And particularly so insofar as act itself as singular is necessarily limited. That is, our act is toward an object, but the very act thereby limits the inclination of our *person* to a fullness. That is why we do not wish ourselves to be judged, to be "known," by any single act or even several acts. For in such judgmental knowing of our person by others, a summary of our acts as definitive of our being, we fear we shall appear only as a "formulated phrase" that leaves us "pinned and wriggling on the wall," thus forced to "spit out all the butt-ends of [our] days and ways." We are more than such a summary. We resist being taken to be so simply measured by our singular acts in aggregate. How can we appear other than a "do-gooder" in our devoted pursuit of the common good?

And that is why to act at all is in some degree heroic, insofar as the agent (the acting "I") knows that the single act while determinate is not exhaustive of potency. Not only does the hero act beyond his knowing; he acts with the knowledge that the world must judge his *being* from his *acts* and can never fully know the *person* acting. We have quoted Eliot's Prufrock, who fears that any word he may utter may serve as a pin to leave him wriggling on the wall. He chooses then, in Sophocles' or Aristotle's or Dante's view of the world, to be merely member of the chorus as opposed to attempting to be hero.

Eliot, by his portrait of Prufrock, suggests that Prufrock has replaced the hero in the modern world, wherein the common good is nevertheless still at issue. We should learn from Prufrock a central lesson in relation to act, beyond his fear of act as reductive of being: Prufrock recognizes that action is always a single movement toward an object, a movement possible only in this present moment of the will's choice. Insofar as his act presents itself as spectacle to the world, the closed world of the tea party, by spectacle he will be judged. Given his vanity and pride, he concludes it were better to have been a "pair of ragged claws" than a man. For he cannot value the effect of a constancy of act upon his personhood, the necessary habit of being in relation to an ultimate end. He has long since succumbed to mediate ends as final. By the time he writes *The Waste Land*, Eliot himself has begun to understand action in relation to final end. The significant actions are not likely to be spoken in words by those for whom spectacle is actuality. The actions significant of being, through which alone "we have existed," are "not to be found in our obituaries."

If by action there is a reduction, or seeming reduction, toward a limited movement of the soul in time and place (those circumstances of being to man as a created creature), one must accept that necessity because one must act. It is helpful, then, to find terms that will serve a distinction regarding the agent of action in respect to those inclinations that on the one hand seemingly narrow person to contingent being and on the other seem to open person toward full potency. That agent *through* act must attempt to move beyond the limited singularity implied in speaking of the *individual* as inclined to the *common good.* We know, in respect to our knowledge of ourselves, that somehow our "life" is an aggregate of our actions that point beyond that aggregation to our perfection. Ourself as a Whole is greater than the sum of our parts in the whole, the sum of ourself remembered by the world in our obituary. It is only in a weak moment of the will (for this reason) that we suppose ourselves content if we and the world accept some grand heroic act as speaking our full essence. And that is the terrifying realization that comes to Eliot's Thomas à Becket when he cries out, "This is the greatest treason: To do the right thing for the wrong reason."

And so, how shall we speak of this deportment in act, this inclination of the "I" which is the "I" but is not the "I" in its fullness? And how shall we speak of that full simplicity of our being, the fullness of the "I" that is richer and more resonant than the "I" signified by an act or acts? It is in the light of the complexity of saying the nature of our being that I have chosen to adopt the terms *individual* and *person.* For we recognize at once a resonance of being through the connotations in the term *person.* But such is our sense of ourselves as *individual*, out of long uses of the term born from its root meaning, that it signifies a delimiting. It is as if *person* speaks of the intellectual creature from within that creature itself, with an enlarging openness implied. But it is as if *individual* is spoken from a point exterior and delimiting, as by observation of persons in action in the contingent world. To speak of *individual* is a limited assent to *person*, implying some distance. To speak of *person* implies a consent, a *sensing along with* which involves us in the difficulties to person out of necessary acts within the contingent world.

It is the will in act that makes variableness, while the inclinations of person through speculative intellect guards against a rest of the will's desire in the contingent world. It is a rest prevented, Thomas says,

> first, on the part of the object, when the object is not the ultimate end but is ordered to something else [i.e., to the ultimate end]; secondly, on the part of the one who desires the end but who is not yet possessed of it. Now it is the object which specifies [once more, "makes species of," makes "specific"] the act, but the manner of acting depends upon the agent, and hence is perfect or imperfect according to the condition of the agent.

The will, incapable of possessing the end in the contingent world, is therefore contingently restless, turning intellect speculative out of practical,

practical out of speculative. Even when will is most at home in the contingent world, its hunger remains, its desire for a rest in a perfection possible only beyond its residence in contingency. Such conditions, though tempting the will to premature rest in proximate ends as if ultimate end, is nevertheless not a presence in misery within the contingent world, insofar as it is right will. For Thomas concludes that an "enjoyment of the ultimate end not yet possessed is enjoyment properly speaking, though imperfect because of the imperfect way in which it is possessed." (*Summa* I-II, Q. 11, A. 4) Our willful discontent with the limited joy in such limited, imperfect possession gives us all our misery in life as intellectual creature. Such misery is but a joy from which consent is withheld.

XIX

Given this Thomistic understanding of *person*, a term for an actuality which is at last beyond the full comprehension of its own intellect, we are nevertheless required to a full exercise of the practical intellect in support of this mysteriously limited creature, a creature like the gods but not a god. It is an obligation to the self, despite our usual protests that God is "unfair." For such is not the necessity to other particular creations, to "poisonous minerals" or "lecherous goats" or "serpents envious" because of their given natures. "Why should intent or reason, born in me," make my failures of intent or reason heinous? The answer given by orthodoxy, as Donne knows in his pained cry and as St. Thomas explores in his great monuments on the question, is at last Love. At the proximate level of the question as engaged by the practical intellect, what we encounter is the explicit requirement that we must love our "self" in relation to its given nature if we are to riddle the otherwise oppressive burden of our particular existence as a reasoning spiritual person.

In that initiation of our journey, out of the restiveness of intellect characterized by its "why?" we discover anew that reason is always limited by the proximate ground of being, that ground we have termed the matrix of creation. In the closest proximity to that ground as we are able to experience it, and know the experience to be of a reality, it is the specific nature of our *self* as reasoning creature that we know best. And *specific* here is a technical term, as we have said, meaning that each discrete soul is a species by virtue of its unique existence as known perfectly by God. We advance, or pretend to advance, our understanding of the *self* as an actually existing creature by the (usually) facile attempt at our particularity registered in a term like "subjective" to describe the immediacy of our experience. But that is to have supposed already an "objective" detachment from that anchoring ground. The play of terms between *subjective* and *objective* becomes a source of considerable confusions to the self in its attempt to believe itself a particular, unique, actual, real existence. Through that play of terms, we introduce by indirection the uncertainty of a "relativism" of experience, which in its extremity leaves us not even believing in the existence of our "self." That is why St. Augustine, long ago, countered with the proposition that, whatever my assumption as intellectual creature, even its very error certifies my reality. For if, he said, I am deluded about my own existence, I must first *be* in order to be deluded. This is the reality of a firm necessity to intellect, whatever errors of intellectual action may follow from it.

We use the term *specific*, then, in designating the reality of a person's unique nature, recalling as we do St. Thomas's argument about that specificity as related to the soul. The soul, he says (*Summa* I-II, Q. 51, A. 1), "since it is the form of the body, is the specific principle." It must follow therefrom that the specific creature – this "intellectual animal" – differs each from any other precisely because each is specific. Therefore each differs in respect to its powers as specific being, and most centrally in respect to its intellectual power to engage both its own nature and its circumstantial place in time as a specific being. Thus, as we know from experience, some persons know themselves and their powers both responsibly and more fully than do others. A failure of such knowledge we may even conclude constitutes the moral failure of that person. Indeed, a less-gifted person may be more fully realized out of his potentiality than a more-gifted person, for the failure of potentiality is not determined by the specificity of the gift itself, but by the active engagement of that given specificity which we (following St. Thomas) call the habit of being.

Without engaging the complexity of actuality in relation to appearance, we will recognize nevertheless that our epithets often register a truth about particular persons in relation to the possibility of their "character." That is, we speak of "good country people" or of the "good worker." We speak of the "poor little rich boy" or of the person "born with a silver spoon in his mouth" which has become tarnished by acidic self-love. What is implicit in such attempts at naming reality, though often imprecisely applied (*pace* Prufrock), is the valid assumption of those persons' responsibility to their gifts, independent of the magnitude of any particular gift. We *know*, though we may abuse that knowledge through a failure of understanding of the things known, that some persons deal more reasonably with the circumstantial conditions of their personal being than do other persons. And this is to say that some persons accept their discrete gifts regardless of the relative magnitude of their gift. They prosper through that acceptance, in a prosperity independent of those measures restricted to the material conditions of their existence. They are reasonable in their expectations.

Our reason must, within the specific limits of our particularly given nature, operate within the proximate grounds of our discrete existence which we have termed the matrix of creation. But most fundamentally, reason operates within the limits of that most specific thing we know, ourselves as limited in being. It is within this arena that one "finds oneself," an arena whose borders are determined by the power of the specific soul at its primary level of intellectual action. One establishes onself through the soul's circumstantial relation to creation, but at a secondary level. For this specific creature man must deal with both his own given nature and the limits of his action within contingent creation. That is, within this arena and through reason as guided by will, the *person* must deal with all the problems of his individuated being peculiar to himself as person. In doing so, *person* discovers the field of action as primarily limited by its own specific nature, and only secondarily by circumstances.

In coming to terms with these limits we discover what we speak of as our "calling." Both the discovery and the exercise of that calling are through actions of practical intellect extended toward creation, for we can act only *now* and in this *place*. And it is this extension of intellectual action that we call a *making*. By the intent of that making, it is necessarily the common good that is the proximate end. We need to say here, lest we be misunderstood as generalizing the "common good," that here we mean the good common to the intellect in its act and to the single object of its act. That is the elementary beginning always of any action in the common good, which may thus soundly become enlarged cumulatively by the multiplicity of action in the arena of intellect's circumstantial existence.

Since our primary concern in the present argument is with this *making* of a good in common as the principal habit of the *being* of the particular *soul* under its responsibility as steward of being, we are at the central point of our argument here. We are concerned to argue that this *making* is affective of our being, so in any making whose proximate end is such a common good, there is a concomitant making of the self in relation to ultimate good. The proximate act, rightly made, is in the relation between intellect and object, but the tendency through such act is toward ultimate good. By a right habit of making, there is effected a fulfilling of person through acts of making; that is, through those acts oriented outward from the self by an intent to a common good. Any act, we are saying, not simply affects the agent, but in some respect effects the agent as well, since the act either increases or diminishes that agent in relation to the validity of the intent occasioning his act.

This means that, in attempting to understand the nature of intellectual action, we must at some point contend with any act's proper relation to *virtue*, as *virtue* is considered in the spectrum of its own aspects, its particularities relative to the good of the soul. What we discover as the *calling* of the discrete person to the fullness of being is a calling to act, virtuously undertaken. Now from the position of the maker, his concern is most properly with the ordinate relation of the virtue of *prudence* to the virtue of his *art* as that art is his peculiar gift. Habits proper to both virtues, prudence and art, are necessary to the discrete soul, understood always as out of its specific nature. The relation of prudence to art is complex, and indeed is difficult to consider in an age which has so resolutely divided prudence from art. For we have elected to establish a quasi-mystical explanation for the gift of art in discrete persons which divorces art from person, at least at the theoretical level. That attempt, through that psychology of mind which has replaced the muses as explanation of art, has thoroughly distorted the subtle *moral* dimension of any art as a calling of intellect.

I do not mean here the moral nature of the art object itself, for that is a separate question. Here the concern is with the effect of making upon the soul of the maker, a different center of attention. To simplify the question at issue, we may ask whether a bad man can make a good poem. In doing so we find ourselves engaged in a secular version of Donatism. But in doing so, pointing to undeniable "masterpieces" by scoundrels, we may have lost our central concern once more. If we concentrate upon the bad or good poet in relation to his poem, we easily lose the most important issue. For we become concerned, not with *person*, but with "*personality*." And in doing so, our inclination becomes to consider a particular art, which is credited as the effect of a particular maker of art through his proper calling, as the ultimate good of that maker as person. But that is to reduce, and ultimately to materialize, one's calling as person.

Such a dislocation of prudence in relation to art very easily follows from modernist dislocations of intellect from being, the movement whereby intellect at last declares itself autonomous and so "beyond good and evil." But if intellect is autonomous in this Modernist assumption of its nature, then any position of any intellect as it regards art's relation to prudence must be considered definitive by that intellect. The ambiguity of the person's relative gift to absolute good is rejected, but not the assumption of the absoluteness of its own perspective upon the question. It is when there emerges, as there must, a contention among such absolutes for dominance of one artist over another, with power at the material level of existence being decisive, that there enters the attempt at uneasy truce among contending intellects in the interest of a truce avoiding the risk of standing on principles of truth. It enters as we might anticipate under the vague designation of "subjectivism" as the last justification of self-autonomy whenever material power is not decisive. But that will prove only a temporary strategy allowing the discrete intellect, in its relation to other intellects, the public stance praised generally as "tolerance." But such tolerance can serve only to protect a given soul's private assumption of its absoluteness. Because the position is a fiction about reality, it means that reality will overcome that fiction in the end. It does so, through the contribution of this pretense to reality, in the disintegration of community toward a "pluralism" – a term used in a delaying attempt against intellect's submission to reality. More and more we will recognize that such "plurality," whether oriented to social or political concerns or to art and science, yields as actuality in community only anarchy, which is the death of community. In that extremity of anarchy, brute power will always emerge as decisive of what is to be taken as truth.

We have neither individually nor as a remnant of the body of community been comfortable with this relativistic self-assurance which is based in the tacit assumption of absolute autonomy. Such is the relativism opposed to that relativism of the person's relation to Being Itself, the relativism of participation deployed in proper proportionality as St. Thomas might put it. Especially we are restive in regarding art's role in its service to the artist in his calling, or of art in relation to the larger world in which his made thing becomes a present reality encountered by other intellects and inescapably affecting those intellects. Indeed the question of the *personal* in relation to the requirements of the thing made by a *person* has been a constant Modernist problem, conspicuously illustrated by the poet's pursuit of a rest through his making. It is a pursuit in which he would escape "personality." But person reduced to personality is a reduction of both person and his made thing to the accidents of the making. The final dislocation is of the poet himself, his loss of *person's* relation to making. Such an attempted escape was the tack T. S. Eliot took initially, though its falseness forced him to clarify *accident* in relation to *essence*. For him the result was that he returned to an acceptance of person as central to the person's making. (This is the journey in Eliot which I explore in detail in "T.S. Elliot and the Still Point of Consciousness.")

It was also the tack pursued by that very excellent lyric poet, Wallace

Stevens. Stevens, for instance, insists through most of his career that in making a poem (as he puts it succinctly), "one writes for one." But that assertion upon examination proves most ambiguous, and its inadequacy troubled Stevens. We might in the same words, as we have already done but with quite opposite intent, assert that indeed one does any act for one's own good. We have explored a possible meaning in such words sufficiently to know that "for one's own good" may designate either a selfish, self-centeredness of gnostic intent toward the transcendent godhead of the self, what Dante dramatizes as perverted love. Or it may on the other hand designate an open giving of the self to the good of the thing made, that self-forgetfulness called love which is at last the proper love of the self. It is the proper love of the self in that it *effects* the being of the loving self. That is the condition to love as operative in creation, the action of love which underlies the second great commandment to love our neighbor. For we are to love our neighbor as we love ourselves, in which relationship of love the whole nature of our being as steward of being, as maker, is revealed.

The loss of perspective upon the relation of love to intellectual action is a steady theme in many poems and fictions in that literature we call "modern," as it is sometimes even a presence in literary criticism. It is an assumption in political and social activism of a wide variety, though here, as in our literature, the careful grounding by thought in the relation of prudence to action is obscured by "feeling" as a substitute for thought. On every hand, action purports a common good, but action as intellectually grounded is so vexing to thought that it is little wonder any person hears his own vexation in Prufrock's lament. If one could but have been a pair of ragged claws, one would not be troubled by the dissociation of "the dancer from the dance," let alone vexed by the tangled question of the "common good."

The dilemma of thought in its relation to aesthetic questions, as any "maker" of things must discover, deepens to the inescapable depths of moral questions, despite the maker's best attempts to divorce the virtues proper to making from the virtues proper to the existential realities of his existence as a person. One cannot at last *simply* write for oneself. Wallace Stevens, that highly sophisticated Modernist, comes at his life's end to see this truth through his spiritual trauma, and it leads him, as it had earlier led Eliot, to become a Christian.

The problem of prudence in its offices to our making, as our habit of being in the world, is a general problem to mankind, whether poet or politician or priest, and not specific to the poet only, though we have for the economy of our argument been using the poet as representative of man as maker. But whoever the person, the issue always is that of his proper exercise of the specific soul's calling as specific being, whose common relation to other specific beings of a kindred nature is revealed through whatever actions of making, whether with gestures of the body in dance, or with words, or with wood or paint, or the making of machines or the growing of vegetables. The exercise of one's calling within the contingent world, we said, affects the created world, but it affects the acting soul as well, whether the effect be as palpable as a poem or a landscape or a prescription of words such as a political constitution directed outward toward community good in the social body, or in any political or social or scientific aspects of that community. Intellectual action, then, is to good effect when for a common good, or to bad effect against the common good. But most decisively it affects the active agent since actions by that agent imply a good in which he participates through his will to a common good.

We here argue that an action of practical intellect is itself form a-making, indeed a *made thing* in respect to intellect itself. That habit becomes in some respect a resident immaterial form to intellect, signifying being to the contingent world as the general deportment of that intellect to things, whether we speak of thing as an idea refined by intellect or an executed thing such as a poem or stone or institution. But the question lingering in our concern is the proximate effect upon the agent himself consequent to the habit of making. We have posited as a principle, recognized as known to us from experience, that the specific soul by its very existence is called as maker. Created in God's image, it images itself not as creator absolute but as maker. One *makes*, each according to his gifts. This is a truth of all of us, as *persons*, but if we take the poet as an Everyman because his attention is so steadily recalled to his making by the immaterial cause of his thing, the words making his poem, we find that the poet must, whether he would or not, engage the relation of prudential virtue to the virtue of art in itself.

Since the poet's material cause in his making is our fund of common signs – words – deliberately representative of his engagement of, or refusal to engage, those virtues in their conjunction in his poem, we may find in such words paradigmatic representations of our common actions. That is, his is an imitation through words of the action of making which is common to humanity. That is why, perhaps, the poet is such an inviting representative of that formal presence in our common word. The poet as the user of words well represents for us *person*, man as created in the image of the

Word. The poet, then, intends as an immediacy in his action of words some representation of a present experience through his words. His made thing, the poem, will reflect our common encounter with being by the agency of our own intellect. It seems especially representative if he is lyric or dramatic poet. And it is no doubt this office of the poet as Everyman that prompts C. S. Lewis to argue, out of a long life as academic, that literature is the most central subject to academic training. It is literature, Lewis says, through which we discover "the only possible escape from a world divided between wolves who do not understand, and sheep who cannot defend, the things which make life desirable." ("The Necessity of Chivalry") "The gold," Lewis says in another place, "behind the paper currency is to be found, almost exclusively, in literature." ("Is English Doomed?")

To introduce this concern for the poet as Everyman is not to abandon the philosopher, needless to say. It is only to remind us that the philosopher himself tends to observe the poet as a suitable figure of man in intellectual action. From Plato to Eric Voegelin, the philosopher appeals to the poet. For one good reason: The poet risks himself in words, gives himself to words sacrificially as if indifferent to the consequences of his action. He is less likely to observe the cautionary distance required of other makers, whether we mean philosopher or politician. And his actions often lead to dramatic presences of the poet as person in the words themselves as opposed to merely the presence of his poems as detached objects. That has proved especially true of our recent poets, as our allusions to T. S. Eliot or Wallace Stevens or Ezra Pound have suggested. That is why we well remember, in order to see how steadily the philosopher is dependent upon the seemingly reckless poet, how much given Plato is to being a poet himself, or how respectful Aristotle is of the poet. How often, among our recent philosophers, does Husserl turn to Rilke, or Eric Voegelin to Eliot. The nexus of making, in which the poem and the person of the poet are coincident, lies in the aspects of virtue at last, in the conjunction of prudence in the poet in relation to the good of the thing made, the poem, a "creation" which consequent to the making proves existentially independent of that maker, though never quite so in the end. It is this nexus that is our center.

XX

What, then, is the proper relation of prudence to art? How does the soul come to terms with its proximate calling as maker, when its ultimate calling is to a perfection of its own being? For the relation between the useful good and unqualified good is so complicated that reason is sore pressed to discover the ordinate relation. On the one hand, the soul is called at once to the exercise of action for a common good in the contingent arena, under the auspices of a right will and through the prudential guidance of the practical intellect. On the other, it is called to a perfection of its own being, to the rescue of and sustenance of its specific nature beyond the conditions of its contingent arena. Thus, by the reality of its very specific and discrete nature, it is set apart from the limits of the common good by its ultimate end.

How may it reconcile its actions of love through the ends proper to useful, proximate good in an unselfish devotion to the common good, and yet not succumb to the temptation to make such a devotion a substitute for the ultimate good? For by its actions of love directed to the proximate good, it may lose its final end. On the other hand, in fear of that error, it may turn instead to its ultimate end in such a way as to neglect its responsibility to the proximate. It may do so out of a fear that its highest interest is sacrificed to actions dispersed in the world, at the seeming expense of the soul, with no discernible return to the soul in respect to its perfection. Through which inclination of intellect is the person lost by an exclusiveness of inclination? The dilemma is not unlike the one we encounter in discovering the intellect itself as intuitive on the one hand and rational on the other, with the accompanying temptation to exorcize the one at the expense of the other.

Certainly the soul's actions for the common good may distort the actions of the practical intellect, strengthening thereby a seeming antipathy between the practical and the speculative. So possible is this reduction of the soul, accompanied by such spectacles to the world as those displays of religious fervor detailed in the daily press, that the soul may even seem to have confused itself with Christ in its operations of charity in nature and society. At least sectarian "gurus" exhibit such a deportment. We know the epithet sometimes applied to such a soul, or at least to a soul perceived as overcome by that confusion, the term already used. The "do-gooder" is so named with pejorative intent, suggesting the pretense of such a person as savior of the world. No doubt those same judges of the "do-gooder" (ourselves) may also find an alternate target, that soul so withdrawn to itself as to appear at least aloof, withdrawn – in short, "selfish."

We know, of course, that the temptation to judgment of such souls through the evidence of spectacle in the context of circumstances is risky, especially if the judge is himself reduced to a mere spectator of action. Such a reduction may be evidence of an atrophy of spirit in the judge as well. But for the active soul, in its concerns for the relation of proximate to ultimate good, the dilemma to action is not likely to be resolved by such temporal judges of circumstanced actions as we are inclined to become. That is why that concerned soul must always be learning both to care and not to care, but it must learn always within the arena of its own given nature. The difficulty, that soul must conclude lest impasse arrest the struggling soul to inaction, is resolved only through grace, although a dependence on grace is not passive. That is, the struggling soul must continually engage the paradox which declines the conditions of its coming to be, the necessity of caring and not caring.

If we accept the unrelenting dilemma between actions as related to proximate and ultimate good as the inescapable condition of the soul's life in the world, we may therefrom discover that it is the habit of prudential virtue which is required to that soul's enduring its special and continuous concern for present action. In the necessity, it is little wonder that the poet becomes obsessed, on occasion at least, with whether art may prove his means of salvation. It is an inclination out of desperateness, and instances of such attempt are many among our poets, especially since the late eighteenth century. John Keats and Wallace Stevens are emblematic of those poets. In the arrest of the moment by the power of imagination as dominant in the making, art – the thing being made in this moment – the thing itself too easily becomes an apparent end independent of the larger prudential concern for the self in its relation to unqualified good.

Perhaps we may better understand the temptation to the poet when we reflect that the act of art has a certain finality. Consequent to the act, the made thing *is*, where it was not before the act of making. The thing, a being at last present in existence, seems to its proximate cause, the poet, a purchase made upon a good for the self. Again, poet is representative here, and we need only remember the moment of satisfaction experienced from time to time consequent upon our own work well done, whatever we may have made to share in his temptation. It is a moment of rest, differing in kind but perhaps echoing as if a suitable analogy, that moment best remembered in *Genesis*, God's seeing that what He had "made" was good, and His resting on the seventh day of creation. We experience in such a moment, at the end of satisfying labor, a self-justification through the act of our making. In that moment we may find ourselves, if but distantly, related to Him in whose image we are created. The analogy is shadowy at best, though tempting to this free agent, intellectual man, whose freedom is most evidently registered in his actions of making.

If our made thing becomes, out of our pleased delight in it, an end rather than a proximate end, the inclination of the soul may well be to rise by climbing upon the made thing as it were and thus rise beyond the proximate arena appropriate to the soul, in which arena prudential wisdom must govern the inclination. Or at least it is so governed when prudence is the established habit of being. We have been presented with many instances of this presumption, in relation to art, we suggested, since the rise of Romanticism. And as thus related to recent history we might see it a development as a reaction to the reductionist rationalism of gnostic thought that comes to dominate in science, at the expense of art, out of eighteenth-century rationalism. But the rationalistic inclination is itself analogous to the distortion here characterized as "Romanticism." For there is a symbolic rectitude in seeing in our intellectual history since the eighteenth century a contention between the poet's intuitive intellect and the scientist's rational intellect as a division improper to intellectual nature. Too seldom do we recognize both as reductionists of intellect, since we are likely to be partisan of one or the other. Indivisible, intellect is nevertheless represented in actions signifying on the one hand the intuitive and on the other the rational. But the poem and the chemical formula are more seemingly disparate things than they are in their original mediate causes, in the given intellect who "makes" the one or the other. (This, we recall, is the central concern in *Romantic Confusions of the Good*.)

We add a suggestion, relative to this allusion to the spectacle in recent history of Western thought of that impasse between "two cultures." Either "culture," as a rule, will consider itself escaped from the errors of the reductionist thought it detects in the other. But we must remember that the separation occurs earlier than the eighteenth century and may be traced at least back to the theology grown out of the Reformation. The caricature of that religious thought is usually termed "Puritanism," a term pejoratively taken in naming the putative enemy of both art and science by some minds. What we might suggest is, not that the alarm over so-called "Puritan thought" is not a proper one, but that the reaction to that thought tends to be but a species of the same reductionism of reality exercised as opposition. If we see in the poet, for instance, his desire that the poem become the vehicle of rescue to his intellect, or if the scientist takes the formula as the necessary instrument of that rescue, either action may be but another species of the principle underlying the "Puritan work ethic." That is an "ethic" destructive of rescue insofar as it supposes that by its own making it is self-rescued. In any of these inclinations, whether of the scientist or poet or religious, there lurks the gnostic position, whether the putative concern is a transcendence or an immanent control of being, or some combination of control. That is why we return from time to time to the necessity of recognizing the support of grace, knowing as we do so that this reality of grace is not readily acceptable to the contemporary intellectual.

The temptation to presume autonomous power through the effects of our making follows in part from our recognition that the thing we have made is good. But to take the good of the thing made, which is the proper concern of the artist, as ipso facto evidence of the good of the maker is to blur the incommensurate distance between God as creator and man as a maker, who is himself made in the image of God. It is a confusion which makes art as a habit a substitute for virtuous habits of being in the artist. Let us here approach this concern for the complex nature of virtue in making from a slightly different perspective. The relation of faith to works, which has been a question of contention since St. Paul, is reconciled, not by the making of argument whereby argument itself establishes the truth. It is rather a reconciliation in which love is exercised ordinately, through our caring and not caring, in the action of making. And that center for the soul's reconciliation to its own existence is kept alive to intellect always through our knowledge. Knowledge, we must at last recognize, is given through the agency of grace. In prudence's relation to art lies the wisdom of limit to the gifts of our making as a discretely gifted person. That is a thing *known*, when we reflect upon the concern. But works as the absolute moral principle of our being leads to the distortion of a prudential constancy, leaving the soul consumed with its making as itself the principal means of its rescue. Even so, in rejecting this "Puritan work ethic," whether as practiced by the priest or pastor or poet or scientist, we have not yet restored a perspective upon the ordinate relation of prudence to art, for we *are* makers.

In one species of art understood as rescue of person, the question becomes whether art is to be subordinated to the common good as a means of a general rescue of the world, of the social body. In this wandering from the way, art derived from the "Puritan work ethic" reaches a severe secularization. In substituting the virtue of art as determinate of the poet's being, to the exclusion of prudence in relation to the poet's soul, one arrives at an extreme, the art-for-art's sake worshiper who is indifferent of necessity to the common good. At another extreme lies the art-as-social-mechanism poet, who understands the subordination of art to policy as the desirable use of art in structuring political community. On the one hand the "personal" of the artist becomes (but only apparently so) the end of practical intellect's actions in the world, the artist being indifferent to the common good. On the other hand, the personal is denied altogether. The extreme positions here suggested emerge in contention with each other in modernist thought, and they do so largely because we have lost the distinctions between *individual* and *personal* being, as we have lost the distinction between *practical* and *speculative* intellect. And so we see the poet increasingly turn to art as personal savior. Or we see the political activist turn to art as an instrument of power over being.

But on either hand, we must realize at last that art as savior is at best savior of the *individual*, whether as citizen in the city of man or as a forlorn name continuing awhile in time by its association with an artifact. Art can never be the savior of *person*. This confusion of art as savior leads in the nineteenth century to art's being juxtaposed to science as the only balance possible to particular beings in time, as if science were not itself an order of virtue in the practical intellect and of the same species as other arts of the practical intellect. The confusion of poetry and science as essentially distinct virtues of intellect became intellectually popular through the arguments of critics like Matthew Arnold. Arnold, we might say, anticipates the fault in culture, a fissure which is to widen to our own concern for the "Two Cultures" in contention, science and art. Arnold's concern, we must note, is for the common good. In a sense that concern for art as instrument to the common good, unjustified by metaphysics, leads in our century to a capitulation of art to science in the name of the common good. Or rather, to a capitulation to a pseudo-science. Thus art becomes handmaid through pragmatism to the restructuring of society, at last submitting to the dictatorship of Marxist ideology on the one hand, or to serving disordered appetite through advertising techniques on the other, techniques increasingly required to create appetite for ill-made things in our consumer society. Art thus becomes redefined as a mode of science, specifically a mode of psychological science. In respect to the virtues of the practical intellect as supported by the speculative, in response to intellect's encounter of realities, either art or science were better understood as actions of the practical intellect to mediate concerns in the context of a larger speculative understanding of ultimate end. But that is an approach to art or science seldom encountered in the considerable speculative literature that attempts to justify one or the other or both appropriations of art to appetite.

As for the poet, the artist, does he "save" either himself or others through art? The question will not go away, especially given our age of intellectual confusion in which art as social instrument ends often enough in supporting horrors. For the subversiveness of propaganda, the manipulation of reality by the art of making, has supplied us with an overplus of arresting horrors. We need only recall "imaginative journalism" in support of Hitler and Stalin, championing social determinism whose fundamental principle (when run to ground) is that man is a mechanism to be adjusted within the larger mechanism of the state. What, then, is the poet's proper relation to the body of community? It is a question whose resolution requires our recovering an understanding of the poet's proper involvement in the common good, the proper action of the poet whereby his art does not become his final end but is art nevertheless. That is, the poet's art (he discovers) is an end *in itself*, but not *in the artist*. Nor is his own end in his art. Again a delicate distinction, out of the *intellectus* as supported by the *ratio* insofar as possible. For this mutual support in modes of intellect is necessary to any prospect of stilling, at least for a moment, those insistent questions the poet, and by our extension any person, cannot escape.

Let us begin anew on old ground, by recalling the distinction between the virtue of prudence and the virtue of art – virtues whose separate orders concern separate proximate and ultimate ends. We observe that the soil feeding those ends are the same – namely, the matrix of being which is first of all the discrete soul in its striving for those virtues in pursuit of its beatitude. That soul, rooted proximately in creation, is the same subject out of which blossoms both of these virtues which we speak of as if separate orders of the soul, the virtue of prudence and the virtue of art. The subject of the virtue of art and of prudence, we must make emphatic, is the discretely created soul existing within a discretely created world. And, given common root in the discrete soul, the aspects of this soul we speak of as *individual* or as *person* may not by the separation of terms be supposed as unrelated to each other. It is by our act of categorizing that we use such terms as *person* or *individual* and thereby seem to separate the thing itself as if speaking of separate beings, rather than of aspects of a single being, the person. By such categorizing, we give an appearance of severing, as if naming independent orders and ends by the autopsy of words. But speak of them we must, in the interest of the finite intellect's understanding of its simple existence. Meanwhile, we continue alert to the point that the reality of the soul's simplicity is not itself affected essentially by our naming, by our surgery of terms.

Of necessity, because of the gift of intellectual finitude, we must name dimensions of the simple existence of the soul through such categories as *individual* and *person*, *practical intellect* and *speculative intellect*, *intellectus* and *ratio*, and so on. For always, because of its *very* nature, intellect is committed to categorical acts of intellection in pursuit (through terms) of the simplicity of being, a simplicity which is nevertheless always beyond any full comprehension by the finite intellect. However much it irritates the will to say this truth or however tedious to repeat it, the powers of finite intellect never allow intellect's full understanding of simple being, short of glimpses through an enabling grace in moments of vision. Such is the fleeting promise of a state of beatitude. Intellect cannot even comprehend its "self," let alone any other explicit being. Given our fallen nature, it is no surprise then that this limit to the power of finite intellect is exactly its own given, intellectual being. It is this *givenness* which intellect, directed by will, most stubbornly and perversely opposes. Thus intellect is tempted to stand against the Giver of its very being. For it is always wrestling with its envy of the Absolute Giver, wishing in both open and hidden ways to be "as the gods." What it wishes is that it might be *creator* and not *maker*.

XXI

We have argued that the good of the *doer* is the ultimate issue of intellectual action, because of the order of his special being, his nature as intellectual creature whose proper habit of being is intellectual making. That making is out of the practical intellect, we said, the proper governor of the art of making. But the virtue of art, as the poet must know, is focused proximately in his making, since he is making a thing within temporal and spatial restrictions upon his deportment as a maker of things. The good proper to that focus upon a proximate making is in relation to the thing under construction. The maker's immediate responsibility as governed by material limits to his immaterial vision of the thing he would make is the good of the envisioned thing. It is a responsibility accompanied by a second: that he not violate the good of that with which he makes his envisioned thing. For since he is a maker, and not a creator in the sense in which God is creator, he must appropriate the pre-existent to his making, and his appropriation must be ordinate to both what he takes and what he makes of what he takes. The poet's disquiet in relation to this responsibility we encounter often enough, from Chaucer's retraction to Hawthorne's suspicion that the devil is in his inkwell.

In discovering self-governance in relation to the gift of making, the poet learns his relation to the thing he makes, not always easy for him to accept, since it follows from his role as "coadjutor" of being. What he learns is that, within the purview of art as a practical devotion of intellect, the made thing has as its own end, not the good of the artist, but its own good, and that is the proximate good for which the artist is responsible in his making. This must be so, because unlike God as Creator, man by his nature cannot focus action at once upon himself as primary and the thing made as secondary, though primary in its limited nature. The poet, in other words, wavers in his making when his concern shifts from the good of the thing he would make to his own good as consequence of his making. We have considered that, though one might desire no shifting, no shadow of such turning, such a turning is an inescapable consequence to the nature of the created thing, this coadjutor, this intellectual and spiritual man. It is a restlessness out of his inescapable turning, we suggested, that hints of a state desired beyond temporal conditions to action, that hunger in the soul for beatitude. Man by his created nature, fallen since Adam, oscillates in his spiritual quest for certitude of being between mediate and ultimate ends, and it is this oscillation that is fundamental to the nature of art itself insofar as art is attributable to the practical intellect.

The oscillation, the shifting from an attention to the proximate good of the thing made to an attention to the ultimate good of the maker – who is maker in that he is a thing created in God's image whose proper end is in glorifying God – that oscillation gives rise to the necessity of his ordering ends in relation to willed desire. St. Thomas remarks that, in relation to our literal act of seeing with the body's eye, "[I]t is impossible for the primary thing seen to be the very act of seeing, because all seeing is of some visible object." In that remark lies a figurative description of the dislocation of intellect which is possible through the oscillation we have spoken of. For the poet, as observed in another context, the problem of the "I" in relation to the object of its attention becomes debilitating of intellectual action in some instances. It is the problem of the "recessive I," in which the relation of a seeing by an "I" to an awareness that "I" am seeing introduces a new level of the "I" attempting to look at itself looking at an object. (The poet who perhaps best reveals the dilemma to us, I have suggested, is Walt Whitman.)

But let us return to St. Thomas's remark: "[I]t is impossible for the primary thing seen to be the very act of seeing, because all seeing is of some visible object." He adds, by analogy: "[I]t is impossible that the primary thing desired, which is its end, be the act itself of willing." (*Summa* I-II, Q 1, A. 1) Such is an ancient observation, self-evident, which gives the lie to the existentialist's pretense to the contrary which has intruded upon art with dislocating consequences to the artist. One cannot will to be what must be taken as an already accomplished end in order that it may be willed, and if one attend Jean-Paul Sartre's intricate concern for a *present* willing of a future *being*, in which the nature of time itself is distorted from a present, one sees the circular entanglement of the pretense.

Concerning St. Thomas's observation in respect to our own present concern, we may say that the poet's primary object is the poem being made. To shift from that object to a primary attention to the perfection of the maker's intellect itself is a confusion of proximate goods, though one of those proximate goods, this moment's perfection of intellect, is in effect a distortion of good. That is, the suitable concern for the perfection of the intellect is properly an ultimate and not a proximate good. It is in this distortion of ends that worldly ambition, for instance, may arise, affecting the fulfillment of the proximate good of the thing being made.

What may occur in this aspect of intellectual oscillation is a shifting from an openness of action by finite intellect toward a good beyond itself, but not *transcendentally* beyond itself – the good of the made thing. It becomes instead an act of closure mistaken as a transcendent opening. Hence the conclusion that the danger is in a confusion of unqualified good reduced to proximate good – a reduction of the transcendental end of the soul's journeying to a temporal end of self-perfection, which is necessarily a closing upon the self as its own end when it supposes that end effected by its own will. That is the condition of assumed autonomy, whose reality is an alienation of the soul from reality, both proximate and transcendent reality. It is only through such a confusion that the poet can accept the illusion that by his act of creating the poem he rescues himself. What will suffer most evidently, that is, at the level of spectacle in the proximate world, is the good of the thing made, the poem. Or at least that is a strong probability, let us say, since the maker of the poem will have in some degree abandoned his responsibility as maker of the poem, his responsibility to the good of the thing itself, in the interest of his own good. This is to say, then, that our acts of making partake of sacrifice to the good of the thing made, a sacrifice which must nevertheless be controlled ordinately, in that the sacrifice must not be taken as a sacrifice to an ultimate. For to take it as ultimate is to succumb to idolatry.

If man were God, as through temptation he is sometimes led to desire to be, then the action of his making would be out of a precedent perfection of his intellect such that the thing made might be necessarily good, since God does not create an evil thing. (Thomas reminds us, to this point, that evil is the absence of good.) The popular confusion of the poet with God, encouraged as often as not by the poet himself, is out of the unfocused desire of the maker, which when unfocused would have it that finite acts of making be "original" beyond the limits of reality. That is, the desire is for an originating perfection by the poet whose effect is a perfectly made thing supposed absolutely dependent upon the poet's own "originating" perfection. This is the position, in its extremity, whereby the poet denies any givenness, most especially his own as *created* person. In pursuit of that desire, what is set aside is reality: For in truth the poet operates within restrictions of his own finitude so that practical intellect is the necessary and restricting mode to the making. That is, the practical intellect accommodates the action of making to the limits of finitude whereby the poet, analogous in some respects to God as Creator, partakes of that analogous relationship but only distantly, that is, in St. Thomas's word, "proportionately." Most succinctly, man as maker acts out of the givenness of his own nature within the givenness of complex creation, so that only God may be said absolutely "original."

Art's end, we must conclude, is its own good and not the good of the artist. But even so, in relation to prudence as a necessary virtue in the person who acts by making, his making has an inescapably prudential effect upon himself. For his actions of making cannot be divorced from the effect of his action upon himself. One who has devoted himself to making as an artist knows all too well that making may be "an expense of spirit." Any agent of art (and so every person, since making is central to the nature of person) is at risk in and through his actions of making. Risk is an inevitable condition, since will is the initiator of practical intellect toward proximate ends. The periodic fascination with "automatic writing" as art, which seems to rise at periods when the general community is confused and dislocated as a community, would seem an attempt to escape the consequences of the will's judgment in making or not making a thing. The attempt intends, at its most radical level in respect to the nature of the artist, to escape the effects of making upon the person of the artist, and it would do so by denying the role of intellect in art. But most particularly, it would deny the role of the practical intellect whose responsibility is to bring reason to bear upon intuition, thus establishing a government by the will itself to an ordinate action of the maker. At most, such a position of the artist in his responsibility to the thing he makes as it is represented in the extreme of automatic or spontaneous art will allow only an ungoverned speculative intellect, with intuition thus elevated beyond reason. It is a condition very likely spoken of and even justified as the mode the biologist speaks of *instinct*. For it is not likely that the advocate of such art will in the end submit to any transcendent cause of his making, an initiation of the act of making by either muse or the Holy Ghost. Better animal than *anima* agency, since the soul once granted as an existing gift raises most disturbing questions to the Modernist gnostic intellect.

Pure "inspiration," whether granting to the inspired a locus of inspiration as animal nature or spiritual nature, posits an *in-spiriting*, whereby the thing that is possessed by a mysterious force is reduced to mere instrumentality. Thus, even if art is reduced to the level of instinct, perhaps finding its analogue in nature in the bower bird, the recognition of analogy, the positing of that analogy and the articulation of it, puts the intellect presiding over such an analogy in the inescapable position which Gilson speaks of as "meta-physical." That intellect is dealing with the transphysical and with assertions of truth that are themselves trans-physical, though the intent may be to locate the cause of that truth only in the material reality by the authority of an autonomous intellect presiding over being. In such an impasse, little wonder the welcome we seem now to give the gene as an interior cause of our formal being. The gene itself is at once so remote as to lie on the border of the material and immaterial worlds, but it has the authority of science that it is materially existent. It is the most elemental level of material-spiritual existence, but it seems to yield itself primarily to physics, to the relief of gnostic intellect, thus escaping the necessity to the mythologizing intellect of accounting for its immaterial dimension as an actuality beyond imputations of intellect itself.

Caught up on the one hand by the wonders of new sciences but let down on the other by the abandonment of the rigors of philosophy, the poet finds himself struggling to reconcile the experiences known in and through intellect, his rational and intuitional experiences of reality. It is a knowledge uncomfortably present to intellect, uncomfortable in that intellect cannot quite trust itself in its own knowing, so that it may well feel relieved in taking its actions of making as instinctive, and only when severely pressed by hard philosophy against its hard science will it confront the mystery implied in its intuitive nature. There is a comfort in concluding oneself as intellect merely instrumental. We recall that it was this earlier version of the poet as instrument which Plato is at pains to reject in the *Ion*. It is this version of the poet he finds dangerous in his own great poem, *The Republic*. It is the version of the poet, whose presence among us is not to be denied, which Plato sets aside in the *Phaedrus* in favor of the poet as *philokalos*, the lover of the beautiful, and as proconsul to community with that lover of truth of things, the philosopher.

If we consider that the action of making when properly focused toward the good of the thing made effects a good in the agent through prudential virtue, we are led to a further concern for the distinction between man as maker and God as maker. For in such a conclusion about our making we acknowledge an imperfection in ourselves as maker. We move out of our precedent actuality of being, whereby potentiality becomes actual, in a movement toward perfection of the discrete gift of being to the particular intellectual creature so moving. In God we do not suppose a complex relation of cause and effect, of maker to made thing, with apparent secondary effect: namely, a coming to be of God as the agent beyond the actual beginning state of Being Itself – such is our concern for finite limits as explored by practical intellect, speculative intellect telling us that this is a necessary distinction of man from God. And, indeed, from the perspective of speculative intellect, we might not consent to the description of making upon the finite maker, the effect of a coming-to-be of the poet through his action as poet, as a secondary effect. For it is an effect whose reference is to ultimate good. The perspective of practical intellect, in relation to the action of making, is oriented by the proximate good, the good of the thing made. Out of such meditations, supplied in our thought by speculative and practical intellect in concord, we acknowledge a necessity: Since in God there is an antecedent perfection of being, questions of mediate and ultimate good are not relevant questions, except insofar as they may suggest the reality of man as maker in the realities of his circumstantial existence. That is the reality of what St. Thomas speaks of as man's "participation."

The relation of the Creator (God) to the created creature is a simple one. The contingent perfection of potential being in the creature is dependent in its given nature upon its responding to circumstantial contingencies in the created world of which it is a part. Thus God's relation to his creature is not strictly analogous to the poet's relation to his creature, the poem. We acknowledge nevertheless a certain likeness, not explicable by direct positive analogy, since we accept the mystery of man's existence as created in the *image* of his Maker. It is this relationship of the made creature man to Maker which is so easily abandoned or distorted, and perhaps more easily by the poet than by other makers. The gardener or brick-layer, for instance, is constantly reminded of the antecedent material cause to his making as he delves earth or hefts bricks. But the poet's material cause is, upon reflection, discovered to be rather an immaterial cause, namely the word.

Insofar as the voice or symbols on a page relate to the actual immaterial cause, the word, the poet will be the first to recognize them in their material dimensions as accidental to the actual immaterial cause. It is thought formed, and the voicing or the setting down is in a separate dimension of reality from the essential nature of the poem, as Gilson argues in *Linguistics and Philosophy*. We discover this an important distinction when we compare the voicing of a poem by one person as compared to the voicing of that poem by another. And we even know that the poet who himself makes the poem may, in voicing it, do less than justice to its reality, to the good it enjoys in itself so to speak. Even more obviously, we know that ink and paper are not properly considered material cause to the poem. This is not to overlook the attempts at shaped poems – poems about a tree or swan constructed on the page in the shape of the tree or swan. Such poems as novelties fascinate the eye, but they do so largely because of a wit in the maker whereby there is the attempt through spectacle to integrate differing modes of art – painting in relation to word. Herbert's angels shadowed by ink displayed on the page are nevertheless accidents even in Herbert's intention, for he is committed, not to the spectacle, but to the reality of angels in relation to which the spectacle is inadequate, even as discursive words are inadequate. In this respect, Herbert differs from our century's devotees of "Concrete Poetry" in that his is a shaping of poem on a page less concerned with display of wit than a concern to suggest the ineffable.

A making dependent upon wit, even as a making dependent upon irony, is a dependence which we may discover related to either an assumption of will to intellectual autonomy or an acceptance of alienation in a retreat from responsible action. The one we can illustrate from the poetry of Wallace Stevens, the other from the early poetry of T. S. Eliot. The one poet is committed to the pleasure of wit, the other to the self-protection of an isolated awareness through the defensive shell of irony. There develops for either poet, however, a problem to intellect which he cannot easily dislodge. The question rises whether his willed autonomy or his despair in alienation, is dependent upon his own action in having distorted reality. If so, then reality is not fully submissive to the distorting act, since intellect yet knows reality as precedent to the distorting act. The position of willed autonomy holds that one may either write a poem or not write a poem, accountability for action or inaction solely referred to the "creative" agent. It is a position positing an absolute freedom, independent of contingent reality, since otherwise the agent must acknowledge the problem of his dependence in reality. As for the alienated intellect which takes its alienation as not intentional but accidentally random, it must in the end consider that if not itself intentional, either it is such a random accident or it is an effect of an intentionality other than itself. Either conclusion raises questions unsettling to the proposition that itself as awareness is an existence of an outer, a detached darkness, so to speak. That is the emerging realization in T. S. Eliot, we have suggested. And by that realization he moves from the isolation maintained by irony into an uncertainty to the self. That is, he moves toward risking the self, in relation to reality. In that risk, thought can only accommodate the mystery of existence through paradox, through diverse knowings of reality not fully reconciled by understanding. But in that new recognition the inadequacy of irony as a deportment of the alienated self is recognized in its inadequacy.

Once the dilemma to the assumption of the agent's existence as either autonomous or alienated is acknowledged, it becomes probable that the precedent gift of its own being will be a necessary reality with which it must come to terms. The ground of its actuality must be accounted for beyond the simplifications of the initial assumption of autonomy, of its intentional disjunction from the complex of reality as the cause of its existence. In a last attempt to maintain autonomy, a further problem is likely to arise, turning the intentionally autonomous intellect back to reconsider the ground of its assumption. If intellect asserts its accountability in either making or not making as only absolute to itself and independent of reality other than itself, the question arises at last of the actuality of the autonomous agent himself. What relation, then, is implied between the thing made or refused its possible being and the agent? There is already an implied potential being, a possible poem, which is therefore in some respect already a certain "thing." We may say that it is a thought in the autonomous agent and as such already a thing. The agent, by an act of will, may deny its coming into words, but it nevertheless has a certain existence beyond the agent's power to will that it either exist or not exist. For he has already granted its potential being by his thought. Intellect finds itself powerless in respect to potential being, if by *power* it understands itself as the determining God of a thing's existing or not existing. A thought is, and one may *forget* it, but that is not the same as to make it *not to be*. Since it has come to be a thought in the agent, it has already escaped the power of the will to deny its existence, however resolutely the will would suppress it. To think at all, we are saying, is to call in question the absolute autonomy of intellect, and even of "free" will if we would suppose the will absolute, though will is intricately clever in the manipulation of intellect in response to the threat of thought to will's absolute autonomy.

A considerable dilemma, this. And it suggests that we take recourse to St. Thomas once more. For in considering the virtues of intellect in making, or not making, we must also consider the role of grace to action or inaction. Considered in the limited perspective of the agent's relation to the thing to be made, Thomas asserts that "[a]rt does not belong to moral knowledge, which concerns things to be done (*agibilia*), since art is right reason about things to be made (*factibilia*)." Thus the *Summa's* "Prologue" to Questions 1–16 in II-II. In this series of questions, Thomas affirms that "The way proper to human intellect is that it apprehend the truth by combining and dividing." This is to say that intellect's action is discursive in relation to the simplicity of existing things, since its limits of knowing make discursiveness proper to it by its own nature and not as a consequence of the action upon object. This is the province properly governed by the intellectual virtues: prudence, wisdom, understanding, knowledge. For it is the end of these virtues to bring the discursive intellect into a relation to *being* as simple, to *truth* as simple, and not divided. But, says St. Thomas, these virtues are gifts of the Holy Spirit, operative as gifts in the present moment of discursiveness and as such they sustain the natural gifts of intellect. Thus the thing believed, "about which faith is had," is not complex. But "on the part of the believer," the agent, it is complex "in the manner of a truth-bearing statement," which truth-bearing statement is the summary of the necessary intellectual actions of combining and dividing in reaching an accommodation of simple truth to the simple essence of a thing.

Thomas distinguishes in these questions the appetitive and intellectual powers of the person, the appetitive including passions and will. The appetitive provides access to knowledge by the nature of our personhood, a knowledge from our experience of our own existence as *a* being ordered to an end. Now truth, says Thomas, is "the good of the understanding, it is not the good of the appetitive power." In his own pursuit of truth through dividing and combining by intellectual actions focused upon, Thomas would touch by intellect the known thing which is truth supplied intellect by experience. Thomas builds on his faith in the reality of that known thing as possessed by intellect. It leads him to say that the "virtues that complete the appetitive part do not completely exclude the false," for a person "can act justly or temperately while holding a false opinion about what he does." It is in this respect that we might suggest that the poet, presuming his autonomy as maker, may by a passionate will nevertheless act in a consent to the good of the thing he makes, the poem. The opinion may be wrong, but the consent to the good of the thing to be made may accomplish that good through a making beyond the failure of opinion. It is a condition to making which is graced, and the analogy we might introduce is that of the priest's relation to the sacraments he celebrates. He need not, as the Donatist heresy contends he must, be himself perfect for perfection to reside in the thing he "makes" through his celebration.

The poet as maker, though his understanding and even his knowledge may be defective, may act falsely in relation to the truth as that truth is a possible good of intellectual powers, though he may also act justly or temperately in respect to intention of his appetitive powers. The complexity here, raising the perennial dilemma to the actions of persons in community of the relation of justice to mercy in respect to the truth of things, is the relation of good effected by an intention to the good, though the intentional agent fail intellectually through defective knowledge or understanding. That is the tragic dilemma played out in *Oedipus the King*, as we have suggested, whose good effect in us is a consent to the limits of understanding in relation to intent to the good. That is an aspect of what Aristotle terms *catharsis*. Thus what we are properly recalled to, through tragedy, is the importance to our unity as a person of our intellectual powers which must ordinately support our appetitive powers. It is an intellectual act of faith, then, that makes Thomas say that "faith completes the understanding," while hope and charity complete the appetitive part. Thus hope and charity cannot be "reasoned about in the same way" as we reason about faith. Faith initiates the intellectual powers, in that intellect consents to the reality of the already known, for to know is precedent to the intellectual justification of the known through reason. Hope and charity, we see by intellect's combining and dividing the question, appear separately, as when we say with Thomas that "it belongs to charity to love God in whomever he might be" although it "does not matter to charity whether God is really in the one who is loved because of [our love for] God."

We may seem to have gone considerably afield from our concern for that intellect whose faith rests in its assumption of its own autonomy, as well as from that more desperate condition of the alienated intellect whose effect is despair beyond hope. But we have done so in order to arrive at that dilemma which intellect encounters in attempting to deal with the mystery of thought itself. A thing thought has an existence beyond the power of the will to deny the thought itself its existence. The dilemma must lead an intellect toward a possibility of its participation in being relative to its thought, a participation that can only be accounted to grace. The progress through prudence from knowledge to understanding to this wisdom discovers the progress, given the perspective of Thomistic realism, as under the auspices of the Holy Ghost. That is a conclusion we come to in such a progress from faith. It is thus that intellect is returned to realism as sustaining *of* intellect and not sustained *by* intellect. But it is not an inevitable conclusion to fallible intellect. What we might suggest is a certain support of that possibility on the evidence of certain persons whom we observe in progress, and measured comparatively by our own experience openly engaged. And though we do not intend a prolonged explication of such a progress by dividing and combining known things about at least partially known agents, we shall nevertheless suggest an attention to two poets in whom this progress requires some accounting, poets already introduced, Wallace Stevens and T. S. Eliot. The validity of the attempt will not rest in the end in our certainty about the actuality of their progress as we might know it with certainty, but upon what we experience of our own intellectual progress in the course of this attempt. For it is thus that we come to a better understanding of what we can know only in a limited way, and perhaps know best through exploring the intellects of others through whatever signs they have left us along the way of their progress. That is why it is important to such an attempt to consider conspicuously gifted intellects as witnesses to our common experience of intellectual journeying.

XXII

Let us look at two readily available, well known, poems by Wallace Stevens that are concerned with the principle of intellectual autonomy as the necessity to creating poetry. In his "Sunday Morning," Stevens explicitly questions as illusion the relation of the Word (Christ) to existence. It is a poem which he will later characterize as a "Pagan" poem. The speaker objects to his lady's devotion to an illusion, her religious action whereby she gives her "bounty to the dead" by her Sabbath ceremony. If one look closely at the argument itself at the heart of the art, one finds the protest very like Huck Finn's against the Widow's version of heaven. The reality of human existence (so runs the argument) is that we live "in an old chaos of the sun." We are "unsponsored," therefore "free," and particularly free of that "wide water" that by illusion we navigate in making the journey to "the grave of Jesus." The reality proposed is that we are caught in the "old dependence of day and night," caught in time, allowed within that entrapment only "ambiguous undulations" as we sink "downward to darkness," even as do the pigeons settling out of the "isolation of the sky." If a pagan poem as Stevens says of it, it is hardly celebrative of communal paganism. It is rather an assertion of a separate freedom of intellect against the world, a celebration of alienation whose only means of celebration is the imagination. And that is also the burden of "The Idea of Order at Key West," the concern in that poem being with the word uttered by the poet in support of the imagination. We need to remember Stevens at this point, however, as he insists that the poet writes for himself alone. The uttering is to the uttering intellect's sole pleasure.

As I have suggested elsewhere, this poem pretends to be a monologue, spoken to one "pale Ramon," whose paleness is of such degree as to suggest no anchor in reality. He is an imagined projection, and so is consistent with the argument of the poem. Just why any argument is required if the one for whom the poem exists (the maker of the poem) rests faith in the argument is not very clear.

Nevertheless the evangelical burden of the argument is that the action of intellect alone causes order, where otherwise there is but that "old chaos of the sun." The imagined woman, singing as she strides along the beach, is the "maker of the song she sang," whereby she is declared "the single artificer of the world." In that circumstance to her making, "there never was a world for her/ Except the one she sang and, singing, made." This is a projection of a surrogate poet by the poet, a woman singing as a figure of the singer who is singing the woman's imagined existence. The poet himself as singer now turns to the "material" effect of his making, to the words he uses, the imagistic utterances. But what is asserted, in a moment of rising emotion as if of a religious ecstasy of vision, is that those words signify the spirit of the maker as thus self-made. He is self-made by a "blessed rage for order," specifically "the maker's rage to order words of the sea" – and as the context shows, sky and earth as well. What one makes of dead physics – of color and sound – is the poem. And those words issue from "the fragrant portal, dimly-starred," out of the maker's mouth in a musical articulation of order. The words become "ghostlier demarcations" thereby, despite their being "keener sounds" at the level of physics than the sound of the sea. They are pale indications of "ourselves and of our origins," which is the depth of imagination exercising its self-making of the poet. This is the locus of mystery, set in counterpoint to the "illusion" so attractive to the Beloved in "Sunday Morning."

In "Sunday Morning," the "truth" insisted in conclusion, is from a voice "without sound." That truth is that

> The tomb in Palestine
> Is not the porch of spirits lingering.
> It is the grave of Jesus, where he lay.

The words are subversive of the woman's inclinations, since they are cast as if a temptation by a voice from within herself, a voice she hears that is "without sound." The sardonic irony lies in saying "Jesus. . . *lay*" in that tomb, thus suggesting he no longer lies there, but not because he is risen from the dead but because dissolved in those undulations of dead physics, that sinking downward to the darkness of dissipating matter under the old chaos of the sun. What is necessary to the position thus proposed by the ironic tempter, the asserted temptation a continuous certification to the maker himself of the rightness of the position, is a most strange dependence upon those ghostly demarcations of intellect, signs willed continuously. Words uttered one by one. But why should the sign be necessary to maintain the position? Why must one write even for one? That is the entangling problem which haunts Steven's poetry, giving it the tensional energy which makes it inviting to persons other than the maker himself. For it dramatizes the continuous tension of intellect between its own being and any being not itself, through which tension rises those questions of the cause of being itself that increasingly haunt intellect. That such questions haunted Stevens is made evident by his final deportment as maker, his conversion to Christianity. He argued wittily against Christ through nearly all of his poetry.

When words issue from intellect through those "starry portals," the poet's lips, even if they are not set down in black ink as Shakespeare thought might make them eternal perhaps, the word as word seems not incarnate by its material existence. For the physics of words is a secondary existence. It is hauntingly true of words that truth spoken or written give at best manifestation as a ghostly demarcation from the thought as the actual reality. The mystery is that by its very material representation, its secondary nature, the word seems but the more uncertain in its actuality. Its reality, its meaning, resides somewhere other than in the material representation. This is the mystery of the word which Gilson reminds us leads again and again to the necessity of metaphysical questions. The easy confidence of power by our acts of assertion of material representations of thought – words uttered, inscribed, proclaimed – proves undependable. And that power in the word is undependable precisely in relation to words in their secondary nature as they abandon the truth as determinate of the word's power. This is the shocking discovery T. S. Eliot comes to, the point of that shock, I suggest, in "Death by Water" in *The Waste Land*. Eliot's testimony to his experience as maker one might juxtapose to Stevens's assertion of the downwardness to darkness that closes "Sunday Morning." Eliot's "drowned Phoenician sailor" is (we might suggest) Steven's pagan voice overcome at last by the drowning dark, only to discover that the darkness does not end all.

It is an experience for Eliot, as we have already suggested, whose metaphorical representation in the poem is a baptism, and it is significant that St. Paul issues overtly in the recovery with "Gentile or Jew" in that interval of lines in "Death by Water," that climax of *The Waste Land*, which lies between "entering the whirlpool" and these words from St. Paul's letter to the Romans, "Gentile or Jew." There will follow for Eliot, recorded in the poems that follow *The Waste Land*, a new sense of the word, and of his responsibility as steward of the word. There is no longer the same relation of poet as maker to the word as he had assumed earlier. Earlier, up to *The Waste*

Land turning, he like Stevens had assumed the word as received from the tradition, from precedent "makers" was as a raw matter to be used as willed. In that use the word would acquire whatever "meaning" it might have. That was the intellectual position, which reason maintained as stubbornly as it could. But intuitive intellect would not be stilled, and the effect of that contention within intellect was the event of his "nervous breakdown," which in actuality was a spiritual crisis. Out of that crisis, he turns with new understanding toward the Word, through the word. And it is the difficulty of the word's witness to truth that will concern him from that point on. Truth is no longer relative, though his words are now accepted as at best relative to that absolute truth, the Word.

What we see in Wallace Stevens, almost up to his death, and in Eliot, but only up to *The Waste Land*, is an insistent autonomous relation between the maker and his act, the act represented by the made thing. The maker is God and the thing – his poem – his very Begotten. Given the danger of such an excess, the poet may resist the inclination to idolatry which is implicit in his assumption, as James Joyce for a time attempts to resist it. We ought, in this respect, recall that Joyce was Jesuit-trained, knew his St. Thomas, whom he attempts to de-sacralize by the appropriation of Thomas's arguments on art which Joyce would reduce to the purview of the autonomous maker, the poet, who becomes the God of his made world very like the position Stevens argues in his "Idea of Order at Key West." A difference, however, appears early in Joyce, who recognizes the danger in the made thing of its attraction to the maker. That maker of a poem may become dependent upon the made thing when his intent is its dependence on him. Accepting, and even glorying in, intellectual autonomy, Joyce thus has his young Stephen as surrogate poet reduce his made thing (which is in fact not yet made, only dreamed of by young Stephen). He reduces it by an indifference to it as its maker. He would be serenely aloof from it, imagining himself as a god pruning his nails. If he goes so far as to voice it or inscribe it, he must hold the inscription an accident of the creative act, lest will be forced to acknowledge at least itself as an audience.

One of the ironies of this strain of thought about the poet and his making as we encounter it in modern literature – that is, in our literature since Joyce – is the agony in the actual poet over the necessity of a paying audience, the necessity of publication, so that we have on the one hand a deportment of the poet as maker partially imitative of the Desert Father in retreat, but partially imitative of the Madison Avenue huckster as well. As for the Desert Father aspect, the will as the "god" of making the poem, the being to be created, cannot for its own power's sake as autonomous relent by acknowledging "this is my beloved creation in which I am well pleased." That is because the will, when turned against being in maintaining its autonomy, is a most jealous god, whose jealousy is dependent upon its unjustness. The desire for power is a substitute for love, a desire which can be maintained only so long as it can maintain indifference, even to its own creations.

That is the dilemma, incidentally, that ate away at Wallace Stevens no doubt, for his intuitive intellect was subversive of rational intellect's totalitarian concern for imaginative power. Which is to say that the desire which is love is incipient in Stevens's poetry all along. If it were not, there could not be that tensional drama in it which makes it a poetry of a most engaging kind.

What we are pursuing here is the tangled skein of self-entrapment by thought itself when will turns perverse. In that entanglement intellect will be discovered operating on one principle in one instance and on a contradictory principle in the next. It will be forced to desperate remedy, and it will be so forced by reality itself. For it is reality which is the loving antagonist of willful autonomy. Over actuality the will holds no sufficient control and so the will cannot maintain its dream of self-autonomy. And so in the end the will finds itself besieged by its own thought in its most interior bastion, as Prufrock laments. Additionally, it is buffeted from without. It is subject to both material and immaterial reality, in addition to which it is constrained by its peculiar nature in the agent soul. For it is existent only by virtue of the incarnate soul. However much it would reject the condition of its incarnate locus, by whatever species of Manichaean manipulation of signs, it is always dragged into the proximity of creation as quite distinct from its own makings. It is confronted by circumstantial existence, and that is a necessity to its existence which is intolerable and requires either an embrace of non-existence or a surrender to the necessities of existence that reduces it from its pretense to godhead. *Either* a rejection of Love, a suicide, *or* an openness to Love, through openness to circumstantial reality. This is, as we might recall, the theme developed persuasively by Eliot in "Ash-Wednesday," in an argument turning from the defensiveness of his sardonic irony in the early poetry to the endangerment of the self in paradox by its intellectual deportment. This turning is thematically developed from the impasse of *de-*

sire in relation to *memory*, which seems to prove an entrapment of intellect by history, into a country beyond memory, in which the contention becomes that between *hope* and the temptation to *despair*.

The autonomous poet to the contrary escapes one dilemma, only to find himself in another, and he does so repeatedly. Still he will, or may, cling to his principle, without which a surrender of one sort or another is inevitable, either the collapse to emptiness or an openness whereby his emptiness is fulfilled. He is autonomous by a formal act of intellect, but the only admissible consequence of that act is self-creation by act. Thus the poem serves as a supreme fiction of the self, and for the sole self. The self becomes an actuality demonstrated to itself by its supreme fiction, but it must deny its dependence upon that fiction as its own certification. Otherwise, the fiction is the cause of the maker of the fiction. The thing *made* must be declared at most a by-product of the self-making act. But even *by-product* is too dangerous a concept, since that term already pulls the poem into a reality beyond the self. It must be rather a waste of the act of self-making. As a residue of the poet's becoming, however, it mocks the poet, in that it has undeniably a formal integrity in itself without which integrity – without which good in itself – it would not effect the good of the poet's becoming. Otherwise, without the *formal* act, the informed being of the actor, the poet, would be itself the waste, the residue, the fragment of the old chaos of the sun at best.

One has a rather pervasive presence in modern thought of this radical inversion of the relation of making to being. It has become popularly accepted as a substitute for radical thought about intellect's relation to being, a simplification of the problem easily taken up out of Jean-Paul Sartre, though not comfortably accepted by so honest a mind as Camus. It is accepted by Wallace Stevens and by Joyce and Robert Frost – and by the early T. S. Eliot. Indeed, the inversion of intellect is accepted tacitly in many minds, in a subterranean thought unrecognized and unacknowledged, and with disturbing dislocations of mind. It is, for instance, evident in the growing spiritual unrest of our intellectuals, almost at every hand. Nor does one need to know the "scholastics" of the radical inversion whereby action by autonomous intellect is asserted to be the cause of being. That is, one need not even recognize the name Jean-Paul Sartre. Not only the poet, but any maker may in a community shadowed by this intellectual dissolving take his making as the conditional initiator of his own existence. He might even for a time, but not for long, conclude that the resulting thing made is of no consequence in itself beyond its effecting the being of the maker. We should recall here our own position, since we argue that, in actual consequence of making, the maker's being is indeed effected. But the difference we argue is that the maker is already an existential being before his act of making. The making in its effect upon him is an enlargement of the potential being of the maker. Oaks move out of acorns, but are not the cause of the particular acorn out of which they move, though the cause by participation of subsequent acorns.

This perversion of being by will in its declaration of autonomy is the characteristic principle spoken of as *modern gnosticism* – by Eric Voegelin and others. It is an intent of the self to come to be by its own will, in which the self as a precedent initiator of the intent must be denied, since otherwise the *end* intended is most unreasonably the cause of the becoming. Such an intellectual position is not a mystery but a psychological attempt at alchemy. One sees it in historical perspective as inverted Puritanism, and may reason that Puritanism is one of its begetters, as I have argued in *Why Hawthorne Was Melancholy*. The difference lies in the end posited, the self-salvation by autonomous will, whereas the Puritan attempt is of a making through which the soul is propelled beyond creation into a transcendent rescue from its actual circumstantial existence.

What they (Puritanism and modern gnosticism) share is a necessary indifference to the thing made. Making is the necessity to the maker, but is not governed by the good of the thing made. Existential creation is consequently a means to intellect or soul whereby it *is*, but it is a means to be transcended by an indifference to the means. And this means a rejection of the good of creation itself, which is necessarily good because its creator, Being Itself, is the pre-eminent Good. Thus gnosticism, whether the Puritan or the secularized version, does not reconcile on either hand that intuited necessity of our nature which requires that we care and not care, in the sense of that paradox of our necessary deportment toward existential creation which we have earlier explored. Both are gnostic, in that both reject the stewardship of being as the office of the soul in creation. It is the stewardship designated by the virtue called making. To put the point symbolically, both species of gnostic devour creation though to different suppositions of the end of their devouring of being. For we must recognize that the openness of love is not apparent in the exploitation of nature by the Puritan work ethic as a community principle of salvation. Nor is the apparent love of the world to be concluded actual on the evidence of the secular gnostic's appetite for things, even for the "finer" things, including the "art" thing itself.

What we are saying, then, is that both Puritanism, insofar as it abandons creation as creation – creation as a child of God – and this inverted Puritanism which is secular gnosticism must at least theoretically deny the made thing as of any significance in itself. It is a common position obfuscated when the two come to battle over art itself, as we have witnessed those battles in the final quarter of this century. The early Puritan fathers tended to see the world lying before them as a savage wilderness, requiring a reduction to order whereby a shining city on a hill as the New Jerusalem was to be built. The latter-day descendants tend to elevate appetites whose satisfactions are destructive of that wilderness through the savagery of appetite itself. We are not called to accept one or the other of these false positions, for there is that alternative recognition of the nature of creation which requires no gnostic appropriation, either religious or secular.

When we turn to this alternative, we begin I trust to realize the central, significant effect of making in relation to the being of the maker. It proves analogous to the central issue of sin as dramatized by Dante: What is affected by intellectual action most significantly is the being of the actor. Murder is sin whose most devastating effect is upon the soul of the murderer. The making of a good poem, in which the good of the thing made is the maker's devotion, has as its most transforming effect, the *in-fulling* of the being of the maker. To have said this is not to have pronounced a principle determinant of aesthetic virtues in the poem. One discovers the good of the made thing in relation to its own potential perfection as a made thing. We cannot, however, absolutely divorce the relation of the maker and his own potential from his made thing, for it is an extension of the maker in a sense inappropriately declared of God's relation to Creation. That is a distinction most crucial to make, though we must do so without abandoning a truth of revelation which does not yield its truth easily to reason: the truth that man as maker is himself made in the image of his Creator God.

XXIII

If the maker of a thing is to avoid the error of believing his made thing (and especially a thing made of words) is either *ex nihilo* or is the begotten spirit of his own self-created spirit, he must distinguish between the limits of his power as maker and God's absence of all limit as maker. Unlike the Uncaused Cause, he is inescapably affected by his causing action, since his made thing can in no wise be declared absolute in its origin. One cannot handle stones in making a house without effects of stones on the handling hands. And even if he should be so bold as to deny the transcendent cause of creation, God, he cannot escape the reality of his own limits as maker, except by an excessive will – or if he prefer – an excessive intentionality (whatever its ontological justification). He is, for instance, dependent upon material causes, of which he is himself a special instance though in another aspect also as "coadjutor," the efficient cause of the made thing. Setting aside the poet's dependence upon an inherited language – however distinctive his use of that inheritance – and even setting aside the pre-existing creation out of whose matrix he has his own incarnate being – the reality of his own intellect as an already caused cause in the event of his making denies any conclusion that he can be a pure, an absolute cause of his made thing. That is the argument of distinction by J. R. R. Tolkien in his essay "On Fairy-Stories," in which he distinguishes God's Primary World of creation from the poet's Secondary World of made things.

Experience of our own existence forces us to conclude at last that both the poet and the poem are dependent on pre-existences in actual ways. The poem itself is doubly dependent: first, upon its own proximate cause, the poet, and second upon creation, the Primary World, as the necessary source to the poet's making. There can be no independent origin, either of poem or poet. For except by a willful severance of himself from creation, the poet cannot even maintain that he is autonomous, nor that his poem is. To maintain that position is to ascribe reality to illusion. And to the degree that such a separation is willfully made, the being of either poet or poem is incomplete to our understanding of it at an essential level of being. If it were otherwise, the poet through his made thing might indeed make his own immortality, as poets sometimes dream of doing by their acts of making. But such dreams can but leave the poet's heart "high-sorrowful and cloyed" in the end, for the necessary faith when vested in an illusion of a transport of being to perfection through art can at best but leave the poet wondering whether he is victim of a self-induced illusion. We know the pained question he must put: "Was it a vision or a waking dream?/ Do I wake or sleep?" After Keats, Mallarmé' will attempt to dissolve that sort of question by forcing the poet's relation to words, disjoining words from any relation to reality, not only to intellect itself, but to any lingering traces of a relation to existence other than the poet's own intellect. The word, says Mallarmé, is a "suppressed trinket of sonorous inanity," entrapping the poet who consents to them in "the catastrophe of Therefore." In commenting on Mallarmé's address to the problem of words, Gilson in *Linguistics and Philosophy* observes that, "Like the God of Genesis, he wants to create *ex nihilo creaturae*." But that creature he would create out of nothingness becomes immediately a hostage to the word. What is always necessary is a moment of an absolute beginning, if the word the poet uses is to be freed of that tyranny of an existing reality which is prior to the poet's action itself. That "zero hour," says Gilson, is "the hour of free choice that nothing in time determines. The field is free for the creative decision of the poet, who will try to create poetry out of his own substance and out of that alone." Or such is Mallarmé's intent. By the willed rejection of everything, the poet attempts a zero of intellect which consequently owes nothing to anything except itself, supposing as possible a state of intellect which is "totally unconditional," which is the origin of its action.

That is a point of departure for will, an absolute emptiness of being allowing will its intentional creation. One might well look at Gilson's exploration of Mallarmé, "A Throw of the Dice," in *Linguistics and Philosophy*. For our immediate concern, we are reminded of Descartes's similar desire, reflected in his lament of intellect's precondition whereby it can never quite operate independent of conditioning. If only we could be born grown! But instead, as Descartes laments in his *Discourse*, "We have all been children before being men [and so] governed by our appetites and our teachers." Therefore, "it is almost impossible that our judgments should be so excellent or solid as they should have been had we had complete use of our reason since birth, and had been guided by its means alone." If one needed evidence of Descartes's own "romanticism," these words supply it.

But neither the poet nor the philosopher can lift himself from ground zero by intuitive intellect to a transcendent independence of the "other," of inclusive reality. As sophisticated Huck Finns, they discover themselves rather as tom Sawyers as poet or philosopher. Nor may either do so through a purified rational intellect. Not Mallarmé and not Descartes can rarefy intellect to an independent perfection unbeholden to any cause, either his own appetites or his teacher's. For either poet or philosopher discovers himself to be already a moved mover, a made maker. If a part of that *being made* is the limit of his being by which his gifts of being are those of the poet or philosopher, his recognition of that givenness alone is not sufficient to assure his open consent as a maker to the good of the thing he would make in answering the calling through his gift to a perfection of his own potentiality. The poet, as is true of the philosopher or of any person, by his very nature as fallen person is inclined to willfulness.

This point is of a separate order of concern from our questions of craftsmanship in making, the technical sciences of making appropriate to the particular gift. For one thing, questions of craft are more evidently dependent upon prior existence – upon language itself and upon other poems already existing if one is poet. The will responding to indisputable existence of words as prior to the will's commanding of the words constitutes a problem somewhat different from the will's response to its own existence, over which it may suppose a proprietary office more easily. That proprietary sense suggests to the will evidence of its own causing of the thing it already possesses, the "self," an error of judgment difficult to surmount. "I am my own man" is an assertion ripely ambiguous in its consequences to the asserter, in contrast to "this is my poem." The first asserts a closed system when taken as true by the "I." The second, however lordly the proposition appears, certifies a separateness between the owner and the thing owned, between the poet and the poem. The "ownership" expressed in "I am my own man" is of a different orientation of intellect to existence than "this is my poem." The distinction turns on the perception of originating cause in its participation in the caused thing. We might suggest, for instance, that the words "This is my beloved son *in* whom I am well pleased" speaks a relationship of father to son, which in the specific instance of the words as related to the Incarnation expresses an intimacy of begetter to begotten, to put the matter poorly, as the putting of mystery always is. It is quite different in meaning from the person as father who uses the same words of his natural son. And so it is only within the weakness of analogy that we suggest correspondences between human parentage and the mystery of divine parentage, a difficulty which is partially annealed by the Incarnation, in which annealment St. Mary is our healthful mediator of meaning.

We seem further afield than perhaps we are. For what we are considering is intellect as originator, the concern a poet is more likely to be agitated by than others. Or at least it is the poet who reveals the agitation more publicly, given as he is to public signs. He is "creative," a term so special to his intent as to be appropriated widely. We must have *creative* thinking wherever thinking goes on in our day. But we were moving toward the complexity of the poet as "creative" in making his poem, and need not dwell on the sentimental appropriation of his inclination to a general consumption in the general climate of making which constitutes community consumption in the active consumerism in our day, whether related to making products or social and political structures. The poet's concern for creativity focuses in a measure of his action by what is likely called his "originality." The moment that focus appears, his "originating" powers as maker, such as those Mallarmé would sell his soul to achieve as absolute zero, are at once prevented. For how is he (or we) to conclude his originality? The first attempt is always by analogy to the already existing, and at a level of analogy uncomplicated by the incommensurate levels of the reality of things that are always present in our attempts upon truth through analogy, as in that between God the Father and God the Son on the one hand, or between this person named John and this person named John*son* on the other. Or, in the relation to things made other than in nature, such as this beloved poem, in which I am well pleased. Is it loved because it is "original"? The question brings automatically into the context of the concern a poem by Homer or Dante or Shakespeare or Eliot, and so on. For they are there as poets already. Robert Frost says words appropriate to the point. A poet writes his poem, he says, in the light of all the poems ever written – and he does so (such is the implication) whether he knows all those other poems or not. It is impossible, as this perspective shows us, to move with words from an absolute zero.

The measure of "originality" is in relation to other "original" poems, so that the question of whether this poet is merely an imitator of another poet or an "original" centers in the measure of one made thing against another made thing. Obviously the matter is more complex than as so simply put here. But the point at issue is that such a concern for what we call "originality" is proper, though more properly put when the concern for *made* things is first and centrally a concern for the good of the thing in itself, which the concept of analogue gives some evidence of perhaps. The issue is not first and last, whether Shakespeare is a more original poet than Eliot but, first of all, whether this poem is perfected, is good in itself. There is a considerable range of argument over such a proposition, witnessed by the growing volume of literary criticism since the Renaissance, so we may neither resolve the difficulties in the proposition easily nor undertake extended defense of the proposition. That is not, indeed, our immediate concern. What is our concern is to suggest that suppositions of intellectual autonomy, whereby intellect takes itself as the only maker of its only world, already prevent any reconciliation of intellect to the difficulty with this question of "originality" in making. That difficulty remains so long as the distinction between *making* and *creating* is confused. More importantly that question of originality is itself a secondary concern at best, a concern which will affect adversely the good of the thing one is making when that maker is principally concerned with his own originality.

What is of central importance to the making is the good of the thing being made, we insist with St. Thomas, and not a concern with whether it is better than or less perfect than another thing made by another maker. This is by no means to say that made things are equal. Some poems are better than other poems, even among several poems made by the same poet. But this aspect of concern, unless rooted in the question of the perfection of the specific thing itself, this particular poem, becomes a matter of advertising and not a matter of the intellect seeing the virtue of being in the thing seen, the poem in itself. To proceed intellectually otherwise will be to live intellectually at the level of mere spectacle. That, perhaps, was the gnawing concern to Mallarmé, more than a concern for his "originality" against legions of other poets. For he is too serious in his concern to have been so frivolously concerned as we must otherwise suppose of him. What he feared was the endangerment of words which, by his very inheritance of them, seemed always to threaten a reduction of the poem he would make to the level of spectacle. Words seen thus become the enemy of the poem, and that was the trap Mallarmé was caught by, so that ironically we engage his poetry largely as spectacle.

The poet may, from acknowledgment of proximate dependencies in his making, turn to the power resident in intellect as independent of such entrapment of his desire for originality. He will see his own power as insufficient to create *ex nihilo creaturae*. But, as Mallarmé knew, at the level of craft (without which there is no making) the coming-to-be of the poem consequent to his action of making forces his practical intellect to operate within the given. Its very making therefore requires craft proper to things existing at the level of a Secondary World, not at the level of the Primary World, to borrow Tolkien's terms once more. The poem, of course, even as the table or the house, becomes a part of reality by its existential, by its actual, being once it is made. In this sense, the act of making seems to add to the Primary World. But the problem for the poet as "original" is always that his poem adds to the Primary World, but *out of* that Primary World and in tribute to it. In this perspective, the poet finds himself sacrificial mediator rather than creator, in recognition of which he reflects that art is the child of nature, as the early Renaissance mind (including Dante's) not simply acknowledged but celebrated. In that relationship the poet participated in creation, as St. Paul long ago reminded us is the condition attendant upon our nature as created intellectual creatures.

The sometimes tedious responsibility to craft in making, which engages questions of material and formal implications of the good of the thing under construction, begins indirectly to prescribe the limits of gift in the poet. Just as through gifts of bodily stature, one person has advantage of another in tennis or weight-lifting or basketball, so too are there limits in the gifts peculiar to intellect in its making of things. This is to insist that gifts to specific persons are consequent to their discrete being, gifts being *severally* inherent in persons, though several persons may share a calling. Many are called, but they are not equally chosen in respect to the limits of gift. When an egalitarian disruption becomes a communal principle, whereby it is declared as law that all poems are equal so that it may follow that all poets are equal, the chaos of factionalism erodes community in an awesome acceleration, such an erosion as we presently experience in the reductionism by sentimentality to "multi-cultural" egalitarianism. It does so, because intellect has turned from attention to the good of the particular thing in itself to an abstraction of universal goodness which effects the obliteration of the particular by egalitarian sentimentality. What works against this gnostic attempt at imposing chaos as order, always, is that knowing of truth which is intrinsic to any discrete, particular intellect – whether that knowing is understood or not: The significant reality of existential things is the relation of being to potential being whose measure is the peculiar nature of the particular being itself. It is not to be measured by abstraction, by a universalized reductionism whereby existential things are reduced toward mere identity.

Some persons as poets, then, are better as poets than other persons as poets. We are speaking of the magnitude of gift, conspicuously evident when we are tempted to that bootless comparison of poets in which comparison is confused with moral judgment. If we compare Keats to Dante, rather than the poems of Dante to each other, the poems of Keats to each other, the poems of Dante to the poems of Keats, we shall but exercise a waste of spirit through the failure of intellect. The distinction of magnitude in gifts to discrete persons is a concern quite separate from the question of the common necessity to each of his responsibility to the magnitude of his own gift. For what is common is that each specific person is called to the full exercise of his specifying gift through the practical intellect. The gift itself, in respect to magnitude, is uncommon because *specific* to person as discrete.

This is a responsibility quite removed from the relative merit of things made as that merit may be considered in the arena appropriate to the actions of the practical intellect, the arena of the world contingent to intellect. That is, in the matrix of reality, particulars are relative to each other in respect to the discrete beings in which the particulars adhere. That is why we may at last confidently conclude that some poems are better than others, but first of all in relation to the perfections inherent in the poem itself. That is, we quickly realize the futility of pretending that *The Divine Comedy* is a greater poem that a sonnet by Keats. The very juxtaposition is a violation of both poems, intolerable to intellectual judgment of the truth of things. The attempt is the putting of the wrong question to discrete things. In ordering the relativity of things, then, intellect is forced at last to acknowledge hierarchy in existential reality in the Primary World, despite the attempts of gnostic intellect to reduce diversity to identity. And intellect tells us there is hierarchy in the Secondary World as well. In that recognition of truth, intellect must set about discovering the significance of the orders of being thus encountered experientially.

The poet, not as poet simply but as person, requires the zeal and industry through which he may fulfill his limited calling, whether he is Dante or Keats. It is a requirement regardless of the magnitude of his gift, but it is a requirement whose exercise must not be confused by mistaking magnitude in the gift with an obsession of competition in pursuit of "originality." The question of magnitude is crucial to proximate actions of the discrete poet, not in a comparative arena, but in relation to potential gift in the exercise of intellect toward the good of the thing being made. The question of a poet's "originality" becomes irrelevant in respect either to the perfection of person or to the perfection of the good of the thing undertaken in itself. One sees a recognition of this responsibility in Keats perhaps in his desire to be dramatic poet but his subsequent discovery of and acceptance through his making of poems of the perfection suited to his gift as other than the gift of a poet like Shakespeare. He did not write poor plays, then, he wrote great odes. In this perspective, the concern for perfection is not relative to other perfections at all, as if we were to consider Keats a failed Shakespeare. It is a concern for an absolute in the sense that the perfection of gift in the discrete person lies in the full realization of that potential given in one's being, his actual and potential being as discrete person. It is in this respect that we may say that a person must be absolute in his being, through grace.

Our common necessity, which binds us at last in a community of concern for the common good, is that each person is obligated by the gift of his existence to exercise a consent to the thing he is called to make in the proximate world. That thing will be, by his right will, if not directly effective of a common good, at least not contrary to it. The consent is required because the discrete agent is not the ultimate cause of the good he would effect. Through his action in perfecting that good, he participates in arriving at his own proper end. It is in support of this fundamental necessity to the discrete person that community itself exists. Therefore, auxiliary to the poet's necessary consent to a responsibility toward the discrete existence of himself as person is his concern for the common good in the proximate world, his concern for community. That is a consequential responsibility which St. Paul speaks of as the mystery whereby we are members one of another.

Our *in-memberment* in the body of humanity is formally in respect to the specific nature of each as person, differing as persons. "For," says St. Paul, "as we have many members in one body, and all members have not the same office; so we, being many, are one body in Christ, and every one members one of another." Having gifts differing through grace, each ministers as member – teaching or judging or governing or philosophizing, or declaiming in respect to gifts discretely appropriate. The gifts as appropriate, however, are not appropriate to community except in a secondary sense, in respect to our particular existence in time and place. It is a distortion of this primary appropriateness of person of the secondary role as individual in community in declared primary. With the elevation of the civil state over the body of community, that modern gnosticism dislocates persons from true membership. That has been the formal dislocation of the relation of community to person since Hegel, whereby the secondary is declared primary.

Even if one does not admit the relation of the body to a community in Christ, it is only through sheer anarchy as social policy that one may deny the necessity of gift ordinately serving social body. Ezra Pound finds an acceptable principle in Confucius, for instance, preaching it as necessary to polity. In Canto XIII, Pound's Kung declares the principle: "[E]ach in his nature" is required to pursue "order" in the self, family, state. It is to be pursued with a "brotherly difference" to the specific nature of the discrete individual. If we insist on a purely mechanistic, as opposed to spiritual, reading of social order, the principle of service to the state advanced through arguments of mechanistic necessity can only be concluded an accommodation of discrete accidents of being to the state, so that in the end the state is the ultimate end, to which person must be sacrificed. The reduction of person as spiritual being, and the consequent dislocation of his proper end in the community as ultimate makes inescapable the totalitarian mechanic of the state such as a Hitler or a Stalin advances. Pound, finding a traditional justification of that direction in Confucius, is easily led to elevate Mussolini as philosopher-poet-king. It is an error more general than the spectacle of Pound as traitor reveals. For when the principle of individual gifts is appropriated to the ordering of the contingent world as the ultimate office of "talent" in the person, an accompanying distortion of person will follow. That is why the dangers are as great in "democratic" ideology as in "totalitarian" ideology insofar as the value in the being of the discrete person is at issue. In either distortion, what is denied is the Cause of all order, which is to deny the person's potential perfection as person by a reduction of that potential to the service of a proximate, secondary end as if his ultimate end.

It is a wise shibboleth, then, which says that one is called to be what he may be, in that it recognizes the obligation to a perfection of the discrete being, an actualizing of a specific potential. We are arguing it as necessary to the soul's passage to its ultimate end, an imperative to the soul's discrete becoming which is indifferent to such questions as that of magnitude, of "talent," but which rests the limits of the soul in a happiness that results from the fullness of its being. In our generally willful age, of all the losses to the possibilities of the person's coming to be the one which is most destructive to the common good itself within the proximate arena is a failure of the person's habit of consent to the good of the thing in the making in relation to his gift as maker. We lose the capacity both to support and to declare that, in the contingent world where actions of the practical intellect occur, each is limited in magnitude, but also that each differs one from another in gifts as suited to particular actions in the contingent world. At every turn in community we meet denial of this reality, a denial usually advanced against the realist position I hold under the devil term "elitist." The argument is a deliberate or a thoughtless confusion common sense of our actual experience of the contingent world. When deliberate, it is advanced by the gnostic ideologue as a gambit of words to obscure our recognition of the truth of distinctive existences, necessary to reduce persons to controlled units of power. Thus the *several* are declared *equal* not only in potentiality but in explicit particularized nature, the argument denying each person to be a distinct and separately created creature. It is in the name of abstract equality that persons are destroyed as if identities, to integers, reduced to units of power intended to be manipulated collectively.

But those who are actually unequal, even as measured by the abstract relativism of the argument against personhood, will recognize the deception, more or less clearly. Depending upon the clarity of the recognition of this disparity between reality and description of reality by false words, the person will be less or more susceptible to the pride or envy occasioned by a false comparison of one "self" with another "self." It is the distortion of reality through false perceptions of reality which allows and furthers the manipulation of persons whereby persons are persuaded not only of a common but of an equal right to being, not as measured by the distinctive gifts of being as a person, as *this* person, but comparatively among persons in relation to the abstract formulations of a vague "justice" unrelated to truth. One's actual being is thus turned against itself by the dislocation of its potential since one's being is measured by the imagined being of some other, by a posited abstraction. When the measure leaves the measuring self short, the effect is a feeding of envy. When the measure leaves the measuring self superior, the effect is a feeding of pride. Thus the sins of envy and pride are actions of will made possible by a dislocation of intellect from reality. It is one of the social ironies of our day that we find that the egalitarianism now rampant is itself the principal cause of unbridled pride and envy in discrete persons.

In respect to the discrete nature of the person to be manipulated in distorting intellect's relation to reality, thus dislocating the person from his progress to ultimate good in favor of some limited good, the gnostic manipulator will quickly perceive the advantage of a reduction of the principle of particularity in the person. Thus the necessary elevation of egalitarian identity of persons by gnostic thought. But in order to effect this intellectual shell game, it will be necessary to establish an illusional final end. The reduction of persons to identity is a reduction of the actuality of hierarchy in being, of those orders of being which are actual to particular creatures by the very nature of their particular existence. It is possible that such a distorted secondary end elevated as final end may borrow a legitimate term to name it an illegitimate thing. Thus it is possible that the gnostic manipulator may declare the final end a rescue of the *person*, beyond time, to some heaven, and do so with such persuasion that the eager person may not notice the worldly advantage of power gained by such a "preacher." The history of certain evangelical Christians, though not *all* of them, will supply ready illustration, or the "preacher" may be intent on characterizing a Utopian Eden in the world, to a similar end, even sometimes self-persuaded of that end. And certainly the many "preachers" of the absolute sanctity of the political state since Hegel illustrate the procedure whereby a collective support directed to a questionable end is managed through the sacrifice of individual persons to an idealized identity of persons subservient to a false end.

Thus egalitarianism, whereby particularity is dissolved to identity, is made a moral imperative. The ploy is, whatever the name given its end, radically anti-Christian, in that it must deny the particular nature of each person as created in the image of its Creator, ordained to its particular fulfillment when it moves in an openness of its being through participation in being toward its Creator and not toward a lesser end mistaken as ultimate. Failing of this proper end, the effect becomes that which would otherwise be the proper love of existences in their reality. In the end, that love turns back upon the loving agent if that agent fails to break through toward the proper end. This is to say that self-centered love results in that alienation whose spiritual climate is a cynicism whereby existence itself is at last repudiated. At its extreme the repudiation will be of the very self, the very soul of the dissolving person.

We argue in contrast to this distortion that the moral agent, the divinely created person as maker in creation, is properly called by created nature to love the particular for its very particularity, which particularity is an evidence of that abiding and sustaining Love, the Creator of all things. This is quite different from that attempt to love the particular because it is the *same* in every particular. One is called to love the *what* of a creature, not the *that*, for love is of the explicitly discrete as an evidence of the omnipotence of the Creator of the discrete. In loving, St. Augustine says, one must adhere lovingly to something for itself, even as God loves each something. We may see, then, that the gnostic deconstruction of reality to deceive the perceptions of discrete intellects, necessary to accumulated power through consent of disparate intellects, is a sacrilege. The appropriate encounter of love with the particularity of existential things is transgressed as a matter of principle. The actual particular is reduced to an idea, which in turn is subsumed to the ideology of egalitarianism in which all *person* is lost. The final resolution of such reductionism intends the reduction of existentiality to a sort of prime matter to be manipulated by the gnostic will in the restructuring of being itself. In respect to the manipulation of persons, the necessity to gnostic power is that discriminate persons must be reduced to amorphous *that*s, to zeros.

Not that such ideology is suited absolutely to the restructuring intended by the gnostic manipulator. One need only look closely at the unfolding actions of the Soviet state at the close of our century to discover how quickly, once the ideology becomes generally accepted as requiring the faith of the believer, reality reasserts itself against the distortion. But we must observe more closely the lesson here, and may do so by relating the recent collapse of the Soviet empire to the collapse of the Third Reich. Hitler from the beginning accepted the necessity of hierarchy as ordering the power accumulated to gnostic intent. That he was by violence overthrown from without made it possible to give too much weight to the spectacle of hierarchy as he misrepresented hierarchy. His ideology of a racist spectacle as camouflage of gnostic subversion of persons, by which I mean a subversion of persons employed in advancing the racist spectacle, distorts the truth about the orders of nature. It is not the reality of hierarchy as inescapable to the orders of being that is the difficulty, but the perversion of the orders of being.

That perversion is made more evident by that second manifestation of secular gnosticism elevating the state as absolute good, practiced in establishing the USSR. Once the ideology out of Hegel and Marx becomes emotionally effective to the worship of the state, requiring the faith of the believer, reality reasserts itself again. The pretense to egalitarian principle, to the reduction of persons to identities, may continue only so long as the reduced persons do not see the emerging orders of inequality of individuals. One may rise from the proletariat to office in the name of the proletariat, but there is nevertheless a *rising*, in which action one is taken out of the order of being designated by the term proletariat.

Toward the close of our century, it becomes more and more evident from within the USSR that an hierarchy existed under the dense shadow of perverted language pretending to egalitarianism. It emerges more evidently as economic reality becomes inescapable, so that the advantage of an elitist position becomes generally conspicuous to the growing discontent of the populace. Since the interior hierarchy constituting the state depends upon the degree of power siphoned from the people to the office, and since that power has no legitimate reference beyond the mechanistic actions within the contingent world in the name of the disembodied god, the state, that power increasingly operates against the principle upon which cumulative power was justified: the ideology of egalitarianism. The breach between "haves" and "have nots" proves not always measurable in terms of things made, but under the stress of reality comes at last to focus upon the power possessed and exercised over things, in this instance persons reduced to *things*, but not in our sense of that term whereby we mean by the term *thing* a particular created existence requiring a sacramentally oriented love of that thing for its very self. Rather, *things* in the gnostic view are material existences to which no spiritual reference is allowed. In this necessity, we more fully understand why it was expedient to the Soviet state to eradicate religion insofar as the old religion found orientation in the spiritually transcendent as the cause of things. The strategy is to relocate the religious necessity, intrinsic to person by his nature, to a worship of the state. The gnostic, let us remember, unless naive, knows that the necessity to worship beyond the self cannot be removed from the creature man, even by genetic manipulation. It can, however, be relocated to a proximate end which will give, though but only for a brief spell (such is the tyranny of reality), the illusion of ultimate end as the focus of that modern worship of the state.

Power thus exercised has, for the moment, a continuing consent from the "have nots" who are themselves that power's source. The old promise that one will feel good through a sentimental faith in idea is for a time appealing. Until, that is, it becomes apparent through common sense that idea so taken is a violation of reality and is therefore itself an illusion of reality. The social body as a "classless society," in which all members are indiscriminate, is a fantasy possible to sentiment when intellect desires relief from its own particular gift. I should have been a pair of ragged claws,

Prufrock fantasizes. The Marxist ideology intends as its end exactly that reduction of all persons to Prufrocks. What we observe at this moment, in the final political agony of our century, is that in the USSR and its satellite states the recognition of a responsibility of particular persons to particular gifts reasserts itself. It does so, not by denying hierarchy, but by rejecting a false hierarchy – that is, a hierarchy which perverts the reality of the orders of nature under the ideological pretense of denying the orders of nature. It is a lesson not yet appreciated in the West, though it is deeply learned from within the collapsing system itself, which is why some rescue of the West may in fact reside in the emerging recoveries in the Eastern states from Russia to Yugoslavia. The disintegration into political chaos is accompanied by attempts to recover order founded in reality, and especially founded in the reality of persons as discrete, particular, unique creatures differing one from another by the nature of gift as person. It will be long, one fears, before this discovery becomes viably recovered here in the West, where denials of the orders of nature have also been necessary to the maintenance of political power in the ambiguous name of "democracy." One need only examine closely the political campaigns in the United States to illustrate the observation. Or one need only look closely at Western foreign policy settled in upon "ethnic" chaos in Africa and the Balkans.

That is why we must say that – sentimentality being contagious where there is no firm intellectual community committed to reality – that gremlin of history, Irony, finds sentimentality yet dominant in the intellectual community of the West though dissolving rapidly in the East under the acid of reality. Thus there is the lingering nostalgia for Marxism in the West which will not abandon the old illusions despite the overwhelming evidence that it is an illusion about reality. One finds such sentimentality very close at hand, centrally within those institutions whose proper responsibility is the health of the intellect, the academies. And that is an added, almost a bitter, irony. Already the academic intellectual seems well on his way to a recovery from that initial panic at the collapse of the USSR. In the American academy in particular the "best minds" still maintain an odd position. On that academy's playing field, the egalitarian principle is an intolerable presence as principle. Under the banner of tolerance as falsely understood, egalitarianism is declared primary to the nature of intellect itself. Football players are not equal, but all minds are. Therefore, it becomes necessary to exercise a Nominalist strategy of redefining difference as sameness, in respect to intellect, by a pretense at egalitarianism that attempts to deny difference by such distortions as "differently abled" to describe the physically or mentally "handicapped." One need not be cynical to conclude of such attempts to establish the dogma of the "politically correct" that a collapse of intellect is immanent. For intellect, and especially in its academic aspect, is responsible only when it discriminates among particularities and when it does so in service to the ordering of members one to another in a social polity governed by reality, in support of the common good. We witness increasingly an arrest of the life of the social body, now almost moribund in the West. It is so because tranquilized by ideological denials of its own reality. Where intellect slowly awakens in that body looking eastward, it begins to find itself fascinated by the return of life to some of those social bodies in the East, even though that recovery is accompanied by convulsion here and there. A present reality in event appears reminiscent of old events now but vague in memory. It is highlighted, for instance, when President Havel of the Czech Republic, a poet, addressed a joint gathering of our Congress with words summoning our own history, out of the last quarter of the eighteenth century, reminding us of truths about the nature of the state in its proper relation to persons which the Founding Fathers knew but which we have largely abandoned and then forgotten.

XXIV

We have characterized a sentimentality toward existential reality as a deportment in which, moved by the inclination to love existence, the person may not support that inclination by intellect. In that confusion, one does not act as person, does not act out of the nature given toward a fulfillment of that nature. We might observe in such divided response of intellect to existence a dependence on "feeling," since thought is reduced to a dependence on a residue of abstractionism in intellect which is taken – at least tacitly – as justifying feeling. Such is that "dissociation of sensibility" which T. S. Eliot saw as a defect in the unfolding of our literary tradition since the Renaissance, though he subsequently discovered this dissociation of sensibilities as more fundamental than a merely literary concern. In the dislocation a presence of the existential creature as intellect in the enveloping context of the contingent world becomes obscured or lost. That is, we lose that sense of immediacy in our encounters with things that is consequent to any open consent to being by intellect.

One does not have to read far in our literary criticism before encountering a concern for this immediacy of experience of intellect to thing. The poem itself is such a thing recalling immediacy. But the concern central to immediacy is not simply aesthetic, a management of thought and feeling in the instrumental sign, through which there is a control of re-encounter in the poem through the poet's mastery of "objective correlatives." There is, we have been concerned to argue, a sense in this seemingly literary shibboleth which is founded, not in the sign as used by the poet – though that use is important to the good of the poem – but rather founded in the experience of intellect with thing, whether a poem or a tree or person. It is a complex response to objective, separate things on the part of intellect, but a response ordered in its complexity by the nature of the responding intellect. We quoted St. Thomas on the point (*Summa* I-II, Q. 11, A. 4): While "it is the object which specifies the act [i.e., determines its species], the manner of acting depends upon the agent, and hence is perfect or imperfect according to the condition of the agent."

The *manner* is crucial, since through that manner the agent responds ordinately to the existence of the object. It loves the thing insofar as it recognizes the thing as proper in its being, which means that it does not love the thing as an ultimate good. To mistake the thing as ultimate is to become disoriented from the ultimate good. That is a lesson aptly put to Dante by Beatrice in their first words on Mt. Purgatory. She chastises him for his false love of her. If there is a lingering unformulated realization of the possibility of excess, it may consequently result in a "manner" whereby "feeling" is rested in the object, but with a detachment, a reserve, in the encounter, lest one become absorbed by the thing through the response. That constitutes a turning away from the thing in itself. By this attempt, one might undertake a protection of the self, with the ironic consequence that feeling becomes the wall setting the person – the "feeler" – apart from the object in its actuality, which is the nature of Beatrice's rebuke of Dante for abandoning her at her death. (*Canto* xxx, lines 121 ff.) What we notice about that person who appears governed by sentimentality in response to existence is the absence of discrimination, and that absence speaks to us of a reduction of all existing things toward identities of each other, to an appetitive use by the reductionist. To love all existing things equally proves at last to be a false action in which no thing is loved, save the safety of the person pretending to a love of things.

But to be open to a thing, to respond to existential reality, is to risk the self, and one of the risks at issue is the loss of prudential governance of that openness whereby ordinate ends are held in relation to these actions of openness, these actions of love. Sentiment, we insist, is necessary – an inclination to the being of things other than the self. But sentimentality, which is sentiment disoriented, proves a species of self-love at the expense of the purported object of the act of love. The danger may not be denied, but risking that danger is the necessary gesture of intellect toward its own ultimate good. It is a direction possible only through proximate goods, since by its created nature intellect must move through the proximate toward the ultimate.

St. Thomas attempts to guide us in our dilemma over what constitutes the proper conduct of intellect in its correlative deportment to the object of its encounter, intellect's recovery of the "objective correlatives" to its journey through the created world. That section of the *Summa* II-II, Questions 1–16 whose thematic development is the relation of faith to the actions of the rational intellect are pertinent to the journey, but we must be content to cite here only Question 9, which explores the meaning of *knowledge* as a gift to intellect. Knowledge, he argues, is that effect upon intellect from our apprehension of "human or created things." Knowledge is a gift distinct from wisdom, in that knowledge is "only about human things or created things." He adds (Reply Obj. 1) that though faith may be rested in divine or eternal things, faith itself is "a temporal thing in the soul of the believer." It is for this reason that he says that for a person "to know what is to be believed belongs to the gift of knowledge" in the intellect. But since belief, faith in a thing, is in the limited province of intellect as a finite thing, there is the possibility of that dislocation that has concerned us, the loss of the objective correlation of the agent who is *knowing* to the object which is *known*. That is why there is the necessity of a higher accomplishment through grace, whereby intellect achieves wisdom beyond knowledge, though wisdom is thus achieved through the encounters of things whose initial effect is knowledge in the intellect.

It is at the level of knowledge, however, that we observe a mystical dimension in the encounter, understandable only as an action of grace. It is precedent to the intellect's possession of its knowledge of things. We *know* (says Thomas) "the *believed* things in themselves, by a kind of union with them." That is the knowledge of essence of the thing encountered, possessed as knowledge in intellect precedent to the active response of intellect to the knowledge it thereby possesses, the actions for instance of rational intellect in its formulation of concept of the thing known. This "union" of intellect with object, St. Thomas says, "pertains to the gift of wisdom," that gift which "answers more to charity, which unites the mind of man to God." Knowledge, then, involves the action of intellect in respect to judgment, whereby things are maintained in their particularities by discriminating reason. It is charity as a virtue of intellect which orients this judgment to that transcendent Judge, by Whose making the created things are specific in themselves. That deportment of charity toward things at the elementary occasion of encounter with things we might well see as what we ordinarily speak of as "common sense," and in saying this, we appreciate the position taken by such scholastics as Maritain or Gilson, who find common sense the ground out of which philosophy rises toward metaphysical vision. As Gilson puts it in *Linguistics and Philosophy*, "[C]ommon sense is, in the order of the intelligible, philosophy in the unworked state."

We have taken this route through sentimentality, with a resummoning of St. Thomas in relation to those literary categories very popular in modern criticism since T. S. Eliot called our attention to them: the "dissociation of sensibility" which requires a commanding authority of the poet in his use of the proper "objective correlatives" in his poems. Eliot's is an emphasis on the problem which is actually elementary to intellectual action in any time or place, though at the time of his criticism he could see it only in relation to modern poetry. It is a concern fraught with dangers to intellectual action, wherever or whenever. The particular danger of sentimentality as an abandonment of intellectual responsibility has been of concern to the modern poet, to Joyce and Eliot and Pound, since it is such a general intellectual vice in our century. It occurs to intellect through its fearful or diabolic manipulation of its own experience of reality – either from a fear of losing the self or in order to distance the self so intellect may manipulate the thing encountered. What is distorted is the experience crucial to common sense, the experience of a certain "union" with the thing encountered whose effect is our knowing it in its thingness, knowing it in itself. Such knowledge, St. Augustine would say, is the beginning of love.

If we are so easily capable of this dissociation from the thing which already exists, while supposing our manner as agent in the encounter proper to the existing thing, there is a similar but even more chancy concern of intellect in its relation to the object which it intends to bring into existence by its own agency, the made thing. For if the danger of sentimentality is so apparent in intellect's relation to created things in which it does not participate as maker, that danger is more considerable in its relation to a thing yet to be – the object which is not yet an object but is in the making by that intellect. It is in this relationship of maker to thing that the maker's manner as agent may easily lose a primary responsibility to the good of the thing to be made. Thomas puts the concern clearly (*Summa* I-II, Q. 57, A. 3): "Art is nothing else but the right reason about certain works to be made. . . . [The good of these things] depends, not on man's appetitive faculty being affected in this or that way, but on the goodness of the work done. . . . Art . . . is an operative habit." He adds, let us not forget, that art also "has something in common with the speculative habits: since the quality of the object considered [by speculative habits of intellect as a made thing] is a matter of concern to them also." It is not, however, a concern as to "how human appetite may be affected towards that object" of art. For that reason we may not blame the work of art as the cause of failed virtue in the receptive agent, the audience. The speculative concern centers rather in the question of the good of the made thing in itself.

Pornography has been a vexing problem to us, much debated in relation to the common good. It is in dealing with this problem that St. Thomas's distinction may prove helpful. For if we lose sight of the distinction he makes, if we overlook the nature of the speculative intellect's role in our response to art, or mistake that role as properly concerned for the "quality of the object considered" in itself, we will have lost our proper address to the problem of pornography. We may end by condemning art and not by condemning a pretense to art. Or we may fail to find the error in the receptive agent, the audience, in its appetitive dislocation. We must therefore consider that, while art is reason in the making of things and so the special province of the practical intellect, prudence as a virtue embraces both practical and speculative intellect. Prudence shows a "need of a moral virtue, which rectifies the appetite. On the other hand the good of the things made by art is not the good of man's appetite, but the good of those things themselves: wherefore art does not presuppose rectitude of the appetite. . . . Rectitude of the will is essential to prudence, but not to art." Thomas concludes, "Accordingly it is evident that prudence is a virtue distinct from art."

The point may be put, as it has often been put, in the form of a question: Can a bad man make a good thing? We are not so likely to pose the question when we consider the carpenter or similar artists of palpable, material art things. But when we turn to painting or music or poetry, the question seems to become more problematic. St. Thomas, of course, insists that a bad person may as artist make a good thing. As we noted earlier, this is a question at issue in the Donatist heresy of the fourth century, which insisted that an unworthy minister could not "make" a valid sacrament. What we must distinguish here is an attention to the made thing in relation to its own good, its existence in the orders of being as actual beyond its mediate cause, the good or bad poet. That attention we give separately to the poet himself in relation to his making. Prudence as a virtue governs the poet's being in its entirety, including his actions as maker. We might put it thus: The virtue of prudence is irrelevant to the good of the poem, but not to the good of the poet. Additionally, we must remember that we are dealing with the limited "creator," with man as "coadjutor" or steward of being, as maker, and not as creator *ex nihilo*. Creation is good, insofar as the created thing *is*, since its ultimately originating cause, God, the Cause of its being, is good. Man as maker, as distinct from originating cause, is not perfectly good. The effect of his imperfection in relation to his nature as maker we must consider most carefully. In this respect, the caution necessary is that we not "blame" the thing of art as if it were somehow the originating cause of defect in any thing separate from that art thing itself, whether the maker or his audience. For, insofar as the work of art is good in itself, it may not be considered the cause of defective appetitive response of its receptive agent, its audience. And insofar as it is good in itself, it is so despite any failures of personhood in its mediating agent, its maker. It is, in and of itself, what it is, once made, and it is in relation to its own potential good, toward which even a bad man may devote himself. Its good or failure from its potential good is measured in relation to its own nature as a made thing and not by its effect as used to measure its active or passive agents in their encountering it, either the poet or his reader. It was in response to this truth about made things, then, that the so-called New Criticism emerged, one of whose principals was Eliot.

The relation of human appetite to art is anciently confusing, in that historically art is praised or condemned as the cause of appetitive delight or moral decay. Though the question is pursued in sophisticated manner perhaps, we must be careful that the manner not reduce the question of the good or evil of art as is done, for instance, in decrying the good or evil of alcohol, in which the intemperate Temperance advocate declares the evil in the bottle and not in the person abusing the bottle. It is this complication of our appetitive nature in relation to the things of creation that engaged Eliot early on, so that in his concern for the right "objective correlative" he was concerned to disengage the "personal" from art. He had not yet recognized the depths of person, seeing "personality" as merely an aspect of appetitive nature, fearing an erosion of art to the sensually private. It was a concern made particularly necessary to Eliot in his attempt to overcome that degenerated Puritan inclination to the Donatist heresy. For Eliot had to wrestle long and hard with his New England Puritan inheritance.

In our concern for the poet as maker, as distinct from the poem made, we say of that poem that it is an effected thing, properly a thing effected by reason in making. Its province, in relation to intellect as agent to its being, is the practical intellect. But the tendency has been, since the Renaissance at least and rising to a principle widely supported by the poet himself after the abuses the poet sees of the practical intellect by the Enlightenment, to have it that the poem is primarily attributable to speculative intellect. It is especially so as speculative intellect comes to be represented by that popular term for the poet's intellectual deportment, the "Imagination." But if we take the poem as an effect of the speculative intellect, in whose operation intuition is considered dominantly operative, reason in support of the practical intellect may become unduly subordinate. Such a distortion proves an adequate preparation in that intellect for that manner of its deportment toward existence we called sentimentality.

Intellect may become "sentimental" about the desired end, a thing made, while neglecting the responsibility of practical intellect for the good of the thing to be made. Thus the poet may rest his "feeling" in the act of making itself, where reason is properly required. Thought, reason in relation to the making, may thus tend to a contentment with the intuitive, supposing this a speculative action sufficient to the making of a thing. Any poet who has labored at his making of poems will know how difficult the transition of his attention. He must turn to the making which is necessary in moving from the intuitive prospect upon a thing to be made. He must engage, in other words, the practical necessities of making. One may be moved initially as if by an epic thing to be. In the subsequent labor proper to the "vision" of the thing to be made, one may discover that its proper limit is the sonnet. Or it may prove to be something quite other. There are those remarkable words of Dante, for instance, on his finishing his *New Life*: "Just after I wrote this last sonnet there came to me a marvelous vision in which I saw things that determined me to say no more of this blessed one [Beatrice] until I should be able to treat of her more worthily. . . . So that, if it be the pleasure of Him in whom all things live that my life continue for some years, I hope to say of her what has never been said of any woman." One cannot know from these words, nor is it likely that Dante himself knew, the magnitude of his intended "saying," which in the event became his gift to us, *The Divine Comedy*. Nor do we remember that poem primarily as Dante Alighieri's tribute to Beatrice Portinari.

When the intuitive has its way over the rational, when the practical intellect is reduced from its proper office in the making of a thing, the dislocation of the order of thought proper to the making may easily result in the maker's pleasure in himself as maker. For the concentration of intellect upon the good of the thing made is a humbling responsibility. The maker is necessarily a "craftsman," an office hardly allowing him much comfort as the "god" of the thing he makes. We know the temptations to a glory in being "inspired," in being somehow elected to a particular making. We know, for instance, the experience of having made a thing which we recognize as good in itself. That recognition leaves us with the awkward relation of our self as maker to the thing in which we take uneasy pride as maker. It is as possible to the artist after the happy event to disengage himself to an anonymity in relation to the thing he has made as to assume that lofty indifference which Stephen Dedalus announces he shall assume, if ever he writes the supreme poem. The important principle here is *awe*, for the maker of the good thing may sense his relation to the thing he has constructed of words or colors and lines as somehow an action encompassed beyond his powers as maker. It is from this sense of wonder in relation to artistry that we encounter the mystery of inspiration in the artist. As "inspired" maker, we might hesitate to engage the unsettling question about what it means to be "inspired," content with the tradition of the muses, less a metaphor than a self-deprecating allusion to the *awe-full* effect of our making. But the question does not surrender itself, either to such convention or to the modern substitute, those elaborate psychological structures of subtle ingenuity that would explain man's "creativity." We may lamely accept the "creative" act, then, as "inspired." But if inspired, by what or by whom are we thus "in-spirited"? If inspired, is the maker therefore but an instrument at the disposal of some intentionality not properly or immediately attributable to his own operative intellect? It is a question, whether one speculate on the muse or the gene as the "inspiritor."

Since the rise of Romanticism with its emphasis upon intuitive intellect, the question haunts some poets. For if there is a reluctance to submit to the Holy Spirit on the one hand, or to a deterministic inevitability out of mechanistic materialism on the other, there is also a lingering fear that the inspiration may be merely a self-deception by the poet himself, a distortion of his being in relation to the truth of things. It is a concern for Hawthorne, for instance, who fears the possibility of the "Devil in the ink pot." It is a concern underlying Baudelaire's making, a presence in his *Flowers of Evil.*

Though not explicitly so perhaps, it is also in Mallarmé's concern that, as poet, he must gain a "zero point" from which to dictate over rebellious being, especially as represented in signs, in words. This "Romantic" attention of the poet to himself as maker, which seems to him an office ill-served by too great a dependence on rational intellect, submits more easily to the intuitive. In its extreme version, the intuitive is supposed a means to spontaneous making such as Hawthorne feared it might be, thus making the poet less than human – less than intellectual creature. In the development of this "Romantic" response to Hawthorne's problem, we come at last, through Henry James's dissociation from Hawthorne's problem through a theory of "realism," to James Joyce, whose young poet Stephen boldly puts his allegiance clearly and explicitly: *non servium*. The Devil in the ink pot as a disturbing possibility to Hawthorne becomes a welcomed ally.

But what if the suspicion rises that such an ally is false, even as Hawthorne feared. That is what T. S. Eliot will come to believe. The ink pot itself is not the Devil's, though he may inhabit it in intellectually disoriented times. Even the Devil is dependent, then, and scarcely a dependable patron of art, whether taken as muse or god. And lest the clever poet too quickly recognize this handicap to him in his dependence upon a false patron, as Baudelaire says perhaps the devil practices a very clever strategy. It is not enough that the absolute autonomy of intellect must be assured by pronouncing the death of God. The death of the Devil is necessary also. For only thus may the poet as autonomous intellect be comfortable in assuming an autonomy beyond good and evil. As for the Devil, says Baudelaire in a "Preface" to *Flowers of Evil*, "Everyone smells him and no one believes in him. Sublime subtlety of the Devil," this presence to the appetitive nature of man, while man's speculative nature busily denies his existence.

We have been arguing that intellect may lose its habit of assent to being, which is a habit out of experience itself – a sense of common existence, a sense of being as actual, discovered through particularities of explicit beings encountered through our own discrete particularity. In that loss we may be self-deceived by sentimentality as the decayed manner of intellectual deportment toward being, the effect of which is that we make the self the end, even though this shifting to self-love may be tacit rather than deliberately conscious. Or there may be degrees between the tacit and deliberate. We know from experiences of both our own manner and the manner of others that a person may be selfish without realizing overtly that his deportment reveals him as selfish. We depend on manners to restore us from such selfishness.

We might put it that, given the undeniable reality of our specific nature and given the force of ideology in suborning intellect to self-worship, the particular soul desperately seizes upon itself as at least one dependable reality, in an action closing the self to alienation from being. The self as primary object of worship is an inevitable consequence of a denial of discrete particularity beyond the self, a denial of the obligation of intellect to discriminate in response to being. Too easily in consequence, the self is elevated as a complex of appetites, which we may observe at this juncture as supplying a variety of industries for marketing the self. Goods to please appetites become the function of society. In that climate of action, the self quickly is burned out. If ours is a "consumer-oriented" society, as we generally concede, we find that it is society itself which is increasingly consumed, increasingly unsatisfied by appetite as its end. Little wonder, then, that particular dismembered members of community in that dissolving body seize upon evil as certifying some aspect of being beyond mere appetite. Flannery O'Connor gives a persuasive portrait of such a member in her Misfit in "A Good Man Is Hard to Find."[1] The Misfit is, from the perspective of that intellectual reductionist of reality who takes man as constituted of animal appetites only, a pathological killer. But in him is evidence that mechanistic nature has broken down. In a larger perspective, from St. Thomas's for instance, he is much more than a defective element in the machinery of society. He is a disoriented moral agent, intuitively seizing upon evil in a world which denies both moral good and evil. It is as if by that action he touches upon a truth he cannot understand: Evil depends on good. If there is evil, then there must be good. Therefore, so long as there is the actuality of evil, man is more than an accident of mechanistic nature. That is

---

1 Miss O'Connor's Misfit speaks poignant words in her story "A Good Man Is Hard to Find": "Jesus thown everything off balance. . . If He did what He said, then it's nothing for you to do but thow away everything and follow Him, and if He didn't, then it's nothing to do but enjoy the few minutes you got left the best way you can – by killing somebody or burning down his house or doing some other meanness to him. . . . I wisht I had of been there. . . . if I had of been there I would of known . . ." There is a striking echo here of an old argument, one version of which we find in the eighteenth-century poet-critic-philosopher Lessing, whose influence on Romanticism through Coleridge (especially of his *Laocoon*) is well known. Lessing, himself influenced by Leibniz and Spinoza, remarks in an essay, "Argument of the Spirit and Force," on modern man's difficulty with Jesus' miracles. "Prophecies fulfilled and which I have witnessed are one thing. Prophecies fulfilled and of which I have only an historiographical account are quite another. . . . If I had lived in Christ's time the prophecies his person fulfilled would certainly have drawn my attention to him. And if I had actually seen him work miracles and if there had been no doubt that there were true miracles, then . . . I would really have had such faith that I would have willingly subjected my intellect to his. . ." (Quoted in "The Miracle of Masonry" by Antonio Socci, *30 Days*, No. 2, 1991.) Christ anticipated the concern in a lament and rebuke of the "intellectuals" of his day: "An evil and adulterous generation seeketh after a sign." (Matthew 12:39)

why Flannery O'Connor herself observes of her Misfit that he is on his way toward becoming in the end "the prophet he was meant to become." Within the story itself he stands as a rebuke to that sentimentality of intellect which would explain him as a defect, either of nature or of society. That sentimentality paraded as intellectual understanding we are concerned with as destructive to art, of course, but it is more largely destructive than merely to the good of any thing made, such as "pornographic art." (In Thomistic context, as we have suggested, "pornographic art" is a contradiction in terms.)

As Flannery O'Connor remarks, remembering Hawthorne and his concern with sin in relation to his calling as artist, "When tenderness is detached from the source of tenderness, its logical outcome is terror. It ends in forced-labor camps and in the fumes of the gas chamber." "Tenderness detached from its source" is what we have spoken of as the manner of intellectual deportment characterized as sentimentality. Walker Percy, in his *Thanatos Syndrome*, puts similar words in the mouth of his fictional Father Smith: "Don't you know where tenderness leads? . . . To the gas chambers." Both poets, O'Connor and Percy, recognize a dislocation of the proper end to be pursued in pursuing the common good, whereby in the name of the common good, reality is adjusted to accommodate feeling as separated from a profound thought anchored in reality itself. It will, inevitably, find a reflection through the artist in the thing made. For art as an imitation of the action of nature (not an imitation of nature) is in the end inescapably an imitation of the nature of man as maker, and in the most proximate relation, that of the nature of the particular maker of the particular thing. That is why, in the end, though prudence is concerned with moral virtues, it cannot be absolutely severed from effect upon the good of the thing made by the moral agent, man. The recognition of this profound truth is conspicuous in the fictions of both O'Connor and Percy. We may not conclude, of course, that the recognition itself certifies their work therefore as good. It is exceptionally good, in my view, but at last to be so declared in relation to itself, in relation to the mastery of making by the poet, however dependent upon vision or inspiration is that making.

XXV

When our personal understanding of the common good is so far fallen from any communal understanding of reality as related to being, then the common principle is likely to emerge that each individual is autonomous. That becomes the only acceptable principle of existence, and one which does not admit of a critique of principle by dispassionate rational intellect. Each soul is at first flattered by the illusion of its autonomy, though it may continue to give hollow acknowledgment to some imaginary common good. For under the principle of autonomy, each soul is necessarily the center of the only significant universe. Its consent to a common good can extend only so far as the level of "individual rights," the vague border of the contiguous universes of separate selves. That border is always in contention in the name of the local contending self. But there is at least a lingering aura about that self of a moral universe. We need only note the moral outrage of any person who feels his "individual rights" have been transgressed, however difficult it may be to the outraged self to justify the outrage in any authority of moral virtue generally acceptable to the plurality of selves.

What we are concerned to notice as both a problem and an evidence encouraging hope is this moral aura. It suggests as still extant a vague desire for a perfection of being, though the disturbed self in its revolt against a supposed transgression has only a sentimentality about its "rights" as a justification of its vague desire. There can result from such constriction to plurality only a chaos of moralities in contention over the borders between sovereign selves. Meanwhile, the protestations grow louder and louder through an empty rhetoric about the common good. For in this distortion of circumstantial existence of the self to community, the common good can be understood only as a special privilege. The contradiction is hardly noticeable in the uproar. We find this evident, whatever sector of the chaotic social moil we look to in this moment.

It could hardly be otherwise, and the very frenzy of voices is out of the desperation in separate souls separately hard-pressed by the realities of the soul's nature. In the sleight-of-hand whereby the self thus self-loved would posit a common good, establishing the absoluteness of selves as separate, the rhetorical argument tends more and more to a reduction of selves to identities in a pretense of naming things with discriminating intellect. Letter dominates over spirit. To deny the particularities of discrete beings, upon which depends the orders of being in a unity determined by being itself, is to challenge particularities in a contest by intellect already doomed to failure. For the argument comes to rest necessarily on a final denial of particularity as discriminatory, which is to deny the discrete being of the self which engages in the denial. Such is one aspect of the abolition of man, not dependent upon technology but only upon a misappropriation and misuse of signs by abstraction from reality, a denial of the word's relation to reality as inescapably known by intellect, but denied through self-love.

The denial of reality by the actual, discrete intellect, however the denial may be projected as in the interest of a common good, destroys at last not only the possibility of a common good but the possibility of the good of the discrete intellect as well. Consider the danger reflected in our present political climate. In the United States, it is now established as an absolute principle of social responsibility that one accept the judgment that any person "is as good as any other person." To deny the proposition, even on the inescapable ground that *good* in the proposition is so vague as to deny any particularity to separate persons, is to risk being declared inhuman. Or in the terms more common, a chauvinist or racist or elitist. But in the proposition, whether maintained on the authority of the law of the state or as a supposed religious doctrine, the complexity of good is denied our proper exploration by the practical intellect. The principle is acceptable only as a "feeling," whereby vague feeling becomes the highest intellectual virtue. The operative principle to such a thought is a dreamed illusion, destined to disappoint any soul struggling for that good which is the desired reality to its perfection.

At least it must prove disappointing to any soul that attempts to maintain that principle short of the temptation to an excess of power over being, which in the event always means a power over *other* beings. We have remarked the procedure of gnostic manipulation through the sophistic principle of egalitarianism, which in our century has led again and again to the community subsumed by totalitarianism. We see in our own locales a species of that distortion, as for instance the activity of special interest groups operating with totalitarian intent in the name of animal rights or tree rights or earth rights. Thereby existence is reduced to a single dimension having no content. The authority is that of an abstract, unexamined "right" unrelated to the complexity of being, as it must properly be related through God's plenty of particularity. God's plenty is lost to the activist sentimentality whose gnostic address to particularity, through which the plenty is recognized, prevents the soul's adhering to particular beings lovingly, for themselves. To champion a *category* of beings in the name of *rights* violates the "personhood" of persons and the creatureliness of animals or trees or stones. In this putative moral world thus established, where the sense of morality is residual and so not an active element in the practical intellect, most selves will become victim to the wily, whose manipulations of being hinge on an imputed sacredness of the self based on the assumption of the self as autonomous. The consequences are predictable, one of them illustrated by the following.

As I write, I have the current mailing of the *Georgia Farmers & Consumers Market Bulletin* (May 18, 1988). This weekly serves individuals across the state who in one way or another are understood to be closely allied to the land, as gardeners or farmers and so on. The first item in the regular "Ag Consumer Line" says "I . . . recently bought some new ducks to add to the flock. I penned them up for a short time, then let them out. An older, very aggressive drake chased them off. He has also killed a dozen or more hatchlings. What can I do about his undesirable behavior?" The concern for a social rehabilitation of the drake suggests that the correspondent is a member of some division of the social bureaucracy, until we realize that both the sentiment and the vocabulary have become pervasive of public discourse. The concern is for the drakes "civil rights," and the "official" response cites expert opinion in the matter: "According to our poultry expert, you must either get rid of the drake, or pen him up if you wish to keep other ducks around. It is unlikely that his aggressive behavior will change." The same advice would be given no doubt by the experienced criminologist about Miss O'Connor's Misfit. The practical intellect in the correspondent, who is concerned for his Misfit Drake, is so decayed that he (or she) is removed from reality to the vaguely disturbed climate of decaying sentiment. One attuned to reality would be more direct: Ring the drake's neck and serve him to the county agent when next he visits. The final query in this issue's column is more metaphysical: "Do you know of anything I can do to prevent my new garden tools from rusting and wearing out too soon?" (The best answer is to use them.)

A willfully effected confusion in the popular mind, engineered by the gnostic lords of power, hinges on a residual sense of the sacred which is skillfully dislocated to a single sacred, the autonomous self. The confusion is about the meaning of *good*, and it is willfully effected by some autonomous beings who are self-convinced they are more autonomous than others. Such gnostic drakes dominate the flock of those who have neglected or abandoned their natures as intellectual creatures. That the observation is generally true in our century requires no extended catalogue of those autonomous selves as self-elevated to power over other selves. They are, as we observed, those gnostics whom Eric Voegelin speaks of as "lords of power," and they have been most prolific and omnipresent among us, both as demagogues in "democratic" societies and as dictators in totalitarian societies. What is always necessary to their success over us – always and anywhere – is our losing, as intellectual creatures, an understanding of the relation of proximate good to unqualified good, the relation of proximate ends achieved by practical intellect to our ultimate end perceived by the speculative intellect – the relation of actuality to potentiality in the discrete existence and a sense of the possibility of a perfection of being as our final end. We have observed, and often must: What is lost in these abandonments is the reality of being itself, but most decisively lost is the reality of the being of our abandoning self.

We raised the question earlier of the effect of a confusion of intellect resulting from the reality of relative magnitudes in discrete beings, among poets or athletes or (in the evidence above) among ducks. That reality, whether effected by nature or accident, affects each creature's address to the good of the thing he would make, and we cannot escape evidence of the destructions of particular souls among us caused by the failure to address differences of magnitude in the gifts among discrete creatures. This is the failure to come to terms with the orders of nature. That is the proper exercise of our own intellectual gift, through which we may come to understand the difference in beings, and learn thereby the principles of contingent effects upon diverse beings consequent upon those differences. If we may in fact learn something of the sensible nature we share with creatures such as ducks, we may not rest content in reductions of all creatures to that limited common nature, an identity obscuring discriminate differences lest judgment be required of us. We must distinguish between "undesirable behavior" of drakes or children, dogs or colleagues. It is a responsibility required by our given nature as intellectual creatures.

We may be said to be, even as humans, in some respects like ducks, but that is a beginning to the practical intellect in its pursuit of understanding its own nature through understanding the orders of nature. Metaphor, such imputation of likeness between our selves and ducks, speaks at most a partial likeness in things which are *essentially* unlike. For by being, by existing particularly, each thing is discretely unlike other things. The unlikeness that continues a challenge to intellect, after its partial advance through metaphors of likeness, continues in the creature despite our enunciated concepts, an unlikeness to be pursued by intellect in coming to love any thing in itself. We must love the thing for itself, not because it is "like" some other thing, though in likeness may be a beginning of love. The ordinate love of a thing is not because it is *like*, but because it *is*, however helpful a careful attention to likeness and unlikeness in unlike and like things may prove in leading us to see the thing in itself. Intellect rests in a reductionism such as metaphor affords only at its own peril, especially in a world where Misfit Drakes and Misfit Humans exercise divisive power when not recognized in their actualities – when they are not seen with the intellectual eye in their limiting gifts of particularity whereby, though they may be lord of any realm, they are not the Lord of Creation.

Intellectual creatures who avoid this necessity experience destructions of their potential being. We need only recall homely and local instances, as when a concept like "marketability" comes to dominate the virtue of a making whose specific end is properly the good of the thing made and correlatively the good of the maker. For the marketability of a thing easily becomes destructive of both maker and thing. Such a concept may intrude upon the pieties of craftsmanship, for instance, as our daily experience of made things will testify from the shoddiness justified as an economic necessity of the "throw-away" thing. Still, we must consider that nevertheless the effect upon the good of the made thing in itself, consequent upon the intrusion of the principle of "marketability," though it may complicate the proximate end of our making (the responsibility to the good of the thing we make) is not *necessarily* reflected in the thing made. There is the possibility that a thing is good in itself, even though it may not effect a good in the maker of the thing, who may be uneasily aware of submission to a principle not conducive to art, namely "marketability." The relationship crucial to the maker is that of the conjunction of the virtue of prudence and the virtue of art, and that conjunction occurs in his actions as maker. But the made thing exists at last as a reality, and its own virtue requires our recognizing it as a thing in the order of its own being. That a thing has been made in the name of "marketability," through abstract technology for instance, does not mean that it may not be good in itself.

What we discover is that the good that is in the thing itself is a dimension of that made thing's formal perfection. That is a realization of its being as thing intended by intellect as its formal cause, regardless of the intrusion of concepts like "marketability."

If we understand the distinction here, we may escape a sentimentality about mass-produced things that rejects them because they are mass produced, rather than because they are not good in the order of their own being. That sentimental reaction rises, of course, because so often such things are *not* good in themselves, either through failures out of their material cause or formal cause. An automobile may be formally appealing, materially defective, or materially good but formally flawed. It follows that in either case such a thing is not good in itself, since the perfection of a thing in the order of its own being implies an ordinate relation of causes in it: efficient, material, formal, final. The made thing is perfected through its material and formal causes, and whatever good it possesses in itself resides there. It is the efficient and final causes that give us as makers difficulty. When the material and formal causes are at odds, the source of failure lies in the efficient cause, the maker, in that he has not exercised a sufficient power in the making, focused by a concern for the good of the thing being made, for whatever reason it is made. If one is killed by an automobile defective in itself, the efficient cause comes under pressure in our courts for violating the common good. But if one is killed by excessive speed in relation to contingent circumstances, the defect lies in final cause as exercised by the self-victim. In either event, the clarifying principle comes to rest upon the uses by the practical intellect as it is either efficient or final agent in relation to the made thing.

This is an old point, explored with precision by minds from Aristotle's down to our own day. We engage it here since it is too vaguely a part of our thinking about the implications of good as applied to our making or to the thing made and to our uses of made things. That vagueness spawns a variety of dislocations in our perceptions of being. In a notorious series of events in our history, we find whiskey is declared evil, as we observed in another context. Rum becomes "demon" rum. Or a particular weapon becomes, in itself, evil. The well-made thing, perfect in the order of its own being – that is, perfect in the order of art appropriate to its nature – may have proved an expense of spirit to the maker in the prudential order, or it may prove destructive of the world's body in respect to its final cause. But what we must require of intellect in addressing the implications of good in respect to causes, if we are not to end up attempting to establish a right-willed intellect by energy spent futilely on the symptoms of willfulness, is that intellect respond to reality in orderly practical actions.

We shall then recognize an ancient truth: The proximate effect of good or evil out of any art object is not a good or evil in the thing itself. Such is the distortion and confusion within intellect resulting from a false understanding of the relation of art and prudence as virtues of intellect. In our moment, that confusion makes it almost impossible to come to terms with many impinging concerns, from drakes to pornography, from atomic energy to the energy of genes. Old-fashioned Aristotle as explicated by old-fashioned St. Thomas might leave us less terrified in the presence of such realities no doubt, and help us deal more realistically with the actuality of energy from atoms, for instance, perhaps turning it to the common good at last. Now the well-made thing – one in which formal and material cause are such that it is one undivided thing – may be a proximate good achieved by the maker at a considerable expense of spirit to that maker as we have said, even when that thing is a poem and not an atom bomb. That is, considered in the prudential order of its relation to the maker it may cost spirit. Artisans in our day are notoriously disturbed and unhappy with their makings. It becomes easy to blame historical circumstances for this disquiet, given that our world is one in which technology threatens to supersede and subordinate all makers, even those who make our songs. But to repeat, it is not necessarily because the thing made is not good in itself. For the artisan, limited in reflective vision, limited in the inclination of intellect whose concern is the perfection of being in the artisan, may nevertheless make a thing superlatively good in the order of the thing's own being, though restless as maker because of the limited vision and understanding.

The point intended may perhaps be clarified by recourse to Thomas once more. For the general context of our thought here is concerned with the relation of the artisan, the maker, to the common good in his pursuit of the good of the thing he makes, and it needs emphasizing that the concern is not primarily caused by the artist's time or place. Thomas observes that "[w]hen man of himself acts for an end, he knows the end, but when he is moved or directed by another, that is, when he acts at another's command or is moved at the instigation of another, he does not have to know the end." (*Summa* I-II, Q. 1, A. 1, Reply Obj. 1) When man acts in such a limited capacity of his intellectual being – when he is moved or commanded toward an unknown end – he may do so by suspending the authority of his own will and its responsibility to an end. We may speak of such a person in act as suspending, for the moment of the act, his will's responsibility in the name of a common end. This is to suggest that such a common end is proximate and not ultimate. Such is a requirement, for instance, in the soldier. When soldiers act, submitting to the direction of another's command, they become a thing in the sense in which an instrument is a thing. They become a *team*, as we might say, a body directed to a proximate end, in which respect they differ from that communal body directed to ultimate end of which St. Paul speaks in exhorting us as members one of another.

We do not say that soldiers become a community, a body, in which they are members one of another in the sense of body as a living unity, desirable as a *community*, another term for St. Paul's *body*. There is an obvious difference, for instance, in a well-ordered family as a body and a squad of soldiers as a body. This is not to say that the individual soldier does not retain some sense of proper end, though he surrender his will in proximate act for a common end. The camaraderie famous among soldiers speaks the contrary, though we might observe that the soldier recovers that residual community sense separate from his action of consent to proximate end when he surrenders his will to his corporal or sergeant. It is more nearly the stuff of barracks friendship, the stuff of campfire tales and of soldier remnants gathering after old wars. What is recovered beyond the submission of will to a common act as a unit or instrument in war is the recognition of service to a calling, a calling whose proximate circumstances require in the event itself a surrender of individual will to the direction by another will.

Having made his observation about this surrender of will whereby one intellectual creature is directed by another, Thomas adds, "So it is with irrational creatures." One can argue nevertheless, from our example of the soldier, that the soldier is an artisan whose concern is the making of an instrumental agent, the squad or platoon or company. In that making he may be devoted to the perfection of that instrument without an understanding of the proximate end. Loyalty, pride, courage – soldierly virtues testify to that sense in the separate soldier that he is moved by an act of intellect toward a perfection through actions accepted as a common good, though his is not fully the intellectual act. With the soldier as with any man, the proximate good may become confused with unqualified good. Soldiers are notorious for this confusion, as the history of war-time atrocities reveals. But common to such a commitment to instrumental calling is a sense of an end beyond the proximate end, even if that end is not recognized as proximate and mistaken as ultimate. That is, the soldier in suspending his will surrenders his intellectual being to a higher authority. He serves a commander or a state, acting in the name of a common good. It is not to the immediate point that this common good may prove otherwise, for we are concerned here with the sense in which to surrender to the authority of another is not essentially irrational, not merely animal-like. One may make grievous mistakes through rational error, but only man as reduced to automaton may be declared irrational in respect to his actions.

And that brings us at last back to the general unrest of artisans in our century, of makers who, having surrendered to the authority of another in order to exercise themselves as makers, find no content either in their making or in the thing made. The builder surrenders to the architect, resting a faith in the architect's practical intellect insofar as it is attuned to the reality of being. It is a faith to be sustained and justified by the builder's seeing that attunement in the architect's plans. The building rises as a thing in nature and thus becomes a part of nature. When it rises pleasingly (i.e., when its formal and material being are in concert and its being in itself in contextual concert with place and time) it has done so in a harmony with the contingencies of circumstances in the place of the making that complements its being in itself. But what happens to the builder's own content with his making when what he is called to make is not in due concert with reality? When prefabricated repetitions are commanded upon a denuded and leveled place? Though the builder may comply insofar as he is prudential being as well as artist, and thus susceptible to imprudence, he knows a disquiet. An indifference to the reality of the particularized place, through which autonomous intellect imposes form regardless of the given material cause he would inform, violates being at the expense of the intellectual creature. A builder so disturbed judges the architect, and thereby may recover to himself something of the proper relation of the responsibilities of efficient cause to formal and material cause – toward that harmony of being of the thing and of the maker which is the desirable proximate end of any making.

But this prospect of recovery has become more and more problematic to the artisan since the Industrial Revolution. One need not deny that useful things result from that revolution. There is a good in running water and indoor plumbing, though we should be careful to deny that the quality of life itself is determined by such a progress of good things. But in respect to a calling of the person who is the maker, there has been a more considerable expense to spirit than commonly understood. This is not the place to pursue the point at length. Let us observe only that such has been the price that the artisan as ordinarily encountered in the developed West has largely lost the satisfying recognition of his calling to be a maker. The concern he has for his own prudential being is shifted to a concern for fringe benefit – for vacation and insurance and the like. The end toward which he is apt to yearn is not a perfection of his own being through proximate actions of making but – retirement. He surrenders his will to a making whose good is problematic more often than not in respect to that common good which by intuition he is inclined to serve. That does not mean that the thing of which he is a party to the making is not good in itself necessarily, as we have said. It is rather that he has surrendered his authority and responsibility as maker to a process, to an abstraction. The company logo associated with such a making very often is advertised through spectacle in an attempt to woo not only the buyer's money but the artisan's devotion as well. To take the point, observe TV ads for the latest automobile model. But while one may love the thing he makes, it is not so easy to love the "company and its sign." The proper relation of the virtue of art and the virtue of prudence in the person – proper because implicit in the nature of person – becomes dislocated. Prudence separates from art. Retirement benefits become increasingly paramount, as making becomes drudgery. Thus the one hope of perfection lies in that condition called "retirement," a point where one is his "own boss" and can have a garden or fish and loaf to his heart's ease.

Such is the reduced sense of a final end, a lingering desire for a perfection of being. That there remains an intuitive knowledge that such attenuated life is not proper to this created intellectual creature man is signaled again and again to us by such events as the sudden violence among artisans, baffling when not seen in such a context as our argument advances. In a subtle gesture, a worker may put a loose bolt in an inaccessible place in the body of the car being made, so that there is a mysterious rattle. Not a matter of random malice, it is rather a comment on the loss of the person's openness to the good of the thing he makes. More spectacularly, there is the actual violence widespread among artisans collectively committed to unsatisfying labor, especially where people are concentrated about plants. Suicide, murder, the general wild destruction reported in the Monday news in heavily industrialized centers. On the other hand, there has emerged, and grows gradually, a new artisan. He is most likely to be, though not necessarily so, a college graduate or college drop-out, and his presence is reassuring, since it means that intellect is still viable, though his institution does not and should not claim credit for intellect thus stirred. I mean that young artisan who finds a certain content in the good of the task he undertakes as carpenter or mason or mechanic. He (or she) is most probably independent, in business for himself as he puts it. But he is more than an entrepreneur in that the object that commands him is not primarily or exclusively the money he receives for his making, but the good of the thing made. I am happy to number many of these among my friends.

It is not that I advocate as necessary to the spiritual recovery needed in our civilization that all persons so redirect themselves, that all become carpenters or plumbers. That would be to deny the reality of the circumstantial world. Among other errors, it would be to try to deny the past three hundred years of history, and many of the young intellectual artisans I otherwise applaud tend to make that sort of mistake. In the 1960s the now-notorious "awakening" of our youth tended to become programmatic in its reaction, intended to replace one established process of being with another, regardless (because intellectually shallow) of the necessary grounding of actions of making in complex reality. In its insistent rejection of what it called "The Establishment," it rather imitated its antagonist than recovered a proper ground of action to personhood. As we enter the twenty-first century, we shall more and more, I suggest, discover the "awakening" of the 1960s – in the instinctive rejection of the so-called Establishment, in a proper stirring of intellect, and in the errors following from that vague hunger for the truth of things – as parallel to that other Great Awakening in our history associated with Jonathan Edwards. What is needed in it to its recovered health is our bearing witness more clearly and firmly to the truth of things as necessary to the soul, through a habit of the practical intellect suited to the good of things as mediate ends. Otherwise we shall but establish a new sort of Puritanism in which the realities of the spirit are displaced by an infatuation with the world, with mediate ends as final, the obverse of the old Puritan deconstruction of the soul whereby soul was separated from both the human body and the body of the world by intellectual actions, although that separation was momentarily refuted by the actuality of the contingent world.

In this respect, ours was a second Great Awakening in the 1960s, evangelically political more than religious on its surface, but with a considerable presence of religious self-righteousness in the movement such as we more usually associated with apocalyptic religious hysteria. One might well notice, for instance, as a substitution for the Second Coming, the recent terror of the Bomb, and as that terror fades, a substitution becomes necessary for that recent apocalyptic remnant – acid rain or the widening ozone ring. To make such a comparison is not to declare such agents of apocalypse purely fictional (although we have not examined them with sufficient rigor) but to call attention to the increasingly distressed address to realistic problems by intellect when it is disjoined from the complexity of reality. It seems, for instance, a betrayal and denial of the psychological comfort of alarmism when the scientific evidence accumulates against industrial waste as *the* cause of acid rain, even as it appears anticlimatic to a religious ecstasy, associated with "nature," when reasonable, and relatively inexpensive, solutions to such problems as acid rain become feasible. As the family fishing pond may be maintained through proper fertilizers, so does it now appear that larger waters may be similarly recovered without the crusade of massive federal monies. That will mean, in such event, the collapse of bureaucratic managements excessively funded by congressional largess, those who have an entrenched, vested interest in alarmism.

Out of such witness, we must try to recover to the artisan – that is, to each person in his character as maker – a sense of personhood larger than his actions of making as final end, even when he finds himself on an assembly line in a factory. Otherwise we shall certainly succumb to that ultimate spirit spawned out of the Enlightenment principle of the autonomy of intellect which evolves as process in the "industrial revolution." We shall become more enslaved to that unholy spirit sprung from autonomous intellect, Technology, than ever soldier was to sergeant or field hand to planter. Jacques Ellul, in *The Technological Society*, is an extreme Calvinist on the point, contending that the genie technology once let out of nature by autonomous intellect is now the ravenous master of all personhood, beyond containment. Perhaps. But the witness of the young artisans I value is to the contrary, and a certain stirring of discontent with the reductions of intellect by the academy itself are abroad in even the popular mind – however limited that mind in its ability to say the truth of how things stand in respect to person and to community. And that, of course, is why our argument about making as our proper habit of being is so crucial. What must be recovered to that popular mind is an understanding of the person as intellectual creature, since the general failures of community so widely ascribed to the machinations of "intellectuals" has given intellect itself a bad name. That is, intellect as popularly understood is not a proper understanding of its reality. We must recover the truth of how intellect must stand in the contingent world, recognizing that we each and every one by the gift of our nature is by our very nature an intellectual creature.

XXVI

If we are to recover intellect to its proper, proportionate offices to the good of ourselves as persons, and thus recover a viable deportment toward the common good, if we are to think clearly about our condition as a civil community in rapid decay, we must return to a better understanding of man's discrete nature as intellectual creature. It is out of such an understanding, if at all, that a civil community becomes possible. We must recover to our self, as the ground of order to that "self" which is a spiritual creature, a responsibility to an effective relation of practical and speculative intellect. And in that recovery lies the rediscovery of the relation of the virtue of prudence to the virtue of art proper to any person, since every person is by nature a maker. Such a relation assures the health of the discrete soul whose reality we speak of as *person*. In the recovery of person it becomes possible to recover the proper order of persons called community. In understanding truth as the good of this recovered intellect, our judgment, whether as person or more generally as persons in community, will be commensurate to truth, will be just.

It is through our attempt at this recovery that we must consider the made thing in respect to its perfection in itself, whether we mean by *thing* a poem or garden or an institution established in support of community. We shall thus be able to understand what degree of loving adherence is required of our will to our made thing, a love for itself as it exists among the orders of existing things. This is to say we shall then once more be able to distinguish. And it will follow from the just response of distinguishing among the degrees of good in existing things that we may affirm of any made thing that it is supportive of or stands in the way of the good of the soul. That is a distinction relative to ends, whether the concern is for the soul of the maker or of makers or of any soul affected by the made thing, insofar as its existence becomes a part of the circumstantial conditions to the affected soul. We shall then be prepared to consider more wisely the relation of the good of things to the good of persons. Such is the recovery of prudential virtue, consequentially supportive of the good of persons. With such clarification of our will in its relation to the truth of things, to the good of those things willed, we shall be more likely to deal effectively with the problems agitating civil disorder, as for instance pornography or acid rain.

But we need not attempt here to plunge into that complex of problems, about which the daily press gives us the latest evidences. For the first necessity is to recover our own ordered thought about the nature of thought itself, about intellect as the special gift of our nature through which our being as discrete creature may be restored to order in a community with being. Let us take as a point of departure here, not that contradictory thing already adverted to, pornographic art, but begin rather with a respectable and respected poem: Respectable in that it exists with a sufficient good proper to itself and is respected by just responses to it as a thing by intellect. It dramatizes the soul's attempt to recover that order we are contending necessary to the recovery of the reality of creation itself. I have in mind a poem already present to our thought, Eliot's "Ash-Wednesday," from which we chose at the beginning our governing epigraph to these speculations and meditations upon our intellectual nature – "teach us to care and not to care."

It is evident from our use of these borrowed words so far that we have not been primarily concerned with an aesthetic question, with the good of the poem in itself as poem. Whether the words in their context speak the general virtue of the made thing "Ash-Wednesday" is sometimes debated. But that one is drawn to it again and again because it is there, because it exists as a thing in some degree of perfection as a thing, seems hardly debatable. The degree of its perfection need not here concern us, though we ought to acknowledge that it exists to a sufficient degree of perfection as a made thing that it can recall us to it. We do not here approach the poem from a perspective strictly limited by its order as art, then, but rather as it bears evidence of the maker's own attempt through his making to recover prudential intellect.

Indeed, we might observe that some other intellect might borrow our epigraph to an end quite different from our own. We must be guarded in our use, therefore, lest we distort the good of the thing by dismembering its words from whatever unity it possesses as a made thing. When a made thing, or a portion of such a thing, is dislodged from its order of being for uses tangential to its existence in itself, the whole or the part may suffer abuse, whether an abuse intended to the general good or to the good of the self appropriating the thing. One might use the words we have borrowed as epigraph, for instance, to embellish an advertisement which intends to exacerbate sensual appetite, so that one is urged to "care" for the automobile pictured (usually with an attractive female torso associated with the image) at the expense of other "cares" in the prudential order.

Copyright laws aside, we might properly object to such a use as an abuse of the poem itself, as a willful distortion of the burden upon *care* within the complex of the poem itself. We might nevertheless grant that the abuse of *care*, which in the poem centers upon the concerned commitment to the truth of created things by a created soul, is turned by a certain wit from the expectations established by the poem itself. What the ad writer would recognize as effective to his purposes is the jangling juxtaposition of serious reflection to the inclination of appetitive excess. Indeed, that is why it might "sell" a car, not to the careless, but to the sophisticated. If it "works." (If it "works" as "ad" however, it probably does so because it flatters the would-be owner of the latest sleek car, one who is bent on satisfying appetite with "the good things of life.") The strategy of wit in varying degrees is standard in the advertising "industry," whether in support of drinks, food, cars, cosmetics, headache remedy or social or political causes. We have probably all seen one instance worth taking as a measure of our inclination to recovery: A cosmetic ad presents a self-absorbed Aphrodite who, admitting her excess, the luxury of the product, declares, "But I'm worth it." Such catering to self-indulgence proves more effective, no doubt, than our whimsical ad using words from "Ash-Wednesday," since it goes so simply and directly to the inclination of our appetitive nature but turns on self-flattering words to justify the disproportionate value of the Aphrodite's person to herself in the fiction of the ad. It is a species of abuse of personhood more fundamental than its spectacle of ambient sexuality. Our sensual worth is raised to expectation of perfection in the sensual, by the mere use of a soap or a perfume – which as we have said may in fact be good in and of itself as a made thing, to its proximate end as soap or perfume. What is involved is a confusion of an intuition to perfection of being, proper to our nature, by directing it to a mediate good exhibited as if ultimate. That is why the pretense of person as goddess proves especially subversive. That it is cynically perverse needs only the "research" of observation of the women who buy such products in comparison to the carefully selected goddess of the ad.

The error of such appropriation of residual desire, through made things presented as desirable means to false "ultimate" ends, is the inappropriateness of the end proposed to the desire. The lesser good is exaggerated as if a greater. Our coming-to-be is affected. This is true if by *desire* here we mean that desire native to us for an ultimate good. And our insistent contention is that this deepest of all desires is with us in consequence of our given nature. For the end intended in our making is that we know and love and worship God, not ourselves as our own god or goddess. If intellect does not support that desire, the desire does not cease. It rather finds inappropriate object. We are here describing a truth about our nature as human creatures which is seemingly recognized more clearly by our manipulators than by ourselves, as the history of our submission to consumerism of several species suggests, in the political, social, economic, religious spheres of our actions.

The safeguard against the abuses of art or nature engineered by willful misappropriations lies always in our understanding of the relation of virtues that in concert dispose the will to right action. Again, that safeguard lies in the manner of the agent. External restrictions upon that manner, as by the law, will not prove sufficient to rescue the agent to its own good, however necessary such restrictions may be to establish external order. For we must understand that a perverse agent may appropriate our prayer "teach us to care and not to care" as a motto, as a directive to transgression in the face of prudential virtue. It may become, in effect, a reminder to him of the pragmatic advantage of a caring demeanor hiding the intent to deceive. One remembers here the conman's self-congratulation on victimizing his "mark": "He was a stranger, and I took him in." And when we recognize the intent of such a will and consider it separate from whatever evil effects may be registered in the external world by its actions, we must still return to that most devastating effect of all: the *self-destruction* in that perversity of will. That is the sorrow of the Fall, over which "Jesus wept."

As for the proximate effects of perverse will, we must acknowledge them and deal with them as we may in support of community. But we need not conclude ourselves substantially reduced by their effects, even when we are principal victim. If we suffer an evil effect upon our soul it will be because we have failed to distinguish proximate and ultimate good, not because something untoward has been done to us by some other. Neither the manipulating agent nor his instrument may be suitably charged as the cause of our own spiritual failure in our response to the ways of the world. Socrates, through reason, arrived at the same conclusion: A good man cannot be damaged essentially by a bad man. And to that reasoned argument, as its justification as legitimate argument, we have advantage beyond Socrates. We have the good offices of revelation certifying the goodness of being because of the supreme goodness of that supreme Being in whom is no shadow of turning. It is in this reasoning toward discovery of the precedent truth of revelation that we may come to understand the distinction necessary in *good* as suited to our finite existence. Otherwise we will not understand sufficiently the point St. Thomas makes about these two goods. "The useful good and the unqualified good," he says, "are not on the same level, for one is good in itself and the other in relation to another." Even less may we understand St. Augustine's remark: "What we here call the end that is a good is not that which is consumed so as not to be, but that which is brought to completion so as to be fully." (*City of God* xix, 2) These reminders alone prove sufficient to any intellect so that it should be able to understand why in a "consumer" society which is increasingly dependent on made obsolescence, man himself becomes jaded – becomes the final obsolescent thing.

By a willful excess, by the desire to possess the good, we turn a proximate good into an illusion of "unqualified," ultimate good. That is the procedure whereby intellect turns idolater. Even so, the thing thus worshiped as ultimate by that worship ceases to be the thing it is, insofar as the worshiping intellect may respond to it. By the mistaking of its own being, then, the intellect separates itself from the actual and is left with an illusional residue taken as actual. That is the effect of idolatry upon the soul. And so the thing in itself, clutched by willful desire, proves not gold, but fool's gold. Once possessed it is "consumed so as not to be," leaving the will unrested in its desire. Turned restive, restless in the world, the will becomes ravenous as well, like Dante's she-wolf famished by the act of gluttony itself.

What we must insist to the point is that each person by nature has a sufficient and immediate ability to judge his own will as right or excessive, guided as is most anciently testified by conscience. But given that sufficiency, whether or not the person has an intellect sufficient to advance the concerns of conscience to a communal consent may be another matter. Differing as members one of another, each is not gifted as philosopher-poet or poet-philosopher. Intellectual gift is particular and not uniform, despite the Albigensians of Modernism, the egalitarians. That is why we recognize and treasure superlative intellect in action, memorialized in "monuments of unaging intellect," as Yeats described them. So, at least, is the testimony of poets and philosophers, nor is this a circular assertion but rather an assertion of the self-evident. Thus we are reassured by Plato or Aristotle, by St. Thomas or St. Augustine, by Dante or Shakespeare. But alas, as Thomas himself puts it (*Summa* I-II, Q. 14, A. 1, Reply Obj. 3): "Things which are most certainly good according to the opinion of wise and spiritually minded men may not be certainly good according to the opinion of the multitude, or of a sensually minded man. Consequently, counsel can be given about such matters." In good conscience, we listen to wise counsel, willfulness suspended.

Under such counsel, we recognize that a made thing, a creature which is an effect of man acting out of his nature in his contingent world, may be good in its own order of existence, though it may be used to ill effect upon intellectual creatures. For in the order of prudence, it is always the soul at risk and not the thing at risk, whether good or bad in the order of its own existence. Such is the distinction crucial to the problems of the common good. As "marketability" may intrude destructively upon one's address to the good of a thing he makes (whether his labor is that of the craftsman of the car of the poet-advertiser of the car), so a maker's indifference to the good of the thing under construction (car or advertisement of the car) is consequential in his being – consequential to that inherent desire in him for a perfection of his own being. Restlessness of spirit is always in some respect a consequence of intellect's not pursuing through the proximate good the unqualified good. That such unrest distorts the good of the things we make as a community of souls needs only our observing the shoddy condition of marketable things in our world, as we have reminded ourselves, or the abuses of person that is the increasingly unrelenting operative principle in advertising.

Our artisan's attention to the good of the thing made has been largely shifted from that good to the actions of the making. We have already named one effect of this shift: the artisan's increasing unhappiness with himself, to escape which he focuses his own attention peripherally from his central responsibility as maker. The most important concern for man the maker thus becomes his working conditions, his insurance benefits, and the like. His proper desire for good is not fed by any good in his making as revealed to him in the thing itself and that is why desire comes to anticipate a rest, not a fulfillment, contracted as vacation time or retirement. In that relation of his being to his making, the maker becomes an element of a process, and will be spewed out by process as obsolete in the end. Whether he is on vacation or retired, the process continues unaffected by his absence. Out of this abuse of our being as maker, at the level of national policy, the concern accelerates for the old, the retired. The concern for "health" is removed from any relation to a fullness of being through ordinate becoming through the gifts of making. The "psychological" problem of the old and retired may be sometimes considered, but the emphasis is upon bodily health, at times almost as a refusal of the complexity of the circumstances of persons "superannuated" by process. The enlarged attention to substitute process, to "recreation" for the old, signals again the loss of spiritual dimension to existence requiring our recognition of the proximate to the unqualified good as affecting a person's being. We say, rather, that the machine when at rest, rusts. Such is the likely analogy summoned to a concern for the "senior citizen," who must be kept busy if he is to be kept "alive." Little wonder those extensions of that view of human existence is the growing practice of disassembling of the body as machine to recover usable parts, in one way or another. Such an address is inevitable when man as autonomous must be concluded at last a mere mechanism whose operations are limited and whose final value beyond participation in process is as salvage in and for the world of society as machine. If to become an organ donor is the final end, can euthanasia be far behind?

That such an argument is not merely an obsolete Jeremiad is testified to by a considerable literature advocating that view of mankind. And against it stands good counsel given by a growing number of persons defending person, among them Gabriel Marcel, Jacques Ellul, Eric Gill, Ortega y Gasset, Miguel de Unamuno, Jacques Maritain, Etienne Gilson, Donald Davidson, Richard Weaver, Eric Voegelin, Alexander Solzhenitsyn. One could easily summon recognized champions who, by the virtues of intellect, stand against the reduction of man as maker to the level of an element or a component in a process, a reductionism dependant upon mechanistic Darwinism. And in our summoning, here, we have not even included those good soldiers of the true and beautiful, the poets.

XXVII

Since we share with each other through our nature the means to that becoming we have named as making, and since words are the most portable evidence of that making, words traveling through both time and place in a seemingly enduring journey in relation to the perfection in them in the order of their nature, perhaps we may reflect once more on the poet as an appropriate figure for man the maker, his office as steward of words. In his prudential action to the word's fulfillment he makes a suitable figure representative of mankind. Now as the poem becomes a reality, out of his making, and thereby a thing among things in a complex of created existences, the poet himself may consider it with an excessive regard, or he may be indifferent to its existence. For he is not merely a figure representing mankind. He is a person. He might, for instance, perceive the poem's reality as exclusively an other-worldly one, since it seems not strictly a thing of a palpable nature as we remarked earlier. Is a thing of words a reality at all? Is a thought a reality? Questions the philosopher must deal with through rational intellect. The poet as philosopher – given the completion of his making whose result is the poem – may consider his poem a spiritual extension of other-worldly dimensions, a thing regardless of the existential world.

The poet may, in consequence, become dominated by that native movement of being in him for immortality, for a perfection of his own being, and so conclude the poem a creature which, if not registered in heaven, is at least above the reach of nature. He may cling to it as his rescue to the transcendent. Several of young Shakespeare's sonnets raise this possibility as theme to the poem under construction, the relation of the good of the poem to the immortality of the poet himself. Sonnets 55 and 65 touch the concern. What the voice of the sonnet engages is a mystery whereby the sonnet itself exists as a real presence in the mind, a reality whose substance is in no wise material. And, though the mind is circumscribed by its context of time and place as materially manifest, beginning with that little earth which is its own body, the mind in its particularity seems destined for oblivion, "unless this miracle have might,/ That in black ink my love may still shine bright." At the most immediate level, of course, "my love" alludes to another person, but the action of rescue of that exemplary beauty of person devolves upon the making action of the poet. And, insofar as there is an immortality of that beauty rescued out of nature, it must mean that through these words, the poet's voice continues always in an actual present to a subsequent mind. So far, we might say, the miracle of those voiced words of Shakespeare's indeed continue in their might, since our mind is enlivened by that present voice, historically several centuries stilled, yet still alive.

But, though "Not marble nor the gilded monuments" of princes may be said to outlive powerful rhyme – Homer's voice a present to us while Agamemnon's palace is long since dust – the assertion of an immortality of his words and through them the poet himself rings hollow and rather desperate in his own ears at that first moment of his making. Nevertheless, there is at least a hollow insistence that his being continues beyond the limits of nature through the action of mind itself, even when that *beyond* is understood as somehow contiguous to nature and not to a transcendent. The poem serves a personal desire that is also a universal desire. That is, it serves a desire personal to the discrete mind in any time and place. If Brice Parain, given the same subject as Shakespeare in his sonnets, declares that words are immortal precisely because they *feed* upon existence, primarily the existence of the articulator, who is thus but a food to words as flesh or grass to bacteria, the poet will resist that conclusion, as if such a philosopher were poetry's principal antagonist.

We find the two in contention, a Shakespeare of the sonnets or a Brice Parain of *Metaphysics of Language*, at a level somewhat lower than the poet's concern for his own immortality in words when we turn to the relation of the poem to the common good as addressed by the philosopher of the common good. For if we turn from the poem as an enduring icon of a particular voice to the poem as a cause of action in the common world, we seem to enter a different order of concern. The poet, should he give himself to that order, is likely to cease from poetry and become polemicist. But the trapped philosopher must say at last, I think, that regardless of whether the poet turns or not, the thing he makes has proximate effect and so is part of that arena in which we pursue the common good far beyond the poet's concern for his own person. He may even object that, given the reality conscribing Shakespeare's attempt at magic over nature through words, the poet may be cause for a subsequent dislocation in other minds, those who are caught up by that voice and give a consent to an end at variance from the actualities of being. Only by a sort of ventriloquism, he might say, on the part of the present mind may it be said that the voice of the poem is a present reality, and if that enacting mind in this present moment does not realize the point, he falls out of reality. The argument is fascinating in its complexity, a complexity we are contending to be riddled only by our understanding the proper nature of the intellectual creature man in his relation to the contingent world, through which he must pursue that proper end of his desire, a perfection of his own being.

Let us reduce, for the moment, this high and fascinating question of words in service to final ends to a more proximate question prominent to the concern for the common good at this present time. The question continues to be whether the work of art has effect by its own being in the contingent world, whether the poem is an object decisive to the actions of the practical or the speculative intellect, or both. Whether words, because of their very being, of and in themselves, are dangerous to the common or the personal good. Such is the matrix of questions within which we attempt to define such a dimension of the world as revealed in that "art" we call pornography, the most spectacular of the attempts to manipulate appetitive nature. The dilemma of art's "immortality" as it affects this passing show of persons haunts our age with peculiar intensity, focusing at this present moment in the academy, the refuge of intellect in which a responsibility to reality through the word is in alarming decay. Can the thing perceived through the thing of art be exorcized by an abolition of the art? Can the proper action of intellect, one might say (if he is poet) be achieved by destroying all mirrors? Alas, that seems the present course of action in our academies.

The poet struggles with the problem, and he is likely to maintain that art may raise that which seems prudentially unacceptable and rescue it by his art. Pornography as art is opposed (so he may conclude) by unpoetic moralizers. In declaring his own authority on the question over that of philosopher or theologian, he may also insist on more ancient credentials in the question, pointing out that Homer and Sophocles and Aristophanes come before Aristotle. The poet, thus, is father of the philosopher. Art raises the prudentially unacceptable above prudential concern; thus other-worldly values are reserved to art, though the precise relation of that other-worldliness to this present-worldliness is not always clear. The aesthetic sensibility to which art speaks is inescapably anchored in the sense, however abstractly a Shelley may insist that intellectual beauty is the omnipresent "Spirit of BEAUTY." Shelley's "awful LOVELINESS" is contained by "every form," though form itself appear to the uninitiated the decay of nature and so stir in such an intellect a desperation not governed by beauty. That fleeting presence for Shelley, then, cannot be (as often argued by critics) an intellectual beauty perceived by "spiritual illumination" rather than "by the senses." His apostrophe to that spirit in his famous "Hymn to Intellectual Beauty" even as in his "Ode to the West Wind," clings desperately to the fading sensual world to verify his own mind as the ultimate center. The furthest reach of will for Shelley beyond the self can be at last only toward the common good, but that good is defined ultimately by his own intellect. In short, his is a closed world in which his intellect only is omnipotent. The rest which is longed for by will's desire is projected as achieved by its own actions in an ascending trinity: "Love, Hope, and Self-esteem." The somewhat frantic gesture toward an absolute through this sequence, it is clear, ends in the self, leaving a very lame directive to this worshiper of Beauty "[t]o fear himself, and love all human kind."

It is not arbitrary choice that brings Shelley into the poet's argument with prudence here. The poet whose words we use as epigraph to our concerns, T. S. Eliot, remembers that in his own discovery of his calling as poet, it was Shelley he chose as patron saint, carrying a dog-eared selection of Shelley everywhere. This is the time of youth out of which he comes to write that portrait of Prufrock, a portrait we might conclude to be the end of "self-esteem," an inevitable end to that approach of intellect to the contingent world which Shelley advocates. It will be only after a journey of recovery out of Shelley's shadow that Eliot will be able to pray: "Teach us to care and not to care." Now "an aged eagle" unable to fly above the world by an imaginative will to transcend the world – having come to the middle of his journey – he turns *to* the world as Shelley has tried to turn away from it. For what Eliot has concluded at last is that it is not art that saves us from the sordid perceptions of the soul in its appetitive degeneration, the dissolutions in our sensual matrix that tempt the poet to become an alchemist of being through the magic of words. For there is no miracle of transubstantiation of being in the power of art itself, and so the poet cannot through art be savior of any being, and certainly not of himself. The illusion, whereby art is supposed as superseding prudence by elevating mind to an order of being beyond the complexities of created being, fails. That is the poignant testimony of Keats. More than aesthetics is involved, then, when Eliot after "Ash-Wednesday" rejects Shelley, celebrates Keats, and affirms Wordsworth among the English "Romantics," in his Harvard lectures in 1932–1933.

In this present theme of "pornography" baptized and raised by art, seemingly given imprimatur by the National Endowment for the Arts on occasion, our concern has not been with the crafty manipulators of pornography. They present their products as if simply a marketable product of the imagination, like automobiles or cosmetics, complaining that their "good" products are still suffering a "bad press" from lingering Puritan objections in the popular mind. It is usually put by the purveyors thereof very much in this vein with shibboleths like "freedom of expression" as the new moral law justifying whatever one wills to do to reality with words. Through such wily justifications, the poet himself is recruited to testify that art has precedence over prudence, prudential concern thus indicted as an outmoded, untenable enslavement of mind. It remains true nevertheless that the poet in such a stance is awkwardly exposed. For what he insists is that art itself is the highest prudence, that whatever effect art has in the existential world is a good effect simply because it is an effect of art. We ourselves have been arguing that art properly seen always speaks prudentially, but it does so within the arena of a prudential concern for being and is subordinate to being. And that is an order of concern quite separate from the order of art.

Art is not prudential *of itself*. If it were, then the poet would prove, as Shelley believed, our best legislator. If it were, then an Ezra Pound would be right in advocating the poet as king, over Plato's argument for the philosopher as king. The inescapable prudential dimension to art, which moves it beyond its order of art in respect to the contingent world, is out of its own dependence upon created reality in the first place. In the second, its prudential effect rises because, by its existence, in its own order, art is but a mode of making within the orders of creation in service to the fulfillment of passable existences. It is a mode of intellect contingent in man as maker, whose actions within the proximate arena of creation are to be governed ultimately by man as steward of, as coadjutor of, being.

And so it is a mode of encounter by intellectual creatures inhabiting that world, creatures who must struggle to relate the prudential virtue proper to that intellectual action of making as a power of intellect. No work of art as an existing creature in the complex of creation can be declared a transcendent rescue of nature in and of itself. We may go only so far as to acknowledge, with Horace and Longinus, that a work of art as an existing thing is long in its relativistic relation to the single, particular life of the poet himself. Even Shakespeare's assertion that powerful rhyme outlasts sluggish stone does not make the rhyming poet immortal, though every poet no doubt at times dreams of singing his favored immortal lines in some Elysian Field. It cannot be that, through art, one is gathered "Into the artifice of eternity" as Yeats asserts in his powerful incantation of art's omnipotence. For the poet is neither king nor priest in his calling, though his sense of power over being through his gift with words leads him again and again to that illusion.

What the poet's calling allows at last, is not an alchemy through the magic of words, but a prophetic office in which he helps recover to us known but forgotten things. Poems are existent things, and we are served by them in our recovery of what Eliot called the "permanent things," but they are not themselves of that high order. Through them at last, by grace in aid of the reflective intellect, we may reach that perfection of being that is spoken of by true priests and philosophers and poets as the state of beatitude. Neither art nor nature can be the rescue of the intellectual creature from what Shelley calls "This dim vast vale of tears, vacant and desolate." That rescue lies through the Word that is at the heart of Shelley's desert, though he does not recognize Him, the Word within the word that Eliot at last encounters in both art and nature, the Word Hopkins celebrates as "fathering-forth" being, out of "a beauty past change," through Whom change is reconciled, change is transcended to an unchanging perfection. That unchanging perfection is to be discovered by intellect as it is related to the perfection possible in the gift to its own existence, its own potential as a being past change in that state called beatitude.

XXVIII

We remarked that the poet may or may not reflect in his poem his awareness of, or concern for, the effect of his labor upon himself as person or the effect of his poem upon another person. It is often a characteristic of the so-called "Romantic" poet, however, that he has a decided belief that he must have an effect on community. His calling seems a religious one to him in a world in which the offices proper to "altar, sword, and pen" (in Wordsworth's phrase) are decayed. For, with that decay, persons in community have lost that "inward happiness" which sustains a person in his exercise of his calling in the world. (The term *person*, we remember, intends to name a transcendent calling of the soul in its participation in the social world as *individual.*) But we have also ventured that if the poet does succumb to a concern for effect as the principle in his act of making, he may become distracted from the proper concern for the good of the thing a-making. He may violate the order of art, the virtue of the poem as poem, and become tractarian. For a concern for the effect of the poem upon himself, or upon others as beneficiaries of his making, easily perverts art. We recognize this tendency and speak of a species of poem as "occasional" to indicate the recognition. It is not an easy thing for the poet not to care for the effect, to care only for the good of the poem itself. It is difficult to resist looking over his shoulder toward his audience. The carpenter building a house, if he does the like, will hit his thumb with the hammer or saw a finger – effects of his action of making that are accidents, but not accidental, since they are a consequence of his shifting the attention of practical intellect from the good of the thing made, or rather from the good of the thing *being made*. But the signs in the poem of such a turning are not so conspicuous as the blood stains on a window frame.

Of course, the very matrix of proximate reality within which the poet or carpenter lives and breathes as necessities to the exercise of his calling makes it virtually impossible for him to separate the complex of ends proper to the thing and implicit in the making. A purification of the actions of making allows no orderly purity of deportment in the making. In addition, there are always the sidewalk superintendents watching, the critic spawned by art. Or there is perhaps the restless family anxious to move into the house before leaves fall. For the carpenter of words, there is always the editor pushing a deadline – even if that editor be only the poet himself anticipating the publication of his voice. And this series of complications has not touched at all the problems with material cause, the supply of timbers and glass or the nature of the supply, the necessity of metaphor here or image there, the aligning of music. These are considerations most demanding even without the intrusion of changes in schedule or on the blueprint that may prove inconsiderate of the implicit relation of material and formal cause. We must declare, however irritating the declaration to the carpenter or poet, that such complexity of means is the price he pays to reach his ends, especially the price of his particularity discovered through the exercise of his calling. He is challenged by his being, which is further circumscribed by those particularities of the circumstantial matrix.

It little helps to know, under the pressures of immediate actions of being, what we must come to know reflectively if we are not to be at last overwhelmed by intrusive circumstances: Circumstance is the inescapable condition of being. If he were God, rather than carpenter or poet, his making would be a simple act not conditioned by circumstance. Indeed, circumstance is an actual effect of the simple creation of the primary world, God's making, and since the carpenter's or poet's own making is dependent in that world, that very dependence requires his contending with circumstance. He is himself a circumstantial creature, in that his finite existence is itself accidental *to* the created world. A particular intellectual creature finds himself living in this time and this place, but there is nothing essential in his nature that requires by his essence that he exist in this time and at this place. The particular discrete gifts of his essential being are independent of history. One may, like Miniver Cheevy, long to have been born six hundred years ago. Or one may long to have been born six hundred years hence (and so contract for the freezing of one's body at death so that the possibility of an afterlife in this world can be entertained). But illusion aside, one must engage circumstance out of essential nature. Both essential nature and circumstance partake of "gift," since neither is the essential cause of the other or of itself. Such, then, is the necessity attendant upon the singularity of being, the particularities occurring to existing things as necessities to existence.

St. Thomas speaks reflectively on the point. "The particular conditions of any singular thing are called individuating accidents of it." (*Summa* I-II, Q. 7, A. 1) "Circumstances of human acts should be called their accidents."

These conditions are "outside the substance of an act," though they affect the act. Now *accident* as spoken of here is differentiated from those circumstances that are "wholly accidental," those which "are not taken into account by any art because of their uncertainty and infinity. This randomness is not the same as the accidents of circumstance, having no part in the act as ordained to it." (*Summa* I-II, Q. 7, A. 2) What is crucial in this fine distinction is "the substance of an act," circumstance affecting the actuality of that substance, but not determining it. This distinction reminds us that the substantial nature of human act is will, through which the nature of our intellectual being is brought from potential to actual. Circumstances, then, are not "mere" accidents to being, a random chaos, but ordained to being whereby being *fulfills* through its actualities. It is limited by circumstance but not determined by circumstance.

This is a point perhaps made clearer if we say that for the discrete intellectual creature, any Miniver Cheevy or Oedipus, there comes to be an importance to contingent place and time. But the importance lies in circumstances that make possible a growing knowledge of the circumstances themselves. Thus acts are not subject to a randomness exterior to act, as would be true were there no knowledge of circumstances' limit to act. Still, a Miniver may dream of having lived earlier or later, thus escaping that present moment in which alone any act is possible. When we say *present moment*, we designate thereby the particular place and time, always at a certain still point of the intersection of intellect with circumstance out of which action moves. But the desire in us is for a purity of act that is both timeless and placeless. That is, the desire is for a purity of act possible only to the ultimate cause of all act and time and place, and not to the finite "particular conditions of a singular thing."

The conditions to the singular thing through circumstance, the accidents of its being, is a difficult ground for intellect to deal with. We mean here only to suggest that the poet must make the most of these difficulties to his singing in a fallen world and out of his own fallen state. His singing is necessarily in relation to the realities of being thus circumscribed. The action of the practical intellect is the attendant cause to his song. Thus singing is an act of reason in making, as Thomas says. Pure singing and pure song must be at best figurative analogies to the true nature of perfection, of that state of rest called beatitude. As figure, it is not unlike those figurings of Heaven as a gleaming city with streets paved of gold. Meanwhile there is the more local, accidental, level of difficulty in which contingent ends of making surround the substance of act itself. Of that necessary engagement through making let us argue that, insofar as the poet is engaged in a present making of his poem, he is poet. Insofar as the carpenter is sawing the board or nailing rafters, he is carpenter.

The pen aside, the saw aside, the complex of circumstances to the person who a moment ago was poet or carpenter is of a differing complexity. He does not cease to act thereby, but the contingent effect of his action is different. The intellectual creature's endurance of circumstances of his being, we are saying, is always necessarily through singular acts of intellect, acts not uniformly engaging circumstance by a uniform act whose mediate object is extensively the same. As I write a poem, I am a poet, and the name may follow me into my other conditions of discrete being. But there is a complex of conditions of being to be reconciled only as I am a person and not a poet or carpenter or the like. It is only when I think of myself as poet, separate from my writing a poem, that the title seems appropriate as a general designation of my being, appropriate to a resumé. There are thousands and thousands of poets who do not write poems, as there are thousands and thousands of knights like Miniver Cheevy. Each is poet or hero – at moments of thought. And because of this lure of thought centering upon a calling recognized though not pursued, it becomes seductive to reduce our essential calling as maker to an illusion of a constancy, a continuousness, of act in that calling. In point of our actual endurance of being – that is, continuous actions of coming to be fully – we are makers not simply in the office of our calling as we are called to the good of the thing being made through discrete gift. The poet not making a poem may rather be planting a garden. Or he may be advancing a philosophical argument.

But in either possibility, he is required by the nature of his being to an openness to the good of the thing being made – the garden or the argument – and in relation to the circumstances contingent upon its own order of being. He may not plant lettuce in December simply because he is a poet, nor deal with the relation of accident to being in philosophical treatise because he is a carpenter. But neither may he cease to be intellectual creature simply by ceasing to make a poem or to build a house. If by his nature the intellectual creature exists through singular acts but not continuous act, he is so as person, a term designating an inclusiveness of his nature that makes him specific and unique and not a singular thing closed by circumstance. That is, if one's calling is that of poet or carpenter, he is not by that calling specific. As specific, he is a person.

When the poem is at last an existing thing, when the poet ceases in his making, he steps back from the thing he has made. In doing so, he ceases to be singularly the poet, and so stands in a new relation to the poem. In this new relationship, as the poet or any maker knows, the thing surprises its maker with his sense of it as a new creature, and even though he may hold copyright, it confronts him as well as an independent creature. He rests and beholds it in itself, as good or not. It is at this point of address to the made thing that his reflection on the thing for itself and consideration of its possible effect to the common good becomes a consideration of his intellect. This is to say that we must come at last to acknowledge a poem's actual presence as a thing in the order of nature, though dependent in nature, and most especially as it depends from human nature. It is a thing existing because of a making by a caused cause. To deny the poem some effect within the whole of creation, as if through the poet's singular devotion to its good as a poem he thereby removes it from its anchor in, and continuance in, creation, is not only to deny reality but to be open to decided danger to the denying soul by that action. It will mean a confusion in the poet's dealing with the true relation of his art to the common good.

Let us relate the conditions of our acceptance of the thing for itself, the poem, to our being and to its existence in the contingent world. An act of love reduced by the practical intellect to a simply mediate end to the convenience of our being, as when one gives of the self out of fear or in hope of gain, reduces that act to a level below prudential virtue and results in a reduction of the lover's potential being as well. But an act of love out of neither fear nor hope but rather centered in the justice of affection for the thing itself in itself, as when one would clothe and feed the destitute because they are destitute, such is still not at last full love. Love is larger than any question of need, whether the proximate object in need is the self or some other. But acts of love governed by prudence – that is, acts of love moved beyond mediate ends – will nevertheless have immediate and proximate effect. Acts of love in which the self is removed as object of the effect, the selfless act that radiates through and beyond the proximate object of love (we are saying) affect the proximate, mediate object. The mediate effect is not simply in the name of a larger end. But it is primarily for that larger end, though we may put it, in St. Augustine's words, that we love by acting in the name of God. It may seem as if by that agency we were turned from God in an action downward from God as it were. But the act of love is toward God, though it is made through the proximate end. That is the complication occasioning our prayer for grace in ordering the ends of our action: Teach us to care and not to care.

So it is that we may speak of that act of love whereby the poet is openly directed toward the good of the poem a-making, in which openness he accepts the necessary conditions of that good as restrained by the order of art and of art's virtues. There is a singleness of concern, but it is not removed from an enveloping larger good. In that creative making contingent reality is affected, though the act is restricted to the object of act. For a thing comes into being thereby where it was not before and so necessarily affects the circumstantial world beyond the order of its own discrete being, as we said above. Sometimes "selfless" acts of love, we must acknowledge, are destructive of the general good in the arena in which the common good is the proximate end. Zeal for the common good, when in excess of the practical intellect's knowledge of the consequences of such zealous action for the common good, may prove directly destructive of that common good. Again and again, we know instances of destructive effects of well-intended programs of action in the social or political realm. Such destructive effect, however, while it may be destructive of the common good, may not necessarily be destructive of the soul of the agent. We must repeatedly recognize this point, since our judgmental inclinations so easily move beyond the realm proper to our finite judgment and thus usurp those regions of judgment appropriate only to God. What is at risk is the judging soul, caught up by its presumption. It is in this most ambiguous country of prudential concern that good intentions intersect reality, creating for us those finite problems of justice in relation to mercy and complicating all our actions for the common good, whether the action be in the name of criminal justice or political justice or the like. The relation of justice to mercy in creation is always problematic, so that the pressure upon prudential actions toward the common good is constantly threatened by gnostic solution of common problems. In respect to art, we have already introduced such a problem, that of reconciling or distinguishing pornography and art. Always, even valid principles if abused make clarifications of appropriate lines of action most difficult. But, acknowledging the complexities, we are nevertheless required to act on such difficult concerns as the execution of judgment and mercy for the common good, community order requiring it. (This relation of justice and mercy involving the common good I have written of speculatively in the conclusion of my *Possum, and Other Receits of "Southern" Being*.)

XXIX

It is easy enough to characterize a certain "Puritan" habit of intellect in our culture by pointing to such absurdities as the argument that evil is in drink rather than in the drinker. Still, with those advances of technology upon us that have made us the subjects of an elaborate road system on which we speed to proximate ends, usually as if to an ultimate end, we sometimes meet an end ascribed to the evils of drink, even by a sophisticated citizenry. The evidence of abuse of the fruits of the earth, in their fermented state, brings strict law to bear. Those fruits of the earth, when consumed as fast food heavy with cholesterol, raise additional terrors. In addition, the products and by-products of our technological conquests of nature raise the specter of cancer at every turn, so one fears any encounter of the created world through the senses, unless that thing encountered has been certified officially as not hazardous to one's health. It seems a most dangerous time to live in the world, aside from all our recent concerns for global wars. But once upon a time "nature" seemed glowing with spirit. Even as late as John Keats the poet could allow his fancy to speak of the nightingale as a "light-winged Dryad of the trees." Now everywhere in nature lurk Darth Vaders with carcinogenic swords.

The problem has become for us, how shall we abide? How shall we find our way out of this embalmed darkness that is not only nature but nature reconstituted by our technology? The first step, we have already suggested, lies in recognizing that, in respect to the good of things, the good is properly in accordance with its nature. The consequence of evil effect lies in misuses we make of nature through the practical intellect. And those abuses of things in themselves follow most usually from our mistaking a proximate good as if an ultimate, unqualified good. In respect to the thing made through that virtue of art which is the dimension of our being as maker, the made thing must first be taken in the order of its own being, in its order as art, lest we become caught up in that "Puritan" panic which leads us to locate evil in the thing rather than in the will. If our confusions were not so disturbing in their mediate effect, we might even be amused by the puritan response of liberated minds on this point, minds that have rejected the actual old Puritan ground of gnostic separation of *things* as evil from *spirit* as good. The transcendent anchor of the older Puritan thought, though abused, nevertheless contended that the ultimate, unqualified good was the proper end of man. It did damage most severely by confusing the relation of mediate good to ultimate good, being suspicious of any good in the mediate world and most especially suspicious of the sensual necessities in approaching the unqualified through the proximate world. That is, the Puritan solution would deny our appetitive nature, lacking a confidence in virtues proper to the appetitive.

That species of Puritan gnosticism is subsequently modified so that the transcendent is relocated and redefined in autonomous intellect. Thus "nature" becomes a contingent reality not to be rejected so much as to be transformed by intellect. But when that transformation comes through an unbridled technology, when evil effects at the level of our biological existence become daily more evident, we become possessed by a new puritanism in which nature and things made out of nature become the immediate enemy of our biological existence. Since we have been left with biological existence only, having lost our belief that specific intellectual being is properly transcendent in its ends, the next step must be to call in question intellect itself. For it has been intellect (we sense this if we do not understand it) which has loosed technology as bad genie in nature. But as proper as some of our arguments with "scientists" are, it is improper to conclude that intellect itself is the mad cause of our collective biological woes. From man to whale to elephant to rare plant, we are concerned with endangered species, but at the level of biological survival. It is with great reluctance that we acknowledge such concern as a rather attenuated level of love for things in themselves, one hardly adequate as a vision of creation such as the one given us by St. Augustine and St. Thomas and like minds. And so we are, let us pray, increasingly forced to a recovery of the good of the intellect that we may rediscover a relation between proximate and ultimate ends of intellect. Only by doing so will our vision of being overcome the reductionism of physics or biology. And a recovery of prudential virtue to an accord with the virtue of art is the necessary direction we must take toward that vision, if our making is to be a making rather than a perversion of being.

By analogy to the act of procreation in community, let us say that a loss of prudence in the causal agent does not necessarily flaw the consequent being, the child or product or poem, even though that agent is indifferent to prudential virtue or scornful of it and thus proceeds with his making. To allow this point is a beginning to a journey out of our terror of the contingent world with which terror and which world we must come to terms despite all the dangers. The limits of gifts in the casual agent of either action, the biological act of reproduction, the intellectual action of the making of a poem, does nevertheless speak a limit of being consequent in the "offspring." Now if in either order of creation, the biological or the imaginative, the agent were absolute cause in respect to the limit of being of the caused creature, it would follow as accountable in the causal agent. That is the false position we take in declaring intellect autonomous, or declaring the body the primary self to autonomous man, the most important existing thing. But the perspective of the existential child or poem, we must conclude, rather that parent or poet is itself but a proximate circumstance to the being of that thing insofar as that thing is specified in itself. We speak here of the biological nature of the child, the art nature of the poem. Because we are agents, makers, we are inclined to speak of being, of existing things, from our limited perspective as agents and with a partial understanding of being. That is, we are inclined to speak as if the agent were in actuality a being's absolute cause. If such were indeed the reality of the agent as cause, any incompleteness in the child or poem would then have to be fully accountable in that causal agent, and we should have to say that any failure of being in the thing is caused by that agent's failure to achieve a perfect union of formal and material cause in the created thing, the obligation of will in making to the good of the thing made.

It is a popular position, in respect to our biological existence as makers, that we set aside the agent's will, at the same time denying a transcendent participation to such a primary existence. But thus we are left with the necessary conclusion that existence in nature is random and accidental. Such a confused solution to the finite agent's causal role in creation allows the willful intellect an escape from responsibility to being. It is the intellect's attempt, in a popular figure, to have its cake and eat it too.

In our attempt to resume a responsibility of intellect in its relation to being, whether participating in primary creation or making secondary things like poems or houses, let us posit the following about any discrete creature: Any actual incompleteness in child or poem is properly considered by the reflective intellect in respect to its proper order of being, in relation to the whole of ordained creation. This does not mean that one must exhaust the specific creature in a fullness of the contingencies of all existence forced upon it. We mean only that the intellect's reflective concern is properly in its beginning and end, a consideration of the thing for itself. The thing in itself is the more considerate approach than an initial and primary concern for the causal agent, though the ultimate end of that agent is at issue. When we come to reflect upon the existing thing, it already exists, and its very existence is the proper point of our reflective departure. From the point of view of the specific nature of the thing itself, the proximate agent (poet or parent) is not only a *limited* causal agent but also a *part* of the contingent, the circumstantial reality to its being as well, even as it comes to be. If we move from the creature itself outward to the contingent world in our attempt to understand its being, we are not likely to forget the complexities of circumstance that account for its particularities.

Considering the child: The parents indeed bequeath a limited and limiting biological effect in the child's actuality. What could be more universally recognized than this biological participation in being. But the very immediacy of that participation, from the agents' perspective (the parents'), is already tempted to an assumption of their agency as absolute. The most difficult role of parent is finding the line between responsibilities as agent – a concern for the good of the "thing" one has been a limited causal agent of – and an acceptance of the implicit integrity of that newly existing creature, the child. The anguished love in this new encounter of parent-child grows complicated as the child comes to know intuitively that the parent is more than the proximate causal agent of biological being: The parent is also a continuing circumstantial presence to the child's becoming in ways not to be accounted for by biology. One might recall here Joyce's presentation of this growing awareness in the child, of enveloping circumstances to his own existence. Stephen Dedalus makes a comfortable location of himself as the center of his universe freed for a moment from intrusive discomforts of immediate circumstances. Writing the geography of himself on the flyleaf of his geography book, he justifies himself:

Stephen Dedalus
Class of Elements
Clongowes Wood College
Sallins
County Kildare
Ireland
Europe
The World
The Universe.

But by the time Stephen is a young man, the circumstances of his being appear to him such that he rejects, not only his geography as justification but the complex of intrusive social beings, the church, nation, family. He can shift his place, but he feels more compelled to reject that spirit of place as he finds it reflected in the circumstances of his own history. That he loses both place and history, except as matter for his intended art, is one of the novel's ironies.

As for the poem in itself, in relation to the poet, we have cited Robert Frost's remarks. One writes in the light of all the other poems ever written. This is to say, with a depth I do not think Frost fully appreciated, that in respect to the poem in itself, it exists in a relation of *being* to which all other poems ever written are circumstances to it. This means that the critic, while obligated to start with the poem itself *in itself*, moves outward from that concern in recognizing the circumstantial contingency of other poems to the particular one. That is why the poem as poem is not simply a biographical footnote on the poet. Such is the gift of intellect in considering being that it sees the poet, the proximate cause of the poem, as but part of the complex of circumstances that establish the particularities of the poem in itself. (I said I do not think Frost fully aware of the depths of his true words because he is, despite them, always extremely jealous of his own "originality," a concept we explored earlier.)

Such journeyings of the active intellect as we are trying to orient here, in respect to being, is analogous to the approach to literature advocated by some of the New Critic critics. Here I have particularly in mind Eliot, Tate, Ransom, Brooks, in each of whom there is from the beginning a strong "traditionalist" presence, though they vary in their accommodations to tradition. In each, the struggle is to recover, *through* the poem, its relation to circumstantial reality in respect to its own discrete nature. That is why it is an over-simplification to contend, as some recent commentators on the New Criticism have done, that as a body those critics are interested in the poem only as an existence independent of all else save the engaging mind. While such is an emphasis in some degree by some of those generally described as New Critics, in those I here single out it is quite other.

One need only consider Eliot as critic in relation to Eliot as poet to realize that what is fundamental to his concern is a recovery of his soul's orientation to being. It is inevitable that St. Augustine is important to him in that recovery, and we have observed the presence of that rather ancient "New Critic," St. Augustine, in *The Waste Land*. *The Confessions* is important to our understanding the portrait of the artist that rises out of Eliot's criticism and poetry, figuring not only in *The Waste Land*, but crucially in "Ash-Wednesday." St. Augustine's dramatic work is a portrait of the philosopher as a young man, complementary in its visions of the nature of intellect, upon the callings of the poet. It is especially so in respect to memory and its uses, as well as in its concern for the relation of language to the actualities which language would name. Through a recovery of an orientation whereby the right-willed intellect comes to "adhere lovingly to something for itself," in St. Augustine's words, Eliot at last gains strength to pray, "Teach us to care and not to care." And such is the degree of recovery to things for themselves that the voice of "Ash-Wednesday" can say with a new delight in things in themselves that the "weak spirit" at last recovers the "cry of quail and the whirling plover." Even smell is renewed by "the salt savour of the sandy earth." The questing intellect is thus revealed as changed by its open act toward particular being, so that it becomes more largely actual out of its potential, and in so becoming recovers the way toward the undifferentiated good.

That is the necessary movement of will toward ultimate ends because intellect and will must by their finite limit engage being through singular existences, if the way is to be recovered. And that is the viable principle at the heart of the New Criticism as practiced by those poet-critics I have singled out. They understand that the very nature of finite intellect is such that it must move through singulars, starting with the object immediate to intellect and moving through that object as known in larger circles of its journeying toward understanding, till it breaks through the proximate toward the ultimate in a visionary moment. Again, this is the principle very carefully established by St. Thomas long ago, out of Aristotle and Augustine. (If Aristotle is for Thomas "the Philosopher," Augustine is the "Theologian" surely, as a cursory thumbing of the *Summa* will show.) Thomas insists that it is through the most local manifestation of being to the finite intellect in its desire to approach ultimate being that the person properly begins. It is the senses that provide a movement to intellect beyond the sensual. Rather early, Eliot's Gerontion laments having lost "sight, smell, hearing, taste and touch," recognizing that loss as consequence of an approach to being whereby it would consume being, rather than, as St. Augustine advises, consent to the being of the thing in itself. That is the distinction recovered dramatically to the "little old man" as he is reborn in "Ash-Wednesday."

The proximate good that stirs the will's desire, Thomas says, is desirable not as an object possessed but as an ally to intellect in its journey toward perfection. (*Summa* I-II, Q. 1, A. 8) It is thus that one discovers an affection for the being of the thing, the object *in itself* and not as an object to be consumed by intellect. Again, Thomas remarks that the relation between intellect and its object is that the object *specifies* the act, but the will the *manner* of the act, as we have heard him say. (*Summa* I-II, Q. 11, A. 4) When we realize that the object acts in a specifying way upon intellect, out of that object's singularity, we begin to understand that the unmannerly act, the willful act, distorts in the intellect itself the particularizing effect of action toward the object. This occurs when intellect through its manner would make the object an end in itself to be "consumed" by the possessive act of knowing. The object of the will's act defines the nature of the act appropriate to object, thus ordering the love of things. Since the object cannot be in itself the ultimate good of the act, no rest of intellectual action is possible in the object possessed. For, what if a man gain the whole world by such action and lose his soul? The restlessness of the "successful" possessors of a multitude of objects is a common place in our experience. We usually ascribe such emptiness of spirit to "the rich," but one must not conclude that the owner of multitudes of objects is restless because of the multitude. It is rather because of the *manner* of possessing, and the individual soul may be as miserable holding a single object as in holding many. The "poor," then are as susceptible to losing the soul as the "rich." The restlessness lies in the nature of consort between intellect and being, not in the legalistic categorizing of property as possessed under the abstract laws of property.

Now if one may be miserable whether possessing one or many objects in a manner destructive of the proper office of the will (which is to love being), we must remember it possible because will in its actions necessarily moves toward single objects. If the object of the will's act in itself concerns the nature of act – i.e., the limits possible to act of finite will in response to particularity, the thing itself in its own nature – then from the will's point of view the circumstances of the act concern the individuality of the act itself. (*Summa* I-II, Q. 18, A. 3). This is to say that the moral aspect of act lies in the individuality of the movement of will toward circumstantial existence. The act is individuating of the willing intellect, which means that the movement toward its perfection must be through encounter with the multitudinous circumstances of specific beings other than itself. It is not perfected by an accumulation of those beings, but by the effect on its own being determined by its manner of encounter in its multitudinous acts. That is why a proper habit of its own being must be established and maintained, lest it be turned from its proper end by a faulty manner toward existential reality, the manner whereby it would devour reality. Perfection, then, is not a consequence of numbers in respect to encounter, as in the "bottom line" value of our possessions. It is a consequence of the actuality of the intellectual creature itself, made possible by the consort of itself as being with circumstantial beings. In the end, by right will it transcends circumstantial beings in achieving its perfection as oriented to ultimate, undifferentiated good. That is its hallelujah to its Cause.

Meanwhile, however, the burden remains that such a coming-to-be of the intellectual creature depends *in* circumstance, where it must take existences singularly. For, as Thomas insists and as our moment-to-moment existence certifies to us, "actions are about singular contingent things, which because of their variability are uncertain." (*Summa* I-II, Q. 14, A. 1) Given the uncertainty out of variableness, it is little wonder that the will in action is tempted to seize being out of the order of being to still its own restlessness. For our relation to the singularity of being, while analogous to God's in that we exist in his image, are limited analogously as explained by Thomas's principle of participation.

If we will to possess being, God's is a willing of being of the singular things which by that willed being is contingent to any created intellect. The creative act of God is specific to the thing. But our action of response to the thing is specific in effect upon our own being. That is a relationship, out of God's providence, between intellect and object so that intellect may gain its perfection when in a manner of right will it engages being. Because this is so, we must realize that truth or falseness resides in intellect, not in things, for things, insofar as they *are* by the willing specificity of God, are true in themselves. It is intellect's recognition of that truth in the thing itself that gains intellect's being, and we describe it as a loving adherence to the thing for itself. That is the direction in manner whereby one praises God, loving being for itself because it *is* through the sustaining specificity of God's loving will that it be. Thomas makes this distinction by arguing (*Summa* I, Q. 16, A. 3) that truth in things is *substantially* in their being, while truth about the thing to intellect is *convertible* with the being of the thing. Truth in intellect is the coincidence of thought and thing as truth, the proper response to which is wonder and a new stirring toward perfection by intellect itself as a created and sustained thing.

XXX

Our will, says St. Thomas, "is midway between the intellect and external activity, for the intellect presents the will with its object and the will causes the external action." One must conclude then that "the movement of the will is from the mind to the thing." (*Summa* I-II, Q. 13, A. 5) In another perspective, "Natural things are midway between the knowledge of God and our knowledge: for we receive knowledge from natural things of which God is the cause by His knowledge." (*Summa* I, Q. 14, A. 8, Reply Obj. 3) The knowledge of God is prior to natural things; natural things are prior to our knowledge. The measure of the being of natural things is God's knowledge, then, not our knowledge. Such is the visionary discovery we see in Wordsworth's witness of his experience of natural things in "Tintern Abbey," Wordsworth was a poet rather distant from St. Thomas's formal argument, depending upon immediate experience along the River Wye. But there, Wordsworth has also discovered a problem to intellect with which he must attempt to deal. He remembers a time when, with a fuller power in "appetite," he experienced intuitively "a feeling and a love" of things for themselves that "had no need of a remoter charm,/ By thought supplied, nor any interest/ Unborrowed from the eye" – i.e., separate from a present sensual encounter of being as in the "sounding cataract" or "tall rock" or mountain or "gloomy wood."

Indeed, Wordsworth makes a distinction between this remembered relation of intellect to being and an earlier state, that of the "coarser pleasures of my boyish days." That earlier state St. Thomas would no doubt characterize as exercising "natural appetite," which "arises from the form that is present in the natural thing," a stirring of "boyish days" comparable to the state of our animal existence. (*Summa* I-II, Q. 8, A. 1) The second stage for Wordsworth is that painful one whereby he recollects himself as confused as to whether he is fleeing something dreaded or racing toward something strangely loved. This is, we might conclude, descriptive of the stage Thomas speaks of as "sense appetite," through which the intellect encounters being mediated by the senses. There remains subsequently the "rational appetite – the will – which arises [as does the sense appetite] from a form as known." One cannot read Wordsworth, a poet far removed from such precisions of inquiry about intellect as St. Thomas', without recognizing that both are nevertheless concerned with the same common experience of being. Wordsworth, for instance, in attempting to come to an accommodation of thought by his current appetite of will, talks very explicitly of the relation of form as it rests in mind out of experience to the actuality of the external in-forming object. But such is his delight in that thought that he simplifies the problems of contingent circumstance, as if to insist on an inevitable goodness of the will out of its encounters. For, he insists, through such encounter of objects, the mind becomes a "mansion for all lovely form." What he neglects is that, in the will gone awry, unlovely form may come to inhabit that "mansion."

What Wordsworth is losing sight of is the becoming out of being of intellect itself. Intellect in its finite existence *becomes* in its potential through repeated encounters with actualities made through the senses. There are not three stages of man's being so easily categorized as he would have it in "Tintern Abbey," the last and saddest but necessary one in his paradigm of the evolution of intellect being supplied by *thought*. For Wordsworth here, thought is the will's direction of awareness toward external beings through perceptions. By *reflection*, which he calls *thought*, Wordsworth would regain a state of an unself-aware awareness, but finds that possibility forever fled. Thomistic realism would question this assumption of the nature of thought. Through grace, it would say, intellect acts at a most elementary level, in the context of encounter with reality. Thought, this realist would urge, is already operative in circumstantial encounter, and most especially in that "bounding roe" stage which Wordsworth remembers in his reflection upon past experiences in nature. The immediacy of intellect and object Thomas speaks of as "a kind of union," and those words would very likely be sympathetic to Wordsworth. What Thomas holds, and what Wordsworth does not recognize in his actual experience of things, is a condition within which thought is already operative long before that restricted aspect of thought, reflection, becomes for Wordsworth the whole of thought.

In not recognizing the operation of intuitive intellect in its encounter with beings as a dimension of thought, Wordsworth inclines – through reflection taken as the full nature of thought – to remember past encounter as involving instinct more than intuition. That is, remembering encounter, he sees it as rather a state of animal existence in nature. He is not being fanciful in aligning himself with the roe. He does not suppose his language merely attributive, but that it describes an actual relation of likeness of his youthful state to the state of that free-ranging creature, the roe. This is a serious lapse of reflective thought upon the event, for it turns Wordsworth toward *thought* as if it were late to being. Thought in his view appears on a linear, sequential condition to his existence. But taken in such terms, thought is time-bound limit upon the "self." That is, he does not see it as the Thomistic realist does, for whom thought is an aspect out of intellect's specific nature as an existing thing. It is not evolved in consequence of enduring circumstantial necessities as if an effect of circumstance upon person. There results for Wordsworth a dichotomy between "thoughtless youth" and thinking age so that thought is seen at last as an accident of being attributable to time.

As close as Wordsworth comes to seeing as a realist, and he comes very close, this confusion over the nature of thought arrests him, and in response to that arrest, in reaction to his awareness which finds itself time trapped, he resorts to Platonism as the solution, to an Idealism that sets aside the goodness of existential reality which he had earlier perceived. We see this rather clearly in his famous "Intimations on Immortality from Recollections of Early Childhood." (I have developed this argument at length in *Romantic Confusions of the Good.*) He has prepared his own way to becoming lost in the dark wood of the world, but he has also prepared a way in our recent literature for the continuance of the nostalgic regret we associate with Romanticism as a literary movement. We have argued it a regret for the loss of a state of unself-conscious openness to creation, mistaken as a cause lost by historical limits upon the person. In this time trapped view, man is born and moves through those stages of life Shakespeare memorializes, down to old age and the grave. With the rise of Darwinian evolution, the Romantic inclination seems to gain a certain validity from the new "science," though this view of existence very deliberately embraces a closed history, rejecting Wordsworth's Platonic view, in which we die at birth into nature, and are born transcendent at death. Instead, that vaguely remembered loss of a "state of nature" freed of the necessity of thought is embraced in its animalistic reductionism, a point we saw earlier in Brice Parain's lament for the loss of *A Metaphysics of Language*.

The late Romantic, the Modernist poet, finds himself torn by desire. He is pulled on the one hand to a complete submission to animal nature to escape reflection and on the other hand to a complete rejection of animal nature through intellectual detachment. The detachment, no longer allowed a point of reference of its disquiet in a transcendent rescue from disquiet, finds irony its only refuge. The agony of this dislocation of intellect becomes, as we have said, a continuing theme in art since Wordsworth, which we have given a title touching its pathos in our sociological and psychological concerns, "Alienation." The intellect separated from reality, such as represented by J. Alfred Prufrock, puts the dilemma with a poignancy of despair which irony will not rescue. Rejecting Wordsworth's free creature bounding by rivers and up mountains, that roe who seems like the poet as he remembers his experience as if a fleeing from as much as rushing toward "something he loved," a Prufrock prefers a less ambiguous kinship in animal existence. He would prefer a state of nature like that of a "pair of ragged claws" scuttling sand under silent sea.

Both Wordsworth and the early Eliot are more nearly like each other than either is like roe or crab. Both are confronted by the mystery of intellect itself, an immaterial reality of their being inescapable by the gift of thought, though intellect is related nevertheless to material reality in complicating the mystery of human existence that will not yield easily to thought. The actuality of existence – inexplicable in terms of mineral, vegetable, animal materialities, yet integral to those realities: How can immaterial intellect understand its incarnate nature as a "spiritual animal"? If only it could maintain a constancy of thought uninterrupted by the intrusion of self-awareness. Again, what the realist would say to the dilemma, and Eliot comes to see this way in recovering his nature, is that the nature of intellect is finite in its incarnation and by the limits to its existence by specific gift in respect to both its immaterial and material particularities. It is consequently discontinuous in its actions. For what is desired in the "romantic" state of crab or roe is a continuity freed of the interruption of self-awareness. Intellect is nevertheless always a present condition of this specific being, despite wishful thinking, whether named Wordsworth or Eliot or some other specific person. Even when the will is not presently in act, it is presently existent in potential act. Meanwhile, finite intellect must engage being singularly – *this* act of will toward *this* object – and not inclusively, as is the supposition of the will in its dream of a transcendent perfection when it shall "see God." It must do so, since it is like God in its knowing but only by that principle of proportionality of being. Its acts of love can be but echoes of that perfect love whereby both intellect and all things are willed.

God's action, unlike intellect's, is not discontinuous. It does not withdraw and then go forth. It does not shift singularly from one actuality to another as finite intellect must. That love is perfect knowledge and power. It alone can be *simply* inclusive of multiplicity, in which is included both a present actuality of a specific creature and its potential actuality. Unwavering, with no shadow of turning, God's knowledge of a discrete existence makes of its actual and potential a single and simple existence in a way impossible to finite knowledge and power to fully perceive out of that simplicity of its own limited being. It is within the interval as seen by finite intellect as between actual and potential that operations of the finite will, in respect to its being, can occur. That is why man's "creative" acts as maker are a secondary level rather than a primary, to recall Tolkien's distinction. Man makes only by borrowing an actual potency from primary existence. The possible or probable that Aristotle speaks of in respect to tragedy's relation to history applies more widely to man's "creative" intentions in nature. For only because of an existing potency in nature, through the unwavering and continuous act of God's love, is man able to "make" anything. The point applies to the making of poems rather obviously. But it applies as well to the manipulations in our day of genetic codes whereby new creatures would be patented in our copyright office, but as if a new nature had been created, rather than being a creature brought out of the potency in actual nature. That realization ought, perhaps, restore some sobriety to our suppositions about man as God in respect to biotechnology, lest we make of this new science merely another sort of alchemy in which the limits of potency in nature go unnoticed.

It is because of the loss of our sense of limit in the remaking of natural things that we need to reflect here upon the nature of power. I am fond of quoting Andrew Lytle's remark that the opposite of love is not hate but power. It is a remark sufficiently arresting to give us pause, and in that pause we first should say that, though power may be evil in its uses, it is not necessarily evil in itself. If it were, then the Supreme Evil would be God, since God is omnipotent. Rather clearly Mr. Lytle means to point to power *abused*, a temptation so common as to make power seem inevitably evil. Again, it is St. Thomas who gives guidance in the concern. Power, he says, "has the nature of a principle" and is related "both to good and evil." (*Summa* I-II, Q. 11, A. 4). In making this observation, Thomas is contrasting power to happiness, which "has the nature of an ultimate end," namely "the proper and perfect good of man." Power as a principle in relation to the will is always an actual presence, he says elsewhere (*Summa* I-II, Q. 9, A. 3,

Reply Obj. 2) and when concentrated in act by the will's movement it may move the will to either good or evil ends. What is at issue, at last, is the happiness of the will, for when power is used willfully, it is consequently an action against happiness. It is through power as a principle *allowed* the will by its creation that intellect becomes both knowing and virtuous, but only when the will is ordinate in respect to power. The inordinate exercise of power is the act of willing that intellect exercise dominion over being, whereas the proper exercise is toward an undifferentiated good beyond being itself. For intellect's object is *universal truth*. Both terms, we remember, are "interchangeable with *being*" when spoken of in reference to God.

It is love as itself a power in the will which is will's first movement toward an object. But if that love is disoriented so that its primary object of action becomes the *self* and not the *good*, there is a perversion of that power, such as Lytle intends to castigate. It is the dominant principle in Modernist thought and to be opposed. If will seeks an object because of itself as an existing thing, as a proximate good, so that the ultimate goal may continue to be the unqualified good, this use by will of the power of love is itself good. If on the other hand it seeks that proximate good as its own rest, it will follow that the act of will is itself the end, and not the good. In this disjuncture of the power of love from its true object and a reaction upon the willful self as the ultimate good, the will can but attempt to devour being itself. The will, ravenous over being, is power turned to evil end, in which perversion the assumption of will as autonomous disguises from the ravenous will itself the truth about its own action. Whatever effect it has in the circumstantial reality – and its effects at the material level can be horrendous – it is still dependent upon the potency of being insofar as that potency is an existence out of the unwavering power of God's love. The dominion which the will enjoys is temporary, and insofar as its object is its own rest through its own action, it is an illusion as well. We might give as emblem to the point Alexander's weeping because no worlds were left for him to conquer. Inordinate power, then, is love perverted, dependent still upon the potency-actuality of being in the soul's tensional state as that soul is maintained in its being by the unqualified power of God.

Being-in-act and being-in-potency, let us say with the speculative intellect, are a *one* of being in the creative act of that unqualified power, namely God's love. There is the oneness, since God's unqualified love for that being is continuous, not discontinuous as it must be for the creature thus created. In this respect we might say that the thing is drawn to full actuality through its potential as it were, if we might hazard words out of the presumption of speculative intellect. The *thing-as-being* is drawn to God through that potency drawing its actuality out of its potency. Thus the thing is made actual through the force of Love shining through the potential upon the becoming. From man's point of view, the potential might be spoken of as a contingent shadowing, impalpable to intellect because not yet actual, but it is that very potential that serves to draw man to a perfection of being, to the highest reality of the thing willed by God, the full being of this particular singleness of creature called *person*.

Might we say that in our love for children and young animals we come closest to a recognition of the potential in being as God sees it? In a very real way we thus love the man or woman who is not yet actual except to God. In that visionary movement of love toward the creature who is child, from our position as man rather than child, our love of potency is so directly a gift of God that thereby we love in the name of God. But it is love easily perverted by our attempts to arrest that potency as an actuality beyond any contingent dangers of becoming. Or by its alternative, the forcing of the intuited potency in the child to premature actuality. It is thus that we may be tempted to dress the child as adult, or in a similar way treat the child as adult, as if thereby to avoid all the dangers feared in contingency itself. Or we may treat the adolescent as child. What we attempt is an arrested potency, always doomed of course. But such action is a willful intrusion upon that relation of the continuous will of God to the being of the child. And in its nature, such an attempt is a usurpation of that power of love in our own ultimate interest, not in a devotion to the good of the child, but in the interest of our own will as act.

We may sum the point thus: Power is will in act. When continuous, that power "forces" being. But such an attempt to force being is proper only to the cause of all being, God. Meanwhile man by such an abuse of will attempts a continuous act of being upon an object, though by nature unsuited in his limited power to continuous action. Thus the presumptuous attempt upon God's prerogative. Though the actual center of intent is the possession of an absolute power over being, which is the nature of self-love, the effect intended on the being of the object is to move it beyond the potency that is its own because of what it is in itself. What the will attempts then is an alchemy whereby it would transform being to please its own desire, desire itself becoming a final empty end. We need to remember particularly this perversion of power as we come more and more to contend with power as exercised by the geneticist or biotechnologist in the name of the "common good," reminding ourselves that by action we raid the potency of nature but do not therefore create any *new* reality, however fervently we dream of doing so.

XXXI

Some pages earlier, we were considering the relation between the knowing intellect and the thing known, in relation to the good of the thing known, and we were speaking of acts of making whereby a thing suited to knowing comes into existence. We had used as agents of making the poet and the parent as analogous. Analogy is a very limited strategy of knowing to the intellect, so that we must not forget the unlikeness in terms allied by verbal analogy. Children are not poems, in addition to which the complexity of the being of each in relation to contingent circumstance differ significantly. Yet our point remains: In attempting to know an object intellectually, we must attempt to know it in itself, in its own nature, and then in relation to the contingent world of which it becomes a part by the actuality of its being. Not that those are rigid procedural steps, for we may discover the existing thing in some instances through its contingencies and only in that way come to consider it in itself. To pursue the tiger in its jungle, we sometimes must first enter the jungle. And to engage the tigers of contingency can be sometimes a dangerous undertaking. We do the best we can, in discontinuous actions of our intellect, sometimes positing speculatively the being of the thing in itself as the desirable point of departure, whereupon we attempt by the practical intellect to move by extension of intellectual act from the speculative position.

Thus we say that a poem is good or bad first of all in respect to its existence in the inclusive order of art, not in respect to the limiting order of its mediate cause, the poet as its proximate maker. As for the child, it is evident that the order of its being in itself participates not only in proximate causes of time and place or its proximate origin in its parents as themselves nourished in the matrix of creation. It is primarily a special creation beyond proximate origins. Indeed, the proximate circumstances of its being are more accidental then definitive. This is the point where our analogy of child and poem most clearly fails, since the order of the child's being includes its immediate transcendent nature, as the poem's does not. The sacrament of baptism acknowledges this dimension of a special creation of the child, a sacrament in which the parents accept with due humility not only a limited responsibility but also a subordination of parental power as proximate agents. We might observe with amused irony those pseudo-sacramental rituals in relation to the poem, the publication ceremonies. A further disparity in our analogy: However often a poet may speak of his poems as his "children," however much the published child is celebrated by publication ceremonies, the poem exists at once in a degree of actuality to which any becoming *in itself* is terminated. It is what it is. Not that poets may not revise the published piece, sometimes unmaking more than making, though the poem as is still remains despite an addition, despite the edition of its revised being.

Even so, the analogy of poem to child may continue helpful to our argument through limited correspondences: A child's parents cannot absolutely determine prudential virtue in the child, yielding in the baptismal ceremony itself to an independence of its being, praying that it may more and more come into a fullness of being through the child's right will supported by grace. Nor can the poet determine absolutely the virtues of art in his poem. Insofar as he has been devoted to the good of the poem in his act of making, in respect to the potential of its possible or probable relation to the actualities of primary creation, it is possible that the thing he makes may be at last even greater than the limits of his own gift of making. One knows all too often the puzzlement that rises in considering that this person, an unlikely poet, insofar as we can know him, could have made this poem which is resonant in its being. (We need not name names here.) This is to be reminded that saints do not require parents who are saints and that poets may write greater poems than their "talents" seem adequate to explain.

In respect to art, this is the point Flannery O'Connor is making, relative to the school of writers called naturalists, when she says: "If the novelist is in tune with [the Modernist spirit], if he believes that actions are predetermined by psychic make-up or the economic situation or some other determinable factor, then he will be concerned above all with an accurate reproduction of the things that most immediately concern man, with the natural forces that he feels control his destiny. Such a writer may produce a great tragic naturalism, for by his responsibility to the things he sees, he may transcend the limitations of his narrow vision." He will do so, we are saying, because in being true to the actualities of primary creation in making his thing in *imitation of the actions* of nature itself, he will include in his representation of the possible or probable something of the mystery of being beyond his explicit knowing.

But, we are quick to ask, doesn't a limit of talent in the poet, even as with limits of biological being in the parent, affect the good of the thing made? Certainly. But this is a question quite separate from the agent's limited perspective upon the poem he would cause to be. Most poets, for instance, *intend* the poem to be a superlative being. They desire that the poem find its place in the order of art as among the world's great poems. And insofar as the parent is intentional in his mediate role to the child-to-be, no parent intends a retarded child certainly. Neither do they intend an ordinary "average" child. And so strong is this intentional perspective of the parent that it is a considerable cause of confusion and unhappiness in many families. Parents disappointed in their children's state of being must distinguish in their disappointment as to whether it is out of failure between their own intention at variance from actuality or in relation to the possibilities of being in the child itself. Ambitious fathers and doting mothers have been repeated themes in our art, in imitation of the actions of the nature of families. The limits in the nature of the existing creature will always override intentionality in the agent.

That is why we must concede at last a participation of grace in that making we claim, of which we are but proximate agent. A dimension of the being of the new creature, child or poem, puts it always beyond the strictly determining limit of created, making creatures, whether poet or parent.

It would be otherwise in respect to the limits of making as determined restrictively by the limits of the agent-maker if indeed man were merely "natural" man, his intellect an immanent lord of nature as an accident of an antecedent accidental universe. Or if the artist were himself truly, verily, a transcendent uncaused cause of intellectual act. Modernist faith tends to believe both of these illusions. But if all being is enveloped, permeated, and sustained by an Uncaused Cause, in a perspective rested in being as we intuitively recognize it as caused being, then finite reason itself is led to terms with a reality. It is so led when it acknowledges itself neither the principal cause nor absolute lord of that reality. Thus the good of any finite existence may at last be seen as good in itself and not dependent primarily on the proximate agent of its making or proximate perceiver of its existence. Parents without virtues may have virtuous children, or virtuous parents may have unvirtuous children, the problem of cause and effect rested in the nature of the explicit thing in its own relation to contingent circumstance. Cause and effect are not required in this vision to hold mechanistic, deterministic direction of being. So then, even bad men may write good poems.

Man is, as a principle of his nature, a maker, and he is so because he is created in the image of God. In Thomas's words, this means that man is "an intellectual being who is free to judge what he shall do and has the power to act or not act." (*Summa*, Prologue to I-II) He is in this respect like God, but only in accordance with the "principle of proper proportionality." He is not *very* maker, as God is *very* God. He discovers that his actions of will, moved by love, are through the practical intellect. Those actions are restricted by the virtue of art and by the measure in which he has the gift of artistry. Making becomes an actual virtue of the will through the habit of rightly oriented will, in its address to the proximate good in relation to unrestricted good. But as person, we are quick to add, as a simple being in whom practical and speculative intellect are understood as modes of the will's singular action toward singular objects, this same maker is properly and more largely governed by the virtue of prudence. It is a prudence desirably enlightened by the speculative intellect, as his art is executed by practical intellect. Thus it is that one's child, to speak metaphorically of the poet, cannot save its parent, just as the actual natural child cannot save the natural parent. The poet may be saved only by the growth of his own soul to its potential perfection through the virtue of prudence in response to the hope of grace, manifested though that perfection may be and ought to be by the practices of the virtue of art. This is to emphasize that the artist is not rescued by his art, as at moments John Keats longed to believe possible.

Good art, an order unto itself but within the context of the existential world, does not necessarily require a perfect artist for its perfection, anymore than the good child requires the good parent as cause of his goodness. Nor do parents' nor children's nor poets' actions in the common good – actions required of man's specific nature – presuppose the necessity of a fullness of their being as agents. For the actions in the common good are essentially actions in affirmation of being and not causes of being at the primary level of existence, the province reserved to God. Thus one may do the right thing to good effect, even if for a partially understood reason.

In respect to *good* art we mean nevertheless to speak of good as in some wise related to the artist as artist. But we do so only in the perspective of the order of making. Still, we may also speak of the artist from another perspective in saying that he is good in the order of his prudential being. In this perspective, however, we are speaking of him, not simply as artist, but as person. And we have observed of the poet that, when his poem is made, he occupies a new relation to the poem. The poem has now become a creature independent of him insofar as it continues sustained in its being. Poets die, but poems do not cease in consequence. Meanwhile the poet as person has come to occupy a prudential dimension of being, and he is in no actual way the continuing proximate cause of the poem. Our actions, even those of the poets, are disjunctive. That is why with a term like *good* we must be careful always as to which order of virtue we mean it to apply – whether we are speaking of the artist as artist or as person, of his poem as in its order of being or as it has effect beyond the order of art in the country of prudential beings. The virtue of art as the action of the practical intellect may not have the full support of a prudential right will, though the poem may prove virtuous in itself in respect to art's order of being. It may even have good effect in the prudential order. For a bad person may as artist make a good poem whose effect is supportive of prudential actions beyond the artist. A good person may as artist make a bad poem of either good or bad effect in the prudential order, depending always upon the will of the affected agent. Any combination of causes and effects is possible, but cause-effect is not the determining consideration. Rather, the question always rests in the nature proper to the thing itself, separate from its proximate causes and proximate effects. Now what the poet discovers through his speculative intellect, once the poem is in existence, is that the poem, just as every other existent thing his intellect engages, stands before him in evidence of a desirable full simplicity of intellect in himself. The existing thing, known in itself, is significant to the encountering person's gift as potentially perfect in being. That is why a work of art inescapably affects creation by its existence, though the decisiveness of effect rests in the affected agent. For artifact no less than a creature of nature, by existing becomes a circumstance of proximate existence to the intellect. Thus it may be that even the poet's own poem bears witness to him of the mystery of being itself.

And so beings, existences, insofar as they have being, are good we must say, whether we speak of poem or person. Some poems are better than others. But then so too are some persons better than others. A being necessarily bears witness, and it is an intimidating witness to our willful inclination to deny the reality of being. This is to say that any creature, even a poem, is a dictate to prudence in any maker – any intellectual creature – but it does so specifically in relation to the potential being of the maker. This is a concern separate always from the actual good of a thing made, a point to be recalled again and again. While the act of making requires an openness of the artist to the good of the thing he would make, the artist may yet fail in his own fullness. The failure is particularly dangerous to the artist in that, where prudential virtue has gone awry, he may take his action of making as the final end of his own being. To the contrary, a proper prudence is concerned with the soul's transcendent end. And it is only, at last, by a willful rejection of the testimony of being encountered in particularities – whether in the order of art or nature – that one may exclude his own virtue as artist from any relation to prudence as a virtue of person. To reject this testimony that being is good in itself, thus requiring a prudential concern for intellectual perfection, is to deny the mystery of a simplicity of being in the maker, in the love-sustained existence of a created "creator." In the mystery of a perfection of being that is the soul's final end, practical and speculative intellect no longer signify. And so we rest a moment in a conclusion: Only by wrong-will may man exempt himself from an effect on his prudential existence by his actions of making. Those actions of will are moved toward a singular object in pursuit of a knowing of the good in the object in itself. It is this recognition that Rilke speaks for, on behalf of the poet as person and for the receiver of the poem as person as well. In responding to a visionary moment of his own encounter with a bust of Apollo, Rilke cries out its effect upon him: "You must change your life!"

XXXII

In our poetry since the Renaissance, there are often intimations of the poet's attempt to engage through art a reconciliation of the virtues of art and prudence, where these concerns are entangled in the bordering regions of the moral and the aesthetic concerns of the maker. And often it has been the plastic arts that supply the poet with focal images for his attempted reconciliation of seemingly disparate virtues. Indeed, the plastic arts provide most immediate witness that the thing of art is a being. Thus sculptures and paintings are increasingly conspicuous presences in our thing of words, the poem. Through images chosen from the plastic arts, the poet recalls, first to himself and through his poem to others, his fellow maker's attempt upon the mystery of making in relation to the mystery of the maker's own being. The torso of a god becomes first an omphalos to Rilke in his own becoming, then an imagistic center of a thing he makes with words out of his experience, his poem on the "Bust of Apollo." Thus another "poet's" made thing (the bust) becomes the focus of a present attempt to reconcile the demands proper to the virtue of art and the virtue of prudence in the maker of the poem. The made thing, which in the order of art is its own proper end, is transformed to a means through which (in an actual sense of *throughness* in respect to a movement of the poet's soul) the poet attempts a self-rescue.

We might remember here as well John Milton's "Lycidas," a poem in which poetry rather than the plastic arts becomes the focus of the question whether the artist through the action of art transcends in a movement of self-rescue. By the nineteenth century the concrete made thing – art palpable – becomes increasingly clutched at by the poet, even as the palpable existences of nature are clutched at by words. In the history of our poetry, Milton's poem is a signal turning of the poet to self-rescue through his art, though that particular poet John Milton recognizes and perhaps avoids that danger himself after uttering this dramatization of the temptation, "Lycidas." In respect to the art object as a focus of attempts at self-rescue, we have alluded to John Keats's "Ode on a Grecian Urn," and to Yeats's "Sailing to Byzantium." Later still Auden's "Musée des Beaux Arts" continues the theme. One could make a considerable anthology of arresting poems in which a work of art, encountered in the context of nature, is addressed as a possible opening out of nature to a prudential rescue of the artist. In that collection it might gradually emerge that the word as savior (as opposed to a lost Word) is advanced as the most promising means of transcending the shifting uncertainties of particularities. We have made this point with Wallace Stevens's "Idea of Order at Key West" as example – as a rather direct descendent of Shelley's "Hymn to Intellectual Beauty."

As our anthology would show, the temporally existing made thing, poem or bust or painting, seems increasingly in our recent history of the poets' makings to promise a transcendence. And this attempt becomes magnified, we may discover, as we progressively lose our understanding of the proper relation between the virtues of art and of prudence. What the poet encounters in himself, when disoriented from an understanding of the relationship, is the desperate necessity of a continuous creation, the necessity of a never-ending song. In Robert Frost's version, the poem is a "momentary stay against confusion." The conclusion must be that the poem must be momently made again if confusion is not to rule. The same confusion about the poet in relation to making is in Wallace Stevens, for whom a "supreme fiction" out of his imagination becomes a constant necessity. We cite these poets because each is a considerable witness of the expense to individual spirit resulting from the assumption in Modernist thought that man is autonomous. Man as his own god discovers great price in the presumption: the burden upon intellect of a constancy of the act of "creation," not in the interest of his fulfillment of being but against the equally constant threat of emptiness, of that absence of being, in the self-declared autonomous creature man. That is the root cause out of dislocated thought whose effect is a terror to our spirit in this Modernist world. It is one of the ironies implicit in the reality of being that when God's image (man) would be God, he is forced to a continuous and sustained self-creation. It is a punishment of presumption such as Dante might dramatize in his Hell: this necessity of a constant projection of the self by self-love, with the terror present that if this tortured soul once turns from itself as object it will absolutely cease to be. Thus our juxtaposition: God, in whom there is no shadow of turning in His act of love; autonomous man in whom shadow seems all and any movement toward transcendent light an obliteration.

In individual poems, one may discover tensional poles, insofar as the poem is good in the order of its art – insofar as it executes an imitation of an action of nature. Why this should be so concerns us in closing, though we have touched upon reasons all along. The drama in such a poem is an imitation of a present action of the making intellect in relation to the pulls between the artful and prudential necessities of the soul. This is to say that such a poem is an imitation of the action of fallen man, caught by art as if in a present moment of contention. For, since art is an imitation of the actions of nature, we must consider that the nature whose actions are most intimately imitated are those of the maker himself – the created cause of the poem, the poet. Because this is so, the poet will be much concerned with whether his imitation of action of human nature is of a universal action or only of that specific historical manifestation, himself. He would universalize the personal, and in our century a critical concern, addressed as often by the poet as by the critic, is whether the actual discrete poet imitates only his own actions. The problem of autobiography and art has been a vexed one in this century.

But we are saying that, at some level beneath this so-called "personal" ground of art in the poet (which in the usual critical approach is rather a matter of *individual* than *personal* ground), there is inescapably a concern for the universality of his poem. Insofar as he is true to art's requirements, imitating not nature but an action of nature, he must touch in some degree upon his desired "universal." John Keats testifies to this point when he says of his reading of the *Iliad* that when he reads that great poem he is with Achilles shouting in the trenches. The details of social existence reflected by Homer, so sharply different from those encountered by Keats in nineteenth-century London, does not override the common human nature in an Achilles imitated out of nature by Homer. It is this dimension of art, separate from spectacle, that we are likely to have in mind when we say of a great poem that it is "timeless" or that it is "timely." That is why through his art Sophocles even now releases us in our tensional suspense of soul through *Oepidus the King*.

Since the reader of a good poem shares in this common nature, he discovers in the poem an imitation of his own fundamental actions of being, despite differentiating spectacle that sets Homer's world apart from ours, but only seemingly so. And always what is implicit in the tensional drama of the good poem, to be found in it at some level, is testimony to the difference between the maker as caused cause and the Maker as Uncaused Cause – however oblivious to or willfully indifferent to or quaintly engaged by the tensional condition of the poet's own being from which his action of soul is imitated by the poem. The caused cause (whether poet or reader) is acting through the practical intellect. In this light we say that his art, while it must reflect the demands of the order of art, will inevitably reflect a disquiet of soul in consequence of the demands of prudence upon it, given our fallen nature and given the universal nature of practical intellect as desiring mediate good toward unqualified good.

When these distinct demands are unmediated through the practical intellect in its ordinate relation to the speculative intellect, so that in consequence intellect orders the soul to its proper role as created being, there is suspended in the soul a continuing tensional disquiet with its state of being. It is this tensional reality of the soul that man's art imitates at a most fundamental level. That is, art imitates at its most primary level the action of human nature. In a "good" poem – a poem fully realizing its order of being – the drama in the experiencing intellect finds release in a resolution of tension. That release or failure of release we consider under the critical rubrics of tragedy and pathos. We have long discussed in our criticism the release in tragedy as "a moment of catharsis." (My own attempt is called "In Pursuit of Melpomene," in *The Reflective Journey toward Order*.) We have also recognized an inadequacy in pathos to lead us toward a high comedy as distinct from tragedy, a rescue from pathos through tragedy onto a higher plane, in poems like *The Divine Comedy*. As for the necessity of tensional release, the poet himself may, by an intuition deeper than his deliberate intentions of art, imitate the action of such resolution in the soul. On the other hand, he may willfully turn from imitating such a resolution. This difference in our experience of his imitations of the action proper to human nature, or his turning from that action, is the difference between the cathartic effect of Sophocles' moment when Oedipus gains full knowledge of his circumstances and the turning away from the terror of such a moment when Eliot's Prufrock laments not having been "a pair of ragged claws" rather than man. Prufrock's lament is that he is not a creature existing below intellectual being, but Eliot's poem imitates the action of such an intellectual being through which that being, Prufrock, attempts to turn from his proper nature. Prufrock's "love" song, as we readily recognize, is a "self-love" song, reductive of the being of the "self" through the speaking of words. This moment in a poem, with resolution or lack of resolution of the tensional pulls at issue, separates the literature of tragedy from the literature of pathos, over which species of poems looms as a literary ideal that great healing poem, *The Divine Comedy*.

If the maker of the poem focuses his prudential inclination upon the thing he makes as primarily his own means of rescue, turning aside from the good of the thing he is making for itself, it becomes less an imitation of soul's action than an idol. It becomes an idol raised to fallen human nature, specific in the making poet. But even so, insofar as his art truly imitates such an action of human nature, that art because it has its own made being shares with nature a continuing presence as being. This is so even of such a failed being as Eliot's "Prufrock." For though the action of soul as imitated by art in the poem is not praiseworthy, the poem as poem – in the order of art – is arresting in its being. Thus the poem bears a true witness to a reality, though the poet himself may falter in his own being, as Eliot (one suspects) is in danger of doing at the time he writes his poem. Again we are reminded that since the poem is necessarily, at the deepest level of its own being, an imitation of the actions of a fallen nature – an imitation of man as maker bearing witness to his fallen nature – it is necessarily inadequate *in itself* to the prudential rescue of any created soul. It is as inadequate to that task as would be fallen man if he should directly worship himself, a form of worship endemic in Modernism.

Being, within the limits of creation itself, is therefore dependent ultimately upon the Uncreated Creator of being. Again and again we must iterate this refrain. Nor is being ever completed in itself – never absolutely fulfilled in creation. And so from this perspective we must conclude that art as a species of being can never serve as a sufficient rescue of its maker out of finite being, nor of its beholder. It is nevertheless true that it will effect a change in his life when openly encountered by the soul. But the perfection of the discrete being of the soul lies elsewhere than by art, however resolutely one sail to ancient Byzantium on the willed wings of imagination as Yeats would do or however dogmatically one assert the absolute power of supreme fictions of the imagination as Wallace Stevens would do. Having thus insisted on the limit of art in the becoming of the artist, we once more underline our opening point. For we are not speaking of painter or poet only: Every soul by its nature is maker, is artist, and so every soul is endangered by the illusion of its self-rescue through its making.

In the limits of creation, in the limits of finitude, the finite soul's pursuit is always of an unheard music and unsaid word beyond the senses' and beyond the intellect's finitudes. That is why we conclude now that in our pursuit of a full being out of our fallen nature it is necessary that we sing and louder sing. That is, we are each called to *make* as fully as our discrete gifts allow, so that we may gain a habit of our own being sufficiently open to being that our movement of soul may be complemented by grace. Whatever the singing, it is some mode of "singing" that is the soul's calling – whether we be president or priest or poet in our proximate role as agent to the common good. And in accepting that calling as maker of some song of and to being, the soul sings willy-nilly for the common good or willfully to its destruction, since any singing has mediate effect in creation. Still with right will, whatever the mediate effect of our singing, we are turned by our actions beyond the common good. One sings, knowingly or not, in pursuit of a perfect silence which is the final fulfillment of our singing nature. It is a singing in which one prays for that balance of voice this side eternity – teach us to care and not to care. Our hope may then joyfully anticipate a state in which all our singing this side of eternity is surrendered as but St. Thomas's "straw."